HOLIDAY IN MEXICO

American Encounters/Global Interactions

A series edited by Gilbert M. Joseph and Emily S. Rosenberg

This series aims to stimulate critical perspectives and fresh interpretive frameworks for scholarship on the history of the imposing global presence of the United States. Its primary concerns include the deployment and contestation of power, the construction and deconstruction of cultural and political borders, the fluid meanings of intercultural encounters, and the complex interplay between the global and the local. American Encounters seeks to strengthen dialogue and collaboration between historians of U.S. international relations and area studies specialists.

The series encourages scholarship based on multiarchival historical research. At the same time, it supports a recognition of the representational character of all stories about the past and promotes critical inquiry into issues of subjectivity and narrative. In the process, American Encounters strives to understand the context in which meanings related to nations, cultures, and political economy are continually produced, challenged, and reshaped.

HOLIDAY IN MEXICO

Critical Reflections on Tourism and Tourist Encounters

Edited by Dina Berger
and Andrew Grant Wood

Duke University Press
Durham and London 2010

© 2010 Duke University Press

All rights reserved

Printed in the United States of America
on acid-free paper ∞

Designed by Heather Hensley

Typeset in Warnock Pro by Keystone
Typesetting, Inc.

Library of Congress Cataloging-in-
Publication data appear on the last
printed page of this book.

To my tiny tourists,
AMELIE ROSE AND LILAH MAE,

and to
MS. LORNA WOOD [1938–2006],
inveterate Canadian traveler

CONTENTS

ACKNOWLEDGMENTS

The idea for this volume initially grew out of discussions on tourism after a panel organized for a Rocky Mountain Conference for Latin American Studies (RMCLAS) meeting in Tempe, Arizona. Broader discussion among the contributors was realized in later conference settings including the Latin American Studies Association meeting in San Juan, Puerto Rico, in 2006.

We would like to thank our contributors for their tireless efforts in writing and revising their essays. We appreciate their promptness and the quality of their work, especially by those with other full-time careers (the volume plays host to essays by a practicing lawyer, renowned journalist, administrative director, and a still relatively new mom!).

We wish to thank Gilbert M. Joseph, who believed in *Holiday* from the earliest stages. We also would like to acknowledge Valerie Millholland, Miriam Angress, and Pam Morrison at Duke University Press for their editorial support, as well as two anonymous readers whose feedback helped make the collection a better book.

DINA BERGER AND ANDREW GRANT WOOD

INTRODUCTION *TOURISM STUDIES AND THE TOURISM DILEMMA*

> Tourism, holiday-making and travel are more significant
> social phenomena than most commentators have considered.
> **JOHN URRY**

With its pre-Hispanic archaeological sites, colonial architecture, pristine beaches, and alluring cities, Mexico has long been an attractive destination for travelers and it has provided opportunities for Mexicans to capitalize on their nation's natural wealth and great promise. In September 1936, those gathered at the first meeting of the Mexican National Tourism Committee listened to opening remarks made by the freshly appointed head of the new Department of Tourism, General José Quevedo, who spoke of Mexico's blessings and warned of its potential curses. The revolutionary veteran's comments focused on what he saw as the dilemma of tourism development.

A fledgling industry by the early 1930s, tourism offered the possibility of bringing about much-needed economic growth through the enhancement of roadways, hotels, restaurants, and other related commercial activity. Emerging routes that provided visitors access to proper "national" sites and events such as regional fairs or popular festivals represented the most ideal kind of tourist destinations. Yet at the same time, many worried that tourism had the potential to corrupt Mexican identity and culture. If Mexican hosts catered too much to visitors' demands, tourism might turn their nation into a hedonistic playground for foreigners (Quevedo used the phrase "another Cuba") and might lead to "the death of the nation's soul."[1]

Mexicans have in fact struggled to reconcile market demand with a desire for national sovereignty since the very beginnings of modern tourism in the early twentieth century. Countless citizens have often wondered how to profit from touristic exchange without necessarily compromising their integrity or that of their community, culture, and, ultimately, nation.

Taking a cue from Quevedo, the essays in this volume reflect the complicated history of tourism. In what one scholar has referred to as a "devils' bargain," tourism in Mexico represents a $680 million business with over 21 million international visitors as of 2005.[2] The industry now ranks third in contributions to the gross domestic product,[3] and it provides more than 5.5 percent of total employment nationwide.[4] Yet at the same time, tourism produces a kind of "invisible export" in which nations, locales, environments, and people are marketed as commodities for consumption.[5] As the general forewarned, not only has tourism resulted in economic growth and profit for some but it has also made manifest a number of social, cultural, and environmental consequences.

Spanning well over a century and a diverse terrain, chapters in *Holiday in Mexico* illustrate three major themes: (1) the various ways Mexicans have imagined and promoted their culture and nation, (2) the politics and means through which Mexicans and their guests have interacted over time, and (3) the costs and benefits of tourism. Taken together, the essays presented here offer a detailed and complex view of tourism—a critical topic which has largely been ignored by historians of Mexico.

While travelers have spanned the globe for centuries, tourism as a modern social practice first gained popularity with the advent of the railroad and steamship. In the 1840s, the Englishman Thomas Cook "packaged" tours for enthusiasts eager to make their way south to popular destinations such as Italy and Egypt. A century later, the proliferation of cars, bus tours, and charter flights helped pave the way for our contemporary era of mass travel. More recently, the advent of safe, quick, and more affordable jet airplane travel after the 1950s further revolutionized the ability to travel. Tourists have made the world a smaller place just as tourism has become a truly global service-industrial complex.

Encompassing a vast array of producers and consumers, tourism, unlike other leisure activities, brings into contact people from different nations, socioeconomic classes, and ethnicities. While encounters abound, one is never simply a tourist, just as tourist encounters are never inconsequential. Like the activity one finds behind the curtain of a staged production, tourism involves a host of actors whose labor, money, and time make tourism happen. Host and guest interact—whether face-to-face or in passing—when currency is exchanged, questions are answered, historical landmarks are visited, food is prepared, beds are made, music is danced to, photographs are taken, and countless impressions are rendered. As such, tourism is revealing in that it sheds light on human behavior that is both pleasurable and profitable as well as exploitative and depleting.

In one of the earliest volumes dedicated to the study of tourism, the anthropologist Valene Smith defines a tourist as a "temporarily leisured person who voluntarily visits a place away from home for the purposes of experiencing a change."[6] Tourism, she argues, rests on a combination of leisure time (vacation days), discretionary income (savings), and cultural norms (expectations).[7] The tourism studies pioneer Nelson Graburn expands on this definition to argue that tourism is a leisure-time activity and a form of play that involves travel—the act of getting from here to there. Tourism, he writes, "is *not* work, but is a part of the recent invention, *recreation*, which is supposed to renew us for the workaday world."[8] Inherent in tourism, then, is sacredness, a kind of liminality defined by time away from the ordinary—work, home, and family—as well as a playfulness that comes with leisure activities.

Tourism has also come to represent a rite of passage to adulthood for those who can afford it. The college student who backpacks through Europe does so to assert her independence, to become more worldly and, thus, mature as a result of her experiences abroad. By learning to navigate the streets of foreign cities, by seeing famous sites, and by meeting foreigners along the way, people old and young alike engage in tourism as a kind of path toward spiritual enlightenment and intellectual self-enrichment.[9] For others perhaps less conscientious, tourism is an opportunity to perform identity rather than fit in.[10] In this regard, visitors stubbornly bring the worst of their home culture with them while on vacation, thereby (unknowingly or on purpose) reinforcing negative stereotypes and aggravating hosts.

Touristic experiences are not just about travel but are a product of the postindustrial world where high levels of productivity allow for time off the job, evoke the desire or the expectation to explore, and provide access to means of transportation like the train, the cruise ship, the automobile, and the jumbo jet.[11] Tourism promotion, as a result, involves the sales and marketing of destinations whereby maps, guidebooks, and guided tours shape what people choose to see while on holiday. Thus, in contrast to the sheer act of getting from here to there, tourism is extraordinary and self-enriching.

For academics, foundational works in the field of tourism studies include

Dean MacCannell's pathbreaking study *The Tourist: A New Theory of the Leisure Class* and the anthropologist Valene Smith's aforementioned *Hosts and Guests* both published in the 1970s as part of what would later be called "the cultural turn" in the humanities and social sciences. These works draw our attention to the complicated cultural, social, and economic negotiations involved in tourism. Subsequently, the sociologist John Urry's *The Tourist Gaze: Leisure and Travel in Contemporary Societies* (1990) employs Michel Foucault's charged concept of "the gaze" to emphasize the consumer side of tourism and to remark upon several key characteristics that make up the modern tourist experience. Urry writes that "places are chosen to be gazed upon because there is anticipation, especially through daydreaming and fantasy, of intense pleasures [and that] such anticipation is constructed and sustained through a variety of non-tourist practices such as film, TV, litera- ture, magazines, records and videos, which construct and reinforce that gaze."[12] Thus, our gaze—our decision to holiday somewhere—is constructed by an innate expectation and sense of anticipation of what that place will be like, all of which has been shaped by the media, by images and stories in literary works, by art in museums, and even by word of mouth.

Following Urry and others, it has become clear that the tourist experience is one thought to be distinct from everyday life—a process mediated through an artificial, protected environment developed for and demanded by the tourist. Ironically, tourists nevertheless set out in search of "the authentic." As one scholar comments, "The tourist is interested in everything as a sign in itself [for] all over the world the unsung armies of semioticians, the tourists, are fanning out in search of the signs of Frenchness, typical Italian behavior, exemplary Oriental scenes, typical American thruways, traditional English pubs" and so on.[13] Given this, tourist discourse nevertheless minimizes the "inconvenient" presence of local residents who do not fit a preconceived semiotic frame. Rather, locals only tend to be "of use" when pictured to complement the advertised allure of pristine beaches, stunning architecture, and carefully photographed cuisine.

The essayist and philosopher Alain de Botton reflects on this experience in an account of a trip to Barbados during which his hopes of an imagined, dream vacation suggested by tourist brochures were quickly dashed by the reality of life there. He writes: "Nothing had existed in my mind between the last line on the itinerary and the hotel room. I had not envisioned, and now protested inwardly the appearance of, a luggage carousel with a frayed rub- ber mat; two flies dancing above an overflowing ashtray . . . a white taxi with a dashboard covered in fake leopard skin; a stray dog in a stretch of waste ground beyond the airport." In his anticipation, he comments that "there had simply been a vacuum between the airport and my hotel."[14] Despite the first-world fantasy of vacationing, tourist encounters (conscious or otherwise) usually highlight asymmetrical relations between guests and hosts. Taken from a wider perspective, tourism is not all fun and adventure; it is about power.

The power inherent in tourism reveals sharp divisions between the haves and have-nots and is the source of tourism's many transformations.[15] Economic, cultural, and political influence shapes the demography of tourism, namely, who has the means to travel, as well as the result of encounters over the short and long term. To be sure, anthropologists like Dennison Nash, Kathleen Adams, and Quetzil Castañeda have shown how communities are affected when they cater to the needs of tourists who demand particular services like air-conditioned hotels and Americanized cuisine and who desire to see unchanged indigenous communities and customs.[16] That change, however, is not necessarily always for the worse. As Adams shows, the indigenous community of Tana Toraja in Indonesia used the power of tourism to reinvent themselves as progenitors of traditional Indonesian culture and art and to demand protection, and thus financial support, from groups like UNESCO.[17]

Not surprisingly, tourists typically reject critical remarks linking tourism to the exercise of privilege and power. Disavowals run the gamut from outright snobbism ("I'm not your typical tourist") to sheer insensitivity ("Leave me alone, I'm on vacation"). Examining the ideology embedded in the history of travel, Mary Louise Pratt has employed the term "anti-conquest" in describing tourism's many discursive denials. Generally, she finds that travelers have sought to distance themselves from the crude trappings of imperial domination and the rationalizing rhetoric of empire. Yet at the same time she notes how most have nonetheless enjoyed the ostensibly elite status afforded the modern-day "conqueror."[18] Tourism, in many ways, is ultimately a political endeavor.

Tourism studies critically considers the interaction between people and industry makers in what Pratt has termed "contact zones": spaces of transnational encounter "usually involving conditions of coercion, racial inequality and intractable conflict."[19] The historian Gilbert M. Joseph builds on Pratt's concept by recognizing that transnational encounters happen in "power-laden contexts," but ones that can also yield "interactive, improvisational possibilities."[20] The making and articulation of national identities and even transnational identities is one of these possibilities. Tourism necessitates a marketed national identity that is sold, consumed, and negotiated. In the hopes of attracting tourists, industry makers draw on the uniqueness and the sameness of particular destinations. In so doing, they try to meet the multitude of tourists' expectations from comfortable, familiar accommodations to exotic, awe-inspiring sights.

Tourists also perform and shape identity. The freedom, will, and means to travel as well as where one chooses to vacation usually reflects one's national and cultural identities. When France was sworn off travel itineraries by many Americans after September 11, 2001 (and French fries were renamed "freedom fries"), U.S. tourism there dropped by 31 percent.[21] In contrast, Japanese tourists in Berlin increased by 115 percent in 2004.[22] With strong currency and fewer fears of terrorism, Japanese tourists performed their economic and political will through holiday making in Europe. Tourism can also help forge a kind of transnational or even global identity. Heritage tours, for example, offer organized trips of Israel to American Jews who want to connect with their Jewish kin and adopted homeland, while solidarity or reality tours offer socially concerned Americans tours of Zapatista communities in Chiapas.[23] This kind of travel can galvanize transnational identities rooted in religion and human rights. Essays in this volume are exacting about locating such spaces of neocolonial encounter along with actors' articulation of social identities in negotiating often unequal power relationships.

Tourism research is not social sciences "light." It has the potential to strike at the very heart of key political, economic, cultural, and environmental issues in that scholars use the lens of tourism to examine questions related to development, class, ethnicity, gender, and a vast range of cross-cultural interactions. It is an important pursuit which today brings into focus an ever-widening circle of peoples, places, and industries throughout the world.

Despite scholarly assertions that Mexico's modern tourism industry began as a model for economic development in the 1960s,[24] its development took shape in conjunction with various modernization projects in the 1920s. Undoubtedly, one can find its origins even earlier with the proliferation of railroads by the mid- to late nineteenth century, which provided all-important transportation routes for early travelers. Those travelers, in turn, returned home with snapshots and produced memoirs, all of which helped to form a Mexican imaginary that many sought to see firsthand in the years to come. For excursionists, diplomats, and business travelers of the mid- to late nineteenth century, Mexico offered few excavated sites. Incipient efforts by scientists to uncover and promote Mexico's many pre-Hispanic ruins only began in 1910 as part of a broader effort by the Porfirian regime to attract foreign investment and to incorporate Mexico's indigenous past. Visitors complained of the unsatisfactory accommodations in Mexico City, and travel often proved harrowing: foreign visitors were commonly robbed by border bandits while traversing roads by coach and train, especially in northern Mexico.[25]

The key to any successful tourism industry is peace and stability, two conditions Mexicans did not enjoy until the late 1920s and early 1930s. By then, General Plutarco Elías Calles and the revolutionary family (progenitors of the Partido Revolucionario Institucional or PRI) had consolidated political power through arm-twisting and a string of assassinations. Mexico's last major armed rebellion (before the Chiapas uprising in 1994) was led by Catholics angry with restrictions on religious freedom imposed by the federal government. The revolt eventually ended with peace accords brokered, in part, by U.S. ambassador Dwight Morrow. The real push for tourism development, then, came in the wake of the long Mexican Revolution when government and industry ostensibly joined forces in peacetime.

One of the first changes can be seen as early as 1925 when Calles inaugurated a series of reconstruction efforts, one of which focused on building a system of highways to connect a nation of many parts.[26] In the decades that followed, Mexico's Road Commission helped to build the first major highway from Laredo, Texas, to Mexico City (inaugurated in 1936 as the Pan-American Highway) and built a constellation of modern highways with Petróleos Mexicanos (PEMEX) gas stations from Mexico City to central tourist destinations like Acapulco, Guanajuato, Morelia, Oaxaca City, Taxco, and Veracruz.[27]

The postrevolutionary era also saw a renewed fascination with Mexico's indigenous past.[28] This new interest—particularly among academics and government officials—paved the way for the founding of new institutions such as the National Institute of Anthropology and History (INAH) in 1939 and an ensuing legitimization of what is now a thriving artisan trade.[29] This initiative complemented a new model of economic development that sought to concentrate national development in national hands. The idea of Mexicans profiting from their own comparative advantages like a temperate climate, premier coasts, colonial architecture, ancient pyramids, and proximity to the United States fit well with broader goals of economic growth and with the broader sense of revolutionary nationalism. Mexican leaders wanted profits and progress and looked to tourism as a panacea for underdevelopment. By the late 1940s, President Miguel Alemán shifted the tourist gaze from national treasures to sun and fun, spearheading rapid development in places like Acapulco where success soon led to his officiating over what became one of Mexico's most lucrative industries.

Finally, Mexico's improved relations with the United States during the late 1930s under the Roosevelt administration's Good Neighbor Policy came at a momentous time when world war and extremism loomed. For fear that Europe's troubles would spread to the Western Hemisphere, the U.S. government sought solidarity with its southern neighbors. The U.S. government encouraged Americans to "discover" Mexico in the hope that tourists would help build democratic ties. After the war, the GI Bill paid for veterans' tuition at Mexican universities and colleges. In turn, Mexico capitalized on these opportunities to expand its tourism infrastructure and become one of the primary destinations for U.S. travelers. By the 1970s, Mexican tourism was booming and U.S. tourists accounted for nearly 90 percent of all industry trade.[30]

New state-driven development projects such as Cancún soon led the way. Built in the 1970s, Cancún further illustrates Mexico's long history of collaboration between government and the tourist industry. Since then, however, Cancún's history has been far from rosy, as the site did not generate the profits investors had hoped for or, echoing Quevedo, the kind of refined vacation spot they had envisioned. Nevertheless, the industry today plays host to millions of tourists, including thousands of middle-class Mexicans, who make their way to various leisure destinations each year. Tourists converge on sites ranging from casinos, restaurants, bars, shopping malls, outdoor sporting venues, and parade routes to art museums, colonial cathedrals, archaeological parks, designated ecological zones, and ocean beaches. Rather than the well-worn fun-and-sun development model that has played out in Cancún, Mexican tourist industry insiders along with the state are now betting on exclusive, high-class resorts like Cabo San Lucas as the latest answer to the tourism dilemma.

While Mexico has inspired many well-known travel accounts from the colonial period to contemporary times, relatively little scholarly research on tourism (a few pioneering articles, book chapters, and books notwithstanding) has been produced to date.[31] Presenting original work by a leading group of scholars on the subject, our volume is the first collection of essays dedicated entirely to the study of tourism in Mexico. The collection compiles some of the most recent research on tourism in Mexico from a variety of disciplines including history, art history, cultural studies, and anthropology. Although we could not conceivably include material on every important tourist destination or topic, chapters nevertheless cover the range of tourist destinations from Mexico City to Tijuana and from Acapulco to Veracruz as well as the development of tourism over time, from the 1840s to the present day.

Chapters also cover the multitude of historical actors who constitute the kaleidoscope of tourism: the prototourist soldier in the mid-nineteenth century; the archaeologist excavating Teotihuacán during the Porfiriato; *porteño* business owners marketing Carnival in 1920s Veracruz; American tourists, retirees, and artists settling in San Miguel de Allende; cookbook authors and restaurateurs selling "authentic" cuisine in the U.S. Southwest and Central Mexico; presidents, governors, and local officials vying to develop the next "it" spot in Acapulco, Tijuana, and Cabo San Lucas; service workers migrating from Cancún to their rural villages; *ejidatarios* fighting for their land in Acapulco; art curators organizing the "Great Masters" exhibit; and women hoteliers, tour guides, and market vendors selling services to tourists in Oaxaca. In short, this volume peels away the many layers of an industry that is far from transparent.

Holiday in Mexico provides a critical analysis of the industry by examining its origins, promoters, participants, and power relationships. Our case studies cover this important history in three distinct periods: (1) first tourists, ca. 1846–1911; (2) postrevolutionary developments, ca. 1920–50; and (3) contemporary articulations, ca. 1960–present. Taken together, we hope this volume will appeal to a wide readership interested not only in the history and culture of Mexico but also comparative approaches to travel and leisure more generally.

First Tourists, ca. 1846–1911

The volume begins with Andrea Boardman's essay "The U.S.–Mexican War and the Beginnings of American Tourism in Mexico," in which she argues that to understand modern tourism to Mexico in the twentieth century one must look at one of the earliest phases during the U.S.–Mexican War (1846–48), which brought American troops to Mexico. Young American soldiers ostensibly became tourists in their free time as they waited for the completion of the treaty making and the reconstitution of the Mexican government. Although they had little money, they demonstrated great curiosity to explore. Some even climbed the volcano Popocatépetl. Many, she finds, drew maps of Mexico, wrote descriptive letters home, and recorded their experiences in memoirs. These forms of "mapping" and remembering their sojourn came to shape the way tourists at the turn-of-the-century visited Mexico, particularly the routes taken and sites seen. The soldier-tourists in no small way shaped some of the first imaginings of Mexico in the American imagination.

In "Teotihuacán: Showcase for the Centennial," Christina Bueno examines how the excavation of Mexico's most prized pyramids dovetailed with the centennial celebrations held in 1910. She not only examines the Porfirian state's efforts to tap into the popularity of ancient archaeological sites to promote foreign investment and to associate Mexico with classical civilizations found in Egypt but also shows how excavation of Teotihuacán illustrated much broader debates about the Indian in Mexico and about Mexican national identity. She argues that observers believed the decrepit pyramids to be a site of humiliation, rather than pride, and that excavation helped the Porfirian state to recast Mexico's image as a nation that took pride in its pre-Hispanic past, despite prevalent racist views. Mexico, in turn, would appear modern. Bueno uncovers the contentious and self-serving history of, and the debate around, Teotihuacán, a site that nearly all tourists now visit.

Postrevolutionary Developments, ca. 1920–60

Andrew Grant Wood shifts our attention from the foreign tourist to the national one in "On the Selling of Rey Momo: Early Tourism and the Marketing of Carnival in Veracruz." In his chapter, Wood explores the origins of what is today that city's most prosperous celebration, Carnival. In light of the port city's history of violence and unsanitary conditions, Wood points to the turn of the century as the moment at which state officials and business elites sought to promote Carnival and thus modernize the port city and its tourist infrastructure. By the late 1920s, he argues, local business and political interests coalesced to begin to promote this weeklong, pre-Lenten event by devising a formula that included crowning of a King and Queen as well as musical performances by local *jarocho* bands and national orchestras. A large cadre of tourist boosters, from the shop owner to members of the local organizing committee, helped shape a broader and sustainable tradition of consuming Carnival in Veracruz, particularly through the use of advertisements in local and even national newspapers and through cooperation with tourist pioneers in Mexico City. By the 1940s, Wood shows, guidebook authors and tourism promoters recognized Carnival in Veracruz as a viable tourist destination and as an asset to the larger national tourism industry.

Encouraging us to think about the political uses of tourism, Dina Berger's essay "Goodwill Ambassadors on Holiday: Tourism, Diplomacy, and Mexico–U.S. Relations" examines how tourism and tourists mediated foreign relations on the eve of and during World War II. At a critical point in the history of Mexico–U.S. relations, tourism promoters on both sides of the border promoted American travel to Mexico as the ideal way to get to know your neighbor. Berger argues that tourism emerged as a form of diplomacy that complemented the work of officials and that forwarded goals of Panamericanism and the Good Neighbor Policy. During their holidays in Mexico, tourists performed and thus spread American values of freedom, democracy, and consumerism to their Mexican hosts; conversely, hosts represented the "new" Mexican nation of progress, democracy, and brotherhood. Tourism promoters believed that this encounter between host and guests could help foster mutual understanding and bridge the gap of perceived cultural differences. As World War II began, the United States government worked to build solidarity in the Americas and needed Mexico as an ally, while Mexico was in an ideal position to profit from the tourist dollar by capitalizing on the rhetoric of travel with a purpose.

Eric M. Schantz gets at the underside of tourism by analyzing questions of power, nation building, and transnational relations as he traces the development of tourism in Baja California. His chapter "Behind the Noir Border: Tourism, the Vice Racquet, and Power Relations in Baja California, 1938–65" follows the meteoric growth of border cities as tourism helped create a dynamic underground economy centered on prostitution, gaming, drugs, and alcohol. Schantz focuses on the political dynamics behind tourist development by unraveling the connections between political support and self-aggrandizement of important politicians such as the governor of Baja California Norte (1924–28) and president of Mexico (1932–34) Abelardo L. Rodríguez. Indeed, it was Rodríguez who promoted "family" tourism while growing rich on vice trade at the same time. Yet when President Lázaro Cárdenas decreed a widely publicized ban on casino gambling and the vice resorts along the border, he attacked the economic base of many of his political enemies in Baja. In response, the gaming industry staged a comeback after the *cardenista* ban of 1936 and in doing so mocked the state's attempts to eradicate their business. Gradually, these conflicts gave way to a compromise that allowed for the continuation of regulated vice as long as promoters catered mostly to foreign consumers. At the same time, Schantz shows, tourism boosters tried to promote family attractions, emphasizing the appeal of shopping for *curiosidades*, dining at Mexican or Chinese restaurants, and sporting spectacles such as bullfights and jai alai.

In a similar vein, Andrew Sackett's essay "Fun in Acapulco? The Politics of Development on the Mexican Riviera" looks at the early history of one of the nation's premier tourist destinations. Sackett weaves together a story that traces the connection between state-driven tourist development and its human costs. Focusing largely on the developer of Acapulco tourism, President Miguel Alemán, and the local Junta Federal, Sackett examines the state's gradual expropriation of communal lands (*ejidos*) along the waterfront and the ensuing conflict that took shape between developers and local residents. More broadly, though, Sackett illustrates the many ways that people contested tourist development, from those who struggled to retain their land to those who fought to gain entrance into the tourism market. Acapulco, he shows, presents quite possibly the best case study of tourist development under direct state control by the 1940s, something that we do not see prior to that time. Sackett's study also best illustrates the direct effects of tourism on local people, namely, the state's persecution of ejidatarios and, in turn, their politicization. While Hollywood stars sunbathed, police burned farmland and jailed residents who refused to give up their land for tourist development.

Lisa Pinley Covert's chapter "Colonial Outpost to Artists' Mecca: Conflict and Collaboration in the Development of San Miguel de Allende's Tourist Industry" conversely looks at tourist development at the hands of foreigners. Pinley Covert analyzes how the changing image of San Miguel, Guanajuato, from silver town to exotic and bohemian artist colony distinguished the city from other Mexican tourist destinations. After being declared a national monument in 1926, the city of San Miguel underwent several identity transformations, largely due to foreigners. The first transformation, Pinley Covert shows, began with the opening of the famous Escuela Universitaria de Bellas Artes by the Peruvian artist Felipe Cossío del Pomar in the late 1920s. San Miguel soon became a stopping point for Mexico's most famous intellectuals and artists. By the late 1930s, the school attracted droves of American and Canadian students until it earned such accreditation from the United States and Canadian governments that World War II veterans could study there under the GI Bill. Since the 1950s, the city has been internationally recognized as a trendy haven for cultured travelers seeking an alternative to the more conventional tourist experience in Mexico. Pinley Covert's essay reveals how the trajectory of San Miguel serves as an alternative to other state-led tourist endeavors so prevalent elsewhere in the country.

Contemporary Articulations, ca. 1960–Present

Jeffrey Pilcher's "José Cuervo and the Gentrified Worm: Food, Drink, and the Touristic Consumption of Mexico" uses the practice of culinary tourism as a lens onto the historical construction and contemporary expression of cultural stereotypes between the United States and Mexico. In particular, Pilcher examines the connection between gastronomy, the tourist gaze of foreign visitors, and the national elite, arguing that the consumption of Mexican food and drink has objectified indigenous people of Mexico, especially women. Because both food and drink play such a vital role in the creation of human identities, culinary tourism, defined as the deliberate sampling of unfamiliar ethnic foods, is particularly revealing when considering cross-cultural encounters. The handcrafted nature of tortillas and *moles* in indigenous communities seems to support a view of tourism on the part of foreigners who see the practice as an example of authenticity. Some have complicated this understanding of tourism, however, by showing the commercialization inherent even in ecological and ethnic tourism. To explicate these contradictions, Pilcher examines the cultural projects of culinary intermediaries such as Mexican and foreign cookbook writers as well as Native American chefs. Considering pervasive myths and stereotypes—especially when it comes to Mexico's infamous tequila—Pilcher notes historical cycles of acceptance and rejection of Mexican foods and how they shaped the tourist imagination.

In addressing one of the most complex regions of contemporary tourism, M. Bianet Castellanos returns us to the sometimes harsh reality of industry development. In "Cancún and the Campo: Indigenous Migration and Tourism Development in the Yucatán Peninsula," Castellanos considers the construction of Cancún in the early 1970s as a strategy intended to divert rural-urban migration from Mexico's core to its periphery—thought to be the most effective way to modernize the countryside. Subsequently, Cancún served as a model for the development of other tourist "poles" like Ixtapa-Zihuatenejo in Guerrero and Huatulco in Oaxaca. Through an ethnographic study of a rural Yucatec Maya community and a history of migration to Cancún, Castellanos observes how the building of an international tourist center within a predominantly indigenous region has had a significant impact on local societies. She examines the ideological struggles indigenous communities face as they experience work and life within an agricultural region increasingly dominated by the production of services and the migration of peoples. Castellanos's research suggests that the wages and excitement of Cancún threaten the social, political, and economic practices oriented around *milpa* (largely corn) cultivation in the countryside, and she explores how indigenous migrants and residents struggle to maintain community across the space-time divide generated by international tourism. Noting how indigenous communities have come to rely on new technologies as a way to cement social ties, Castellanos describes how workers use wages earned in Cancún to diversify their agricultural production to preserve the social, religious, and economic importance of their land and culture.

In a more recent example of the way Mexico sells itself abroad, Mary Coffey's "Marketing Mexico's Great Masters: Folk Art Tourism and the Neoliberal Politics of Exhibition" offers a critique of President Vicente Fox's campaign to convert Mexico into a "full service tourist destination." As part of this campaign, Fox's administration pledged $1.6 billion to invest in more than two hundred different projects aimed at tourist development and promotion. Coffey describes how, as part of this effort, blockbuster exhibitions of Mexican art were developed for travel to museums in the United States and Europe. She then details how one such exhibition—the Great Masters of Mexican Folk Art—served not only to draw large New York crowds but also to promote folk art tourism through a slick presentation of "authentic" and "high quality" masterpieces. Coffey observes how criticism of the Great Masters exhibition highlighted concerns regarding ethical questions about the use of Banamex's art collection to further Citigroup's corporate buyout as well as more general anxieties over the commodification of folk art by global capitalism. Going beyond these critiques, Coffey argues that the exhibition also served as a touristic prelude for more extensive corporate exploitation of transnational cultural citizenship. Her chapter thus historicizes Mexican folk art initiatives and exhibitions in order to demonstrate how commercial concerns often dictate consumption and development trends.

In "Golfing in the Desert: Los Cabos and Post-PRI Tourism in Mexico" Alex Saragoza examines the role that the state-run Fondo Nacional de Fomento al Turismo (FONATUR) played in its development of nautical tourism aimed at attracting wealthy Americans with their yachts and SUVs. In a move away from Cancún—vacation spot to the all-inclusive spring breaker or middle-class family—the project called Escalera Náutica (Nautical Ladder) emerged, designed to attract only the most elite tourists and seasonal residents at its resorts and developments. What first began in the 1980s with a vision and with investments by the beer mogul Juan Sánchez Navarro, the Nautical Ladder became the pet project of FONATUR and the Fox administration by 2000. Saragoza demonstrates how Nautical Ladder, with its marinas, resorts, and timeshares, marked a turning point in the nature of Mexico's tourism industry that mirrored the hope of Vicente Fox's presidency and his fresh approach to politics, not to mention his neoliberal bent. Ultimately, the development of Los Cabos has given way to what Saragoza calls "placelessness," such that there is little uniquely Mexican in this premier tourist destination.

Finally, the renowned travel writer Barbara Kastelein rounds out our volume with "The Beach and Beyond: Observations from a Travel Writer on Dreams, Decadence, and Defense." Drawing on her own travels in Mexico while writing stories for *The Herald Mexico* and for assorted travel magazines, Kastelein takes us on an insightful tour of Acapulco, Oaxaca City, and the town of Amecameca located on the slopes of Mexico's famous volcano Popocatépetl. A combination of investigative reporting and academic research, her lively narrative connects with key themes discussed throughout the collection. While in Acapulco, Kastelein wades through the complicated sea of memory and myth. On her travels to Oaxaca City, she explores the success of the tourism industry there, where visitors search for a kind of "otherworldliness" rooted in strong, local indigenous culture and shaped by artists who demand cultural preservation and patrimony. On her final journey, Kastelein takes us to the stagnant tourist spot of Amecameca, largely unknown to foreigners but one that is popular among Mexicans, especially *chilangos*, who go on pilgrimages to the Black Christ of Sacromote or spend the day picnicking at the foot of the volcano. There, she learns that officials in Amecameca are indifferent to tourism, knowing that it has little future in attracting the "right" kind of tourist—foreigners—rather than national ones. Together, Kastelein's vignettes show us somewhat of the arc of Mexico's twentieth-century tourist history from those in ascent (Oaxaca), in decline (Acapulco), and stagnant (Amecameca).

Omnipresent, complex, and ethically ambivalent, tourism is an industry that is here to stay. In acknowledging and evaluating the impact of tourism's ever-expanding reach, we need to be careful not to oversimplify. The history of tourism should be appreciated from nuanced, multiple positions that take larger international structures as well as local experiences and agents into careful account. Similarly, tourists themselves should not all be judged negatively. Not all are the "ugly American" conquerors, backcountry boobs, or yammering yuppies that many snobbish commentators would surmise. Holding on to what today may be cynically seen as just an old-fashioned idea of international goodwill, we nevertheless believe that—given the right conditions—both guests and hosts can have (and have had) much to share, learn, and even profit from each other. Accordingly, the essays assembled for *Holiday in Mexico* speak of this possibility (as well as the many failed attempts) and of the importance of tourism as a vital subject of critical social inquiry.

Notes

1. José Quevedo's speech can be found in the meeting minutes of the National Tourism Committee, September 18, 1936, Centro de Estudios de Historia de México CONDUMEX, Fondo: Luis Montes de Oca, 292: 27012. On the history of tourism in Cuba, see Rosalie Schwartz, *Pleasure Island: Tourism and Temptation in Cuba* (Lincoln: University of Nebraska Press, 1999).
2. SECTUR, "El turismo en México, 2005," no. 5.2 (September 2006), 6. It is important to note that according to this report, over 60 percent of these tourists traveled for pleasure. Also, statisticians attribute the higher than usual numbers in 2005 to natural disasters like the tsunami that wiped out tourist destinations in South Asia, http://datatur.sectur.gob.mx/pubyrep/cargas_manuales/DE/TurMex.pdf (visited May 14, 2007). See Hal K. Rothman, *Devil's Bargains: Tourism in the Twentieth Century American West* (Lawrence: University of Kansas Press, 2000).
3. According to the Mexican Tourism Board, the tourism industry contributes 8.3 percent to the GDP. See "The Mexico Travel News Bureau E-Newsletter" in

2004, published by the Consejo de Promoción Turística (CPTM), http://www.visitmexicopress.com/newsletters/12_04/EndYear04_press.html (visited May 14, 2007).

4. Kathleen Bruhn and Daniel C. Levy, *Mexico: The Struggle for Democratic Development* (Berkeley : University of California Press, 2006), 242.

5. Economists generally refer to tourism as such because it is part of international trade but functions differently largely because tourists do not take a tangible good with them save for snapshots and souvenirs. They consume the product of a Caribbean beach but also a host of products inherent in their holiday such as their hotel room, food at restaurants, guided tours, shops, entertainment, etc. Tourism, then, is not a readily apparent product but the coalescence of countless goods and services consumed. For a textbook explanation of this invisible export, see Robert Christie Mill and Alastair M. Morrison, *The Tourism System*, 4th ed. (Dubuque, Iowa: Kendall/Hunt 2002), 40–42, and Brian Archer and Chris Cooper, "The Positive and Negative Impacts of Tourism," *Global Tourism*, 2nd ed., ed. William F. Theobald (Oxford: Butterworth Heinemann, 1998), 65–68.

6. Valene Smith, introduction, *Hosts and Guests: The Anthropology of Tourism*, ed. Valene Smith (Philadelphia: University of Pennsylvania Press, 1989), 1.

7. Ibid., 1–3.

8. Nelson H. H. Graburn, "Tourism: The Sacred Journey," *Hosts and Guests*, ed. Smith, 22. Emphasis in original.

9. See Lisa Johnson, ed., *Rite of Passage: Tales of Backpacking 'Round Europe* (Footscray, Australia: Lonely Planet Publications, 2003), and Pico Iyer, *The Lady and the Monk: Four Seasons in Kyoto* (New York: Vintage Books, 1992).

10. By performing identity we mean that people travel and are tourists as representatives of their national, regional, religious, and ethnic identification. When Americans travel abroad, they embody American values and ideals, no matter how hard they might try not to. The so-called ugly American reputation of the typical American tourist who does not try to fit into the culture he or she is visiting and who, more often than not, stands out because of casual dress or inappropriate behavior, speaks to American values of informality and self-importance derived from our notions of what freedom and democracy might mean.

11. See Dennison Nash, "Tourism as a Form of Imperialism," *Hosts and Guests*, ed. Smith, 37–52.

12. John Urry, *The Tourist Gaze: Leisure and Travel in Contemporary Societies* (London: Sage Publications, 1990), 3.

13. J. Culler, "Semiotics of Tourism," *American Journal of Semiotics* 1 (1981): 127. Quoted in Urry, *The Tourist Gaze*, 3.

14. Alain de Botton, *The Art of Travel* (New York: Pantheon Books, 2002), 13.

15. The most provocative essay on tourism and power is Jamaica Kincaid's *A Small Place* (New York: Plume, 1989) in which she rails against the inequality of travel and tourism on the island of Antigua.

16. See Nash, "Tourism as a Form of Imperialism," Kathleen Adams, *Art as Politics: Recrafting Identities, Tourism, and Power in Tana Toraja, Indonesia* (Honolulu: University of Hawai'i Press, 2006), and Quetzil Castañeda, *In the Museum of Maya Culture: Touring Chichén Itzá* (Minneapolis: University of Minnesota Press, 1996).

17. See Adams, *Art as Politics*.

18. Mary Louise Pratt, *Imperial Eyes: Travel Writing and Transculturation* (London: Routledge, 1992), 7.

19. Ibid., 6.

20. Gilbert M. Joseph, "Close Encounters: Toward a New Cultural History of U.S.–Latin American Relations," *Close Encounters of Empire: Writing the Cultural History of U.S.-Latin American Relations*, ed. Gilbert M. Joseph, Catherine C. LeGrand, and Ricardo D. Salvatore (Durham, N.C.: Duke University Press, 1998), 8.

21. Jamey Keaten, "U.S. Tourists Warm Up to France," *Oakland Tribune*, August 19, 2004.

22. Ibid.

23. See Stephen Franklin, "Chiapas: An Adventure into Reality," *Chicago Tribune*, May 22, 2005.

24. See Michael Clancy, *Exporting Paradise: Tourism and Development in Mexico* (Oxford: Pergamon, 2001), 2.

25. On business travelers, or what the author refers to as "investor tourists," see William Schell Jr., *Integrated Outsiders: The American Colony in Mexico City, 1876–1911* (Wilmington, Del.: SR Books, 2001), 79 and 117–18. On early travel to Mexico and its dangers, see Aida Mostkoff, "Foreign Visitors and Images of Mexico: One Hundred Years of International Tourism, 1821–1921" (Ph.D. diss., UCLA, 1999). On border bandits, see Paul J. Vanderwood's classic text *Disorder and Progress: Bandits, Police, and Mexican Development* (Lincoln: University of Nebraska Press, 1981).

26. Lesley B. Simpson's famous phrase "many Mexicos" from the book of the same title (1941) illustrates the need to build a united highway network and, thus, a united Mexico after the revolution. On how leaders dealt with this challenge and on road construction, see Wendy Waters, "Re-mapping the Nation: Road Building as State Formation in Post-Revolutionary Mexico, 1925–1940" (Ph.D. diss., University of Arizona, 1999), and Waters, "Remapping Identities: Road Construction and Nation Building in Postrevolutionary Mexico," *The Eagle and the Virgin: Nation and Cultural Revolution in Mexico, 1920–1940*, ed. Stephen

Lewis and Mary Kay Vaughan (Durham, N.C.: Duke University Press, 2005), 221–42.

27. The development of a modern highway system that highlighted tourist spots can be seen in tourist pamphlets, some of which include "Touring in Mexico" (1950) published by the National Tourist Bureau and "Mexico: The Faraway Land Nearby" (1939) published by the Mexican Tourist Association.

28. See Mary Lee Nolan and Sydney Nolan, "The Evolution of Tourism in Twentieth-Century Mexico," *Journal of the West* 27.4 (1988): 14–25. On the role of *indigenismo*, see Rick A. López, "The Noche Mexican and the Exhibition of Popular Arts," *The Eagle and the Virgin: Nation and Cultural Revolution in Mexico, 1920–1940*, ed. Stephen Lewis and Mary Kay Vaughan (Durham, N.C.: Duke University Press, 2005), 23–42, and López, "*Lo más mexicano de México*: Popular Arts, Indians, and Urban Intellectuals in the Ethnicization of Postrevolutionary National Culture, 1920–1972" (Ph.D. diss., Yale University, 2001).

29. For the most important texts on folk arts and crafts, see Néstor García Canclini, *Transforming Modernity: Popular Culture in Mexico*, trans. Lidia Lozano (Austin: University of Texas Press, 1993); Michael Chibnik, *Crafting Tradition: The Making and Marketing of Oaxacan Wood Carvings* (Austin: University of Texas Press, 2003); López, "The Noche Mexicana" and "*Lo mas mexicano*"; and Lois Wasserspring, *Oaxacan Ceramics: Traditional Folk Art by Oaxacan Women* (San Francisco: Chronicle Books, 2000).

30. G. Donald Jud, "Tourism and Economic Growth since 1960," *Inter-American Economic Affairs* 28.1 (summer 1974): 21.

31. José Rogelio Álvarez, "El turismo," *México: 50 años de revolución*, I (Mexico City: Fondo de Cultural Económica, 1963), 61–64; Dina Berger, *The Development of Mexico's Tourism Industry: Pyramids by Day, Martinis by Night* (New York: Palgrave Macmillan, 2006); Nicholas Dagen Bloom, ed., *Pleasure, Profit, and Refuge: American Adventures in Post-War Mexico* (Lanham, Md.: Rowman and Littlefield, 2006); Quetzil E. Castañeda, *In the Museum of Maya Culture: Touring Chichén Itzá* (Minneapolis: University of Minnesota Press, 1996); Clancy, *Exporting Paradise*; Clancy, "Mexican Tourism: Export Growth and Structural Change Since 1970," *Latin American Research Review* 36.1 (2001): 128–50; Andrea Boardman, *Destination México: "A Foreign Land a Step Away," U.S. Tourism to Mexico, 1880s–1950s* (Dallas: DeGolyer Library, Southern Methodist University, 2001); Miguel Guajardo Bonavides, *Relatos y desarrollo del turismo en México* (Mexico City: Miguel Ángel Porrua, 1995); Daniel Hiernaux-Nicolas, ed., *Teoría y praxis del espacio turístico* (Mexico City: UAM-Xochimilco, 1989); Hiernaux-Nicolas, "Cancún Bliss," *The Tourist City*, ed. Dennis R. Judd and Susan S. Fainstein (New Haven, Conn.: Yale University Press, 1999), 124–42; Aida Mostkoff, "Foreign Visitors and Images of Mexico: One Hundred Years of International Tourism,

1821−1921" (Ph.D. diss., UCLA, 1999); James Oles, *South of the Border: Mexico in the American Imagination, 1914−1947* (Washington, D.C.: Smithsonian Institution Press, 1993); Andrew Sackett, "The Two Faces of Acapulco during the Golden Age," *The Mexico Reader: History, Culture, Politics*, ed. Gilbert M. Joseph and Timothy J. Henderson (Durham, N.C.: Duke University Press, 2002), 500−510; Alex M. Saragoza, "The Selling of Mexico: Tourism and the State, 1929−1952," *Fragments of a Golden Age: The Politics of Culture in Mexico Since 1940*, ed. Gilbert M. Joseph, Anne Rubenstein, and Eric Zolov (Durham, N.C.: Duke University Press, 2001), 91−115; Eric Schantz, "From *Mexicali Rose* to the Tijuana Brass: Vice Tours of the United States−Mexico Border, 1910−1965" (Ph.D. diss., UCLA, 2001); Vincent Cabeza de Baca and Juan Cabeza de Baca, "The 'Shame Suicides' and Tijuana," *On the Border: Society and Culture Between the U.S. and Mexico*, ed. Andrew Grant Wood (Lanham, Md.: Rowman and Littlefield, 2004), 145−76; Eric Zolov, "Discovering a Land 'Mysterious and Obvious': The Renarrativizing of Postrevolutionary Mexico," *Fragments of a Golden Age*, ed. Joseph et al., 234−72.

ANDREA BOARDMAN

THE U.S.–MEXICAN WAR AND THE BEGINNINGS

OF AMERICAN TOURISM IN MEXICO

Tourism and war seem an unlikely combination: the bloody cost of combat and the playful serendipity of touring do not easily come together in our historical imagination. Yet soldiers in foreign lands witness more than battles. When responsibilities shift from fighting the enemy to occupying ports, towns, and cities, a natural human curiosity nudges them to explore their surroundings. They soon find themselves becoming a strange kind of hybrid "soldier-and-tourist," like the young Army clerk John Meginness in Mexico City when he "examined the museum and found a large collection of interesting curiosities,"[1] and Captain E. Kirby Smith, who thought that Puebla's cathedral was "the richest and most beautiful in the entire New World,"[2] or Captain Simon Bolivar Buckner, who climbed Popocatépetl, the majestic volcano on the rim of the Valley of Mexico and exclaimed how "we beheld the most remarkable of that mountain chain which stretches, in a glittering belt, from the Gulf to the Pacific Ocean."[3]

In this sense, the experiences of these nineteenth-century soldiers are not so different from those of modern American tourists. "Whether in 1800 or 2000," writes one historian of tourism, "observers found in Mexico a stunning degree of ethnic and regional diversity as well as a dizzying array of apparent contradiction: urban vs. rural, modernity vs. tradition and rich vs. poor."[4] This essay argues that more than 110,000 Americans who went to war in Mexico in the years 1846–48 were the first generation of Americans who in large numbers spent a concentrated time in dramatically diverse parts of Mexico. And although their sojourn on foreign soil was defined by the harshness and unspeakable violence of war, these soldiers nevertheless often found themselves awed by the landscapes, the array of lifestyles, and the rich history they found in Mexico. Many wrote about their experiences during and after the war, sharing their wonderment at the landscape and antiquities and descriptions of people and places, to the extent that these soldier-tourists kept Mexico's attractions in the American imagination for several decades. By the mid-1880s, when two international railroad lines connected Mexico City with El Paso and Laredo, American tourists began to travel to Mexico. In less than forty years, then, the sites that soldiers had marveled at would become "must-see" places and activities on itineraries designed for tourists. By then business and government interests in the United States and Mexico were eager to find ways to work together. As part of this effort, President Porfirio Díaz saw the potential of U.S. tourism and made its development a priority.[5]

The historical impact of these soldier-tourists' experiences for an under-standing of modern tourism has surfaced thanks to a range of richly docu-mented studies that connect the soldiers of the U.S.–Mexican War to such major themes as Manifest Destiny, adventurism, and views of masculinity in the nineteenth century. The list includes James McCaffrey's *Army of Manifest Destiny: The American Soldier in the Mexican War, 1846–1848*; Bruce Win-der's *Mr. Polk's Army: The American Military Experience in the Mexican War*; and the more recent work by Amy Greenberg, *Manifest Manhood and the Antebellum American Empire*, and by Jimmy L. Bryan, *The American Elsewhere: Adventurism and Manliness in the Age of Expansion, 1815–1848*. These scholars, along with others I cite throughout this essay, tapped into the wealth of material written by and about the soldiers and the society in which they were formed. Building on their work, I seek to reach beyond it by attempting to situate U.S. soldiers' war experiences against the background of a budding tourism to Mexico, even as I remain mindful of the terrible cost in civilian and military lives that helped to initiate this cultural shift.

An Overview of the War

The war that initiated the soldiers' travels to Mexico had tremendous conse-quences for both countries as well as for the international balance of power. The Treaty of Adams-Onís in 1819 included in Mexico's domain the land that is today New Mexico, Arizona, Nevada, the southern sections of Colo-rado and Utah, as well as California. With the Treaty of Guadalupe Hidalgo in 1848, which ended the U.S.–Mexican War, Mexico ceded all of that land—529,017 square miles—to the United States in exchange for $15 mil-lion. This is described in several thoughtful studies, including *The Diplo-*

macy of Annexation: Texas, Oregon, and the Mexican War by David M. Pletcher, who lays out the international context in which the United States pursued this war.

The prologue to war began with the Texas Revolution and the defeat of the Mexican army at the Battle of San Jacinto, followed by Texas's declaration of independence in 1836. The Mexican government could not accept the loss of Texas. Political tensions between Mexico and the United States intensified further when James K. Polk campaigned for the presidency in 1844, asserting that his goals included the annexation of Texas and, by any means, the acquisition of California, particularly San Francisco Bay, because it was the perfect seaport for Pacific trade. Polk knew that achieving these goals would risk war with Mexico. When he was elected, Texans did vote to be annexed to the United States—and Mexico was ready to declare war, even though its defenses on the northern frontier were extremely vulnerable, as documented by numerous works, including David J. Weber's *The Spanish Frontier in North America* and *The Mexican Frontier, 1821–1846: The American Southwest under Mexico.*

In late November 1845, Polk's emissary arrived in Mexico City with an offer to buy the provinces of Nuevo México and California, including San Francisco Bay, and settle the Texas question, but a presidential crisis in Mexico City made it impossible for the offer to be considered.[6] Polk then ratcheted up the pressure on Mexico by ordering General Zachary Taylor to establish a U.S. Army base in south Texas on the Gulf coast at the mouth of the Nueces River, while the Mexican army stationed itself near Matamoros on the Rio Grande (Río Bravo del Norte). Both nations claimed the territory between the two rivers as theirs. In March 1846, General Taylor marched into that territory and headed for the Rio Grande, fueling the fire for war. On April 25 when a U.S. scouting party and Mexican troops clashed, Taylor wrote to President Polk that "hostilities have commenced," but before his letter arrived in Washington, the armies started fighting. After the second day's battle, tactically Taylor could declare victory, but strategically it was a draw.[7]

With these two days of battle, which became known as Palo Alto and Resaca de la Palma, named after the areas in which they were fought, the human toll of the war became real, as soldiers and citizens, Mexican and American, confronted loss, pain, and death. Another reality of this war was that over the next two years disease and accidents would kill far more than the battles would.[8] Two historians, Irving W. Levinson and Richard Bruce

Winders, focus on these costs of war as well as the context for this suffering. In *Wars within War: Mexican Guerrillas, Domestic Elites, and the United States of America, 1846–1848*, Levinson explains how the complicated social and political situations in Mexico before and during the war led to battles between different forces within the country as well as against the invaders. In April 1847 while serving as substitute president of Mexico, Pedro María Anaya signed a decree to establish volunteer forces commissioned to operate within various geographic areas. Their mission was to attack U.S. troops.[9] "Having failed to hold the enemy at the frontiers or confine the invader to the coastal plain, the Mexican government would now wage guerrilla war in central Mexico," Levinson concluded. Complicating Mexican defense actions, however, were "agrarian-based revolts against the Mexican government . . . in many parts of the nation." Levinson describes a sorrowful situation: "The Mexican government confronted both an invader advancing upon the national capital and an internal foe of increasing strength. To this bloody mélange—federally sanctioned partisans, spontaneously emerging local guerrilla groups attacking U.S. forces, peasants rebelling against the Mexican government, and regular armies of two nations fighting each other—can be added another consideration: the extent to which many Mexicans divorced themselves from the war effort."[10]

While Levinson details events within Mexico, in *Mr. Polk's Army* Richard Bruce Winders describes the way in which the U.S. Army took shape. General Zachary Taylor had gathered 3,900 regular troops at Corpus Christi: five regiments of infantry, four regiments of artillery, and one regiment of dragoons.[11] Polk asked Congress for 50,000 volunteer citizen soldiers from each state and territory, 20,000 from the western and southern states, and 30,000 to be held in reserve until needed.[12] Those in Taylor's Army of the North marched with him on his campaign to defeat the cities of Monterrey (Nuevo León) and Saltillo (Coahuila). Those with the Army of the West under the command of Brigadier General Stephen Kearny marched from St. Louis, Missouri, along the Santa Fe Trail, the main commercial route into Mexico's Nuevo México, where they took control of Santa Fe on August 18. By the end of 1846 and early 1847, Taylor's army was in control of Mexico's northeastern states, which secured the U.S. control of newly annexed Texas, and Kearny's army, with the help of the U.S. Navy and Marines, had taken control of the key ports and towns of California.

Even though the U.S. forces had won key battles assuring Polk's goals of gaining control of Texas, its southern border, Nuevo México, and California, he still needed the Mexican government to make the U.S. claim on these lands official. To accomplish that, however, he faced a perplexing situation. The Mexican government was in crisis with no leader in a strong enough position to sign a treaty ceding these lands to the United States. Polk decided to increase the pressure by ordering General Winfield Scott to begin his campaign from the Gulf of Mexico toward the Valley of Mexico. Scott landed his troops at Veracruz in early March 1847. When city leaders refused to surrender, he ordered the city bombed until they did. In early April Scott gave the command for his troops to begin moving inland toward Mexico City. General Antonio López de Santa Anna led his troops against them at Cerro Gordo, near Xalapa. The U.S. troops successfully outmaneuvered them and the results were disastrous. The Mexican army disbanded and Santa Anna fled.

Scott decided to station his troops in Xalapa and wait for news about Mexico City and orders from Washington. In the meantime British diplomats assisted with negotiations to try to get Mexican leaders to approve a treaty that would include the U.S. annexation of Texas and relinquish Nuevo México as well as northern and southern California. It soon became clear, however, that there was no hope of a treaty while in Xalapa, so Scott once again tried to increase the pressure for a treaty by marching first to Puebla and then into the Valley of Mexico. After another series of battles, Nicholas Trist, the U.S. negotiator, met with several Mexican leaders in August 1847 but quickly realized that they were not empowered to make a treaty. This failure led to the final battles of the war, which ended with the U.S. Army beating back Santa Anna's troops all the way into the Zócalo, the central plaza of Mexico City. Santa Anna withdrew toward Puebla, leaving Mexico City's leaders to surrender on September 14, 1847.

For the next four and a half months, U.S. troops were stationed in Mexico City. Others occupied Puebla, Xalapa, and Veracruz to the east, and up north, Taylor's army was spread from Saltillo to Monterrey and Tampico, working with city leaders to keep control. Although their presence as occupiers was felt, they were far outnumbered by Mexicans in each place. Then the Treaty of Guadalupe Hidalgo was signed on February 2, 1848, and a transformation began: a shift in the status of the soldiers, many of whom became soldier-tourists in their free time, and a shift in the daily ways Mexican citizens interacted with them. Whether in the capital or in smaller cities the soldiers walked around, observing the daily living of different classes of Mexicans, listening to Spanish and indigenous languages, witnessing the practice of Catholicism, tasting new foods, and learning the effect of the alcohol content of tequila and mescal. They were awed by some of the architecture and evidence of ancient cultures. They visited museums, historic places, and markets. They went on adventures in the countryside, including trips to archaeological sites; they climbed volcanoes and explored caves. They sent home souvenirs, including things they bought, bartered, or took. They were behaving more and more like tourists, although sporadic violence by troops or citizens reminded them they were first and foremost soldiers. One noted: "I venture to assert that there is not one of us to whom the service in Mexico is not a recollection surpassing in interest the most brilliant operation of the Rebellion." The historian Bruce Winders wrote that Lew Wallace, author of *Ben Hur*, served in Mexico as a young man. With enthusiam, this soldier-tourist marveled that "Mexico was a strange land to us all, and full of novelties."[13]

On June 12, 1848, the U.S. flag was lowered and the Mexican flag raised in the Zócalo, the main plaza of Mexico City.[14] The war was officially over and the new treaty would shape the two countries' future relations. In the spring and early summer, soldiers left the capital and other Mexican cities where they had been stationed and headed home. During the course of the war they had traversed historically significant land routes, which would become highways and railways in the years ahead. The country had left its mark on them, as it would for future generations of foreigners.

The "Tourist Gaze" of Soldiers

As a way of exploring how the U.S. soldiers in this war at times became a blend of tourist and soldier, it is helpful to stand in their shoes as they considered their surroundings and interacted with residents. The title of a well-known book on tourism, *Seeing and Being Seen*, resonates with the experience of U.S. soldiers in Mexico.[15] They were unmistakably "being seen," as they moved in groups large and small. To Mexicans they stood out because of their uniforms, weapons, ethnicity, and language. At the same time, U.S. forces cast their own gaze upon the Mexican landscape and people. In the literature on tourism much has been written about the "tourist gaze," a term used to describe a tourist's relationship with the people living in the area being visited. One scholar explains that "the gaze in any historical period is constructed in relationship to its opposite, to non-tourist forms of social experience and consciousness . . . particularly those based within the home and paid work."[16] This was true for U.S. soldiers in Mexico. They were fascinated with daily life in Mexico, constantly comparing how similar activities were performed back home. Another scholar offers a more complex framework: "the *imperial* gaze, the *male* gaze, and the *tourist* gaze." Certainly the American soldiers in Mexico viewed their surroundings from all three of these perspectives.[17]

The Mexicans they encountered viewed the soldiers in a guarded way, men who were the "other," invaders, different in race, ethnicity, physical appearance, language, uniforms, and weapons. During battles, marches, and the occupation, no one doubted they were soldiers in an invading army. But, especially during the occupation, when American soldiers and Mexican civilians began to interact, they could find some common ground in the course of their daily activities. As U.S. soldiers and Mexicans tried to communicate, a general ignorance of each other's language and culture was a source of frustration for both sides and an obstacle for U.S. soldiers who wanted to learn more about Mexico from Mexicans. Without the ability to speak Spanish, soldiers had to try to deduce what was happening around them, so they had to rely on each other for information, much of which was drawn from the books they carried and what was quoted from those books in the military newspapers. It was a clumsy, curious, yet stimulating time.

Certainly the "tourist gaze" of soldier-tourists glimmered with caution. In this context, it took the form of a dual vision—private and public. The letters Captain Ephraim Kirby Smith wrote to his wife offer examples of the private tourist gaze. Early in the war this career officer described how he was struggling to connect Mexico's past and present. After viewing the aftermath of the battle in the city of Monterrey in Nuevo León, Kirby Smith said he had studied the Obispado—or Bishop's Palace—on a hill above the city, where the U.S. troops had won a battle that led to victory.[18] "The Bishop's palace in the distance realizes all I have read and seen in pictures of the old castles of Europe, now standing in ruins, monuments of the feudal ages. . . . There is not a broken arch or fallen column which does not interest me. I would like to explore every ruin and trace in the fragments and shattered sculpture the history of a fallen people, the descendants of the proud and magnificent Spaniards."[19]

The tourist gaze of George Furber, however, was deliberately public and obviously had a commercial goal in mind: selling books. This Tennessee lawyer volunteered for the war and admitted that he could hardly wait to capitalize on a market eager for reports from Mexico. Shortly after his year of duty, he published *The Twelve Months Volunteer or Journal of a Private in the Tennessee Regiment of Cavalry in the Campaign in Mexico.* In the sub-title he announced that it contained a description of "Texas and Mexico, as seen on the march; manners; customs; and, religious ceremonies of the Mexicans."

Furber proceeded to share his tourist gaze, guiding readers with segment titles like "beauty of country south of the Panuco; banana plants; ancient Mexican idol; puros and cigarros; Mexican liquors and method of distillation; politeness of Mexicans; markets of Tampico; sea turtles; style of building; streets; señoritas; Plaza de Armas; hospital; rosca de los muertos, or loaves for the dead; and Mexican ceremonies of marriage." Furber's categories were replicated by many other soldiers whose tourist gaze became apparent in their writings as they observed the differences between Mexico and life at home. They found vivid differences in scenes involving race, class, and religion.

Most of the soldiers were Anglo-American and Protestant, although they varied greatly in terms of class. As most tourists do, they saw and judged people in this foreign land with a sense of their own superiority. They arrived "with a belief in the inferiority of mixed-bloods," observed one historian, enabling them "to predict erroneously what Mexicans would be like. . . . Not surprisingly, the Anglo Americans' expectations were fulfilled."[20] Southerners who brought slaves with them to help in the war faced new challenges together. One newspaper illustration clearly depicts an African American, most likely a slave, fighting side-by-side with Texas Rangers "resisting the Mexican cavalry during the battle of Monterrey."[21] One historian wrote that "the racial justice of the slave South was put under great stress in Mexico, and its finer legal distinctions were sometimes unenforceable there. [Some] soldiers thus engaged in vigilantism to reinforce racial dominance."[22]

In quieter periods, American soldiers, particularly the more well-connected officers, found the harsher edges of the tourist gaze softened by serendipitous encounters when they met Mexicans with whom they had some shared experience that bridged their differences, or Americans who were living and doing business in Mexico. While in Victoria, Tamaulipas, with General Zachary Taylor's army, Maryland volunteer John R. Kenly met Captain Augustine Iturbide, "who had been a scholar at Saint Mary's College, Baltimore, and was now on the staff of General Urrea. He seemed much pleased to meet a Baltimorean who knew some of his former schoolmates." Later in Xalapa, Veracruz, Kenly met and visited with "Mr. James Kennedy, an American gentleman intermarried with a Mexican lady," and "Mr. Henry

Hall, of Poughkeepsie, New York, the superintendent of a cotton factory in the vicinity of town, whose long residence in the country, and familiarity with the Mexican language and character, rendered his society not only agreeable but at all times advantageous to the officers of our garrison."[23]

Although the soldiers' tourist gaze was shaded by their military mission, much of what caught their attention in Mexico, and what they shared with others, were the same subjects and objects that would attract the attention of fellow Americans in the 1880s. By communicating their observations, the soldier-tourists had begun to construct a tourist gaze about Mexico that would provide future travelers with a baseline of familiarity, with which they could agree or disagree.

Mapping Mexico for Readers at Home

Maps are essential for tourism—and for war. In 1846, Mexico's territory included what now are the U.S. states of New Mexico, Arizona, Nevada, California, plus the southern terrain of Colorado and Utah. The military campaigns of the war introduced U.S. soldiers, sailors, and marines—as well as the American public—to a broad swath of this geography. The Americans became consumers of information about Mexico by reading letters and articles written by soldiers and war correspondents traveling with them. Whenever possible, publishers added maps of troop movements and battles. For example, early in the war, the *New York Herald* adapted Tanner's "Travelling Map of Mexico" to orient readers to the country and the *New York Weekly Tribune* offered a map of the Matamoros area, site of the first battles of the war, "drawn expressly for the New-York Tribune by an officer of the U.S. Army."[24]

As General Zachary Taylor's Army of the North conducted their campaign from Matamoros to Monterrey and Saltillo and later on to Tampico, a burst of information—and maps—reached Americans in cities, towns, and farmlands, making it possible for them to follow their countrymen into northern Mexico. Then readers were able to track Colonel Stephen Kearny's Army of the West across the plains into Mexican territory and on to Santa Fé, Nuevo México. After that city surrendered, Kearny led a smaller force, which included topographical engineers, who professionally mapped the terrain, all the way to San Diego, the southernmost point of Alta California.[25] Later these surveyors' maps would become resources for map makers of the new international border.

War-related movements conducted by the Navy and Marines also received attention. After the Mexican surrender of Alta California in January 1847, the U.S. Navy sailed south to the Baja California ports of San José del Cabo, La Paz, and San Lucas, and to the mainland ports of San Blas in Nayarit, Mazatlán in Sinaloa, and Guaymas in Sonora. In letters and memoirs officers and sailors provided news of their military activities as well as their impressions of the varied landscapes and inhabitants around the Sea of Cortés.[26]

On the Gulf Coast, after helping the U.S. Army land at Veracruz and overpower the city, U.S. Navy expeditions then sailed south to Tabasco, Campeche, and the Yucatán to thwart any attacks the Mexican Navy might have attempted against the U.S. troops in Veracruz.[27] As they cruised along the coastal lowlands, where the Papaloapan and Coatzacoalcos rivers flowed into the Gulf of Mexico, those who had read recent books, including *Incidents of Travel in Yucatán* by the archaeologist John Lloyd Stephens and the photographer Frederick Catherwood, knew they were in the area where the Olmec civilization had thrived centuries earlier.[28]

The Navy's other mission, led by Commodore Matthew Perry, attracted the interest of financial investors as well as military strategists. Perry was exploring the possibility of a river and potential canal route across the Isthmus of Tehuantepec that might make it possible for ships to move more quickly between the Atlantic and Pacific Oceans to engage in lucrative trade with "the Orient."[29]

Meanwhile in the north during December 1847, Colonel Alexander Doniphan, a Missouri lawyer, led his First Missouri Mounted Volunteers in a fast-paced sweep through El Paso then south along the Camino Real to Chihuahua, where they battled with Mexican troops, then on to the ancient ruins of Paquimé, also known as Casas Grandes, crossing into Apache and Comanche territory, the desert region of the Bolsón de Mapimí, to finally join General Wool's army in the grape-growing area of Parras, Coahuila.[30] They eventually headed home through Nuevo León and Tamaulipas.[31] In addition to great publicity given them after their return, an unlikely botanist added to the drama.

Dr. Frederick Adolphus Wislizenus had been captured by the Mexican Army while conducting a botanical and geographical study in Chihuahua, so he welcomed the opportunity to travel with Doniphan and his men as far as Monterrey. Wislizenus continued writing detailed scientific notes intermingled with comments on the troops' progress. He submitted his manuscript to the U.S. Senate and released it to the public in the form of a report,

"Memoir of a Tour to Northern Mexico connected with Col. Doniphan's Expedition, in 1846 and 1847—with a Scientific Appendix and Three Maps." His observations added to the stream of information about Mexico for U.S. readers. In prose, he had mapped for them a botanically spectacular and diverse region of the country.[32]

Doniphan's troops crossed through Coahuila, where General Zachary Taylor's Army of the North had fought their last major battle on February 22–23, 1847, on the plains of Buena Vista near Saltillo. The battle of Buena Vista was copiously described, mapped, and celebrated in U.S. newspapers and communities.[33] After General Antonio López de Santa Anna ordered his army to retreat from that battlefield, U.S. soldiers solidified their occupation of the principal cities in the northeast: Saltillo, Monterrey, Matamoros, and Tampico. As an occupying force, these men were among the first to become soldier-tourists. In Saltillo a group of them posed for the only known daguerreotypes of the U.S. Army in Mexico. In one daguerreotype a soldier stands surrounded by a group of Mexican boys in a scene that would be repeated by camera-toting railroad tourists forty years later.[34]

In March 1847, the war shifted farther south when General Winfield Scott landed his Army of Conquest at the port of Veracruz and forced the city's surrender after a siege and four days of bombardment. Three weeks later, on April 17–18, Mexican and U.S. troops fought the deadly battle of Cerro Gordo in the highlands of Veracruz, near Xalapa. Santa Anna's army was shattered and needed to regroup. He barely escaped capture. For the next four months U.S. soldiers traveled in stages along the highway that wound through the states of Veracruz, Puebla, Tlaxcala, and into the Valley of Mexico. In August and September, after a series of battles and heavy losses on both sides, they took control of Mexico City.[35] Each advance, battle, and location was described in letters and newspapers.

Abruptly starting with the truce in mid-September 1847, the U.S. military, with a fluctuating presence of 8,000 to 14,000 in the capital and surrounding area, became an occupying force in a city of over 100,000.[36] This occupation was tense until the news spread that on February 2, 1848, Mexican and U.S. negotiators had agreed on terms of a treaty at the Villa de Guadalupe Hidalgo. New maps would be drawn by a binational boundary expedition, but the results of the treaty were clear: Mexico had lost half of its territory and readers had been exposed to all of it, through maps that explained the course of the war. For two years, Americans had received a lesson about Mexico's geography, a lesson that informed them about the country's contours and attractions, one that would prepare future tourists forty years later.

The Books They Carried

As troops received orders to prepare for war in Mexico, present and incoming soldiers looked at maps and started to read whatever they could find about their various destinations. Three popular books that would serve as travel guides had been printed in 1844, two years before the start of the war. William Prescott's *History of the Conquest of Mexico* quickly became a favorite for U.S. soldiers headed to northern and central Mexico no doubt because "at the beginning of the war, the Secretary of the Navy ordered Prescott's book to be added to every ship's library."[37] Prescott's history of the Aztec empire, the Spaniards' discovery, conquest, struggles, and domination of Mexico fascinated the troops.

For men traveling west to Santa Fé with Colonel Kearny's Army of the West, Josiah Gregg's *Commerce on the Prairies, or The Journal of a Santa Fé Trader during Eight Expeditions across the Great Western Prairies and a Residence of Nearly Nine Years in Northern Mexico* provided detailed descriptions of what to expect along the Santa Fé and Chihuahua trails.[38] For those traveling into northern Mexico, George Wilkins Kendall's *Narrative of the Texan Santa Fé Expedition (. . .) and their March, as Prisoners, to the City of Mexico* provided information about the diverse and intriguing landscapes and lifeways Kendall had seen on a grueling journey. As soon as Kendall was free, he returned to New Orleans and transformed his experience as a prisoner but also as a prototourist into a book that quickly sold 40,000 copies. When the war began in 1846 Kendall returned to Mexico as a war correspondent for the widely read *New Orleans Picayune*.[39]

Soldiers traveling into northern and central Mexico read other books, including two by U.S. diplomats: Waddy Thompson's *Recollections of Mexico* (1846) and Brantz Mayer's *Mexico as It Was and as It Is* (1844).[40] Both included detailed background information on the country's history, government, culture, society, politics, Catholic Church, economy, industry, agriculture, and commerce. Mayer's accounts of Mexico's antiquities intrigued the soldier-tourists, especially when they visited the National Museum in Mexico City. His book contains many illustrations and explanations of items such as the sacrificial stone and funeral vase used by the Aztecs, which were on display there.[41] Soldier-tourists also referenced Mayer's book when they encountered archaeological sites in the Tampico area, in Cholula, and in the Valley of Mexico.

Mayer drew from many sources to describe places he did not visit personally, including *Incidents of Travel in Yucatán* by the archaeologist John Lloyd Stephens and the photographer Frederick Catherwood. It featured exquisite engravings of ancient Mayan architecture in the Yucatán, drawn using a camera lucida. This technological innovation allowed Catherwood to project "the sculpture's image directly onto lined graph paper, where its scale and the complexity of its carving could be captured more easily."[42] The two-volume set stirred the public's– and the soldiers'—curiosity about Mexico, selling "cheaply and in enormous quantity, reaching an unprecedented readership in the United States."[43]

Another Army favorite was *Life in Mexico during a Residence of Two Years in That Country*, written by a witty Scottish American woman. Frances Erskine "Fanny" Calderón de la Barca was the wife of Ángel Calderón de la Barca, Spain's first minister to serve there since Mexico's independence.[44] Documenting her stay in Mexico from 1839 to 1842, Madame Calderón de la Barca offered soldiers an intimate view of Mexican society, including observations about some of the Mexican generals she met at social events, men whom the soldiers would know as enemies.[45]

Soldiers trusted the data and descriptions in Henry G. Ward's book *Mexico in 1827* even though it was about twenty years older than the others they used. They mentioned Ward frequently when they made comments about Mexico's history, government, economy, religion, society, and geography.[46] Ward relied heavily on the "grandfather" of books about Mexico: Alexander von Humboldt's *Political Essay of New Spain* (1811). It was "a massive synthesis of centuries of history, geography, and scientific data and in part was responsible for "the 19th century's discovery of Mexico."[47] Collectively, all these authors did much to shape the U.S. soldiers' understanding of Mexico. In the 1880s tour promoters were still recommending that travelers read these same books.

Sending Home News from Mexico

The soldiers' news from Mexico, supplemented by newspaper reports, reached communities in all mid-nineteenth-century U.S. states and territories. For the first time, war correspondents traveled with the U.S. Army and were in fierce competition with one another to file stories that would entice customers to buy and share newspapers.[48] The newly invented telegraph, which came into use just before the war, the new faster steam presses, and cheaper paper led to the affordable "penny press" that quickened delivery of war news from Mexico to an expanding reading public.[49]

This concentrated flow of information within a two-year time frame helped the American public to "discover" Mexico and develop a degree of familiarity with the country. One way of appreciating the impact of this burst of news from and about Mexico is to indulge in a moment of speculation and do a rough calculation of how many people were exposed to news about the war. With upward of 110,000 Americans traveling in different parts of Mexico, if each had a circle of family and friends of about ten to twenty people—and estimating that in some cases soldiers were from the same town so knew the same people—when multiplied by the total number of men serving in some stage of the war, that could roughly mean that one to two million Americans might have received firsthand information about Mexico as a result of the war. An additional number would have been exposed to accounts about Mexico in newspapers and magazines. A rough estimate of the U.S. population by the end of the 1840s is about seventeen million.[50]

Although it is hard to quantify how many Americans were literate, studies suggest that literacy was growing markedly from the 1820s to the 1840s. There is evidence that parents and communities felt a sense of urgency to educate their young, whether through the common school movement, pay schools, or charity schools. The burgeoning activities of religious publishing companies like the American Tract Society further encouraged the desire and ability to read.[51]

A brief comparison of a volunteer soldier and an officer who served in Mexico suggests that parents used various strategies to ensure that their children became literate. In his memoir, Jacob Oswandel, a volunteer from Pennsylvania, remembered how he not only wrote from Mexico to his family but also to "a farmer in Lancaster county, for whom I used to work when a boy." In his book, Oswandel explained how he was bound to this farmer for food and clothing for nine years. "The agreement [between his parents and the farmer] was also that I was to be sent to school regularly every winter . . . [but] I never got much further in my learning than the Comly's or Cobb's spelling book."[52] Compared to Oswandel, the young Lieutenant Ulysses S. Grant was fortunate his parents could afford to keep him at home in the Western Reserve of Ohio. In his memoir, he recalled that he only had a single teacher in a school that ran "by subscription," but thanks to his father's efforts, Grant was able to advance his education when he entered West Point's class of 1838–39.[53]

Through their letters and memoirs both Grant and Oswandel joined many other veterans in leaving a written legacy of their time in Mexico. The collective impact of their writings helped to root Mexico in the American imagination.[54] A scholar who specializes in American and British perceptions of Mexico concluded that "the literature of one country about another often seems to begin with such travel notes. It is as if more creative work cannot be set easily in a foreign locale until the area has somehow become *domesticated through familiarity*."[55] While this scholar was referring to fiction or poetry, the same can be said about soldiers' letters, memoirs, and newspaper reports from Mexico, because these writings also served to "domesticate through familiarity" and stir interest among readers to see for themselves in time of peace "a foreign land a step away," a term used to attract railroad tourists at the turn of the century.[56]

How Patterns of Interest Become a Tourist Itinerary

Although soldiers' writings added a personalized account of a day's experiences, when viewed collectively, their reactions to Mexico had much in common. The author of one study about American and British writers in Mexico suggests looking for patterns of interest that recur in visitors' observations.[57] For soldier-tourists, those patterns combined their awakening interest in Mexico's history, culture, and life across a dramatically varied landscape, as well as their observations about the relationship between citizens and their leaders. Whether visiting Aztec archaeological sites, a Catholic mass, marketplaces, and community gathering places, or experimenting with a bit of "adventure-tourism" by climbing a volcano or exploring spectacular caves, the patterns of the soldier-tourists' activities tested and shaped an itinerary that fellow Americans would make their own.

The following snapshots of various sites highlight patterns of interest that focus on soldiers' experiences from Veracruz to Mexico City. As they read about, moved through, and recorded their impressions of central Mexico, they were testing and describing what would become a popular itinerary for American tourists in the decades ahead. Soldier-tourists were engaged in a form of "tourist site development."[58] What they did and where they went would later be packaged into the itineraries of organized tour companies in the 1880s.

Soon after General Scott's siege and the surrender of Veracruz in March 1847, soldiers began to explore the city, sending home letters and souvenirs. Soldiers were eager to possess samples of Mexico's material culture in any number of ways and to share those things with friends and family. Second Lieutenant Napoleon Jackson Tecumseh Dana from Maine visited the bombed cathedral and confessed in a letter to his wife how he had obtained the object he was enclosing in the envelope: "Your sacrilegious husband stole from the very altar . . . in the pile of destruction of one of the altars, I found several little consecrated bags which the priests bless and sell to the people, who wear them around their necks under their shirts and shifts as the Indians wear a charm."[59] Other soldiers like Jacob Oswandel shopped around for souvenirs. He had been working as a Pennsylvania bowsman on a canal boat ferrying soldiers on their way to Mexico when he decided to join them. The souvenir that caught his eye was a pair of spurs, which he bought for a friend back home.[60]

While touring Veracruz, John R. Kenly, a Maryland volunteer, spent several hours walking through the eerie dark insides of the fort of San Juan de Ulúa, originally built by Spaniards in 1692. Later he wrote home, mixing the elements of a soldier-tourist's gaze—imperial, male, and tourist: "I have just returned from an exploration of its interior labyrinths, which remind me of my visit to, and recall the wonders of, the Mammoth Cave, Kentucky . . . everything that man as a soldier would require is to be found within these walls."[61] By comparing the fort to Mammoth Cave, Kenly revealed he had visited one of the important American tourist sites of the period, a place where some visitors said they felt an almost spiritual experience of wonder.[62] In the 1880s, when American tourists saw that San Juan de Ulúa was included in their itineraries, they were as eager as Kenly to explore it.

XALAPA

Soon after the battle for Veracruz, General Winfield Scott began moving many of his troops up the coastal range toward Xalapa to escape the yellow fever, which was endemic to the port. Soldiers quickly discovered why Xalapa had long provided a delightful respite for travelers making the trip between Veracruz and Mexico City. It was situated between two climate zones, making it possible for tropical vegetation and mountain forests to coexist.[63] Scott established his headquarters there while he and treaty negotiator Nicholas Trist worked through British intermediaries to try to end the war. In the meantime, the soldiers' relief at being there was almost euphoric. Kirby Smith wrote to his wife that "the climate of this region cannot be surpassed, the soil is exceedingly rich and all the fruits in the world grow in it. If I could have my friends around me and a good government I should delight to pass my life in [X]alapa."[64] Volunteer soldier George Furber, who had also been transferred from northern to central Mexico, continued to work on his "travelogue," reveling in the climate and civility of the city: "[In Xalapa] we saw, in comparison to what we witnessed in the valley of the Rio Grande, just what a foreign traveler would see in the United States, in New York, Pennsylvania, or any of the older states, compared with the frontiers of the west."[65]

Beyond extolling Xalapa's weather and surroundings, soldiers took great pleasure in seeing and writing about the city's beautiful women "of good class." Navy lieutenant Ralph Semmes encountered a mother and daughter traveling from Veracruz to Xalapa. "The daughter was so beautiful, that I was afraid to do more than admire her from a respectful distance."[66] George Furber reported that "the ladies of Jalapa are, with few exceptions, beautiful —strikingly so; and their manners are most agreeable and pleasing." As for the men, he wrote that they were "superior to those that we had before met with; more industrious and enterprising. Several cotton and woolen factories are on the streams about the city, and all the business within it was brisk and flourishing."[67] Tourists arriving in the 1880s would extol many of the charms of Xalapa that had enchanted the soldiers.

VOLCANOES

Where some saw beauty, others saw a tourist destination—for healthy people as well as for those seeking a cure. The *American Star* newspaper, published in Mexico City for the troops, reported that "the Americans astutely prophesied that 'a visit to Popocatépetl will be deemed as great a treat as a visit to Niagara.' Because of the mountain's pure air and water, they all agreed, 'it would someday serve as a resort for invalids.' "[68] The volcanoes also appealed to the athletically minded. During the U.S. Army's occupation of Mexico in the spring of 1848, in what today would be called "adventure tourism," two groups of U.S. soldiers climbed Popocatépetl (Simon Buckner among them) and one ascended the Citlatépetl—or the Peak of Orizaba.[69] By the 1880s, American tourists, as well as American residents of Mexico City, continued to be fascinated with scaling these volcanoes. One group even attempted to ride bicycles, unsuccessfully, up the side of Popocatépetl![70]

PUEBLA

After Xalapa, the next stop on the route to Mexico City was Puebla, known for its churches and its textile industry since early colonial times. In 1827, H. G. Ward had described the city as home to 50,000 and "the seat both of the richest Bishoprick in the country, and of the most extensive manufactures of cotton, earthenware, and wool." Ward wrote that "whether of divine or human origin, the Cathedral is a very fine building, and the riches of the interior are worthy of a country that has produced, during the last two centuries, nearly two-thirds of the whole of the silver raised annually in the world."[71] In the early 1840s Waddy Thompson, in *Recollections of Mexico*, remembered Puebla as "the Lowell of Mexico," referring to the important textile industry in Lowell, Massachusetts.[72] By the time of the war, Puebla's population had grown to 80,000. In May 1847, city leaders opened the gates to Scott's army, not because they were eager to help the soldiers but because they wanted to protect the city itself. Puebla's residents had been through a complicated and painful history with Santa Anna and had no interest in fighting on his behalf.[73]

At the beginning of the U.S. Army's occupation of Puebla, Ephraim Kirby Smith had arrived before his uncle Edmond, who was an officer assigned to a later regiment arriving from Veracruz. In a tourist-like mode they stopped for ice cream (made using ice from the volcano Popocatépetl) and then attended Mass in the Cathedral. He noted in a letter to his wife that it "is said to be the richest and most beautiful one in the entire New World" but this soldier-tourist became a soldier again when he reminded himself as well as his wife: "There have been several cases of stabbing today and one soldier killed. It is dangerous to go about alone or unarmed."[74] Admiring a beautiful seventeenth-century cathedral as a tourist and fearing death as a soldier capture the essence of what it was like to be a soldier-tourist during the war.

The Army's occupation of Puebla was tense although city leaders and military officers managed to sustain a mostly workable coexistence even when the city was attacked at the end of the war by Santa Anna's army. By the 1880s, American tourists eagerly visited Puebla's cathedral and its many other churches. However, fellow Americans who were Protestant missionaries in this bastion of Catholicism were not as welcome as the tourists.[75]

"A well-paved road cut by the old Spaniards, ascends from the northwest corner, with steps at regular intervals . . . to the front of the small, dome-crowned chapel . . . dedicated to the Virgin of Remedios" was how Brantz Mayer described the pyramid of Cholula that so intrigued soldiers.[76] They also consulted William Prescott's and H. G. Ward's books for details. A twentieth-century guidebook gives the dimensions: "At 425 metres square and 60 metres high it's even larger in volume than Egypt's Pyramid of Cheops."[77] Discovering a Catholic chapel on top of an ancient temple, the mostly Protestant soldier-tourists had much to consider regarding the physical layering of belief systems. Cholula was one of the many places where they collected souvenirs. "Like all travelers," observes one historian, "the soldiers were avid souvenir hunters. At Cholula, they carried off bricks with which the pyramid had been constructed, or purchased from Mexican vendors small clay figures that had been recovered from the debris surrounding the pyramid."[78]

In the 1880s when the railroad-tourists began to arrive in places like Vera-cruz, Xalapa, Puebla, and other cities where soldiers had been, they were just as interested in buying souvenirs from eager local vendors or in stores that catered to foreigners. And once they went home, these turn-of-the-century tourists could continue to make purchases through sales catalogues. In 1909, for example, the Francis E. Lester Company of Mesilla Park, New Mexico, advertised "genuine Indian and Mexican handicraft, native gems, etc."[79]

TENOCHTITLÁN

In September 1847, General Santa Anna left Mexico City, in the valley of what had been known centuries earlier as Tenochtitlán, the center of the Aztec empire. General Scott and his officers were well aware of the symbolism of their "conquering" presence but uneasy that they were far outnumbered by the residents of the city and the valley. They quickly worked with Mexican leaders to set in motion the terms of the military occupation and ways in which the citizenry could return to daily life. As tensions eased in most areas, soldiers began touring one of the largest and oldest cities in the hemisphere. They visited the center, the outskirts, including the canals of Xochimilco, and some even explored as far as the pyramids of Teotihuacán to the northeast and Cuernavaca to the south. Their tourist activities increased once news spread that on February 2, 1848, negotiators had signed a treaty and the ratification process was underway. They knew that when it was ratified by the U.S. Senate they would be able to go home.[80]

In his book *Mexico in 1827*, H. G. Ward wrote that after visiting "the great Plaza, the Cathedral, the Palace, and the noble streets which communicate with them, we were forced to confess not only that Humboldt's praises did not exceed the truth, but that amongst the various Capitals of Europe, there were few that could support with any advantage a comparison with Mexico."[81] Twenty years later U.S. soldiers used Ward's descriptions as a guide to places they should visit and shared his enthusiasm for what they discovered. These soldier-tourists also relied on the books by Brantz Mayer, Waddy Thompson, William Prescott, and Francis "Fanny" Calderón de la Barca as they explored their surroundings.

At the city's core, the cathedral was a magnet for soldier-tourists. They had read that it had been built over an ancient Aztec temple, which doubled its attraction for them. Yet their own belief systems tempered their ability to show reverence. Most soldiers were Protestants, and some, including at least one general, were missionaries.[82] The American Bible Society had given Bibles to volunteers on their way to Mexico.[83]

Twenty-one-year-old volunteer John F. Meginness was stationed in Mexico City with Company D of the Fifth Infantry from Lancaster County, Pennsylvania. He had arrived in Mexico as part of the occupation force during the time the peace treaty was working its way through the U.S. and Mexican congresses. On February 19, 1848, Meginness wrote in his journal, "I here make an extract from the [American] 'Star' giving an account of the Gold and Silver ornaments contained in the Cathedral of 'The City of Mexico' which runs thus" and listed many items and their value in dollars. It was a description similar to one found in Brantz Mayer's book.[84]

On February 27, 1848, Meginness noted in his journal that he had found another "excellent extract" in Brantz Mayer's book *Mexico as It Was and as It Is*, about "the physical condition of the country." He made the diplomat's words his own by recording them in his diary: "Mexico is naturally a rich country," he concluded, although "the incentives to labor are scarcely efficient and the race, weakened, on the one hand by a mixture [of a] debased aboriginal population and on the other unfortunately . . . by a strong tinture of Castilian pride."[85] Then, after detailing the gold, silver, marble, and jewels on the dress of the Virgin of Remedios, Meginness referred to Mayer and observed that "around this splendid mine of wealth are half-naked Indians, gaping with surprise, or kneeling to the figure of some favorite saint—the misery of the man a painful contrast with the splendor of the shrine!"[86] Perhaps nothing more clearly demonstrated the extremities of what attracted and repelled travelers than the opulent riches of the cathedral and the beggars who stood outside. American tourists who traveled by train to Mexico later in the century had similar reactions to those of Meginness and many of the other soldiers.

Just as soldier-tourists felt compelled to visit the cathedral, they were drawn to the shrine of the Virgin of Guadalupe, Mexico's patron saint. Brantz Mayer described what it was like attending church services, "crammed to suffocation," on the festival honoring her.[87] Catholic Mexicans were the observed. Protestant Americans were the observers, and in some cases evangelizers.[88] For soldier-tourists and the railroad tourists who followed them in the 1880s, religion would continue to be a line that divided most American tourists from the majority of Mexicans. By the time the railroad tourists arrived, however, more Americans and Europeans had become residents in Mexico City and there were Methodist, Episcopal, Anglican, and Catholic services in English.[89] American tourists could put their tourist gaze on hold and participate in worship rather than watch and judge others.

Beyond observing religious and social differences between home and Mexico, soldier-tourists were eager to learn more about Mexico's antiquities. The National Museum was a favorite attraction on their itineraries. Descriptions by Ward, Prescott, and Mayer as well as those printed in the *Daily American Star* and other wartime newspapers, piqued the soldiers' interest.[90] Young, impressionable John Meginness was one of them: "Visited the city of Mexico, examined the museum and found a large Collection of interesting curiosities. I observed a large collection of stones of different shapes, covered with Hirogliphic characters; some were shaped like men and beasts, and were probably objects of worship among the ancient Aztecs. A large bronzed statue of Charles IV stands in the yard, it formally used to stand in the Plaza mounted on a high pedestal."[91] A fellow soldier from Pennsylvania, Jacob Oswandel, exclaimed that this statue was "one of the seven wonders of the world."[92] By the time of the railroad tourists, the statue had been moved to the new Reforma Boulevard, where it continued to attract tourists' attention, in person and on postcards.[93]

Meginness continued through the museum, stopping at the display of Aztec antiquities: "I, also, saw the ancient weapons of war used by the

Indians, such as bows and arrows, and huge war-clubs curiously carried, representing the deities which they worshiped. The greatest curiosity to be seen is the remains of Montezuma's war-dress, which consists of two blankets of curious construction and a large mantle."[94] Jacob Oswandel provided a few more details of the war dress in his memoir: "It is made of wild duck skins and ornamented with snake skins, etc."[95]

Leaving the museum and crossing the central plaza, soldier-tourists could stroll down the Calle de San Francisco. In the shops along this street and others, soldiers became more relaxed as merchants reached out for their business. Meginness wrote that he "visited the city today in order to 'kill time' and satisfy my prying curiosity . . . I observed that every thing looked gay and active, the streets of this great city were crowded with thousands, passing to and fro in rapid succession. The large mercantile houses made quite an imposing and rich display of goods."[96] One historian noted that "tailors, barbers, storekeepers, bar-keepers, and hotel-keepers, felt the influence of the language of the conqueror, and hastened to substitute for their signs and advertisements other signs and advertisements in the English language."[97] As resignation and pragmatism set in, Mexican business owners advertised in the *American Star* as well as other papers.[98]

The U.S. Army also had its commercial side. Sometimes a soldier-tourist, other times an entrepreneur, Ulysses S. Grant was a young regimental quartermaster and commissary who was faced with a shortage of clothes for the troops, especially for the regimental bands. During the winter of 1847–48, to raise funds, Grant got a contract from the chief commissary to bake bread for the troops, then rented a bakery, hired Mexican bakers, and began to make money to buy cloth for the band uniforms, as well as extra comforts for the troops.[99]

The Alameda Park was the city's most beautiful gathering place for citizens and soldiers. The park became a popular tourist attraction for them, especially on Sundays. Soldier-tourists watched city residents dressed in fine clothes either walk or ride in carriages where they could see and be seen. John Meginness contemplated its refreshing charm: "The Alameda looks most beautifull, all the trees are in full bloom. . . . When we look abroad and to the ruinous effects occasioned by war, astonishment takes hold of the mind, to contemplate that this lovely valley should be traversed by an invading and conquering army, spreading ruin and devastation around. Here you have an opportunity of witnessing the most lovely & beautiful scene. . . . In a fertile country like this every indulgence can be had which human nature could wish for in order to complete its happiness."[100]

During their occupation of Mexico City soldiers found various sources of entertainment beyond touring historical and cultural sites. They attended bullfights, circus performances, theater, concerts, and even dances, arranged by army officers and city leaders. Apparently young Meginness was not hesitant to join in: "Visited the Ball or 'fandango' last night, which was given in this place. I noticed quite a number of Mexican Señoritas present which made the affair pass off quite well. A large number of n[on]commissioned officers and soldiers were present, by the way, they all got pretty well 'blessed' and quite boisterous and noisy." Getting "blessed," or drinking too much, and gambling were also popular ways to pass the time. Meginness described his visit to the New Orleans meson, "one of the most fashionable places in town." He "drank several glasses of brandy—stepped into the gambling [where] there was crowds gathered around the numerous tables—some were trying their luck on the "Wheel of Fortune."... This is the grand rendezvous of all gamblers and follows the Army."[101]

Surrounded by Mexico's great natural beauty, soldier-tourists discovered ways to enjoy outdoor adventures beyond the city limits. Ulysses S. Grant and a few friends decided to visit Cuautla. On the way, they were challenged by the Mexican general in charge of the area and told that they were beyond the limits set by the armistice, but they were allowed to continue to Cuernavaca, where they visited "the tomb of an ancient king." Next they headed for one of the great caves in the area but had to convince a guard they were "a mere party of pleasure-seekers desirous of visiting the great natural curiosities of the country which we expected soon to leave." With "guides, candles, and rockets," they explored about three miles through the cave, using the rockets to light up the chambers and see the "great dimensions and great beauty" of the stalactites and stalagmites."[102] Grant's description could have been influenced by a similar one in Brantz Mayer's account of visiting the "Cavern of Cacahuawamilpa."[103]

In their final months in Mexico City, leading up to their departure in July 1848, soldier-tourists learned as much as they could about the mosaic that was Mexico. They ventured out to see the sights beyond the city, like the canals of Chalco and Xochimilco and the grand pyramids of Teotihuacán. Daily, as they interacted with the citizenry for food, services, and information, and at such public events as bullfights, religious celebrations, concerts, and dances, they added layers of personal experiences to the information they gleaned from books and newspapers. They had already begun to share their stories through letters home. Once they were back in the United States many wrote magazine and newspaper accounts, and as they grew older, they began writing memoirs. Some even returned to Mexico to reconnect to earlier memories and to create new ones.

In 1884 and 1885, with the completion of two international railroad connections, one from El Paso/Ciudad Juárez and the other through Laredo, American tourists had direct access to Mexico. In the fall of 1885, thirty-eight years after leaving Mexico City as a soldier, John Meginness returned as a tourist. By then he was a newspaper editor, with the nom de plume "John of Lancaster."[104] The *Two Republics*, a Mexico City daily, interviewed him and he authored several articles for the *Daily Gazette and Bulletin* of Williamsport, Pennsylvania. Meginness described his visit to Tacubaya where he had been quartered in 1847–48. "Where the street cars stop," he wrote in the *Gazette*, "I found the identical buildings wholly unchanged." However, the *Two Republics* reported that Meginness was pleased with what had changed elsewhere, especially "the presence of electric lights and other modern improvements in Mexico. He was loud in his praise of the magnificent roadbed and rolling stock of the Mexican Central railroad. He has kept up actively with the progress of Mexico, but was scarcely prepared to see such a metropolitan capital."[105]

When he arrived home from this trip, Meginness pasted the *Two Republics* newspaper clippings into the back of his war journal, which he had begun on February 12, 1848. On that day, in fine tight penmanship, he had written his first entry. He described how, in the company of two other soldiers, he "made an excursion through Molino del Rey, and the hill of Chapultepec to view some interesting [items?] of antiquity." Perhaps at that time he had found the sheepskin-covered ledger in which he began keeping his journal. According to Meginness, originally the ledger had been used to record deliveries of gunpowder supplies to the "Fabrica de Chapultepec." The building was also known as Molino del Rey, one of the final battle sites of the war. He then described locating "the ancient Cypress tree called Montezuma, . . . and according to Mr. Ward[']s travels is as surprising to him." He then transcribed and paraphrased sections of Ward's book and gave the citation: "Wards Mexico in 1827 Vol. ii. p. 230."

In 1885, the same year that Meginness returned to Mexico City, New England tourists on a Raymond and Whitcomb packaged tour went to see the same tree in Chapultepec Park that Meginness had visited as a soldier— "the ancient Cypress tree called Montezuma." They gathered around the tree and recorded the moment by taking a photograph.[106]

Raymond and Whitcomb's recommended reading list directed their guests to some of the same books read by the soldier-tourists: William Prescott's *The Conquest of Mexico* and Alexander von Humboldt's *Political Essay of New Spain*. Lists published by other tour companies included H. G. Ward, Waddy Thompson, Fanny Calderón de la Barca, Brantz Mayer, and John Lloyd Stephens's *Incidents in the Yucatan*. But writers of guides and other forms of tourist information for railroad tourists only made slight reference to the war of 1846–48, which perhaps is understandable given that the 1880s were the years when both countries were eager to promote business connections. James Steele's pamphlet *To Mexico by Palace Car* (1884) minimized and distorted what had happened at the battle of Molino del Rey: "The building is still there, but the place shows no marks of the fierce little skirmish that took place there immediately before storming of Chapultepec."[107] That "skirmish" on September 8, 1847, resulted in 2,000 Mexicans killed or wounded and, on the U.S. side, 116 killed and 665 wounded.[108] Raymond and Whitcomb's excursion booklet in 1885 informed tourists going to Chapultepec Park that they would see "a monument to the [Mexican] cadets who fell in defence of the Castle when it was attacked by the Americans in 1847."[109] That monument marked the beginning of Mexico's efforts to display for public memory the country's painful loss of the war and half of its territory.

In February 1880 another war veteran returned to Mexico and gave a boost to U.S. tourism. After his presidency, Ulysses S. Grant became involved in various business ventures in Mexico, including railroads. He sailed to Veracruz, traveled to Mexico City with an escort of government dignitaries and 2,500 soldiers, and participated in parades, banquets, and tours.[110] Among the steps Grant took to promote business and travel in Mexico was an endorsement he wrote for the 1884 edition of *Appleton's Guide to Mexico, Including a Chapter on Guatemala, and an English-Mexican Vocabulary*. The author, Alfred R. Conkling, considered his audience to be "the capitalist, the speculator, the artist, the archaeologist, the valetudinarian [invalid], and the pleasure-seeker, as well as the intelligent and enterprising man of business."[111]

From the time of the U.S.–Mexican War to the time of the railroads, maps of Mexico City and other major cities evolved on paper and in memory, selectively targeting and shaping the business of tourism. The contribution of the soldier-tourists was that they had created a sense of familiarity about Mexico for fellow Americans by describing for them all the terrain the soldiers had covered, the places they had visited, the questions they had asked, and the observations they had shared with family and friends.

In a study titled *Mapping Tourism*, the essay "Tourism Spaces, Mapped Representations, and the Practices of Identity" provides a context in which to view the significance of the activities of the soldier-tourists and the Mexicans who had contact with them. Using a variety of resources and communicating their discoveries through letters, newspaper articles, and memoirs, American soldiers were creating a foundation of maps and itineraries on which American railroad tourists would build: "Like any other map, a tourism map conveys information to us about places," wrote the authors of one study. "And it represents a particular way of socially and spatially organizing places of consumption for tourists and non-tourists alike."[112] The places highlighted on these maps and itineraries "are markers that identify the things and places worthy of our gaze." Such "signposting," wrote one sociologist, "identifies a relative small number of tourist nodes. The result is that most tourists are concentrated within a very limited area."[113] The writings of soldier-tourists "signposted" places for railroad tourists, especially those who were of the same generation as the soldiers or the one that followed.

Although the Mexican Revolution stopped all tourism from 1910 to 1920, by the mid- to late 1920s, when Americans wanted to return, Mexico's government and nascent travel industry reached out to welcome them. Quickly, tourism to Mexico became an important industry for businesses large and small on both sides of the border. The wonderful climate of Xalapa, the temple at Cholula, Puebla's charming streets and many churches, the stunning volcanoes, Aztec, Toltec, and Olmec archaeological sites, Mexico City's great cathedral, the museum and marketplaces, Chapultepec Castle, and the ever popular "ancient Cypress tree called Montezuma" awaited them. What had riveted the "tourist gaze" of the soldier-tourists of the U.S.– Mexican War had become "must see" places on maps and itineraries for future generations of American tourists.

Notes

My deep appreciation goes to David J. Weber, professor of history and director of the William P. Clements Center for Southwest Studies at Southern Methodist University, for sharing his expertise and support; to William B. Taylor, professor of history. University of California Berkeley, especially for his course "Double Eagle: American Representations of Mexico, 1821–Present"; to David Farmer and Russell Martin, former and current directors of the DeGolyer Library at Southern Methodist University, for the opportunity to explore the library's holdings related to the U.S.–Mexican War as well as tourism to Mexico, resulting in an exhibition and catalogue on each of these subjects; to SMU Professors Edward Countryman, for sharing his expertise on American life in the 1840s, and Sherry Smith, for her expertise on nineteenth-century military life; to Dina Berger, assistant professor of history at Loyola University Chicago, for our conversations about her work on Mexico and tourism; to the anthropologist Sylvia Rodríguez, University of New Mexico, for her encouragement to think about these soldiers as "proto-tourists"; to the executive producer of KERA-TV, Sylvia Komatsu, the military consultant George Stone, the historian Miguel Soto Estrada, Universidad Nacional Autónoma de México, and the historian Miguel Ángel González Quiroga, Universidad Autónoma de Nuevo León, who were colleagues in the production of PBS documentary project, *The U.S.–Mexican War, 1846–1848*; to the historian Robert W. Johannsen, whose book *To the Halls of the Montezumas: The Mexican War in the American Imagination* was an inspiration and guide for exploring how soldiers could be seen as tourists. And special thanks to Hermann Michaeli for his steadfast support and to my friends Lucy McCauley and Charles Bambach for their review of the final draft.

1. John F. Meginness, "Journal," February 15, 1848, University of Texas at Arlington Libraries, Special Collections Division, Jenkins Garret Special Collections. A special note of gratitude to Katherine R. Goodwin, former curator, for bringing this journal to my attention.

2. Ephraim Kirby Smith, letter of May 16, 1847, *To Mexico with Scott: Letters of Captain E. Kirby Smith to His Wife*, ed. Emma Jerome Blackwood (Cambridge, Mass.: Harvard University Press, 1917), 166. Also see Jerry Thompson, "Winfield Scott's Army of Occupation as Pioneer Alpinists: Epic Ascents of Popocatépetl and Citlaltépetl," *Southwestern Historical Quarterly* 105, no. 4 (April 2002): 549–81.

3. [Simon B. Buckner], "A Visit to Popocatépetl," *Putnam's Monthly: A Magazine of Literature, Science, and Art* 1 (April 1853), 408. Also see Jerry Thompson, "Winfield Scott's Army of Occupation as Pioneer Alpinists: Epic Ascents of Popocatépetl and Citlaltépetl," *Southwestern Historical Quarterly*, 105, no. 4 (April 2002): 549–81.

4. Jürgen Buchenau, ed. and trans., *Mexico Otherwise: Modern Mexico in the Eyes of Foreign Observers* (Albuquerque: University of New Mexico Press, 2005), 1.

5. Dina Berger, *The Development of Mexico's Tourism Industry: Pyramids by Day, Martinis by Night* (New York: Palgrave Macmillan, 2006), 6–7.

6. K. Jack Bauer, *The Mexican War, 1846–1848* (Lincoln: University of Nebraska Press, 1992), 24–25.

7. Ibid., 57; for a description of the battles of Palo Alto and Resaca de la Palma, see 46–63.

8. Richard Bruce Winders, *Mr. Polk's Army: The American Military Experience in the Mexican War* (College Station: Texas A&M Press, 1997), 145, 147.

9. Irving W. Levinson, *Wars within War: Mexican Guerrillas, Domestic Elites, and the United States of America, 1846–1848* (Fort Worth: Texas Christian University, 2005), 34–35.

10. Ibid., 40, 49, 51.

11. Winders, *Mr. Polk's Army*, 52.

12. Ibid., 69.

13. Ibid., 167.

14. Bauer, *The Mexican War*, 388.

15. *Seeing and Being Seen: Tourism in the American West*, ed. David M. Wrobel and Patrick T. Long (Lawrence: University Press of Kansas, 2001).

16. John Urry, *The "Tourist Gaze"* (London: Sage, 2002), 1–2.

17. Sylvia Rodríguez, "The 'Tourist Gaze,' Gentrification, and the Commodification of Subjectivity in Taos," *Essays on The Changing Images of the Southwest*, ed. Richard Francaviglia and David Narrett (College Station: Texas A&M University Press, 1994), 107.

18. Bauer, *The Mexican War*, 97.

19. Smith, letter of November 2, 1846, *To Mexico with Scott*, 70–71.

20. David J. Weber, " 'Scarce more than apes': Historical Roots of Anglo American Stereotypes of Mexicans in the Border Region," *New Spain's Far Northern Frontier: Essays on Spain in the American West, 1540–1821* (Dallas: Southern Methodist University Press, 1988), 300.

21. "The Texan Infantry Resisting the Mexican Cavalry," from *The Illustrated Sun and Holiday Present*, in *Texas Extra: A Newspaper History of the Lone Star State, 1835–1935* (Edison, N.J.: Castle Books, 1999), 28.

22. Paul W. Foos, *A Short, Offhand, Killing Affair: Soldiers and Social Conflict during the Mexican-American War* (Chapel Hill: University of North Carolina Press, 2002), 98. Also, see Foos's reference to Robert E. May, "Invisible Men: Blacks and the U.S. Army in the Mexican War," *Historian* 49 (August 1987): 464–77.

23. John R. Kenley, *Memoirs of a Maryland Volunteer: War with Mexico, in the Years 1846–7–8.* (Philadelphia: J. B. Lippincott, 1873), 196, 464–77.

24. Robert W. Johannsen, *To the Halls of the Montezumas: The Mexican War in the American Imagination* (New York: Oxford University Press, 1987), 11. An 1846

atlas version of Tanner's map, with its insert of the Valley of Mexico and Guatemala, is at DeGolyer Library, Southern Methodist University: "Mexico & Guatemala by H[enry] S[chenck] Tanner; engraved by J. Knight" (Philadelphia: H. N. Burroughs, 1846), plate 36, color 12″ × 15″. *New-York Weekly Tribune* printed the Matamoros map on Saturday, May 16, 1846.

25. Bauer, *The Mexican War*, 127–44. Johannsen, *To the Halls of the Montezumas*, 159. See Neal Harlow, *California Conquered: War and Peace on the Pacific, 1846–1850* (Berkeley: University of California Press, 1982).

26. See K. Jack Bauer, *Surfboats and Horse Marines: U.S. Naval Operations in the Mexican War, 1846–48* (Annapolis: U.S. Naval Institute, 1969); Tunis Augustus Macdonough Craven, *A Naval Campaign in the Californias, 1846–1849* (San Francisco: Book Club of California, 1973); James D. Bruell, *Sea Memories, or Personal Experiences in the U.S. Navy in Peace and War* (Biddeford Pool: The author, 1886); Don Meadows, *The American Occupation of La Paz* (Los Angeles: G. Dawson, 1955); Samuel Francis Du Pont, *Extracts from Private Journal-Letters of Captain S. F. Du Pont while in Command of the Cyane during the War with Mexico, 1846–48/ Printed for his family* (Wilmington, Del.: Ferris Bros., printers, 1885).

27. See Raphael Semmes, *Service Afloat and Ashore during the Mexican War: By Lieut. Raphael Semmes, U.S.N.* (Cincinnati: Wm. H. Moore, 1851).

28. See John L. Stephens, *Incidents of Travel in Yucatan* (New York: Harper and Brothers, 1843).

29. See Ana Rosa Suárez Argüello, *La Batalla por Tehuantepec: El peso de los intereses privados en la relación México—Estados Unidos, 1848–1854* (Mexico City: Secretaría de Relaciones Exteriores, 2003).

30. For images of the ruins at Paquimé and the Casas Grandes area, see Virginia Fields, Victor Zamudio-Taylor; with contributions by Michele Beltrán [et al.], *The Road to Aztlan: Art from a Mythic Homeland* (Los Angeles: Los Angeles County Museum of Art, 2001).

31. Bauer, *The Mexican War*, 135–38, 151–58; and Johannsen, *To the Halls of the Montezumas*, 159. Also see Joseph G. Dawson III, *Doniphan's Epic March: The 1st Missouri Volunteers in the Mexican War* (Lawrence: University Press of Kansas, 1999).

32. Frederick A. Wislizenus, *A Tour to Northern Mexico, Connected with Col. Doniphan's Expedition, in 1846–1847* (1st ed. 1848; Glorieta, N.M.: Rio Grande Press, 1969), i.

33. Johannsen, *To the Halls of the Montezumas*, 106–7.

34. Martha Sandweiss, Rick Stewart, and Ben W. Huseman, *Eyewitness to War: Prints and Daguerreotypes of the Mexican War, 1846–1848* (Fort Worth: Amon Carter Museum; Washington, D.C.: Smithsonian Institution Press, 1989), 45, 203.

35. Bauer, *The Mexican War*, chaps. 13–16.

36. Donald S. Frazier, ed., *The United States and Mexico at War: Nineteenth-Century Expansionism and Conflict* (New York: Macmillan, 1998), 252.

37. Johannsen, *To the Halls of the Montezumas*, 150.

38. Ibid., 157.

39. George Wilkins Kendall, *Narrative of the Texan Santa Fé Expedition, Comprising a Description of a Tour Through Texas*... ed. Gerald D. Saxon and William B. Taylor (1st ed. 1844; Dallas: DeGolyer Library and William P. Clements Center for Southwest Studies, Southern Methodist University, 2004), xviii.

40. Waddy Thompson, *Recollections of Mexico* (New York: Wiley and Putnam, 1846), and Brantz Mayer, *Mexico as It Was and as It Is* (New York: J. Winchester, New World Press, 1844).

41. See Mayer, *Mexico as It Was and as It Is*, 100, 119–20.

42. R. Tripp Evans, *Romancing the Maya: Mexican Antiquity in the American Imagination, 1820–1915* (Austin: University of Texas Press, 2004), 53. See Mayer, *Mexico as It Was and as It Is*, 108.

43. Evans, *Romancing the Maya*, 3, 45.

44. The personal diary of her husband, Ángel Calderón de la Barca, adds intriguing context to Fanny's observations. It is being edited by the historian Miguel Soto Estrada for publication (Southern Methodist University, DeGolyer Library, MS A88.1509C).

45. María Soledad Arbeláez A., "Mexico in the Nineteenth Century through British and North American Travel Accounts" (Ph.D. diss., University of Miami, 1995), 399–405.

46. Henry G. Ward, *Mexico in 1827* (London: Henry Colburn, 1828). Ward wrote his two-volume work when he was the British chargé d'affaires to Mexico in 1823 and in 1825–27. He was twenty-seven when he first arrived in Veracruz, similar in age to many of the U.S. soldiers, but, unlike the soldiers, Ward had access to leaders and intellectuals, including Lucas Alamán, Carlos María de Bustamante, and José Miguel Ramos Arizpe. See Arbeláez A., "Mexico in the Nineteenth Century through British and North American Travel Accounts," 250.

47. Johannsen, *To the Halls of the Montezumas*, 147–48.

48. See Thomas William Reilly, "American Reporters and the Mexican War, 1846–1848" (Ph.D. diss., University of Minnesota, 1975).

49. Johannsen, *To the Halls of the Montezumas*, 16–20.

50. Dicennial Census, University of Virginia Library, http://fisher.lib.virginia.edu (visited July 12, 2004).

51. Elizabeth White Nelson, *Market Sentiments: Middle-Class Market Culture in Nineteenth-Century America* (Washington, D.C.: Smithsonian Books, 2004), 45–50. Also see Carl F. Kaestle, *Pillars of the Republic: Common Schools and American Society, 1780–1860* (New York: Hill and Wang, 1983), chaps. 3–4.

52. J. Jacob Oswandel, *Notes of the Mexican War 1846–47–48. Comprising Incidents, Adventures and Everyday Proceedings and Letters while with the United States Army in the Mexican War; also Extracts from Ancient Histories of Mexico, giving an Accurate Account of the First and Original Settlers of Mexico, etc. also the Names and Numbers of the Different Rulers of Mexico; also Influence of the Church.* (Philadelphia, 1885), 424, 428, 614.

53. Ulysses S. Grant, *Personal Memoirs of U. S. Grant* (New York: Charles L. Webster, 1892), 1: 24–25, 32.

54. For an extensive listing of memoirs, fiction, and other publications related to the war, see Jenkins Garrett, *The Mexican-American War of 1846–1848: A Bibliography of the Holdings of the Libraries, the University of Texas at Arlington,* ed. Katherine R. Goodwin (College Station: Texas A&M University Press, 1995).

55. Drewey Wayne Gunn, *American and British Writers in Mexico, 1556–1973* (Austin: University of Texas Press, 1974), 36. Italics are mine.

56. [Pamphlet] *Mexico: A Foreign Land A Step Away—The Direct Line.* Missouri Pacific Iron Mountain, 1908. Cited in Andrea Boardman, *Destination México: "A Foreign Land a Step Away": U.S. Tourism to Mexico, 1880s—1950s* (Dallas: De-Golyer Library, Southern Methodist University, 2001), 39.

57. Gunn, *American and British Writers in Mexico,* 252–53.

58. Rodríguez, "The 'Tourist Gaze,' Gentrification, and the Commodification of Subjectivity in Taos," 111.

59. Napoleon Jackson Tecumseh Dana, *Monterrey Is Ours! The Mexican War Letters of Lieutenant Dana, 1845–1847,* ed. Robert H. Ferrell (Lexington: University Press of Kentucky, 1990), 197.

60. Oswandel, *Notes of the Mexican War,* 431.

61. Kenly, *Memoirs of a Maryland Volunteer,* 266.

62. John F. Sears, *Sacred Places: American Tourist Attractions in the Nineteenth Century* (New York: Oxford University Press, 1989), 18.

63. Alfred H. Siemens, *Between the Summit and the Sea: Central Veracruz in the Nineteenth Century* (Vancouver: University of British Columbia Press, 1990), 169.

64. Kirby Smith, letter of April 29, 1847, *To Mexico with Scott,* 139.

65. George C. Furber, *The Twelve Months Volunteer or, Journal of a Private in the Tennessee Regiment of Cavalry, in the Campaign, in Mexico, 1846–7* (Cincinnati: J. A. and U. P. James, 1848), 604–5.

66. Raphael Semmes, *Service Afloat and Ashore during the Mexican War* (Cincinnati: Wm. H. Moore, 1851), 167.

67. Furber, *The Twelve Months Volunteer,* 605.

68. Thompson, "Winfield Scott's Army of Occupation as Pioneer Alpinists," 573.

69. Ibid., 549–81.

70. William H. Beezley, *Judas at the Jockey Club and Other Episodes of Porfirian Mexico* (Lincoln: University of Nebraska Press, 1987), 39.

71. Ward, *Mexico in 1827*, 2: 266, 268.

72. Thompson, *Recollections of Mexico*, 27.

73. Bauer, *The Mexican War*, 270–71.

74. Kirby Smith, letter of May 16, 1847, *To Mexico with Scott*, 166.

75. Charles Drees, *Thirteen Years in Mexico from the Letters of Charles W. Drees* (New York: Abingdon Press, 1915), 103.

76. Mayer, *Mexico as It Was and as It Is*, 26.

77. *Mexico: A Lonely Planet Travel Survival Kit*, ed. John Noble et al. (Hawthorne, Australia: Lonely Planet Publications, 1995), 260.

78. Johannsen, *To the Halls of the Montezumas*, 157.

79. *Indian and Mexican Handicraft* (Mesilla Park, N.M.: Francis E. Lester Company, 1909).

80. Bauer, *The Mexican War*, 386–87.

81. Ward, *Mexico in 1827*, 2: 220–21.

82. "Mexico and Gen. Casey," *Christian World* 66 (May 1866): 152–53.

83. Johannsen, *To the Halls of the Montezumas*, 149.

84. Meginness, "Journal," February 19, 1848.

85. Meginness, "Journal," February 27, 1848.

86. Meginness, "Journal," February 19, 1848; Mayer, *Mexico as It Was and as It Is*, 41.

87. Mayer, *Mexico as It Was and as It Is*, 63.

88. John C. Pinheiro, " 'Extending the Light and Blessings of Our Purer Faith': Anti-Catholic Sentiment among American Soldiers in the U.S. Mexican War," *Journal of Popular Culture* 35.2 (fall 2001): 129–52.

89. Reau Campbell, *Campbell's New Revised Complete Guide and Descriptive Book of Mexico* (Chicago 1909), 120–21.

90. Johannsen, *To the Halls of the Montezumas*, 157.

91. Meginness, "Journal," February 15, 1848.

92. Oswandel, *Notes of the Mexican War*, 424.

93. Michael Johns, *The City of Mexico in the Age of Díaz* (Austin: University of Texas Press, 1997), 24–25; Boardman, *Destination México*, 49.

94. Meginness, "Journal," February 15, 1848.

95. Oswandel, *Notes of the Mexican War*, 424.

96. Meginness, "Journal," April 6, 1848.

97. Johannsen, *To the Halls of the Montezumas*, 173.

98. Conversation with Miguel Angel González, Universidad Autónoma de Nuevo León.

99. Grant, *Personal Memoirs*, 1: 179–80.

100. Meginness, "Journal," February 20, 1848.

101. Ibid., April 7, 1848.

102. Grant, *Personal Memoirs*, 1: 186–88. Grant did not identify the specific location. Perhaps they explored one of the limestone caves near Cuernavaca or perhaps

they went as far as the Grutas de Cacahuamilpa, near Taxco, which were discovered in 1834 by Manuel Saenz de la Peña.

103. Mayer, *Mexico as It Was and as It Is*, 193–95.

104. *In Memory of John F. Meginness, Journalist and Historian. July 16, 1827—November 11, 1899: A Testimonial by the Gazette and Bulletin, The Sun, Pennsylvania Orit, The Evening News* (Williamsport, Pa.: Gazette and Bulletin Printing House, 1900), in the Meginness Papers (GA 119–23), Special Collections, University of Texas, Arlington.

105. *Daily Gazette and Bulletin*, Williamsport, Pennsylvania, October 3, 1885. (Meginness's clippings trim off the heading, but bits of lettering and the mention of his newspaper in the body of the article point toward this newspaper as the source.)

106. Arthur W. and Abby Linder Pope Photographs, Ag88.703.70, DeGolyer Library, Southern Methodist University. Cited in Boardman, *Destination México*, 35.

107. James W. Steele, *To Mexico by Palace Car, intended as a Guide to Her Principal Cities and Capital, and Generally as a Tourist's Introduction to Her Life and People* (Chicago: Jansen, McClurg and Company, 1884), 87.

108. Bauer, *The Mexican War*, 310–11.

109. *Raymond's Vacation Excursions—All Travelling Expenses included—A Tour through Mexico: Leaving Boston February 26, 1885* (Boston: W. Raymond, I. A. Whitcomb, 1885), 42.

110. David M. Pletcher, *Rails, Mines, and Progress: Seven American Promoters in Mexico, 1867–1911* (Ithaca, N.Y.: Cornell University Press, 1958), 157.

111. Alfred R. Conkling, *Appleton's Guide to Mexico, Including a Chapter on Guatemala, and an English-Mexican Vocabulary* (New York: D. Appleton and Company, 1884), iii. For background on D. Appleton and Company in the Americas, see Harry Bernstein, *Making an Inter-American Mind* (Gainesville: University of Florida Press, 1961), 59–63.

112. Stephen P. Hanna and Vincent J. Del Casino Jr., "Tourism Spaces, Mapped Representations, and the Practices of Identity," *Mapping Tourism*, ed. Stephen P. Hanna and Vincent J. Del Casino Jr. (Minneapolis: University of Minnesota Press, 2003), ix–x.

113. Urry, *The "Tourist Gaze,"* 44.

CHRISTINA BUENO

TEOTIHUACÁN

Showcase for the Centennial

M exico's pyramids, along with its beaches, are a major tourist attraction. Even the most hard-core holidaymaker in Cancún will most likely spend an afternoon at nearby Chichén Itzá—"the most spectacular Mayan site," according to one travel brochure. The government has long capitalized on the ruins as a tourist resource. In fact, the nation's first official archaeological site, Teotihuacán, was created for a specific tourist event. The two-thousand-year-old city was rebuilt by the regime of Porfirio Díaz (1877–1910) for the Centenario, the centennial celebration of Mexican independence in September 1910 which drew visitors from around the world. The Díaz government used the celebration to bolster the national image, reconstructing Teotihuacán in order to present Mexico as a unified and modern nation with ancient and prestigious roots. What follows is an account of how this official site was born.

The Allure of Antiquity

One of Mexico's most enduring ideological currents has been the belief in the existence of a "Mexican nation" with roots in the pre-Hispanic past. One only need visit today's massive National Anthropology Museum or tour one of the many archaeological sites to realize that *indigenismo*, "the defence and recovery of Indian culture," has been a major state endeavor.[1] Yet while indigenismo is usually associated with the revolutionary state that succeeded Díaz in 1910, it was the Díaz regime, in fact, that brought Mexico its first concerted effort to preserve and display the Indian past.[2] The government placed guards at ruins, strengthened federal legislation over artifacts, and gave unprecedented support to Mexico City's National Museum. It established the Inspection of Archaeological Monuments of the Republic, the first agency exclusively for protecting the Indian past, precursor of today's INAH (National Institute of Anthropology and History). So, while Teotihuacán was created for the Centenario, it must be understood as part of this larger archaeological project, as antiquity for the Porfirian political and intellectual elite had come to take on a particular allure.

The Indian past had become the bedrock or foundation of nationhood. Prior to this, Mexicans had understood their heritage in dichotomous terms: as either Indian or Spanish. During the Porfiriato, as the state consolidated, so did a new interpretation, one that embraced the nation's dual heritage. The elite had realized that "a comprehensive nationalistic history was sine quo non both for the consolidation of the nation and as a proof of stability and civilization."[3] Indian antiquity became an inherent part of Mexico's official history, essential to uniting the disparate population under a common national identity. And here, not all ancient Indians were considered equal. The government continued a long-standing ideological tradition of exalting the Aztecs as the nation's founding culture, the people of Mexico City, and the historical seat of power.

It was an antiquity, moreover, that brought vital clout to a nation considered backward and uncivilized. Mexico was not only consolidating but stepping out onto the world scene as never before, forging stronger economic links with the nations of the North Atlantic. Yet the dominant Eurocentric racist thought of the times, ideas which the Porfirian elite themselves imbibed, relegated the country of Indians and *mestizos* (people of mixed Indian and European descent) to an inferior status. The Porfirian elite desperately wanted to change their nation's backward image, in part to secure foreign investment and immigration. They used the sophisticated Indian past to dazzle and impress, to put Mexico on a par with those in the canon of the world's great civilizations: with ancient Egypt, Greece, and Rome. The government took steps to highlight the pre-Hispanic past, especially the Aztec past, by erecting the Cuauhtémoc monument on Mexico City's Reforma Avenue; building the Aztec palace at the 1889 Paris World's Fair; gathering the nation's most spectacular artifacts in the Gallery of Monoliths, a new room in the National Museum where Aztec pieces, especially the immense Calendar Stone, dominated.

What might seem odd is that this was also a fiercely anti-Indian regime, one that saw contemporary Indians as degenerate; that stripped them of their land on a scale unseen before; that hunted down the Yaqui and Maya.

While the ancient Indians were glorified in ways that fit Western ideals of progress—as great mathematicians, scientists, and artists—the people considered contemporary Indians were seen in completely antithetical terms. How do we explain these contrasting perceptions of the Indian past and present? To begin, we must turn to the slippery subject of race. While the Porfirian elite imbibed Eurocentric racist thinking, they tailored it to their nation's context in ways both contradictory and pragmatic. Most argued, for example, that Indians were not biologically and therefore inherently inferior but that they suffered from a degraded culture instead. They turned to what Marisol de la Cadena refers to as "culturalist definitions of race," a form of "racism without race," a loophole out of the racist dogma that allowed Mexicans a faith in their nation's future potential.[4] Indians, in this case, could always be "redeemed" through acculturation, by adopting Western ways, and one method proposed (but not enacted) was education. The glorious past, then, offered proof that Indians could be uplifted. There is some evidence for this way of thinking; take, for instance, the statesman and intellectual Justo Sierra's claim that the Indian "race" had "shown signs of colossal energy" in the past and "the precise moment has arrived to awaken it."[5] Following this line of thought, some scholars have suggested that the embrace of antiquity was a sign that the elite had accepted the Indian into their idea of nation.

Yet when observers compared the Indian past and present, they usually emphasized not the link but the disconnect between the two, as if the ancient and contemporary Indians had nothing to do with each other. In their thinking, any connection between the two had been completely severed. Rather than a sign of accepting the Indian, Rebecca Earle believes that the celebration of antiquity was predicated on this disconnect, on the certainty that "any merits such preconquest civilizations had possessed . . . were long vanished, and thus utterly disconnected from the vile *indios*."[6] The past was glorified, in other words, because it had nothing to do with the degraded present. It was a space where Indians could be imagined and reimagined in ways that gave Mexico prestige, unlike the contemporary Indians, whose rag-tag existence was undeniable as it confronted Porfirian observers. If we follow this line of thought, the embrace of antiquity takes on much darker hues; it becomes a retreat from the contemporary Indians, their negation and denial. It becomes yet another loophole to escape the Indian present. In fact, the very projects aimed at protecting the past negated the contemporary Indians, as the government took artifacts from them and eliminated communities from Teotihuacán in order to turn the National Museum and ruins into pristine showcases of antiquity.

Taking charge of the past offered much more—it offered that coveted patina of being scientific and modern. Mexicans equated the protection of national property with a sign of modernity and culture. As the director of the National Museum Jesús Sánchez pointed out, "If the cultured nations like Germany, France, England, Italy and the United States spend large sums acquiring and studying the antiquities of Egypt, Greece, China, and Mexico, then it is only right that we give our antiquities the importance they deserve."[7] Yet at the same time, the global antiquities market was steadily siphoning artifacts to European and American private collections and museums. That Mexico lacked control over its past was "a constant source of humiliation," in the words of Leopoldo Batres, the Inspector of Monuments, whom we will soon meet.[8] It made the nation appear "inferior."[9] It meant it was not modern. Mexico's monuments needed to be conserved, wrote Batres, as "it is usually done in the civilized countries."[10]

Concerns with modernity were thus entwined with concerns about national sovereignty. But here, the aim was to take control of not only artifacts but the actual study of Mexican antiquity as well, which had been largely dominated by foreigners—the Prussians, Americans, British and French—until that time. Archaeology, it was believed, would become the national science, or, as Justo Sierra neatly summarized, it was the only discipline that gave "Mexico personality in the scientific world."[11]

As a result, the government promoted archaeology to legitimize national objectives. The discipline evolved within the context of serving the state, with its political uses often outweighing scientific concerns. This was a nationalist archaeology, what is commonly known as the "culture-historical approach," an archaeological tradition that draws attention to the "cultural achievements of indigenous ancient civilizations" in order to boost national "pride and morale."[12] As in other parts of the world, the state would present the nation's ancient heritage as the "bearer of the national spirit."[13] Teotihuacán was created as a place where foreigners could witness Mexico's modernity and ancient glory, and where Mexicans could rekindle their "faith and belief in the national ideal."[14] It became a place to assert and defend the nation's identity and image, with the Centenario offering a perfect occasion for display and a captive audience.

The site was one of many Centenario settings where the elite projected what Mauricio Tenorio has called "ideal views" of the nation.[15] The year

1910 was "consciously planned to be the apotheosis of nationalist conscious-ness; it was meant to be the climax of an era." It was a milestone year, one that marked not only Mexico's achievements since the outbreak of independence but "the political and economic success of a regime." The month-long centennial celebration included parades, speeches, public ceremonies, and banquets honoring the Díaz regime and the nation's pantheon of heroes, especially Benito Juárez, Miguel Hidalgo y Costilla, and José María Morelos y Pavón. In preparation for the twenty-eight dignitaries and hundreds of thousands of foreigners and Mexicans attending the event, federal, state, and municipal governments carried out construction and beautification projects all over the nation.[16] Everything from streets and statues to penitentiaries and parks sprang up, with Mexico City as the epicenter of the most elaborate preparations and host to the foreign guests.

Apart from the Centenario, Teotihuacán's creation reflected an incipient concern with developing the ruins for tourism. This coincided, moreover, with a general growth in the nation's tourist infrastructure, a "construction fever" of hotels and restaurants.[17] The government made the ruins more accessible, clearing roads as well as debris to make them more "attractive to tourists."[18] This was a concern of one young student in the National Museum, Manuel Gamio, who would go on to become the revolutionary government's most prominent archaeologist. As a student, he created a guide to the principal ruins. Organized state by state, it gave advice on transportation to sites, from the cost of train fare to renting a mule. It offered tips on food and lodging, warning visitors to Morelos, for example, that "the food is pretty cheap and bad."[19] It even suggested the best season to travel and pyramid-climbing attire, as antiquity had come to entice not just Mexicans but foreigners as well.

For Americans and Europeans, touring ancient ruins was all the rage, as steam and rail had made travel quicker, cheaper, and thus a "regular part of human existence."[20] By the late nineteenth century, bourgeois Europeans regularly trekked through Italy and Greece, with the famous travel bureau Cook's Tours hauling them to the Holy Land and to an Egypt which they supposedly " 'did' in little over three weeks."[21] And everywhere they went, they zealously collected relics; so much so that when the great American writer Mark Twain visited Egypt, he thought he saw a wart on the Sphinx's jaw which on closer inspection turned out to be a tourist "trying to chip off a souvenir."[22] Antiquities had become coveted commodities and curiosities, subjects of scientific scrutiny and display; a product of several large-scale nineteenth-century changes, including the rise of the nation-state and modern museum, colonialism and anthropology, the bourgeoisie and consumer culture that turned Victorians into collectors with a vengeance. The objects of "exotic" peoples had become hot items.

Within this context, pre-Hispanic pieces had taken on a special allure for Europeans jaded with the stuff of the rest of the globe. As Elizabeth Williams explains, "The 'oriental' world had lost its feel of utter strangeness and been assimilated into European sensibility through periodic vogues of *chinoiserie*; the 'true' *arts primitifs* of Arctic, African and Oceanic peoples could be unambiguously categorized as the work of savages." But the pre-Hispanic was different. It fascinated because of its "high level of material development" on the one hand, and "its apparent independence from the fonts of Old World creativity," on the other.[23]

This fascination with the pre-Hispanic developed alongside the science of archaeology. Archaeology was becoming a formal discipline in the late nineteenth century, with professional training and organizations and the fieldwork associated with it today. Those who specialized in New World civilizations were part of a growing movement known as Americanism. A broad scholarly field, Americanism can be defined as the general study of both New World continents throughout all historical periods. The majority of Americanists, however, specialized in the pre-Hispanic past, and their most important forum for scholarly exchange was the International Congress of Americanists, a conference held every two years beginning in 1875. Some of the most active foreign scholars of Mexican antiquity at the time were the Prussian Eduard Seler, the Frenchman Désiré Charnay, and the American Marshall Saville. Prominent Mexican archaeologists included Alfredo Chavero, Antonio Peñafiel, and Leopoldo Batres, among others.

It is the archaeologists, in fact, who happen to be the most frequently documented visitors to Mexico's ruins. Interestingly, like other important guests they were often greeted there with live "Indian" shows, what must have been perceived as a "realistic" touch. Officials commonly decorated pyramids with locals singing and playing instruments. When the Mexican archaeologist Cecilio Robelo saw such a spectacle in Xochicalco in the 1880s, the Indians' melodies nearly put him in a trance, with visions of thousands of "slaves" being forced to build the pyramid "by the whips of fanaticism," and even a high priest ripping out the hearts of sacrificial victims.[24]

The problem was, though, that the line between scientist and sacker was quite thin, and some of the most celebrated archaeologists happened to have been some of the most egregious of looters. The Englishman Alfred Maudslay is a perfect example. While Maudslay went down in history as an eminent Mayanist, he also hacked away at the lintels of Yaxchilán, Chiapas, turning them into the smaller, more transportable slabs that he shipped back to the British Museum in London.[25]

It is the nonfamous, the common travelers, who are more difficult to track, both foreigners and Mexicans alike. Some went to the ruins just to acquire artifacts and often got these from the locals. They were frequently antiquarians, like the Spaniard caught leaving Mexico with "various hand-bags and suitcases" stuffed with idols.[26] Others trafficked in the goods, like the woman from Xalapa, Veracruz, who bought artifacts "at despicable prices from the hands of Indians" and sold them "for the price of gold to a company in Hamburg."[27]

An even more elusive group was sightseers. They trekked through the ruins out of curiosity, their visits most likely inspired by what is known as "travel for education."[28] And here, the historical record offers only the occasional and hazy glimpse, like the easily overlooked mention of a "group of Germans" climbing Xochicalco's pyramids in 1900.[29] Yet even this type of traveler seems to have been incapable of leaving without a relic in hand. What drove them to possess these ancient things? Was it that "special source of wonder"? Was there some sort of siren's call these things exerted as embodiments of the "national spirit"? Or were they simply status markers, trophies that proved one had the leisure time and discretionary income to travel? Mementos, like the chunks of Mitla, Oaxaca, tourists supposedly pried off "as a souvenir of their visit"?[30] The ruins were being ransacked and destroyed. They were, in the words of Justo Sierra, in a "terribly deplorable state."[31]

The Mexican government would respond by creating the picture-perfect pyramids of today, beginning with Teotihuacán for the Centenario. As one journalist pointed out, the site had the potential of becoming "the most visited archaeological zone in the Americas." It would attract, according to the American patron of archaeology, the Duke of Loubat, "as many tourists to Mexico as Pompey attracts to Naples."[32]

Teotihuacán

It was bureaucrats and not scientists who decided to create Teotihuacán. Unlike most centennial projects, the idea did not originate with the National Centenario Commission, the ten-member committee established in April 1907 responsible for planning the celebration. Instead, it was Justo Sierra and Ezequiel Chávez, future secretary and assistant secretary of education, who suggested the site's creation in late 1904, a proposal linked to plans for the eventual Centenario. They chose Teotihuacán because it was monumental and impressive, ironically paying homage to a place that Mexico City's long-ago rulers, the Aztecs, had so revered. It was also famous, "one of the most interesting cities in the entire world of archaeology."[33] Unlike other ruins lost to history, it had always been well known, a requisite stop on travelers' itineraries since the sixteenth-century friar Bernardino de Sahagún popularized it in his writings. But more significantly, the choice of Teotihuacán reflected the government's general focus on the cultures of the *altiplano* or central plateau, the area where it carried out most of its archaeological work. It was also conveniently close to Mexico City—just an hour train-ride away for the many guests.

Some of these were prominent archaeologists visiting the capital for the XVII Congress of Americanists, scholars as important as Eduard Seler and Franz Boas, the German American often considered the founder of modern anthropology. The congress for 1910 had originally been scheduled to take place in Buenos Aires, Argentina. Upon the insistence of Mexican delegates at the previous congress in Austria in 1908, however, the conference meetings were split between the two Latin American nations, allowing this important scientific event to coincide with the Centenario. In Mexico, the congress was held in the National Museum, and an excursion to Teotihuacán became part of the program. The museum, moreover, had recently been remodeled and its reopening, presided over by Díaz himself, was likewise slated to coincide with the celebration.

To turn Teotihuacán into an official site, the state called on Leopoldo Batres, Inspector of Monuments. While Batres is often considered a self-trained archaeologist, he had in fact received formal training in Paris under the prominent scholar E.T. Hamy.[34] At twenty-one, he returned to his native Mexico to join the army, traveling much and most likely exploring the ruins. His dabbling in archaeology soon became an official career when he became inspector, a position he held from its creation in 1885 until the fall of Díaz in 1910. Teotihuacán was the culmination of his career, a site he considered "more impressive and elegant than the pyramids of Egypt."[35] It is a spectacular place, a monumental place, what the Aztecs knew as "the place where the gods were conceived." But for centuries it had been so utterly obscured by dirt and vegetation that one had to strain to imagine any sort of monumentality.

Batres had such an imagination. But this, as we will see, would lead him to

1. Workers shoveling soil off the Pyramid of the Sun. FROM *ARQUEOLOGÍA MEXICANA* (MEXICO CITY: EDITORIAL RAÍCES, 2001), VOL. 7, P. 22.

commit a series of mistakes. Standing before the site's massive Pyramid of the Sun in early 1905, Justo Sierra supposedly asked him if he could uncover the structure in time for the Centenario. Batres's answer, of course, was yes. And on March 20, 1905, the Secretary of Education, the ministry in charge of the inspection of monuments, ordered him to begin.

Batres focused on excavating and reconstructing the Pyramid of the Sun, one of the world's largest, nearly 60 meters high, with sides 215 meters long. The job was "colossal," he would later write, "but when man sets out to accomplish something and has the strength of will . . . he defeats all obstacles and executes the task."[36] And he did face a number of obstacles, what he called "problems."[37] There was the dirt problem, the sediment of centuries, "the sea of dirt," in his words, that had to be removed from the Pyramid of the Sun alone. There was the time problem—the Centenario was just a short five years away. There was also the people problem, the *campesinos* who owned the land at the site. They came from at least five villages: San Sebastián, San Francisco Mazapa, Santa María Cuatlán, San Juan Teotihuacán, and San Martín de las Pirámides. Batres estimated they had carpeted the ruins with over 250 "plots," full of crops, *maguey*, and *Pirú* trees. If Teotihuacán were to evoke a mythical past, it had to become pristine, free of any people, especially those considered pesky eyesores like the peasants. They would have to leave.

Batres was no stranger to the locals. In 1889 he had hauled away a sixteen-ton statue known as the "Goddess of Water" amid protests of what he called "angry Indians."[38] On an even earlier excavation, a "mob" from San Martín supposedly "revolted" against him. They took his workers hostage and tried to capture him as well. He escaped by striking the mob's leader in the head with the butt of his rifle, but the experience put him forever on guard: "Knowing the Indian as I do, I made sure they would not sense any sort of fear in me, and from that time on I walked everywhere alone, leaving work well into the night to show them that I feared nothing."[39] He often went about armed or accompanied by the military or *rurales* (the rural police), claiming that their presence served "to promote respect."[40] By the Centenario, a permanent troop of seventeen, a mix of military officers and *rurales*, were stationed at Teotihuacán.

But his visit in 1905 meant something entirely different—it meant the villagers would have to leave. The Law of Monuments of 1897, the nation's most comprehensive archaeological legislation to that date, had nationalized and allowed for the expropriation of ruins. Initially, Batres refused to compensate the locals for their land since, he believed, it should have never been theirs in the first place: it had "belonged to the nation since the time of the Spaniards . . . and it would set a fatal precedent to recognize monuments . . . as private property."[41] For reasons that are not entirely clear, he began his work before expropriating the land, ordering the peasants to stop tending their crops. The first to protest was a Sebero Reyes, the owner of the plot that encircled the pyramid's base. Reyes took his case to the Secretary of Education, requesting to either continue planting or receive compensation for the land. When Batres found out, he relinquished and agreed to the expropriation. But Reyes, it turned out, drove a hard bargain. Although he had originally paid just 10 pesos for his plot, he would only sell for 100. This was the charge for the Pyramid of the Sun—100 pesos, what Batres complained was "the price of gold."[42]

It was now mid-1906, time was passing, and Batres continued working, occupying the people's land. The villagers of Santa María Cuatlán and San Francisco Mazapa protested to the Secretary of Education. Their property, they pointed out, was "inviolable and could not be taken away unless . . . there had been previous compensation."[43] When Batres found out, he again relinquished and agreed to expropriate the lands, but not before he had finished insulting every last villager, or as they explained: "His abuse has become intolerable, he calls us a group of dumb Indians . . . but in words that are less tasteful, and which do not measure up to the standards of a public official."[44] It is not clear what bothered Batres most: that the people had sought recourse in the Secretary of Education and possibly slowed down his work, or that these "dumb Indians" had not only understood but dared to defend their rights.

Within months, Batres purchased the land and carved out the federal site, a process that had required no more than a wire fence, some mineral lime and money, and a bit of patience. He raised the fence to establish the site's boundaries around the main monuments: the Pyramid of the Sun, the Pyramid of the Moon, the Street of the Dead, and the Ciudadela or Citadel. He wanted to ensure that the boundary between the site and outlying private lands was absolutely precise and clear. So he drew a thick line of mineral lime on the ground, marking a buffer zone of two hundred meters outside the fence. He then asked the owners of the land between the fence and buffer zone to come to his office at what became known as Camp Pyramid of the Sun, with their sale price in mind and property title in hand. And then he waited.

By mid-1907, most of the locals had trickled into his camp and sold off their land. Manuel Olvera, for example, had wanted 5,000 pesos for his plot called "Rancho de la Palma," but only got 520; Leandro Aguilar wanted 200 but got 12; Modesto Suárez wanted 500 but ended up with a measly 7 pesos.[45] Batres believed the people's prices were too high, "completely exaggerated."[46] The Treasury of the State of Mexico intervened to determine the property values, which the locals were forced to accept. They had no choice. Had they refused to sell, the expropriations would have been carried out on the basis of "public use in accordance with the law."[47] As one government memorandum made clear: "The property rights possessed by the nation over the land in this case are more important than the property rights of individuals . . . the latter are precarious and ephemeral, while those of the nation by nature are eternal."[48] Ultimately, the National Treasury paid a little over 8,200 pesos for all the properties.[49] And so it was that land that had once sustained villagers passed on to become a showcase of the ancients.

Considering Batres's earlier experiences, we might have expected the locals to unite as a menacing "mob," but they did not. Rather than fight for their land—which would have been futile anyway—they fought for their crops. They asked for permission to harvest one last season. This left the government perplexed. Should it allow them? Should it compensate them for their crops? What was the precedent in such a case? Batres appears to have mellowed, letting the villagers enter the site and tend their crops one last time, "as long as they did not harm" the monuments.[50] After this, however, even the trees and *maguey* became national property, which Batres used in his reconstruction in the most ingenious of ways—as the fuel or combustible material to run his equipment, the "stone-breaking machine, and the pump that carried water to the top of the pyramid."[51]

THE SITE

How does one rebuild a pyramid? There is no manual, no step-by-step guide. There is, moreover, no original pyramid to work from. As the anthropologist Quetzil Castañeda reminds us, "Not only has the original been lost, but the pristine and authentic original never existed." When in a pyramid's millennia of existence is the authentic structure to be found? Rather than representations of originals, ruins are "artifacts of . . . Western science." They are constructs based on "specific criteria and logics of authenticity."[52] What is deemed authentic, therefore, depends on who is doing the reconstructing and why. Recent approaches to archaeology acknowledge this contested nature of authenticity. Rather than reconstruction, today's goal is consolidation: archaeologists restore structures to keep them from further collapse. One example of this approach is Mexico City's Great Temple, which archaeologists have left exposed and restored, but "have luckily not succumbed to the temptation to rebuild the original edifice."[53]

Batres, however, was working at a time when authenticity went unquestioned and "reconstruction" was still the operating word. He was also working at a time when archaeology was not yet guided by rigorous standards. Like most of his contemporaries, his excavation techniques could be summed up in two words: dig and haul. It was not the norm, for example, to use stratigraphic excavation, a procedure which treats an artifact much like a geologist treats a fossil, recording its exact location in the geographic layer in order to establish its relative age. But this lack of scientific rigor or technique ultimately did not matter, since rather than a meticulous archaeological study, Batres's goal was to make the Pyramid of the Sun look grandiose in time for the Centenario.

And while he did not leave a detailed account of exactly how he went about rebuilding the pyramid, from the little that he left, we can glean this much: he began by uncovering the base of its southeast corner, where he conducted a series of what he called "probes."[54] With these he discovered, as he had expected, that the pyramid was made up of superimposed layers, "like the layers of an onion." Batres believed that the layers were designed to give the pyramid "stability." We now know, as many suspected back then,

2. Workers moving soil and excavating in Teotihuacán. FROM *ARQUEOLOGÍA MEXICANA* (MEXICO CITY: EDITORIAL RAÍCES, 1993), VOL. 1, NO. 1, P. 32.

that this superimposition so typical of Mesoamerican pyramids marks the succession of dynasties and rulers. Underneath the exterior crust of dirt and rubble lay a first layer which, according to Batres, was "entirely ruined." Four to six meters below this, however, lay a second "well preserved" layer which, if uncovered, would reveal "the shape of the legendary temple."

Here, Batres faced a dilemma: he could either leave the pyramid untouched and "mute forever," or excavate and risk destroying the first layer. He chose the latter, and when he began digging, the pyramid's entire first layer "immediately" fell apart as expected. In his rush to uncover the pyramid, legend has it that he resorted to archaeology's biggest taboo—he used dynamite. While this has never been proven, he had used dynamite at sites before, and he did have it at Teotihuacán—it is listed among his supplies.[55] He ended up pealing off the pyramid's first layer on the north, south, and east sides, leaving the retention walls at the apex of the structure exposed, which led him, in turn, to his next mistake.

Batres mistook the retention walls for remnants of a terrace and proceeded to reconstruct the pyramid with an extra terrace, leaving it with five levels when archaeologists believe there were originally just four. The much thinner fourth terrace on the pyramid today is most likely a fabrication. While critics have charged that he falsified it deliberately, it was most likely just a mistake.[56] And if it seemed to Batres that his work could not possibly have gotten any more difficult, it soon did. The second, now exposed layer was not as stable as he had thought—it was fragile, very fragile, made of adobe and stone bound by clay. When it rained, the pyramid began to disintegrate. To prevent this, he covered it with a wooden drainage system with gutters that channeled the water away. He then had his workers replace the clay that held the stones together with cement.

In April 1906, just as he was finishing this work on the two lower levels on the north side, President Díaz paid a visit and gave his whole-hearted approval. He arrived to the sound of "cheering Indians" and tolling church bells.[57] He asked to see the pyramid's layers, believing more accurately than Batres that they were markers of some important "event." It was hot and dusty as the dictator ascended the pyramid, followed by an entourage of military men, municipal leaders, and Batres and his son Salvador. Newspapers marveled at the president's "virile stamina" during the climb, praising him as the first leader to have "made the effort" to unearth the ruins, "monuments that are clear proof of a civilization comparable to that of Egypt."[58]

To orchestrate all the digging, lifting, and hauling in the reconstruction, Batres ran his camp of nearly three hundred workers with the military discipline he had learned as a young man. A cannon shot woke everyone at six in the morning, not a real cannon, recalled a worker, but "a small one, almost a toy."[59] Activities were regulated: breakfast, digging, dinner, all ran like clockwork. Laborers were organized, as Batres clarified, into "brigades supervised by officers and captains, under the command of a general foreman; such supervision ensured that they handled their picks with complete caution so that they unearthed rather than destroyed [the pyramid]."[60] The common laborers—diggers and haulers—earned little over three and a half pesos a week, while the bricklayers who carefully inserted the cement with small spoons into the cracks between the stones earned six.[61] Unfortunately, Batres did not record the origin of the workers. But he usually drew them from the area, if not the site itself, often bringing the more skilled ones, the mechanics and carpenters, from Mexico City. In his view, the common laborer was better off at the site than as a debt-peon on a hacienda. The Inspection of Archaeological Monuments had "helped tear the unhappy workers from the clutches and domination of overlords by giving them a full wage to spend where they please without onerous loans that . . . deprive them of their freedom . . . passing those burdens onto the next generation."[62] He bragged that there was not even a monopoly on the sale of *pulque* at the ruins, as brigade captains brought workers their "indispensable" alcohol daily. And if anyone should overindulge and get out of hand, camp Pyramid of the Sun had a cell for confining those who committed "infractions due to drunkenness, and other types of crimes, while waiting to be brought before the proper authorities."[63]

It is telling that Batres compared the camp to a hacienda, because, like the landed estate, it had an air of patriarchal benevolence. We know little about the labor conditions, but the camp had an infirmary, a public bathroom, and even a public bathtub. It had a spring manned by a guard who distributed water to thirsty workers. It had holiday celebrations as well. On May 5, 1905, for example, to commemorate the nation's victory over the French at the Battle of Puebla in 1862, garlands of flowers and Mexican flags were tied to the digging tools and strewn across the Pyramid of the Sun. Over eight hundred people were said to have attended, shouting "¡Viva México!" and cheering for the battle's famous heroes, Ignacio Zaragoza and Porfirio Díaz. One worker made a speech praising Díaz as the leader who had brought peace, civilization, and progress to the country and "solidified the foundations" of Mexican nationhood.[64] Batres then had workers parade around the base of the pyramid to the beat of drum and bugle. With this curious but symbolic act, the state was not just taking charge of the site but the pyramid itself was being incorporated into Mexico's nationalist discourse and calendar of celebrations—the pyramid, in a sense, was being taught to be Mexican.

But nothing brought more excitement to Camp Pyramid of the Sun than the arrival of the train. While the immense mass of dirt and rubble was initially hauled off by wheelbarrow and then boxcars set on tracks, it was soon removed by train. The transport of debris was costly and time-consuming; Batres estimated there were at least 1,600,000 cubic meters to remove from the Pyramid of the Sun alone.[65] In 1908, tracks were extended from the nearby Mexican Railroad line to the pyramid, with the train hauling rubble at the speed of up to 100 tons an hour and dumping it a kilometer away. The railroad also served the important function of transporting visitors to the ruins. But for Batres the train meant much more: it shored up the nation's modern image, or as he boasted, "With it we will truly have a momentous display which will live up to the expectations for the Centenario."[66]

THE TOURISTS

Batres designed some features at Teotihuacán specifically for tourists. He built a museum, the nation's first state-sponsored on-site museum. With its Doric-style façade and elegant display cases filled with over 8,000 objects from his excavation, the press speculated that the museum would "draw the attention of Europeans and Americans."[67] To allow visitors a chance to rest during their tour of the site, which Batres calculated at eight hours, he had wanted to build "a tourist house and restaurant" but settled for a kiosk for them to relax and have refreshments. But his most fantastic, far-fetched creation at Teotihuacán was a "Japanese garden," complete with waterfall and lake, designed, in his words, "to eliminate the arid appearance of the region and make it more attractive to tourists."[68]

Had we visited, we would have been struck not only by the garden but by the array of signs Batres had posted. While they were meant to inform, many expressed doubt at the same time, like the one in front of the Temple of Agriculture which questioned whether this was indeed the "Temple of Agriculture." Others gave bits of information Batres thought were particularly important, like the one that said: "This is where the rubble reached before the Pyramid of the Sun was uncovered."[69] But his most curious sign was not in Teotihuacán but in the ruins of Mitla, Oaxaca. It was a plaque embedded into an ancient wall with a message that ironically did not teach by example: "Warning: It is prohibited to write on the walls of these buildings, as well as to scratch or soil or pull off their stone."[70]

One problem that plagued Teotihuacán's tourists was the sale of fake antiquities. According to Batres, "two brothers" had converted part of the ruins into a ceramics workshop, complete with kiln, where they cooked up not only artifacts but busts of President Díaz. The falsification business was thriving. All over the country antiquities of all kinds were being produced, from the crude and "grotesque" to faithful replicas, "spectacular works in their own right."[71] Batres painted an unflattering picture of the typical forger. He was an "uncouth peasant," a drunk "who spends his time in taverns." But he could also be a criminal, like the "re-offending thief" who specialized in fake obsidian pieces and picking pockets, until he picked one too many and landed in the Islas Tres Marías penitentiary.[72]

Much as is the case with handicrafts associated with modern tourism, the presence of visitors stimulated the falsification industry. Travelers not only bought phony pieces but some even commissioned locals to make them, like the foreigner who regularly placed orders with one peasant. This same peasant explained: "I've lived off this industry for some time now, making heads, idols, weapons . . . and other things which I design to appear ancient, very ancient!"[73] Museums around the world were plagued with these "very ancient" things. The American archaeologist William Henry Holmes, for example, found, on the shelves of the Smithsonian Institution in Washington, D.C., several donations from tourists who had returned from Mexico. The problem had become so rampant, according to one Mexican press report, "that various American museums" distributed leaflets with warnings to Mexico-bound tourists.[74]

Batres fought long and hard against an industry he thought caused "incalculable damage, not only to the pockets of the unwary . . . but to history."[75] He wrote a book exposing it, his *Antigüedades mexicanas falsificadas*. He built an exhibit in the National Museum that taught how to detect phony pieces. At Teotihuacán, he took a practical and benevolent approach to the two brothers, who, like other forgers, he considered victims of unscrupulous middlemen. Rather than shut down their business, he convinced them to be honest with customers: to warn them of the object's true origin and present it as "a local industry."[76] Teotihuacán's tourists could now go home both with souvenirs and undeceived.

As the Centenario approached and Batres tended to the finishing touches, he decided to make Teotihuacán's guards or caretakers more presentable. Over the course of his lengthy twenty-six-year tenure as inspector, he created a network of caretakers at several sites. Known as *conserjes*, they were always local men. At Teotihuacán, he dressed the two conserjes in uniform. Their "humble Indian clothes," he believed, made "tourists look upon them with even more disdain."[77] Off went their traditional *calzón de manta* (comfortable hot-weather clothing), and on came their new attire: red pants, gray wool coat with gold buttons, a helmet and badge. He also ordered German pistols and sabers for each, to give them "the appearance that befits them as authorities of the place."[78]

Here, as on other occasions, the irony of what he was doing did not come into question: as the ruins of the ancient Indians were being unveiled and exalted, the people considered to be contemporary Indians were being erased from the site and concealed. It was this irony, this contradiction, that was embedded into Teotihuacán's creation and the Porfirian glorification of antiquity as a whole. To make Teotihuacán into a pristine showcase, there could be no trace of what Batres, like the rest of dominant society, saw as "savages."[79] This contradiction would mark Centenario events in Mexico City as well.

Hundreds of individuals were made to dress as Aztecs for the Desfile

Histórico, a historical parade complete with Moctezuma carried on a litter, "lords from the valley's principal city-states, priests, warriors and servants, all dressed in period costume and weaponry." Meanwhile, however, officials did everything possible to keep Indians from public view, forcing them to exchange the *calzón de manta* for "trousers, sombreros for felt hats, and sandals for shoes."[80]

Batres did finish making Teotihuacán into a pristine showcase. He not only rebuilt the Pyramid of the Sun but uncovered the Temple of Agriculture, the so-called Subterranean Buildings, and parts of the Ciudadela. Yet not only did he leave the pyramid smaller than it originally had been and with an added terrace but the cement used to hold the structure together gave it, in the words of a later archaeologist, "an alien, modern appearance."[81]

But Batres would consider the work a "happy success" and so would the Centenario guests.[82] They arrived by train the morning of September 10, 1910, a group of over two hundred, including Mexican officials, delegates of the Congress of Americanists, and "many representatives of friendly nations," a contingent led by the ambassadors of Spain, Japan, and the United States.[83] Batres acted as tour guide and gave, in French, a systematic recounting of all his work. They walked around the Pyramid of the Sun; some climbed to the top for a breath-taking view of the Valley of Mexico and the capital in the distance. They toured the on-site museum, which was inaugurated that day. They lunched in the impressive nearby cave, then known as the "Porfirio Díaz Grotto." An orchestra played Mexican and foreign melodies throughout the meal, bursting into anthems of the representative nations, forcing the visitors to stand at attention every now and then. Mexico's minister of foreign relations, Enrique Creel, gave a toast to all the "cultured nations" that had sent representatives. Justo Sierra made a speech praising Teotihuacán as one of "humanity's great works," a site that proved "the grandeur of a people."[84] The archaeologists Eduard Seler and Franz Boas commended Batres for his work. Batres was satisfied as well. He had unveiled the city of what he considered the "Greeks of the yellow American race."[85] Years later he would write that Teotihuacán's creation had been part of his larger struggle to ensure that Mexicans not be judged "as illiterates in the realm of science."[86] In fact, his reconstruction was considered such a success that the press speculated the Pyramid of the Moon would be next.

No sooner had the Centenario come and gone than the country erupted in revolution. President Díaz fled to Europe and before dying got a glimpse of the pyramids of Egypt, monuments Mexicans had always compared to their own. Batres, on the other hand, would be forever condemned for his work. He had left the Pyramid of the Sun "disfigured," claimed the new official archaeologist, Manuel Gamio. He was completely "ignorant of all technique," charged the later archaeologist Ignacio Bernal.[87] His reconstruction was fanciful; he had used dynamite; he had allowed the train tracks to cut right through the ruins. The list of accusations goes on and on, and Batres would spend the rest of his life typing emotional statements in his defense.

But while these critiques are valid, they fail to take into account the context of the reconstruction and its aim. The aim had never been to carry out a painstakingly accurate archaeological restoration and study. Instead, the overriding concerns had been political and ideological. The aim had been to quickly turn the ruins into the first official site to showcase Mexico as a great, modern nation with prestigious roots—in time for the Centenario and the many guests.

Notes

1. Alan Knight, *The Mexican Revolution: Counter-revolution and Reconstruction* (Lincoln: University of Nebraska Press, 1990), 2: 94.
2. Mexico has a long history of using antiquity as a source of ideological manipulation, one that stretches back to even pre-Hispanic times. The Aztecs, for example, collected objects from the ruins of Teotihuacán and Tula in order to link themselves to what they considered the most noteworthy civilizations. For a history of state-sponsored archaeology from the conquest through the Porfiriato, see Carlos García Mora and Enrique Florescano, eds., *La antropología en México* (Mexico City: INAH, 1987), vols. 1 and 2.
3. Mauricio Tenorio Trillo, *Mexico at the World's Fairs: Crafting a Modern Nation* (Berkeley: University of California Press, 1999), 68. This comprehensive vision surfaced in Vicent Riva Palacio's *México a través de los siglos* (1889), the nation's first work of historical synthesis, which opened with the statesman and scholar Alfredo Chavero's volume on the pre-Hispanic past and went on to examine the colonial and modern periods.
4. Marisol de la Cadena, *Indigenous Mestizos: The Politics of Race and Culture in Cuzco, Peru, 1919–1991* (Durham, N.C.: Duke University Press, 2000), 4.
5. *Obras completas del maestro Justo Sierra*, comp. Augustín Yañez (Mexico City: UNAM, 1948), 8: 256.
6. Rebecca Earle, "Nineteenth-Century Historia Patria and the Pre-Columbian Past," paper presented at the Institute of Latin American Studies, London, June 2003, 8–9.

7. Archivo General de la Nación, Instrucción Pública y Bellas Artes, caja 165, exp. 57, f. 3 (hereafter cited as AGN, IPBA).

8. AGN, IPBA, caja 150, exp. 2, f. 3.

9. AGN, IPBA, caja 169, exp. 8, f. 4.

10. Archivo Leopoldo Batres, Subdirección de Documentación, Biblioteca Nacional de Antropología e Historia, f. 278 (hereafter cited as Archivo Batres).

11. Justo Sierra, *Epistolario y papeles privados*, ed. Catalina Sierra de Peimbert (Mexico City: UNAM, 1949), 290.

12. Bruce G. Trigger, *A History of Archaeological Thought* (Cambridge: Cambridge University Press, 1989), 174.

13. O. Hugo Benavides, *Making Ecuadorian Histories: Four Centuries of Defining Power* (Austin: University of Texas Press, 2004), 13.

14. Ibid.

15. Mauricio Tenorio Trillo, "1910 Mexico City: Space and Nation in the City of the *Centenario*," *Journal of Latin American Studies* 28 (February 1996): 75–104.

16. Tenorio lists the nations that attended the centennial: six with special diplomatic missions (Japan, France, Germany, Italy, Spain, and the United States); eighteen with special envoys (Argentina, Bolivia, Brazil, Chile, Costa Rica, Cuba, El Salvador, Guatemala, Honduras, Panama, Peru, Uruguay, Austria, Belgium, Holland, Portugal, Russia, and Norway). Three countries appointed residents in Mexico to represent them (Colombia, Venezuela, and Switzerland), while Nicaragua's envoy was the poet Rubén Darío. Great Britain missed the celebration due to the death of King Edward VII. Tenorio, "1910 Mexico City," 90. For another thorough analysis of the Centenario, see Michael J. Gonzales, "Imagining Mexico in 1910: Visions of the *Patria* in the Centennial Celebration in Mexico City," *Journal of Latin American Studies* 39 (August 2007): 495–533.

17. Héctor Manuel Romero, *Crónica mexicana del turismo I* (Mexico City: Textos Universitarios, 1977), 170.

18. AGN, IPBA, caja 149, exp. 23, f. 5. One government project, for example, was the construction of the first staircase and bridge to the Tepozteco, the hilltop pyramid outside of Tepoztlán, Morelos. Before this, tourists had risked their lives scaling boulders to the summit, where a slip of the foot sent the unlucky soul on a fatal plunge hundreds of meters below.

19. AGN, IPBA, caja 153, exp. 48, f. 2.

20. Gilbert Sigaux, *History of Tourism*, trans. Joan White (London: Leisure Arts, 1966), 82.

21. Maxine Feifer, *Going Places: The Ways of the Tourist from Imperial Rome to the Present* (London: Macmillan, 1985), 193.

22. Ibid., 195.

23. Elizabeth Williams, "Art and Artifact at the Trocadero," *Objects and Others:*

Essays on Museums and Material Culture, ed. George W. Stocking Jr. (Madison: University of Wisconsin Press, 1985), 148.

24. Cecilio A. Robelo, *Xochicalco* (Cuernavaca, 1888), 13.

25. Unlike most looters, Maudslay left a detailed account of how he mutilated the lintels of Yaxchilán (then part of Guatemala). See his *Archaeology: Biologia Centrali-Americana*, reprint edition (New York: Milpatron Publishing, 1974), vol. 5, 42–43.

26. *El Imparcial*, December 19, 1907, in Sonia Lombardo de Ruíz, *El pasado pre-hispánico en la cultura nacional (memoria hemerográfica, 1877–1911)* (Mexico City: INAH, 1994), 2: 403.

27. *El Monitor Republicano*, May 22, 1879, in Lombardo, *El pasado prehispánico* 1: 73.

28. Valene L. Smith and Maryann Brent, *Hosts and Guests Revisited: Tourism Issues of the Twenty-First Century* (New York: Cognizant Communication Corporation, 2001), 4.

29. AGN, IPBA, caja 149, exp. 3, f. 6.

30. *El Monitor Republicano*, September 13, 1896, in Lombardo, *El pasado prehispánico*, 1: 299.

31. AGN, IPBA, caja 111, exp. 31, f. 19.

32. *El Imparcial*, April 10, 1906, in Lombardo, *El pasado prehispánico*, 2: 283; AGN, IPBA, caja 149, exp. 6, f. 2.

33. Leopoldo Batres, *Teotihuacán ó la ciudad sagrada de los Toltecas* (Mexico City: Talleres de la Escuela Nacional de Artes y Oficios, 1889), 13.

34. Formal archaeological training in Mexico did not begin on a regular basis until 1907 with classes at the National Museum. Prior to this, scholars had either studied archaeology abroad or come to the discipline from other more established fields, especially history, medicine, and law. For a biographical sketch of Batres, see Eduardo Matos Moctezuma, *Las piedras negadas: De la Coatlicue al Templo Mayor* (Mexico City: Consejo para la Cultura y las Artes, 1997), 47–62.

35. Leopoldo Batres, *Teotihuacán: Memoria que presenta Leopoldo Batres, Inspector General y Conservador de los Monumentos Arqueológicos de la República Mexicana al XV Congreso Internacional de Americanistas que deberá reunirse en Quebec el mes de Septiembre 1906* (Mexico City: Imprenta de F. S. Soria, 1906), 21.

36. Archivo Batres, f. 215.

37. Archivo Batres, f. 219.

38. Archivo Batres, f. 391. As on most occasions, Batres did not bother to specify who these people were, referring to them simply as "indios."

39. Archivo Batres, f. 492.

40. AGN, IPBA, caja 171, exp. 23, f. 8. Security forces also served to watch over Batres's equipment, which he claimed locals were more apt to steal than any ancient treasure discovered. Although he failed to mention when these forces arrived, they were present by at least May 1907.

41. AGN, IPBA, caja 152, exp. 19, f. 6.

42. Archivo Batres, f. 216.

43. AGN, IPBA, caja 171, exp. 2, f. 1.

44. AGN, IPBA, caja 171, exp. 2, f. 8.

45. AGN, IPBA, caja 338, exp. 2, f. 35. Unfortunately, we do not know the plots' dimensions since they were recorded by name rather than size.

46. AGN, IPBA, caja 338, exp. 2, f. 14.

47. AGN, IPBA, caja 338, exp. 2, f. 4.

48. AGN, IPBA, caja 338, exp. 2, f. 6.

49. Lombardo de Ruíz and Ruth Solís Vicarte, *Antecedentes de las leyes sobre monumentos históricos, 1536–1910* (Mexico City: INAH, 1988), 82.

50. AGN, IPBA, caja 338, exp. 3, f. 6.

51. AGN, IPBA, caja 338, exp. 10, f. 3.

52. Quetzil E. Castañeda, *In the Museum of Maya Culture: Touring Chichén Itzá* (Minneapolis: University of Minnesota Press, 1996), 104–5.

53. Andrew Coe, *Archaeological Mexico: A Traveler's Guide to Ancient Cities and Sites* (Emeryville, Calif.: Avalon Travel Publishing, 2001), 19.

54. The following account is from Archivo Batres, f. 217–19.

55. See, AGN, IPBA, caja 168, exp. 11, f. 5. At other sites such as the Tepozteco, Batres had used dynamite not on the actual structures but to clear roads.

56. Batres is accused of intentionally falsifying the terrace by the archaeologist Rémy Bastien in his "La pirámide del sol en Teotihuacán" (thesis, Escuela Nacional de Antropología e Historia, Mexico City, 1947).

57. The following account is from *El Imparcial*, April 9–10, 1906, in Lombardo, *El pasado prehispánico*, 2: 275–89.

58. Ibid.

59. Leonardo Manrique Castañeda, "Leopoldo Batres," *La antropología en México*, ed. Carlos García Mora and Enrique Florescano, 9: 252 (Mexico City: INAH, 1987).

60. Archivo Batres, f. 222.

61. AGN, IPBA, caja 168, exp. 11, f. 1.

62. AGN, IPBA, caja 171, exp. 2, f. 11.

63. Archivo Batres, f. 157.

64. *El Imparcial*, May 6, 1905, in Lombardo, *El pasado prehispánico*, 2: 241.

65. AGN, IPBA, caja 171, exp. 18, f. 53.

66. AGN, IPBA, caja 171, exp. 18, f. 54.

67. *El Imparcial*, December 26, 1909, in Lombardo, *El pasado prehispánico*, 2: 567.

68. AGN, IPBA, caja 171, exp. 18, f. 54.

69. Archivo Batres, f. 162.

70. Matos, *Las piedras negadas*, 55.

71. Leopoldo Batres, *Antigüedades mexicanas falsificadas: Falsificación y falsificadores* (Mexico City: Imprenta de F. S. Soria, 1910), 4.

72. Ibid., 14–15.

73. *El Monitor Republicano*, July 8, 1887, in Lombardo, *El pasado prehispánico*, 1: 139.

74. *El Imparcial*, January 13, 1906, in Lombardo, *El pasado prehispánico*, 2: 256.

75. Batres, *Antigüedades mexicanas falsificadas*, 13.

76. Ibid.

77. AGN, IPBA, caja 111, exp. 27, f. 1.

78. AGN, IPBA, caja 112, exp. 84, f. 3.

79. AGN, IPBA, caja 167, exp. 31, f. 3.

80. Gonzales, "Imagining Mexico in 1910," 512 and 510. As Gonzales explains, these attempts to alter native dress also occurred in the provinces and everywhere "proved unenforceable." They were part of a more general Porfirian attempt to "civilize" and "modernize" the popular classes through the regulation of dress, which, according to Tenorio, "reached extreme levels" during the Centenario as foreigners inundated the capital, "1910 Mexico City," 91. For "hats and pants laws" that required men to wear trousers and employees to wear uniforms, see William H. Beezley, *Judas at the Jockey Club, and other Episodes of Porfirian Mexico* (Lincoln: University of Nebraska Press, 1987).

81. Sigvald Linné, *Archaeological Researches at Teotihuacán, Mexico* (Tuscaloosa: University of Alabama Press, 2003), 32.

82. Archivo Batres, f. 264.

83. Genaro García, *Crónica oficial de las fiestas del Primer Centenario de la Independencia de México* (Mexico City: Talleres del Museo Nacional, 1911), 229.

84. *El Imparcial*, September 11, 1910, in Lombardo, *El pasado prehispánico*, 2: 634–35.

85. Archivo Batres, f. 502.

86. Archivo Batres, f. 271.

87. Ignacio Bernal, *Historia de la arqueología en México* (Mexico City: Porrua, 1979), 141. For Gamio's critiques, see his *La población del valle de Teotihuacán* (Mexico City: INI, 1979). Other archaeologists, especially foreign and more contemporary ones, have come to Batres's defense. The Swedish archaeologist Sigvald Linné, for example, acknowledges that Batres did use "far too heavy a hand" but that the pyramid is "more or less accurate"; Linné, *Archaeological Researches at Teotihuacan*, 32. As Leonardo Manrique Castañeda points out, Batres had used the techniques of his time, the same that were being used in Mesopotamia and Egypt; see his "Leopoldo Batres," 253.

ANDREW GRANT WOOD

ON THE SELLING OF REY MOMO

Early Tourism and the Marketing of Carnival in Veracruz

Veracruz breaks into a nine-day party before Ash Wednesday each year. Starting the previous Tuesday, there are brilliantly colourful and imaginative parades through the city every day, beginning with one devoted to the "burning of bad humour" and ending with the funeral of "Juan Carnaval." Other organised events include fireworks, traditional and modern dances and music, children's parades, a mini-marathon, and handicraft, food and folklore shows. The informal side of the proceedings is equally attractive, with most people hell-bent on having as good a time as possible and a festive atmosphere taking over the whole city.

LONELY PLANET GUIDE TO MEXICO, 1989

The makings of what would become a robust tourism industry in the Port of Veracruz after World War II began to take shape around the turn of the century. At that time, a growing number of sojourners made their way from central Mexico to the Gulf Coast.[1] Taking advantage of promotions offered by the Interoceanic and Mexican Railroads, travelers came to the port from the nation's interior as well as neighboring cities such as Puebla, Orizaba, Córdoba, and Xalapa.

Some came in response to suggestions regarding the health benefits of outdoor, and particularly ocean, recreation. Seeking active relaxation in the port's tropical environs, they first arrived by train, but then increasingly journeyed by car as workers gradually completed construction of the first modern roadway connections between select Mexican cities in the late 1920s and early 1930s.

Responding to the rising tourist tide, porteños hosted excursions around the Veracruz harbor, the San Juan de Ulúa fortress, and nearby Isla de Sacrificios. The Veracruz Yacht Club and Villa del Mar seaside establishments also sparked tremendous interest.

Early tourism in Veracruz formed a part of a larger project promoted by state officials and commercial elites in Mexico as a whole after the revolution. In this endeavor, boosters headquartered for the most part in Mexico City worked diligently to transform the nation's image abroad from a "backward," "lawless" nation to one that crafted a combination of the folkloric and modern. Yet while many in the fledgling industry endeavored to attract foreign tourists, others took steps to develop a domestic tourist market in places like Veracruz where today the bulk of tourist revenue is generated through national rather than international exchanges. This essay considers ways in which porteños first promoted their city—and particularly the pre-Lenten Carnival festival—as a desirable destination to other Mexicans.

The Cultural Geography of Contemporary Veracruz

Today, Veracruz enjoys a well-deserved reputation as one of the most entertaining and hospitable regions in all of Mexico. Close to a number of ecological as well as archaeological sites, the Port of Veracruz serves as a headquarters for tourists desiring access to a wide range of possible excursions. At the same time, the Veracruz/Boca del Río conurbation has much to offer visitors at almost any time of the year. Most would agree, however, that the most exciting opportunity to experience the city and its people at their best is during Carnival.

The annual celebration of Carnival in Veracruz is one of the largest popular festivals in the Americas.[2] A spectacular event for the city, Carnival, as is true elsewhere in the Americas and Europe, celebrates the last days leading up to the Catholic observance of Lent, which begins on Ash Wednesday.[3] In Veracruz, the festival of Rey Momo attracts close to a million tourists annually.[4] Somewhere between 75,000 and 100,000 stay in hotels located in the area that runs from the historic city center along the coast to Boca del Río. Others shack up with friends or simply sleep in cars, parks, and on the street. Having a drink in the legendary Portales de Lerdo (cafes and bars situated along the north end of the main plaza), enjoying a meal at the traditional Café Parroquia, visiting the new seaside aquarium, exploring the colonial San Juan de Ulúa fort in the Veracruz harbor, or promenading along the malecón where hundreds of vendors hawk their wares: tourists find many opportunities to enjoy the fabled *jarocho* hospitality.[5] Although the majority who come to Veracruz for Carnival are Mexican (estimates figure around 95 percent), a growing number of foreign tourists arrive each year to enjoy the festivities. Combining the income of restaurants, retailers, street vendors, transport operators, entertainers, and other businesses linked in one way or another to the event, Carnival is thought to bring a much needed infusion of approximately 25 million pesos to the local economy.[6]

The Plaza de Armas and adjoining Portales is ground zero for partying in Veracruz. From midday to late in the evening, hundreds congregate for food, drink, cigar smoking, and people watching. It is an alluring, casual space where tourists, navy personnel, homosexuals, transvestites, and locals mix long into the tropical night.[7]

At the west end bordering Independence Avenue, itinerant mariachis for hire and other musicians playing the regional jarocho style with harps and small *requinto* stringed instruments gather. Added to the mix is an eclectic collection of marimba bands, norteños playing ranchero music, and classic Los Panchos–styled guitar trios all politely competing for tips. Shoeshine, balloon, candy and cigar stands dot the perimeter of the plaza, where an army of mobile vendors selling watches, jewelry, hats, nuts, roses, model ships, sketches, Polaroid photos, DVDs and other assorted items circulates through the plaza. On any given night a handful of young kids (sometimes with no more than a scrap of PVC pipe and a stick for accompaniment) will interrupt conversation as they sing for spare change. Meantime, waiters at each of the many bars try diligently to fill their sections and then hurry to fill drink orders for their customers. Despite their hard work and significant sales, however, the late night tip tally is usually a disappointing one.[8]

The malecón lies two blocks to the east of the main plaza. Along this boardwalk visitors can promenade while enjoying the sea breezes and soft streetlight illumination. During Carnival, a mass of micro-entrepreneurs hoping to cash in on the festival's good feeling camp out in this corner of the old city, selling masks, hats, t-shirts, jewelry, CDs, kitchen utensils, hair braids, candy, cut mangoes, hot dogs, tacos, sandwiches, beer, flavored ices, temporary tattoos, turnover pastries, and a host of souvenir items.[9]

Added to this informal economic activity is a significant investment in the industry by public agencies. Most importantly, the state of Veracruz recently dedicated 50 million pesos to the promotion of tourism.[10] This initiative appears to be reaping immediate returns according to the head of the Veracruz/Boca del Río Hotel Association, Faustino Silenceo, who confirms that hotels are 99 percent filled during the peak periods of Carnival

1. Jewelry and clothing saleswoman. PHOTO BY ANDREW GRANT WOOD.

and Easter week. For his part, the Director of Economic Development and Tourism in Boca del Río, Armando Noriega, indicated that revenue generated by the festival in 2004 increased nearly 30 percent over the previous year.[11] Indeed, not only are hotels filled but so too are the many restaurants and various nightspots as thousands come to Veracruz for the festival.[12] Today, tourism is clearly big business in Veracruz and proof that efforts to develop a robust local industry over the past century have largely paid off. Yet given the city's historic reputation as a dangerous way station for travelers journeying either to or from higher ground in central Mexico, how was such a transformation achieved? To begin to appreciate this process it is necessary to consider larger modernization and civic reforms realized around the beginning of the twentieth century.

Modernizing the City

In line with his freewheeling conquest agenda, Hernán Cortés first founded the town of Veracruz during Easter Week of 1519 in a largely ceremonial gesture just prior to the Spaniards' long and bloody march toward the Mexican interior. Shortly thereafter, the colonizers then located "Veracruz" north to what today is a largely desolate village named Punta Villa Rica and then again to another site that would become known as La Antigua. The Crown subsequently called for a final transfer of the settlement at the beginning of the seventeenth century southward to the Playa de Chalchiuhcuecan (across from the age-old ceremonial site known to the Spaniards as San Juan de Ulúa).

From that permanent location, Veracruz served as the principal Atlantic port for New Spain.[13] It was the transfer point for travelers on their way to or from the Mexican interior, and most unseasoned outsiders rightly understood Veracruz as a pestilent place as it played host to any number of contagious diseases including the dreaded black *vómito* or yellow fever. Few, with the exception of a modest population of Africans, assorted "castas," and only a determined white minority, lived in Veracruz until the late eighteenth century, when increased commerce coupled with a series of urban reforms made the city a slightly more attractive place to live. In the meantime, intrepid travelers who passed through the port during the colonial period rightly feared for their lives before they could make it to higher ground further inland.

Nevertheless, an assortment of visitors—*prototourists* perhaps—came to Veracruz. The English Dominican Thomas Gage proved one of the first to record his impressions. Reflecting on his visit in 1625, he noted the port's extremely unhealthy environment and vulnerability to violent northern storms (*nortes*) in the winter months.[14] The renowned traveler Alexander von Humboldt observed the persistent insalubrity of the port and commented in his *Political Essay on the Kingdom of New Spain* (1811) that Veracruz had consistently been plagued by yellow fever from the first recorded outbreaks in the late eighteenth century. Appointed by U.S. president James Madison to report on conditions in Mexico, Joel Roberts Poinsett determined that danger from disease most threatened foreigners unaccustomed to the harsh conditions of Veracruz. Poinsett wrote that "no precaution whatsoever will protect the stranger from . . . illness and many have died in Jalapa who merely passed through the city."[15] Subsequent visitors during the early national period including Fanny Calderón de la Barca echoed many of the same concerns. After a storm delayed her arrival in Mexico for sixteen days, de la Barca regarded Veracruz as simply a "miserable, black-looking city."[16]

Yet despite the well-earned reputation Veracruz held as one of the most pestilent places in the Americas, local merchants organizing in conjunction with a declaration of "free trade" in 1789 stimulated the city's economy and sparked a corresponding need for urban reform. The city council, enlightened merchants, and other civic-minded individuals helped pave the way for the collection and disposal of refuse, relocation of burials, hanging of streetlights, and other sanitary measures around the turn of the century.[17] Following the chaos of the independence wars, the Veracruz state legislature entrusted convicts with street cleaning in the port in the early 1830s. Still, these measures proved inadequate as the city would suffer yellow fever epidemics in 1867, 1872, 1875, 1877, 1881, 1889, and 1899–1900. Making matters worse, a cholera epidemic broke out in the middle of 1833—yet another highly contagious disease that would haunt Veracruz for decades to come.

In an effort to combat the high incidence of disease, city elites called for the razing of the Veracruz City wall in 1873. Subsequent construction of several new public buildings and later modernization of the port facility by Weetman Pearson's engineering corps in 1900 represented important urban renewal achievements. In this endeavor, new water service and a sewer system delivered by Pearson helped improve the quality of life for those residents living in the city's central districts. Yet despite renovating the port and city's central district during the last years of the nineteenth century, officials found they could not keep pace with the demand for urban services in other areas of the city. Attempting to remedy deteriorating conditions in outlying districts, Veracruz lawmakers soon established new sanitation codes that they hoped would alleviate problems for many of the port's working-class residents. In conjunction with municipal efforts, state legislators passed new laws that identified popular housing sites as "foci of infection" and required landlords to provide for basic sewage and sanitation. These measures represented some of the first efforts by elites to address the condition of popular housing. In the midst of various urban reform efforts, an outbreak of yellow fever in 1902–3 signaled that it would still be several years before Veracruz would be freed from the ominous threat of epidemic.

To the shock and chagrin of Veracruz residents, U.S. forces invaded Veracruz in April 1914 and subsequently occupied the port for nearly eight months. Once hostilities had ceased, the occupiers' command dispatched a company of 1,000 marines to "clean up" the city in good *yanqui* fashion. The occupying force endeavored to sweep every street, inspect all residential areas, collect refuse and transport it to a designated area to be burned. Troops sealed old wells, dug ditches, drained stagnant pools, and sprayed nearly 69,000 gallons of petroleum in an attempt to kill off insect larvae understood to be the root cause of local pestilence. The army quartermaster distributed cans to be used for refuse in hotels, restaurants, and public areas. The *gringos* also added public toilets, flytraps, and screens while occasionally repairing broken windows, doors, roofs, walls, and floors. Every night, sanitation agents rinsed the main public areas of the city with seawater. To help realize their plan, they hired hundreds of local laborers.

The imposed sanitation campaign significantly affected the city. Reporting on the situation, a sympathetic writer for the *New York Times* proudly stated that the American "house and street cleaning department has made a great record."[18] Veracruz, the correspondent asserted, "today is the cleanest place in the tropics as every house has been cleaned; every puddle has been filled; every street and by-way have been flushed clear; all refuse has been incinerated, and every mosquito breeding place oiled or abolished."[19] Not only did they comb the city; they also imposed strict sanitation regulations—a matter that infuriated many residents. To the reporter's dismay, some vendors appeared unwilling to cooperate.

In spite of foot dragging in the market as well as more generalized resentments felt toward the invaders elsewhere in the city, strong anti-American feelings generated by the invasion of 1914 would soon be tempered by other important local concerns including a growing housing crisis and the outbreak of two new public health epidemics in the early 1920s. Dealing with these emerging problems, public health experts soon came to realize that, for better or worse, the North American occupation had served as an important precedent for local sanitation work in the 1920s.[20]

In May 1920 Dr. Mauro Loyo detected what he thought was the reappearance of bubonic plague (*peste bubónica*) in Veracruz after nearly a seventeen-year absence.[21] By the end of the month the local newspaper *El Dictamen* had reported several cases.[22] Once notified of the outbreak, authorities from the Public Health Department in Mexico City dispatched Dr. Octaviano González Fabela. Quickly, officials suspended traffic in and out of the port and created a sanitary cordon around the city.[23]

By the second week of August the epidemic had largely been brought under control.[24] Still, some thirty-six people had perished. Some nevertheless felt that the *peste* had proved less catastrophic than initially thought. Rumors circulated that officials had exaggerated the seriousness of the campaign. Moreover, given the trouble residents had endured, the fact that health workers had failed to improve significantly the condition of the city only added to popular frustration. When yellow fever returned to the port that summer, naysayers' complaints carried even greater weight.

The first case of yellow fever in nearly twelve years appeared in July 1920.[25] Quickly, the fever spread throughout Veracruz while also traveling north to Papantla and Tuxpan and south along the Gulf Coast to Yucatán. By the end of the year, 148 porteños had died. The return of yellow fever required that new and more vigilant measures be taken. Initially, the revolutionary government under President Álvaro Obregón took steps against the disease by assigning the Mexican public health officials to the job. The Mexican campaign first began in June 1920. At that time, of the 505 cases counted nationwide, nearly two-thirds were reported in the state of Veracruz.

From June to December 1920, the Mexican Public Health staff worked to bring the outbreak under control through the practice of spraying oil (and sometimes kerosene) in rain water barrels, cisterns, wells, gutters and other water containers where bacteria was found to be most prevalent. Outside the city, serious infection developed in neighboring areas to the north including Papantla, Tuxpan and Tampico; in various sites along the Interoceanic and Mexican Railroads to the west and nearly every area to the south near the Papaloapan Valley.[26] Responding to the situation, health workers inspected the city's water supply and hundreds of storage containers. Sanitation agents also sprayed thousands of gallons of petroleum on stagnant pools in an effort to prevent the breeding of mosquitoes. Gradually their efforts during the summer and fall of 1920 paid off—effectively reducing the number of yellow fever cases by approximately 80 percent.[27] Soon, an agreement between the Obregón administration and members of the Rockefeller Foundation International Health Board established a new binational commission to battle the disease.[28] Jointly, they set the ambitious goal of not only controlling but also eliminating yellow fever in Mexico altogether. By mid-decade their work had proven successful. In turn, their achievement allowed porteños to confidently reopen the port to visitors.[29]

Postrevolutionary Leisure and Incipient Tourism

The section on Veracruz in the *Blue Book of Mexico* (1923) provided detailed information on the city for prospective business, government, and more casual visitors. The *Blue Book* gives special attention to several individuals engaged in a number of different professions—most of them making up the ranks of Mexico's growing middling classes after the revolution. Brief profiles of Veracruz customs house employees, for example, listed the year and place of birth, their education, marriage status, military service (if any), membership in local clubs, and travel experience. Similarly, *Blue Book* editors featured lawyers, doctors, merchants, and various military personnel residing in Veracruz. Photos present all the men as professionally dressed in suit and tie. With the exception of a handful of teachers and nurses, information on prominent women in business, government, and civic service is scant. Despite this shortcoming, the purpose of the *Blue Book* presentation is to create an impression of Veracruz as a progressive, accessible, and modern urban society.

Similarly, the *Mexico City and State Directory* also provides important information on postrevolutionary Veracruz.[30] Issued nearly every year by a U.S. firm based in Mexico City, this compendium of local government and business details a broad spectrum of Veracruz society. Included is a listing of people working at government offices, theaters, churches, grocery stores, customs houses, liquor outlets, automobile dealerships, banks, bazaars, pharmacies, cantinas and billiard halls, various recreational facilities (i.e., dance halls), import-export houses, candy shops, hardware stores, photography studios, hotels, printing presses, engineering firms, musical instrument dealers, jewelry shops, stationery sellers, lumberyards, furniture stores, bakeries, barber shops, cigar factories, restaurants, clothing retailers, tailor shops, travel agencies, and shoe stores. Like the *Blue Book*, the *Mexico City and State Directory* includes professionals such as doctors, dentists, opticians, and lawyers.

Alongside the listings in each of these publications are hundreds of advertisements for typewriters, automobiles, tires, shoes, drugs, perfume, banks, petroleum products, trading houses, stocks and bonds, printing companies, various types of machinery as well as several other products and services. The publishers of these texts, which serve as a virtual Yellow Pages for 1920s Veracruz, endeavor to create an impression of the city as a dynamic business and consumer center. Advertising for hotels, restaurants, even travel agencies also suggests significant transformations in the local social and cultural life of the port. Hoping to transform the city's reputation as disease ridden and deadly toward one more life affirming and progressive, boosters began to promote Veracruz as a thriving business and recreational center "animated by civic spirit."[31]

Indeed, the emergence of what porteños called "bohemian" Veracruz during the early 1920s saw a growing participation in various recreational and leisure-time activities. Increasingly, residents attended sporting events, joined in boating and swimming activities, and enjoyed social dances, numerous concerts, plays, variety shows, and films.[32] People flocked to the Club de Regatas swimming and boating center to the south of the city as well as an adjoining Villa del Mar recreational facility as both centers provided needed relief from tropical heat as well as an important forum for social interaction. Extremely popular from the time the first trolley cars made their way along the Veracruz waterfront in 1918, the Villa del Mar hosted regular dance parties as well as a number of special events throughout the year. Beautifully designed with terraces surrounded by seaside gardens, lawn areas, and palm trees, the facility featured a grand salon with tables around the outside. Sundays proved to be the most active day as couples made the short ride from the Plaza de Armas to the Villa in the early afternoon.[33]

Meantime, several steamship lines including the Ward Line (to U.S., European, and Cuban ports), the Compañia Trasatlántica Española (primarily to and from Spain), and the Hamburg American Line (Northern Europe), as well as a handful of Mexican companies, had been servicing Veracruz from around the turn of the century. By the mid-1920s, printed notices of arrivals (often with a description of the number of passengers and cargo) document the arrival of three to four steamships each day.

With the increase in overseas traffic, a growing number of Mexican nationals also began to make their way from central Mexico to the Gulf Coast in search of warm weather and ocean recreation, which was thought to "relieve anemia, fortify the blood and strengthen one's appetite among other things."[34] Seeking relaxation in the tropical sun, they took advantage of promotions offered by the Interoceanic and Mexican railroads as they traveled from larger cities such as Mexico City, Puebla, and Xalapa. As workers gradually completed construction of roadway connections between various Mexican cities in the late 1920s and early 1930s, more and more tourists came by auto.[35] Often visiting during the week of Semana Santa as well as during other religious holidays, many stayed with family or in one of the few established hotels in central Veracruz.[36]

According to the Veracruz historian Bernardo García Díaz, the number of visitors to the port in 1926 was approximately 6,000. By 1930 this figure had increased to 8,000. By then, hotel infrastructure expanded to include the Hotel Colón, Hotel Imperial, Hotel México, Pasaje, Zaragoza, Terminal, Diligencias, Buena Vista, Rex, Oriental, America, Palacio, Alhambra, and Astoria, as well as the La Victoria, El Cairo, La Vista al Mar, La Española, and El Bosque guest houses (among more than twenty others).[37]

2. Women on the beach in Veracruz, ca. 1930. Photo by Joaquín Santa María. PHOTO COLLECTION OF ANDREW GRANT WOOD.

Porteños responded to the rising tourist trade by offering excursions around the Veracruz harbor and to nearby islands. Promenading along the malecón remained a late afternoon and early evening pastime. Meantime, *El Dictamen* regularly published a society page that chronicled the influx of travelers by listing the date of departure, itinerary, and purpose of more notable Mexican travelers on their way to and from Veracruz. In growing numbers, many came to the port during what would grow into one of the city's biggest attractions: the annual celebration of Carnival.

Revived in 1925 after years of official nonobservance, revolutionary turmoil, and local labor unrest, the local pre-Lenten festival gradually evolved into a promotional formula that creatively combined elements of postrevolutionary nationalism, regional tradition, and local commerce.[38] In growing numbers, Mexicans boarding passenger trains or taking to the expanding network of roads as "excursionists" in motor cars came to Veracruz for Carnival. Newspaper advertisements increasingly used the event to feature products and services for sale while editorials testified at the time that the event proved not only an extraordinary opportunity to promote civic pride but was also extremely "good business" for the city. In opening their city to a new cohort of postrevolutionary visitors, porteños also helped aid in the development of Veracruz as a tourist destination.

Anticipating the big event, the editors at *El Dictamen* busily prepared for

Carnival in late January 1925. A critical component in festival production, their coverage made details of nearly all public activities available to a wide readership. Daily reportage of the celebration played an important role in encouraging residents to feel a part of not only a local but also the larger Mexican postrevolutionary nation.

As early information appeared in print, festival promoters made frequent use of the paper to promote their idea that Carnival represented a means by which the people of the greater Veracruz community could come together in civic celebration. With the festival drawing near, editors printed a message sent by the Carnival Organizing Committee to President Plutarco Elías Calles that proudly proclaimed, "For the first time in over forty years, *veracruzanos* of all classes are eagerly awaiting the celebration of Carnival [and] you are cordially invited to attend." The same day, the paper also published a letter sent to the recently elected Veracruz governor, Heriberto Jara, urging him to join in the festivities.[39] Making this kind of official communication available to the Veracruz reading public, *El Dictamen* assumed a powerful role as the official publicist for the city celebration. Diligent and detailed reporting on the selection of the Carnival Queen in the weeks leading up to the festival came first. Following this, daily encouragements calling for the "participation of all *veracruzanos*" made it clear that *El Dictamen* editors— in conjunction with the Coordinating Committee—saw Carnival as a perfect catalyst for the making of a new civic culture.

In the days leading up to the event in 1925, the Veracruz chapter of the National Chamber of Commerce (Cámara Nacional de Comercio de Veracruz) recommended that all commercial establishments close their doors February 23 and 24 to honor the holiday.[40] Yet despite what appeared to be considerable anticipation for the festival, few Carnival-related entertainment, commercial, or touristic promotions appeared in 1925. Newspaper announcements featured notices of coming attractions to the city, including a stint by an itinerant comedic troupe led by the dancer María Tubau at the Principal and Eslava theaters. For those in the mood for something a little more sporting, the paper informed readers of a "World Champion" *lucha libre* wrestling revue opening at the Ring Coliseo as well as a polo match to take place on Saturday, February 21, 1925.[41] Only a few retailers incorporated the Carnival theme in their print advertising.[42] And apart from news that a group of law and medical students planned a visit from Mexico City, little mention could be found in the press in regard to any tourists coming to the city.[43] Clearly, organizers envisioned the festival's first year as largely a local affair. In the coming years, however, this situation would begin to change as porteños developed Carnival into a multifaceted postrevolutionary holiday bustling with political, cultural, and commercial dynamism.[44]

As porteños crowned Lucha Fentanes the Queen of Carnival in 1926, organizers added new elements to their successful formula.[45] Expanding the reach of the festival's appeal, they invited municipalities throughout the state to select young women (embajadoras) to become part of the Carnival Queen's entourage. As a result, a host of female representatives and their families visited from Veracruz towns including Alvarado, Acayucan, Coatepec, Coscomatepec, Cosamaloapan, Catemaco, Huastusco, Puerto México, Soledad de Doblado, Paso de Ovejas, Misantla, Papantla, Río Blanco, and Tierra Blanca, as well as from the larger cities in the state, including Xalapa, Orizaba, and Córdoba. Adding to the festival outreach, organizers realized a special young people's gathering in Ciriaco Vázquez Park complete with costumed kids and miniature floats.[46] Deepening the satirical side of the event, residents also chose an annual "Ugly King" (Rey Feo) who would—as he does today—help keep spirits high by serving as a friendly joker in the Queen's court.[47] In addition to the newly created role of Rey Feo, first-time participants in the 1926 gala included a chorus of students from the Francisco J. Clavijero School who, under the direction of their band director José Acosta, performed on the night of the Queen's coronation. Traveling all the way from Yucatán for the second year in a row was a group of young performers known simply as "Alegria."

By 1927, the Coordinating Committee had even established a publicity subgroup (Comisión de Cohesión y Propaganda) to aid promotion and organizing efforts. Leading candidates for Carnival Queen participated in a show (velada) at the Carrillo Puerto Theater meant to offer the public a chance to see the young debutantes in person.[48] That same year, various associations got in on the act, including the Veracruz Sporting Club, which sponsored a charity soccer and baseball game. Keeping with the festival theme, the announcement declared that Carnival Queen Raquel and her court "honored" the athletic contest while all proceeds went to local hospitals.[49] In 1929 the Organizing Committee announced that each neighborhood in the city would elect a young woman to represent them in the initial Carnival velada.[50] Expanding the number of male roles, porteños crowned a "Shark King" (Rey Tiburón) the first night of Carnival.[51] Further adding allure to the festivities, that year the renowned Mexico City orchestra of Miguel Lerdo de Tejada performed at the Queen's coronation.[52]

By 1930, organizing for each evening gained even greater coherence as the Carnival Committee publicized a "Program for Carnival Nights" with short descriptions of special events held beginning on Friday, February 28, and continuing through Fat Tuesday, March 4. That year, the coronation took place in the company of three dance bands and a host of costumed well-wishers armed with an ample supply of confetti. Sunday, Monday, and Tuesday nights offered much of the same with music, dance, and frivolous merrymaking in a variety of central Veracruz locations including the 5 de Mayo Avenue and the malecón.[53]

By this time, locals had become practiced in the art of organizing neighborhood Carnival *comparsas* (crews). Similar to parading groups seen in New Orleans and Rio de Janeiro, residents—many of them coming out of some of the poorest areas in town including the famous La Huaca *barrio*—selected an artistic director, made their own costumes, and developed dance routines as they made ready for Carnival. Once festival time was upon them, they competed—as they do today—with other rival groups for honors.

1931 saw a local impresario, Pepe Fraude, devise a satirical "Carnaval de Locos" meant to provide residents with a truly popular take on the pre-Lenten festival.[54] Apparently, Fraude and others felt that Carnival had taken on too much of an elite air, for which his crazies would provide somewhat of a tonic. Meanwhile, regular Sunday fashion features in *El Dictamen* depicting various "modern" young women anticipating Carnival provided further evidence of a festival tradition taking on an increasingly commercial character.[55] Interestingly, the newspaper produced not only extensive coverage on the festival and various style features but also a growing number of Carnival-themed advertisements for retail establishments. Their efforts would help pave the way for the development of tourism in the city.

"Keeping Mal Humor Away": Retailers Catch On

Amid all the Carnival commotion, local businesses began to create various promotional materials specifically designed for festival goers. An advertisement appearing in 1926, for example, announced a new perfume called "Luz" (after the previous year's Carnival Queen) for sale in a shop on 5 de Mayo Street. Various stationery and printing businesses advertised confetti and streamers. Expecting increased demand from residents preparing for Carnival balls and street parades, clothiers Natalio Ulibarri and Company announced a sale on costumes and special gifts for the occasion. The La Galatea fabric store listed a wide variety of materials "with special Carnival prices."[56] Outfitting Carnival goers, the La Imperial shoe store boasted their usual "low prices" refrain while promoting gold and silver women's pumps "especially for *las Reinas y Embajadoras del Carnaval*."[57] Marking the rising tide of leisure tourism among the middle classes, several ads for Kodak cameras appeared, encouraging potential consumers to capture the colorful spectacle—as well as any number of other scenic situations—on film. Subsequent commercial tie-ins included the displaying of several new Ford automobiles outside the Hotel Diligencias on the eve of the 1928 Carnival.[58] Clearly, festival commerce, fashion, and transportation all nicely came together under the rubric of Carnival fun.

While *El Dictamen* regularly featured year-round advertisements for a host of health products and various remedies, everyone knew Carnival afforded residents and tourists alike the opportunity to engage in full-time pleasure seeking before the advent of Lent. Thus, as expectations ran high, the fledgling over-the-counter drug industry cleverly seized upon a fantastic promotional opportunity. For example, the pharmacy "Cruz Blanca" did much to set the correct tone by claiming "Mal Humor is always the cause of poor health."

Accordingly, residents could maintain good health and "keep Mal Humor away" by using medicines available from their shop. The New York–based Ciencia Products Corporation promised that their capsules provided renewed "Health and Strength" to men weakened by overwork, heart trouble, and other unnamed maladies. Droguería Veracruzana offered a product called "Sexocrin" which promised "up to date glandular and neurological relief" for sexual dysfunction. In a similar vein, an injection simply titled "Carrie" gave sufferers of gonorrhea renewed hope while the makers of "Hepaline" offered comfort for individuals suffering from burning or bloated stomachs. "Schering" tablets allegedly fought pain brought on by rheumatism, gout, and urinary tract irritation. Perhaps most appropriately, the marketers of Bayer Aspirin made a special appeal with an illustration featuring Carnival dancers and the inscription "happy times." With the help of their product, the ad read, Carnival could be enjoyed to its fullest with virtually no fear of painful after effects the next day.[59] The Bayer ad copy the following year declared: "Finally the hour [for Carnival] has arrived [to rescue us from] the pain and suffering, anxiety and struggle, monotony and sadness of everyday life! [. . .] All these unwanted feelings are forgotten when it is time for the magic happiness of Carnival."[60] Clearly everyone—at least according to the Bayer copywriters—figured on having a good time.[61]

As the festival tradition grew in the ensuing years, more and more retailers got in on the action. In 1930, the distributors for Discos Brunswick announced having just received a new shipment of tambourines, castanets, whistles, and other noisemakers. With this assemblage of festival fun-making equipment, the owners encouraged readers of El Dictamen to "Prepare Themselves for Carnival."[62]

Keeping with the spirit of the season, RCA Radios fashioned a Carnival ad using images of two musicians and a dancing, costumed woman to promote their product. Claiming the latest in acoustic fidelity, the sketch depicted one man dressed in traditional jarocho style with another in a top hat and tails. Here, Carnival advertising in Veracruz resonated with promotion schemes elsewhere in the republic that increasingly commodified the regional hybrid jarocho identity while perhaps also mediating the difference—and often tension between—"traditional" and "modern."[63]

Judging from newspaper reports, the growing number of participants, promotions, and sponsoring organizations in Veracruz caused a sensation throughout the nation. One journalist from Mexico City commented extensively on the commercial potential of Carnival. "The restoration of the festival," he wrote, "has put in motion a remarkable enthusiasm and energy not only in promoting public spirit but also a prosperity that benefits each porteño to some degree or another."[64]

Taking a cue from their eastern neighbors, organizers in the nation's capital sought to emulate the success of Veracruz organizers by "resurrecting" Carnival. Perhaps not surprisingly, Mexico City boosters confirmed the appeal of the postrevolutionary Veracruz formula by promising nearly all the same elements engendered in the porteño affair. Moreover, several other Mexican cities (including Campeche, Mérida, and Mazatlán) also sponsored Carnivals.[65] As in Veracruz, various local coalitions formed among business, civic, and labor leaders hoped to develop civic pride as well as new sources of tourist revenue. In 1926 the Veracruz city of Córdoba initiated its own celebration complete with a contest to decide the Carnival Queen.[66] The following year, residents of the Veracruz towns of Puerto México (today Coatzacoalcos), Otatitlán (near Tierra Blanca), Coatepec (outside Xalapa), and Tlacotalpan (south of the port) organized festivals.[67]

As the Veracruz event grew during the late 1920s, the editors of El Dictamen took notice of the many people from neighboring areas coming to the port to join in the celebration.[68] A February 1927 headline in *El Dictamen* proclaimed "Numerous Visitors to Assist with Carnival Festivities."[69] The article described how enthusiasm for the event had begun to attract tourists to the port—many of them by train from Mexico City. In other coverage, the paper told how some brave souls had even come to Veracruz on bicycles.[70] Preparing for what they hoped would be a rush of incoming visitors, businesses came up with an assortment of special promotions. The restaurant Hotel Terminal, for example, advertised a special menu for Carnival days and assured clients an atmosphere filled with "music, light and happiness."[71]

As voting tabulations for Carnival Queen came to a conclusion the next year, *El Dictamen* eagerly commented that many outside the city had made known their plans for visiting the port.[72] A few days later, the paper ran a short piece titled "Carnival Will Boost Local Business." Anticipating a wave of visitors to Veracruz, the reporter went on to relate how a number of commercial establishments had been working to make the 1928 celebration the "biggest yet."[73] A similar article claimed that "people from other cities such as Xalapa, Orizaba and Mexico eagerly await the coming of Rey Momo . . . and soon [they] will be traveling to Veracruz to take part in the festivities."[74]

Actively working to attract out of town business, hotels and guesthouses in 1928 offered a 20 percent discount on their regular rates.[75] Various merchants, such as the Farmacia Moderna, sponsored Carnival comparsas while other establishments showed their civic pride by collecting ballots for the selection of Carnival Queen.[76] Echoing earlier sentiments regarding the positive commercial effects of the festival, an editorial titled "Carnival, A Good Business" offered the following commentary:

> While the fun and frivolity of Carnival is now well recognized as a welcome break from the yearlong work routine, we may cautiously note that the event can bring to the city one of the most important economic activities of the present age: tourism. Many splendid cities in Europe and America already attract a great number of visitors each year who in turn find the necessary facilities and services to insure a satisfying visit. If only Veracruz would dedicate herself in a similar manner—for surely we certainly do not lack our own tourist attractions which—among other things includes the enchantment of the sea, the refreshing weather this time of year, the charming character of our people and the simultaneously rambunctious yet elegant festival of Carnival.[77]

The writer for *El Dictamen* argued that if residents treated visitors to the city during Carnival with special care, a growing tourist trade would benefit porteños. Noting that the weather in Veracruz during the late winter usually proved attractive for visitors, he reasoned that it only made sense that Carnival be treated as an essential component of the national tourism industry. "Today," the reporter figured, "the festival draws people not only from neighboring communities but also many from central Mexico who yearn for the kind of attractive vacation we can offer them here in Veracruz." The piece in *El Dictamen* made an appeal to "all businessmen" in the port by emphasizing a main point: "We should view Carnival in a commercial light because the festival is not simply a chance for people to blow off steam and be happy, it is also a genuine business opportunity that can profit many and, in the process, transform our city."[78]

Another editorial from February 1927 echoed these sentiments, stating that Carnival offered porteños tremendous commercial potential:

> [Carnival] signifies an annual gathering of new elements, of renewed energies that give rise to more than a few products and benefits for the entire population. . . . Because the organization of a festival like Carnival creates an extraordinary degree of commerce, various transport services, hotels, commercial houses and entertainment providers will see tremendous economic benefit. Subsequently, Veracruz will have the opportunity every year to improve this situation by beautifying its buildings, parks and avenues thus making the city a more attractive tourist destination. With this effort, the city will no doubt [again] become the indisputable first port of the Republic in the Gulf region offering all the conveniences and progressive touches that one would hope to find in any country.[79]

Clearly, Veracruz residents anticipated the arrival of visitors from around the state as well as other areas across the nation.

Wanting to protect the city's growing reputation as a tourist destination during Carnival, in 1928 the City Council discussed ways to avoid "abuses" practiced upon out-of-town visitors in past years. To avoid unnecessary trouble, they decided to outlaw the carrying of firearms during the festival.[80] In advance of the big event, councilmen also discussed what they felt should be reasonable taxi fares as well as fair hotel and guest house rates for the season. Figuring that they did not have sufficient information to act, however, municipal officials decided to survey local accommodations before deciding upon any type of citywide regulation.[81]

As Carnival tradition became more established each year, a host of local organizers continued to make various adjustments to the festival while looking for ways to expand its commercial appeal. Preparing for the pre-Lenten celebration in 1929, the editors at *El Dictamen* once again hoped for a "truly sumptuous affair" that would bolster the incipient tourist trade. As always, the "delicious" climate and "natural *alegría*" of the Veracruz people served as fundamental ingredients in the Carnival formula.[82]

With the event gaining attention, preparations for the 1930 Carnival included the usual Organizing Committee meetings. *El Dictamen* printed advance notice regarding dances hosted by the Red Cross, the Casino Veracruzano, and the Centro Español. Meantime, candidates for Carnival Queen solicited support as the annual selection process began. With great anticipation, the staff at *El Dictamen* expected "numerous visitors from diverse cities across the nation." One reporter confidently stated that tourists would no doubt be "attracted by the prestige the Carnival now holds as well as the fine seasonal weather."[83]

The potential for local tourism came into even greater focus in 1930 as the Veracruz representative for the Mexico City paper *Excélsior* proposed the formation of a tourism association in the port. During an initial meeting with interested businessmen, Eduardo I. Aguilar explained how a host of commercial associations tied to the travel business planned on coming together for a new committee to promote tourism. Imagining the profit potential for the fledgling industry, Aguilar suggested the group work together to publicize the city as a destination for travelers during Carnival and Semana Santa. "As many Mexicans have recently come to know," he declared, "tourism can be a significant source of income and each city now has its various organizations to help facilitate growth whether it be in conjunction with the Commercial and Industrial Association (Cámara de Comercio e Industriales), the railroad companies, steamship lines or whomever."[84] Proposing that with the help of state and national officials the industry could prove highly successful, Aguilar then pointed out that he felt Carnival offered a particular allure for tourists. Especially critical in the equation, however, would be the cooperation of hotel and guesthouse owners who Aguilar believed should contribute what they could to a citywide promotional fund. Counting on the Commercial and Industrial Association to help facilitate a coordinated marketing campaign that would include advertisements in various local, national, and foreign newspapers, the *Excélsior* agent pitched a few Carnival promotional ideas.[85]

To follow up on these efforts, the National Chamber of Commerce met in Mexico City on February 25, 1930. Various individuals representing shipping, rail and automobile interests along with an assortment of government officials gathered to discuss the potential of Mexican tourism. Perhaps because of its newcomer status, the development of motor tourism attracted particular interest during the discussion as Eulalio Vela (an engineer), Luciano Ortíz Bertheley (a Junta Civil member), and Ignacio Martínez (president of the Red Cross) pointed to Mexico's growing network of highways as the base for the new tourism. Identifying the construction of an international highway between the United States and Mexico (completed in 1936 and eventually termed the Pan-American Highway), Martínez reckoned that a travel circuit linking Mexico City, Veracruz (whose own highway connection with the capital via Orizaba was also under construction), and the United States would be well established in only a few years. Confident that new roadways would pave the way toward a profitable future, those assembled also spent considerable time figuring how they would market Mexico to both national and foreign tourists.

In preparing a promotional strategy, Ignacio Martínez proposed publicizing "all that Mexico had to offer." Taking up the case of Veracruz, many believed that the city held much in store for visitors "not so much as a modern city but as a place of historical interest with beautiful beaches and a pleasant surrounding area that tourists will certainly want to experience."[86] If the volume of hotel space could be expanded and the cooperation of the state government assured, many thought they had a successful business plan on their hands. To this end, the administration of Governor Adalberto Tejeda would soon commit funds to the building of a statewide transportation infrastructure intended to serve the growing tourism industry as well as any number of other commercial uses.[87]

Catching wind of discussions in Mexico City, an *El Dictamen* editorial from February 26, 1930, considered the tourism situation in Veracruz. While not declaring it impossible, the writer asserted that local promoters faced several challenges. *Veracruzanos* needed to do many things. To begin with, basic infrastructural improvement including public health, communication services, and hotels needed to be addressed. If these challenges could be overcome, no doubt the natural hospitality and friendliness of the locals would shine through. For a city so well positioned, the editorial concluded, Veracruz should take advantage of its potential and get to work.[88]

Especially keen on progress realized in the development of the fledgling

Veracruz tourist industry, *El Dictamen* almost never failed to point out various groups of excursionists arriving from out of town. For the most part, these travelers came from other areas in the republic. By the late 1920s, however, a handful of foreigners began to make their way to the city as well.

In mid-February 1929, for example, *El Dictamen* described the VIP treatment a group of three hundred American tourists from Chicago, St. Louis, and New York aboard the English steamer *Lapland* had received after arriving in Veracruz. After being whisked through customs, the entourage enjoyed a special train tour around Veracruz for the afternoon, taking in a number of city sights as they surveyed the central plaza, malecón, customs house, post office, train station, and fortress San Juan de Ulúa. *El Dictamen* commented that the group represented a growing number of American tourists traveling to Mexico who came in response to advertising produced by the national government and Mexican railroad and international steamship companies. Apparently, the *Lapland*'s parent company (the White and Red Star Line) had recently joined forces with Wells Fargo and the Mexican National Railroad to provide the most up-to-date arrangements for the American travelers. Among these was a ten-car passenger train (complete with sleeping accommodations) that took the group to Mexico City and then back to Veracruz.

Asking some of the Americans what they thought of the city, the newspaper reported that many were very impressed by Carnival. Enthusiastic about what they saw, some commented that the festival compared favorably to Mardi Gras "celebrated in Brooklyn, at Coney Island at summer's end." According to *El Dictamen*, these tourists even believed the Veracruz event to be *más alegre* because the local celebration seemed more "passionate and contagious."[89]

A year later, the esteemed newspaper publisher Cornelius Vanderbilt Jr. arrived in Veracruz with members of the St. Louis Advertising Club on their way to Mexico City. Talking with a reporter from *El Dictamen*, Vanderbilt shared his thoughts on the potential for tourism in Mexico. "Mexico has much to offer," he told his companion, "and tourism is a splendid business to get into." Mexico possesses a number of historic points of interest, Vanderbilt opined, and already many North Americans travel to Europe each year to see cathedrals and other structures whose equivalents existed in Mexico. The only problem, the visitor told his Veracruz host, was the fact that few knew much about Mexico in comparison to other destinations such as Cuba, Puerto Rico, and Florida.[90] Above all, Mexico needed to present a more positive image of herself to the North American audience because of lingering perceptions of the countryside being filled with bandits and other unsavory types. Indeed, the *El Dictamen* reporter replied, traveling in Mexico could be a real adventure—even dangerous at times.[91] Yet while promoters of foreign tourism had their work cut out for them in the coming years, thousands of Mexican nationals less inhibited by fears of tourist travel continued to make their way to Veracruz, particularly for the annual Carnival event.

Developing the festival year after year, promoters hoped Carnival would help establish the Port of Veracruz as one of Mexico's most modern destinations for national, and to some extent, international travelers. Their efforts soon paid off as Veracruz clearly became a recognized tourist destination by the start of the 1940s. Evidence of commercial development can be seen in the somewhat more extensive city directory listings at the time.[92] Moreover, the opening of larger hotels such as the Hotel Mocambo on the Mocambo Point Beach 5 kilometers south of the city further tied the future of the city's economy to the growing tourism industry.

By the time the Mexico City journalist Fernando Benítez visited in the late 1940s, the port of Veracruz, with its oceanfront breezes, fresh seafood stews, deliciously rich coffee, sea-shelled souvenirs, Caribbean music, and warm jarocho hospitality, had earned a distinguished reputation as a tourist destination. Travelers like Benítez could marvel at the sensuous atmosphere available both night and day.[93]

The tropical *ambiente* that Benítez enjoyed developed thanks to the informal partnership established between Veracruz businesses, leading labor organizations, and journalists in the staging of Carnival and subsequent encouragement of tourism in Veracruz beginning in the second half of the 1920s. Establishing a successful formula, each year organizers subsequently pursued the design and execution of Carnival with growing enthusiasm. As they had done from the start, they requested the presence of the president of the Republic. And on most occasions various governors made a point of traveling from Xalapa with a sizeable entourage to the port to take part in the festivities.[94] Of course, the state's highest elected official was not alone in his Carnival sojourn as many others increasingly journeyed from all parts of the state and from as far away as Yucatán and the Federal District to take part in the pre-Lenten festivities.

3. Member of the Mexican Naval Band. PHOTO BY ANDREW GRANT WOOD.

As is the case today, government employees, schools, and most businesses (with the exception of those such as hotels, guesthouses, restaurants, grocery stores, and cantinas, which stood to benefit directly from Carnival) went on vacation the Monday and Tuesday before Ash Wednesday.[95] Perhaps the establishment of Carnival as a national holiday gave a new generation of Mexicans their first opportunity to travel as tourists.

Indeed, modern Carnival's formative years and, ostensibly, the selling of Rey Momo, laid the groundwork for the development of tourism by establishing an informal partnership between local businesses, print journalism, and leading civic organizations. Hardly limited to hawking party supplies and corresponding hangover cures for exuberant festival goers, Carnival in Veracruz has turned into big business as porteños continue to find ways to cash in on the fun. In the process, a soon-to-be-robust tourism industry took shape. Today, that industry is alive and well as each year the city welcomes people from all over the world to their weeklong pre-Lenten party.

Notes

1. Many travelers' accounts of the region are compiled in Martha Poblett Miranda, ed., *Cien viajeros en Veracruz: Crónicas y relatos*, 11 volumes (covering 1518–1967) (Xalapa: Gobierno del Estado de Veracruz, 1992).

2. Of course, Carnival (or Mardi Gras in the United States) festivities in Rio de Janeiro and New Orleans are well known. In Mexico, the Pacific port town of Mazatlán hosts an exuberant Carnival that began in 1898 and continues to this day. In the Yucatán, the residents of Mérida have also maintained a Carnival tradition for over one hundred years.

3. The literature on Carnival is vast. See, for example, Roberto Da Matta, *Carnivals, Rogues and Heroes: An Interpretation of the Brazilian Dilemma* (Notre Dame: University of Notre Dame Press, 1985); David Samuel Kinser, *Carnival American Style: Mardi Gras at New Orleans and Mobile* (Chicago: University of Chicago Press, 1990); Joseph Roach, *Cities of the Dead: Circum-Atlantic Performance* (New York: Columbia University Press, 1996); Henri Schindler, *Mardi Gras in New Orleans* (Paris: Flammarion, 1997); Max Harris, *Carnival and other Christian Festivals: Folk Theology and Folk Performance* (Austin: University of Texas Press, 2003).

4. The Roman god Rey Momo is generally understood to be the mythical king of carnival.

5. The term *jarocho* signifies the regional blend of indigenous, African, and European heritage while also insinuating a close connection to other Caribbean cultures.

6. Veracruz Subsecretary of Tourism Mauricio Guillaumín Croda, quoted in "25 mdp, derrama económica en hoteles," *El Dictamen*, March 3, 2003. At the same time, festivals in neighboring Veracruz communities (i.e., Xalapa, Cardel) add further income to the overall state economy.

7. For recent commentary on the environment of the Portales, see, for example, Enrique Vila-Matas, *Lejos de Veracruz* (Barcelona: Anagrama Press, 1995); and Horacio Guadarrama Olivera, "Los Carnavales del Puerto de Veracruz," *La Habana/Veracruz, Veracruz/La Habana: Las dos orillas*, ed. Bernardo García Díaz and Sergio Guerra Vilaboy (Veracruz: Universidad Veracruzana; Havana: Universidad de Habana, 2002), 449–67; and Guido Munch Garrido, *Una semblanza del Carnaval de Veracruz* (Mexico City: UNAM, 2004). Complementing this work is a fascinating study of the Portales as well as several dance halls and nightclubs by Genaro Aguirre Aguilar, *Los usos del espacio nocturno en el puerto de Veracruz* (Veracruz: Universidad Cristóbal Colón, 2001).

8. On a good night, Rolando, a waiter at the Caliente Sports Bar, makes about 400 pesos weekly (base salary plus tips). Testifying to the often close family connec-

tions in the Veracruz workplace, Rolando's father don Manuel tends bar at the Caliente. Nearby, Susana, a nut and seed vendor (accompanied by her nine-year-old daughter Dulce María most nights), brings in between 200 and 600 pesos weekly. Income generated by Olivia, a cigar seller (together with her twelve-year-old son José Naun), varies more significantly because, in addition to buying Cuban product from a local distributor, her husband owns a small tobacco farm down south in Los Tuxlas where he makes his own cigars. Interviews conducted by the author in March 2005.

9. The Holland America line of cruise ships has begun to include a short stop in the Port of Veracruz as they make their way from Cozumel to Key West. For a look at the festival, see my documentary film *Carnival in Veracruz*: http://www.personal .utulsa.edu.

10. "Promoverán turismo regional en el estado," *AZ*, February 22, 2004.

11. "Creció la derrama 30% en el Carnaval," *Imagen de Veracruz*, February 25, 2004.

12. "Chilangada en bola" is an expression used by porteños to describe the somewhat unwanted invasion of thousands of tourists who come from Mexico City to Veracruz for Carnival. It mixes several expressions including, for example, *en bola* (in a group), *armarse la bola* (creating a disturbance), and, of course, *chingado* (screwed) added to *chilango* (usually a derisive term referring to people from Mexico City). "Carnaval ha comenzado," *Milenio*, March 2, 2003.

13. On this early history of Veracruz, see Hipólito Rodríguez and Jorge Alberto Manrique, *Veracruz: La ciudad hecha de mar, 1519–1821* (Veracruz: Instituto Veracruzano de Cultura, 1991).

14. Thomas Gage, *The English American, A New Survey of the West Indies*. Quoted in Paul V. Murray, "Veracruz and the Veracruzanos as Seen by English and American Travelers." Paper presented at the Congress of History, Xalapa, Veracruz, July 26, 1956. Reprinted in *Antología* 1200 (1956): 365.

15. Joel Roberts Poinsett, *Notes on Mexico*. Quoted in Murray, "Veracruz and the Veracruzanos," 368.

16. Fanny Calderón de la Barca, *Life in Mexico*, quoted in Murray, "Veracruz and the Veracruzanos," 374.

17. See Pamela Voekel, *Alone before God: The Religious Origins of Modernity in Mexico* (Durham, N.C.: Duke University Press, 2002), 106–45. As Voekel so interestingly notes, the effort to relocate burials from churches and convents to the new cemetery on the city's periphery toward the end of the eighteenth century proved highly contentious.

18. *New York Times*, May 15, 1914.

19. Ibid.

20. Dr. Ambrosio Silva, "Profilazis Antimalarica," *Revista Medica Veracruzana* 2, no. 12 (June 15, 1922). See also an earlier article titled "La higienización de Veracruz" from April 18, 1919.

21. Bernardo García Díaz, *Puerto de Veracruz: Veracruz: imágenes de su historia* (Xalapa: Veracruz, Archivo General del Estado de Veracruz, 1992), 189–90.

22. See *El Dictamen*, May 31, 1920, for a report that counted four dead and four sick in the infirmary. Established in the Port of Veracruz by the journalist Francisco J. Miranda (1872–1925), *El Dictamen Público* (as it was initially called until 1904) began publishing in early September 1898. Critical of the Díaz administration in its last years, the paper's editorial bias generally reflected a pro-business, more conservative view since the revolution. For a brief history of the paper during its early years, see Miguel López Domínguez, "Continuismo y modernidad: *El Dictamen* de Veracruz, 1898–1911," *Rompecabezas de papel: La prensa y el periodismo desde las regions de México, Siglos xix y xx*, ed. Celia del Palacio Montiel, 175–200 (Mexico City: Porrúa/Universidad de Guadalajara, 2006).

23. *El Dictamen*, June 2, 1920.

24. Ibid, August 10, 1920.

25. "Fallecimientos por fiebre amarilla en la Ciudad de Veracruz en los años de 1901–1923," Rockefeller Archive, Records of the International Health Board (hereafter IHB), RG 5, series 3, box 148, folder 323.

26. Dr. Bert Caldwell, "The Conduct of the Yellow Fever Campaign in Veracruz and the Second Yellow Fever Zone, 1921–22," IHB, RG 5, series 2, box 33, folder 197, p. 1.

27. T. C. Lyster, "1921 Annual report to the Rockefeller Foundation," IHB, RG 5, series 323, box 147, file 195, p. 7.

28. Many details regarding the yellow fever campaign can be found at the Archivo Histórico de la Secretaría de Salud in Mexico City. See Fondo de salubridad III, boxes 15–35, for materials relating to Veracruz.

29. For an account of the yellow fever campaigns in the 1920s, see Francisco Castillo Najera, "Campaña contra la fiebre amarilla," *Revista Médica Veracruzana* 1 (December 1921): 188–205.

30. *Directorio de la capital y de los estados (Mexico City and State Directory) 1921* (Mexico City: American Book and Printing Company S.A., 1921).

31. This phrase is borrowed from Catherine Cocks, *Doing the Town: The Rise of Urban Tourism in the United States, 1850–1915* (Berkeley: University of California Press, 2001), 151. Cocks discusses how early tourist boosters crafted the idea of a city "personality" constituted by the urban environment in combination with its residents "animated by a civic spirit."

32. The first recorded baseball game in Veracruz took place on September 16, 1903. Playing to the south on a makeshift field next to the waterfront, members of the Juárez and Aguila teams faced each other for nine innings. In the 1920s, baseball became extremely popular as a number of talented Cuban stars came to the port.

33. The Villa del Mar had actually opened officially in 1919. A hurricane damaged

much of the Club de Regatas facility in 1926. García Díaz, *Puerto de Veracruz*, 229–32.

34. Quoted in ibid., 227.

35. For a discussion of highway construction, see Dina Berger, *The Development of Mexico's Tourism Industry: Pyramids by Day, Martinis by Night*, as well as Wendy Waters, "Re-mapping the Nation: Road Building as State Formation in Post-Revolutionary Mexico, 1925–1940" (Ph.D. diss., University of Arizona, 1999). On motor tourism in Southern California, see Kevin Starr, *Material Dreams: Southern California through the 1920s* (New York: Oxford University Press, 1990).

36. This paragraph draws on García Díaz, *Puerto de Veracruz*, 226–32.

37. Domingo Muñoz de la G. et al., *Directorio Nacional de la Republica Mexicana, Seccion Veracruz* (Mexico City: Directorial Nacional de la Republica Mexicana, 1930).

38. Most likely Carnival in Veracruz began as a part of the Corpus Christi celebration and then grew into a distinct pre-Lenten celebration from the seventeenth through the late nineteenth centuries. Adriana Gil Marono, "Vida cotidiana y fiestas en el Veracruz ilustrado (siglo XVII)" (thesis in history, Universidad Cristobal Colón, Veracruz, 1992); Martha Cortés, *Los Carnavales en Veracruz* (Veracruz: Instituto Veracruzano de Cultura, 2000).

39. Comité Organisador de las Fiestas de Carnival to President Plutarco Elías Calles, February 19, 1925, *El Dictamen*, February 20, 1925. On the appeal of revolutionary nationalism and the forging of "official" history, see Frederick C. Turner, *The Dynamic of Mexican Nationalism* (Chapel Hill: University of North Carolina Press, 1968), 163–69, and Thomas Benjamin, *La Revolución: Mexico's Great Revolution as Memory, Myth and History* (Austin: University of Texas Press, 2000). For a trenchant critique of certain revolutionary programs, see Alan Knight, "Racism, Revolution and Indigenismo: Mexico, 1910–1940," *The Idea of Race in Latin America, 1870–1940*, ed. Richard Graham (Austin: University of Texas Press, 1990), 71–113.

40. The exceptions to this were those establishments providing articles of "primary necessity," which had been allowed to open for two hours in the morning. *El Dictamen*, February 22, 1925.

41. *El Dictamen*, February 17, 22, 24, 1925.

42. Establishing what would become a citywide practice, the owners of "La Imperial" shoe store offered a special Carnival sale.

43. *El Dictamen* noted in its issue of February 23, 1925, that most were staying in various homes in the Santa María de la Rivera neighborhood.

44. As can be seen in surveying *El Dictamen* over the years from 1910 to 1930, advertisements for automobiles, radios, cameras, and other relatively new commodities increased gradually and soon complemented more traditional printed promotions for drugs, clothing, and local services.

45. The voting for Carnival Queen was tallied throughout the week and subsequently announced in *El Dictamen* on January 31, 1926.

46. See *El Dictamen*, February 10, 1929, for an extensive listing of children (sixty-eight) and floats (fourteen) registered. In 1929 the event moved to Zamora Park (known today for its weekly *danzón* exhibitions).

47. *El Dictamen*, January 24, 1926. Carlos Puig ("Papacito I") served as the first Rey Feo in 1926. Ana María Silva Martínez, *La historia de una alegría: Veracruz y sus carnavales* (Mexico City: Author's Ed., 1973), 10.

48. *El Dictamen*, February 12, 1927.

49. *El Dictamen*, February 20, 24, 1928. In 1929, *embajadoras* assisted in a baseball game organized in honor of that year's Carnival Queen. *El Dictamen*, February 3, 1929. In 1930 the Sporting Club again organized an event. This time they collaborated with La Cia. de Luz in hosting a game between the Aguila and América teams in Aguirre Park on February 5. *El Dictamen*, January 28, February 5, 1930.

50. *El Dictamen*, January 25, 1929. On January 31 *El Dictamen* designated several neighborhood "zones" (eight in total). On February 3 the paper reported that "more than thirty-five candidates" had presented themselves before the Carnival Organizing Committee after parading through the city soliciting support.

51. *El Dictamen*, February 8, 1929.

52. Ibid.

53. *El Dictamen*, January 28, 1930. That same year, a spot on the Carnival court was established for representatives from Jalapa and Orizaba. *El Dictamen*, February 7, 25, 1930.

54. Anselmo Mancisidor Ortiz, *Jarochilandia* (Veracruz: Author's Ed., 1971), 122–29.

55. See, for example, "Titina, Flapper y Presumida, Se Marcha al Baile de Carnaval," *El Dictamen*, February 14, 1926.

56. *El Dictamen*, February 24, 1927, January 25, 1929.

57. *El Dictamen*, February 3, 1926.

58. *El Dictamen*, February 8, 1928. The same year, in its issue of February 12, *El Dictamen* noted that members of the Farmer and Rancher's Union in conjunction with the Cowboy and Peasant Association as well as the local milk distributors had been invited to form a *charro* honor guard to accompany the Carnival Queen in Sunday's parade.

59. *El Dictamen*, February 14–15, 1926.

60. *El Dictamen*, February 27, 1927.

61. Anticipating the holiday closure of local pharmacies, the Sunday edition of *El Dictamen,* February 7, 1926, ran a short article listing all drugstores offering special weekend hours before Monday and Tuesday's festivities.

62. *El Dictamen*, February 2, 1930.

63. For a discussion of jarocho identity and its representations, see Ricardo Pérez Montfort, "El jarocho y sus fandangos vistos por viajeros y cronistas extranjeros

de los siglos xix y xx," *Veracruz y sus viajeros*, ed. Bernardo García Díaz, Ricardo Pérez Montfort, and Daniel Sánchez Scott (Mexico City: BANOBRAS/Gobierno del estado de Veracruz, 2001).

64. *El Dictamen*, February 16, 1926. Reports in *El Dictamen* from February 1926 describe the Mexico City Carnival taking place in Chapultepec Park and along Reforma Avenue. On February 17, the paper reported that five people had died during the celebration.

65. Carnival in Mazatlán is today a huge event and probably the largest in Mexico. Begun in 1825, Campeche's Carnival claims to be the oldest in Mexico. Other celebrations attempting to lure tourists include those in Ensenada, Guaymas, Tepic, and Chamula.

66. *El Dictamen*, February 9–10, 1926.

67. An article in *El Dictamen* on March 2, 1927, reported, "Nearly all towns of any importance in the state celebrated the festival of Carnival." "La celebración del carnaval en todo el estado."

68. *El Dictamen*, February 3 and 5, 1927.

69. Notice of the new Department of Tourism and Publicity was made official in Governor Jorge Cerdan's Informe to the Veracruz Legislature in late 1943. Carmen Blázquez Domínguez, ed., *Estado de Veracruz Informes de sus gobernadores, 1826–1986*, vol. xiii (Xalapa, Veracruz: Gobierno de Veracruz, 1986), 7175–76.

70. Remembering highlights from the previous year, *El Dictamen* told how members of the Orizaba-based bicycle clubs Hércules and Radio had made their way to the port just prior to Carnival. *El Dictamen*, February 2, 1927.

71. Ibid.

72. *El Dictamen*, January 31, 1928.

73. *El Dictamen*, February 1, 1928.

74. *El Dictamen*, February 12, 1928.

75. Of course this practice stands in sharp contrast to today, when rates generally increase approximately 30 percent.

76. *El Dictamen*, February 1, 1928.

77. *El Dictamen*, February 6, 1928.

78. Ibid.

79. *El Dictamen*, February 18, 1927.

80. Ibid.

81. *El Dictamen*, February 14, 1928. Silva Martínez comments that visitors to Veracruz enjoyed reduced railroad and other transport fares as well as promises by the Organizing Committee that hotel rates would remain reasonable. *Historia de una alegría*, 14–15. The same day, *El Dictamen* ran a short article titled "El costo de la prohibicion" informing readers that eight years of Prohibition had cost the federal treasury in Washington approximately $170 million in lost revenue.

82. *El Dictamen*, January 25, 1929. A short essay titled "La gran locura de febrero" by

"Edmundo H. Fentanes," published on January 31, further legitimated the local affair by linking the Veracruz celebration to ancient Greece and Rome.

83. *El Dictamen*, January 20, 1930.

84. *El Dictamen*, February 14, 1930.

85. Ibid.

86. *El Dictamen*, February 26, 1930.

87. Brief remarks on road-building progress can be found in Tejeda's "Informe que rinde el Ejecutivo del Estado ante la XXXIII H. Legislature el 5 de mayo de 1931," *Estado de Veracruz informes de sus gobernadores*, ed. Blázquez Domínguez, 11: 6146–47.

88. "Un ambiente propicio para el turismo," *El Dictamen*, February 24, 1930.

89. *El Dictamen*, February 13, 1929.

90. On comparisons to Cuba, see Schwartz, *Pleasure Island*, and Berger, *The Development of Mexico's Tourism*.

91. *El Dictamen*, February 27, 1930.

92. *Directorio General del Estado de Veracruz: Comercial-Industrial-Profesional, 1941* (Mexico City: n.p.), 9–41 (copy courtesy Biblioteca Archivo Municipal del Puerto de Veracruz). Gobierno del Estado de Veracruz, *Enciclopedia Municipal Veracruzana* (Xalapa: Gobierno del Estado de Veraruz, 1998), 394–401, lists a total of eighty-nine hotels in the city—not including neighboring Boca del Río— ranging from one to five stars.

93. Fernando Benítez in Martha Poblett Miranda, ed., *Cien viajeros en Veracruz: Crónicas y relatos*, vol. 11, 203–6. Later, Benítez, along with José Emilio Pacheco would write a history of the port dealing mostly with the colonial period: Fernando Benítez and José Emilio Pacheco, *Crónica del Puerto de Veracruz* (Xalapa: Gobierno del Estado de Veracruz, 1986).

94. *El Dictamen*, February 26, 1927. Governors included Heriberto Jara in 1926, Abel S. Rodríguez in 1927 and 1928 (whose group that year totaled approximately eighty people—see *El Dictamen*, February 17, 1928), and Adalberto Tejeda, who came in 1928 as Minister of Gobernación and subsequently became governor in 1929.

95. While almost all businesses had been closed for Carnival in 1925, 1926, and 1927, grocery stores and cantinas in 1928 began staying open day and night (rather than supplying customers only between the hours of 10 and noon as before). This, according to *El Dictamen* (February 17, 1928), reflected a more general desire of expanding business in the city during the festival.

DINA BERGER

GOODWILL AMBASSADORS ON HOLIDAY

Tourism, Diplomacy, and Mexico–U.S. Relations

In 1944, the head of Mexico's Department of Tourism, Alejandro Buelna Jr., met with officials from the Office of the Coordinator for Inter-American Affairs (OCIAA) in Washington on his way to represent the Mexican government at various Pan American Day celebrations in New York, Philadelphia, and Boston. At this meeting, Buelna told officials that Mexico "has given special attention to the development of tourism, not so much because of [its] pecuniary benefits . . . as of a desire to strengthen cultural relations and understanding between our two countries."[1] Echoing this sentiment in a report to Stanton Robbins of the same office later that same year, Buelna wrote, "We may say with satisfaction that we have been able to improve our friendly relations with the United States to a degree that would have required many years if it had not been for the tourist industry."[2] According to Buelna, and many others who repeated this message, tourism acted as a vehicle of foreign relations, as a nexus of cooperation between the United States and Mexico, particularly during World War II. This chapter illuminates the unofficial ways that people (tourists), like institutions (universities) and organizations (Rotary Club and Pan American Round Table), carried out broader policy agendas, diplomacy, and international affairs during the era of the good neighbor when friendship and cooperation toward Latin America replaced U.S. interventionism by the mid to late 1930s. By placing this study of Mexican tourism in a broader discussion of cultural relations and diplomacy, it demonstrates how a leisure-time activity like tourism, in which people from different nations encounter each other, can actually promote transnational and transcultural understanding and thus improve international relations. While it is impossible to prove the overall impact of such exchanges, it is worthwhile to consider tourism as more than just a form of imperialism, exploitation, or profit, and, instead, as a form of potentially positive encounters.

The development of tourism in Mexico by the 1930s was advantageous because it was profitable, modernizing, and democratizing. Since the mid-1920s, Mexico's revolutionary government began to consider tourism as a viable industry for economic growth. For the next decade, members of the revolutionary family—presidents, ministers, governors, and businessmen—devised strategies for its development.[3] By the 1930s, a combination of domestic will, entrepreneurship, and partnerships with well-heeled, pro-Mexico Americans from engineers to hoteliers resulted in widespread construction of highways, hotels, and a tourist infrastructure more broadly that could accommodate the burgeoning industry.[4] It also laid the groundwork for widespread modernization in the 1940s and 1950s. Tourism's moderniz-ing effect meant both profits and stability for Mexico and, ultimately, for the United States. For a far-from-stable nation prior to the 1930s, tourist de-velopment in Mexico was forecasted to bring in consistent revenues, par-ticularly from the U.S. consumer-tourist.[5] At the same time, the tourist dollar would drive what would become a mass tourism movement by the 1950s. Although ideologies like modernization theory shaped U.S. foreign policy during the Cold War, there was indeed an understood connection between economic, political, and hemispheric stability that might explain why the U.S. Office of Inter-American Affairs, for example, studied the viability of tourist development in Latin America.[6] Profitable and stabilizing, tourism development also played a role in the democratization of Mexico, because it is only viable in stable and hospitable conditions, requiring ami-ability in the domestic and foreign affairs of the host country.[7] It is no wonder that President Emilio Portes Gil publicly declared Mexico's inten-tion to develop tourism in 1929 only as the Cristero conflict came to an end and as revolutionaries consolidated their power in the National Revolution-ary Party.[8] American tourists played a role in spreading democracy: on their holidays in Mexico, they not only disseminated their earnings but also their values of consumerism and leisure time—those highly treasured, American cultural practices. Tourism, then, was equally important to the U.S. and Mexican governments, for it meant economic and political stability.

Tourism also made strides toward fulfilling goals of hemispheric soli-darity as outlined by Roosevelt's Good Neighbor Policy—a policy since the 1930s that swore off military interventions in Latin America and laid the groundwork for cultural relations—and by the promise of hemispheric defense on the eve of World War II. As María Emilia Paz points out, the Mexico–U.S. military pact of the 1940s and broader hemisphere defense agreement made through the Lima Declaration of 1938 was uneasy given the historical rift and distrust between these neighbors.[9] Outside of official capacities, tourism helped fill the gap of misunderstanding and even distrust to realize the goals of Pan Americanism, or a united Americas. Through the act of travel, by Americans vacationing in Mexico, Mexicans and Americans could get to know and understand each other. This mutual understanding, officials hoped, would build bridges of solidarity never before seen and, perhaps, ones that could not be built at state levels. Tourism, then, served a very real purpose: to massage and improve relations between Mexico and the United States, especially during World War II. Meanwhile, guests and hosts did the work of diplomats. As Mexican and U.S. officials worked out their disagreements behind closed doors, tourists and locals could do their part to ease tense relations, for example, on Mexico's beaches, in nightclubs, and at pyramids.[10]

The role that tourism has played as a vehicle of cultural relations and diplomacy is not new to scholars. In her study of U.S. tourism in Cuba and Hawaii, Christine M. Skwiot demonstrates how the politics and culture of tourism in these U.S. "appendages" shifted according to policy goals and, in the mid- to late nineteenth century, to the desires of constituent groups like American planters and nonplanters.[11] Tourism, for example, was used as a tool by annexationists to sell the idea of incorporating Hawaii and Cuba. In both cases, Skwiot shows how the way in which travel writers represented islands as deserving of the "civilizing mission" and hospitable to whitening played into political campaigns and eventually shaped foreign policy.[12] Tourists affected broader policy agendas at the time, which centered on annexation and race. In his study of U.S. tourism in France, Christopher Endy demonstrates how American tourists vacationed in France not only to escape the Cold War but also to play the role of ordinary ambassadors of friendship.[13] To enhance the rebuilding efforts of the Marshall Plan and to model American values of consumerism and democracy more broadly, tourism promoters encouraged tourists to carry out "consumer diplomacy." A holiday in France, then, was as much about experiencing the "other" as it was about fulfilling a broader state agenda that sought to save postwar Europe from communism.[14] Likewise, Helen Delpar explores the roles that artists, intellectuals, and institutions played in strengthening cultural ties between Mexico and the United States in the interwar years.[15] Her study shows how philanthropic organizations like the Guggenheim Foundation and journalists like Alma Reed brought together Mexican and American intellectuals and artists through fellowships and art exhibits.[16] The coming together of minds and talents, she argues, helped foster cultural understanding, appreciation, and collaboration at a time when formal avenues did not exist.

As these works reveal, and especially in light of Emily Rosenberg's contention that ordinary people have always affected foreign relations outside of official capacities,[17] by the late 1930s tourism was an unstated strategy of public diplomacy—those government-sponsored or private programs and activities that have an impact on foreign relations, whether purposeful or not.[18] As this chapter and other studies show, diplomacy—whether cultural, economic, or political—can be performed officially or unofficially. In much the same way as the U.S. government today sponsors young people from the Middle East to study and live for a year in the United States, tourists, through pleasure travel, learned what made Mexico tick and learned to appreciate cultural difference and likeness. Since the Cold War, public diplomacy has been used by governments to win the hearts and minds of potential enemies. Programs like Voice of America, Worldnet Television, the Fulbright program, and Culture Connect Ambassadors are just a few examples of the ways in which the media, sports, dance, research, and music are used by governments to introduce foreigners to American culture and values. But these strategies had antecedents. One need only examine the activities of the Committee on Public Information during World War I or the programs of the Office of the Coordinator for Inter-American Affairs during World War II to see the way in which the state used culture and the media to shape public opinion.[19]

In comparison to such programs, tourism offers a unique case study as another form of informal diplomacy for a variety of reasons: first, it was not a unilateral project emanating from the United States. Rather, both the Mexican and U.S. governments encouraged American travel to Mexico as a way to build friendship between nations. Franklin Delano Roosevelt named 1940–41 the year of "Inter-American Travel" and Lázaro Cárdenas declared it "the Tourist Biennial."[20] Private individuals echoed their call. For example, Mexican and American hoteliers founded the Inter-American Hotel Association to serve as, in the words of its secretary, a "benefit to the [U.S.] government in its Good Neighbor Policy."[21] Likewise, the Office of the Coordinator for Inter-American Affairs made some effort to study tourism, as did the Pan-American Union's Travel Division.[22] A second reason for its uniqueness is that tourism was far-reaching, because it includes the coming and going of tourists and the many people who made their stay possible, from the restaurant and hotel owner to the tour guide. In many ways, then, it is one of the most diffuse and recognizable forms of engaging and encountering new people. Better yet, because officials and industry leaders imbued tourism with purpose, as something that could bring about hemispheric fraternity, those who enacted it seemingly played some role in forwarding foreign policy agendas, whether aware of it or not. Unlike purely state-driven propagandist efforts of, say, radio or film, tourists and their hosts carried out "the cause" alongside government agencies and private organizations. Taken together, tourism was a much more diffuse, subtle, and ordinary strategy of public diplomacy because it could be carried out in the course of a normal activity—vacationing—and by ordinary people.

Public Diplomacy, Cultural Relations, and Tourism

Diplomacy has traditionally been understood as formal negotiations between nations via diplomats—ambassadors, envoys, and consuls—representing governments who aim to foster communication and to promote cooperation between their home and host countries. Scholars have recently moved beyond this state-centered definition to consider more informal and pervasive mediums of international relations by pointing to the ways in which individuals and institutions such as writers, artists, businesspeople, advertising agencies, and brand-name corporations have acted as intermediaries through their contributions to culture and the economy.[23] Whether through flying, painting, acting, dancing, or music, the exportation of a craft abroad—as in the case of Charles Lindbergh, Diego Rivera, Carmen Miranda, Dizzy Gillespie, Louis Armstrong, Martha Graham, and Alvin Ailey—served as a form of communication about culture in an effort to advance relations between people and nations. Likewise, the executives cum dollar diplomats of Firestone, Sears Roebuck, and others who established business ties and invested in new industries also did their part to communicate, negotiate, and ultimately shape corporate values abroad,[24] showing how diplomacy and its goal to promote understanding and cooperation can take place behind the most likely doors and against the most unlikely backdrops.

Tourism can be analyzed as a form of public diplomacy because it is a kind of exchange among non-state actors that, like more formal programs, can shape and even reorient perceptions of other people, cultures, and nations. A term coined at the height of the Cold War by a Tufts University dean, Edmund A. Guillon, at the inaugural opening of the Edward R. Murrow Center of Public Diplomacy in 1965 (one of the many centers in the Fletcher School of Law and Diplomacy), schools of public diplomacy have since opened, perhaps most notably University of Southern California's Center on Public Diplomacy as part of the Annenberg Center for Communication. In the most traditional sense, public diplomacy includes "government-sponsored cultural, educational, and informational programs, citizen exchanges and broadcasts used to promote the national interest of a country through understanding, informing, and influencing foreign audiences."[25] Scholars of public diplomacy typically examine tangible programs like those run by government offices of information and cultural affairs bureaus. Understandably so, the state has proven to be the most central player in public diplomacy through agencies like the United States Information Agency, which since the 1960s created countless programs to wage the Cold War through culture and education.[26]

These official programs of public diplomacy have long been used by nations to make friends, to shore up allies, and to alter popular beliefs. The Cold War in particular became a battleground to win hearts and minds and it was through the dissemination of culture that the East and West battled. The U.S. government, for example, embarked on a cultural campaign not only to fight communism and to build coalitions against the East but also to prove wrong the Soviet's characterization of the United States. Some of the most overt campaigns funded by Eisenhower's Emergency Fund and the State Department's Division of Cultural Relations were organized in response to Soviet condemnations of U.S. racism. Despite the obvious credibility of this accusation at the time of Jim Crow, the U.S. government funded tours of jazz greats Dizzy Gillespie, Duke Ellington, and Louis Armstrong to perform throughout Africa, Asia, Europe, and the Middle East. Their goal, according to one scholar, was to "claim jazz as a uniquely American art form."[27] The U.S. government exported the talents of prominent jazz musicians, predominately black, in an effort to portray American society as colorblind, inclusive, and democratic.[28] These jazz ambassadors played an important role beyond their performances. After concerts, they jammed with local musicians at clubs and cafes, forging friendships through music that superseded race, culture, politics, and nationality.

More recent examples illustrate the continued role that artists and even athletes play in the war of ideas. In 2003, the U.S. State Department published an anthology titled *Writers on America* that was neither for sale nor distribution in the United States but was circulated for free by U.S. embassies around the world. The goal was simple: as one contributor noted, the anthology aimed to "get non-Americans to discard stereotypes [of Americans]" after the tragedy of September 11, 2001, and the subsequent "War on Terror." In this work, writers from diverse ethnic backgrounds such as Julia Álvarez and Michael Chabon reflected on their experiences as novelists in a "heterogenous, democratic" nation. The writer-philosopher Charles Johnson commented in 2002 that he contributed to the anthology because he believed that "as Cultural Ambassadors we can help people abroad understand what American life is like."[29] Likewise, the State Department's Bureau of Educational and Cultural Affairs' Cultural Envoys Program sent two college graduates and NCAA basketball players on a tour to parts of South Asia, the Middle East, and Eastern Europe in 2006 where they would, in the words of officials, use "basketball to increase mutual understanding and illustrate some of the positive aspects of American culture, including teamwork, free expression and hard work."[30]

Like the arts and sports, education has been a premiere form of public diplomacy used by governments to promote relations, particularly as it relates to inter-American cultural relations. In cooperation with Latin American governments, the U.S. government funded in earnest student and scholar exchange programs by 1939, the most well known of which are the post–World War II Fulbright and Fulbright Hayes endowments. But even before the Fulbright Act of 1946 that formally established international academic exchanges, the State Department's Division of Cultural Affairs set out to develop a program that rested on individual Americans. As then Secretary of State Cordell Hull put it, more than the work of diplomats, politicians, and businessmen, mutual respect between nations "must also rest on contacts between teacher and teacher [,] between student and student[, and] upon the confluence of streams of thought."[31] To fulfill this mission, Congress approved US$69,000 in 1940 (equivalent to over US$1 million in 2009) to support educational exchange programs that included funding for Latin American and U.S. students, professors, and artists.[32] By 1942, some fifty Latin American students had received government funding to offset scholarships from American universities, which usually paid for their costly travel expenses to and from the United States.[33] Among the first American researchers and cultural leaders to receive awards to work abroad were three scientists, a novelist, a poet, and a geographer-geologist. Each travel grant funded their missions to meet with Latin American colleagues and to lecture at Latin American institutions. The first graduate student awardees were two women in the disciplines of history and political science who would study in Santiago, Chile.[34] Finally, the Division of Cultural Relations, the Library of Congress, the newly established Office of the Coordinator of Inter-American Affairs, and the American Library Association began a book-exchange program to stock U.S. libraries with Latin American literature and vice-versa.[35]

In much the same way, tourism can and has acted as a medium for improving Mexican-U.S. relations. After all, through the act of travel, members of different nations came face-to-face with one another in a potentially meaningful exchange. And like more formal programs of public diplomacy, a certain image of national identity was portrayed by both host and guest. But unlike these programs, tourism was a less formal, more pervasive way to improve relations, because it could be carried out by both celebrities and ordinary Mexicans and Americans, by the well-to-do and the middle class, often with only gentle urging from both the public and private sectors.[36] Like no other form of public diplomacy, tourism could bring together Mexicans and Americans, businesspeople, and government officials. Once given the impetus, tourism, unlike other formal programs, could operate on its own and flourish into the most diffuse means of exchange between peoples and nations.

Tourist letters and memoirs, official radio programs, tourist association publicity campaigns, and print advertising are some of the many places where one can locate the different players who enacted international relations along the tourism spectrum. It was these individuals who took on the broad task of building friendships and fostering mutual understanding between Mexico and the United States during the world war, which would ultimately pay off in the postwar, mass tourism boom.

"Know Your Neighbor" and Purposeful Travel

Since the formal founding of a modern Mexican tourism industry in the late 1920s, efforts to couch tourism as something that served a broader purpose than mere profit can be found in magazines, official documents, and organized trips to Mexico. In the midst of the Great Depression that gave rise to the Good Neighbor Policy, Mexico's earliest advocates and loosely organized tourist groups tried to promote the value of travel south of the border. In its short life, the National Tourism Commission (1928–1934), for example, published a collection of essays in 1930 in the *National Tourist Magazine*, designed for Mexican and American readers. In it, contributors promoted U.S. travel to Mexico as the best solution for peace between nations. One writer invited Americans to take part in the new, working relationship between Mexico and the United States. Through travel, he argued, good will could replace ill will (i.e., interventionism, banditry, etc.). He carefully emphasized that official groups in Mexico understood the importance of tourism and gave their support to the industry by building modern highways, airports, and accommodations, while railroad companies improved passenger service to Mexico.[37] In the same issue, the president of Missouri Pacific Lines in Mexico, Colonel C. D. Hicks, assured travel-minded Americans that as they searched for new recreational spots, prominent members of Mexico's official and private sectors were going to great lengths to make their nation the top U.S. tourist destination. For Mexico, he wrote, tourism offered a route toward progress that left dollars in the budget to expand agriculture, commerce, and manufacturing as well as to provide employment. In turn, for Americans, tourism to Mexico offered a route toward peace and understanding because they would find a hospitable and welcoming people.[38]

In a more hands-on attempt to promote travel as a way to improve cultural relations, Hubert C. Herring and friends in 1925 organized the Committee on Cultural Relations with Latin America, which offered Americans yearly seminars in Mexico. Through the meeting of open minds and subsequent tours following talks, Mexican leaders and intellectuals met with American professors, doctors, lawyers, teachers, clergymen, social workers, librarians, and businessmen in what Herring and his partner Katharine Terrill called "ventures in international understanding."[39] With great foresight, Herring encouraged the nearly two hundred participants in his closing speech at the seminar in 1930 to take what they learned and to share it with their audience in the United States. In short, Herring encouraged seminar participants to act as everyday emissaries of goodwill toward Mexico upon their return home.

In some cases this strategy worked. A participant in the "Seminar in Mexico" in 1929, Dr. Lincoln Wirt, delivered an address, "The Lure of Mexico," to the San Francisco Commonwealth Club, in which he shared his transforming experience with audience members and encouraged them to travel there.[40] These efforts and others by the likes of Dr. Alson B. Keller, who lectured on Mexico first-hand, and the women of the Texas-based Pan

Siendo Presidente Constitucional de los Estados Unidos Mexicanos, el C. General de División Lázaro Cárdenas, se inauguró el tramo de la Carretera Pan-Americana, entre Nuevo Laredo, (Tamaulipas), y la Ciudad de México, el día 1o. de julio de 1936.

Being President of the United States of America his Excellency Franklin D. Roosevelt; the link between Nuevo Laredo and the City of Mexico of the Pan-American Highway was inaugurated on the first day of July of the year 1936.

GUIA DEL TURISTA

Unión de Permisionarios del Servicio de Autobuses Dormitorios México-Laredo, S. R. L.

1. Front cover of brochure from the Unión de Permisionarios de Autobuses Dormitorios Mexico-Laredo showing female Uncle Sam and female Mexico in a friendly handshake. According to this advertisement, tourism could indeed build friendship between Mexico and the United States. DEGOLYER LIBRARY, EPHEMERA COLLECTION, C2043, southern methodist university, dallas, texas.

American Round Tables, who forwarded mutual understanding between peoples of the Americas, illustrate how ordinary Americans used their positions to promote a new understanding of Mexico. These individuals reached perhaps larger audiences than government officials.

World War II offered a unique opportunity for the promotion of tourism as a building block of goodwill because both Mexico and the United States, perhaps for the first time, shared similar wartime goals of preserving democracy and fighting fascism. Mexico was also on a high: the country was reeling from the effects of oil nationalization that promoted a sense of renewed confidence, self-sufficiency, and pride, and it had a proven tourist infrastructure in place—highways were built, hotels modernized, tour guides trained, restaurants and hotels regulated. Wartime was, as it is now, a period of propaganda machines, calculated language, ideological repetition, and purpose, all of which contributed to the promotion of tourism as a form of diplomacy.

One of the first ways in which this idea was promoted was through radio. In 1941, Mexicans and Americans helped organize and fund a radio program titled *Know Your Neighbor*. With financial sponsorship from the Institute for Latin American Studies (ILAS) at the University of Texas at Austin and endorsement from National Railways of Mexico (FFCCN), the U.S. State Department, and Mexico's Ministry of Foreign Affairs, Texas Radio House began to air the program on July 7, 1941,[41] transmitting twenty-four radio programs, each fifteen minutes in length, that offered listeners traditional Mexican music and informative lectures on government and society.[42] *Know Your Neighbor* broadcasts aired for only a short eight weeks (followed by a new program titled *Guardians of Freedom*) with two weekly programs in English and one in Spanish that were geared toward American and Mexican audiences.[43] According to Howard Lumpkin, then director of broadcasting at the University of Texas, their objective was to build solidarity between the people of Mexico and the United States through cultural programming that introduced listeners to those values, lifestyles, and history found on both sides of the border.[44]

More than just cultural programming, though, guests of *Know Your Neighbor* acted as inter-American ambassadors to audiences on both sides of the border in their effort to illustrate more often than not that Mexicans and Americans were not so different after all and, as such, could be fast friends or cooperative neighbors at the very least. But how would they become friends? In the inaugural broadcast, Lumpkin placed the onus of friendship on ordinary people: "There must be certain responsibilities accepted by the average Mexican and the average American. They must help each other by their conduct and attitudes to learn the right things about each other. At the moment the best avenue for this learning is the tourist in Mexico."[45] Lumpkin continued with some advice for American tourists, asserting that they have a duty to behave appropriately by shedding typical habits of overeating and overdrinking, and that they should not believe false rumors of banditry and revolution. In short, Lumpkin encouraged the American tourist to think of oneself as "an ambassador of the United States . . . whose actions determine in a large measure the opinions to be formed by Mexicans about the United States."[46] While on holiday, tourists, much like formal diplomats, had the power to shape popular opinion of the people with whom they were in contact. Still more, tourism, according to *Know Your Neighbor* writers, creators, and government sponsors, could promote friendly relations and act as a bridge for understanding between nations.

Know Your Neighbor broadcasts prepared tourists for their mission south with knowledge about Mexico from program guests that included southern celebrities like the folklorist and cowboy Brownie McNeil and athletes like Lt. Charlie Marr, the All-American football player and athletic and recreation officer for the flying cadets of Randolph Field, as well as a cadre of Mexican officials particularly from the Foreign Relations Ministry. To promote the notion of ambassadors on holiday, program content centered on explaining the differences and drawing on the similarities between Mexicans and Americans. Programs usually began with banter between characters Mexico and Uncle Sam, who set the stage for that day's lesson. In one such program Mexico and Uncle Sam chatted about contrasting concepts of time. In supposedly typical American fashion, Uncle Sam tells Mexico in Spanish that he is in a hurry. Mexico responds by saying "Creemos que el apresurarse disminuye la alegría de vida" (We [Mexicans] think that hurrying spoils the joy of life). Uncle Sam retorts by telling Mexico that while in his country he will not spoil his vacation by being in a hurry but that while at home, in the United States, he must hurry to keep up with fellow Americans. They amicably agree to disagree, illustrating that values such as time do indeed characterize a difference between cultures.[47]

In other episodes, though, writers went to great lengths to draw on cultural similarities, demonstrating the small divide between peoples. In one episode, for example, Marr, who also happened to be coach of the National University of Mexico's football team, dispelled the myth that bullfighting is that nation's most popular sport and instead reported that, like Americans, Mexicans are most interested in baseball, basketball, golf, polo, and jai-alai.[48] Similarly, in a Friday episode in Spanish, Ignacio García Zavala and Thomas Sutherland, both recipients of a Farmer scholarship that funded educational exchanges between Mexican and Texan students, spoke about the similar value systems held by U.S. southerners and Mexicans. Mr. Sutherland argued that both cultures upheld family values such as loyalty and honor, that both were warm, friendly, and good conversationalists, and that both were respectful and courteous in their treatment of women. García pointed out that people in Mexico misunderstand Americans because they think they are "dollar chasers," impolite, and devoid of family values. To this, the host, Alfredo Vázquez, responded that "it will be a bright day for both neighbors when they learn to accept each other and make use of the best in both cultures."[49] According to *Know Your Neighbor* programs, the best way to do so was through travel to Mexico.

Radio was not the only medium in which tourism was promoted as a way to enact foreign relations. Print advertising—press releases, magazine ads, and tourist posters—promoted this concept too. In September 1942, the Mexican Tourist Association (AMT) sent a press release to U.S. travel agencies titled "Vacationing with a Purpose."[50] Signed personally by Lucas de Palacio, association manager and Mexico City hotelier, this press release made clear that travel to Mexico served a vital function during wartime because it allowed for what Palacio called "an interchange of spiritual values." In the aftermath of the "big test"—Mexico's declaration of war alongside the United States—it continued, their nations now shared a common destiny that could only be sustained through travel to Mexico. Attached to this press release was an advertisement meant for distribution to the general American public. Titled "Your Neighbor and Ally Mexico," it addressed in even greater detail the valuable relationship between tourism and diplomacy.[51] Dotted with contrasting images of Mexico hard at work for the war and images of tourist offerings, this advertisement assured ordinary Americans like Johnny Adams, the foreman at a defense plant, Janice Meredith, female stenographer, and her boss that it was "patriotic to vacation in Mexico." Through diligence and duty, it read, all earned time off the job. Because Mexico offered a holiday that fit any budget it was the ideal wartime vacation spot. More importantly, as a U.S. ally, Mexico understood the strain of war. A vacation to Mexico, then, served spiritual purposes of rejuvenation, increased productivity, and international solidarity.

Tourists as Goodwill Ambassadors

More than mere rhetoric, the idea that tourists could act as goodwill ambassadors and could travel with a purpose was language adopted by both government officials and ordinary folks alike. As war raged in Europe and Asia, the relationship between Mexico's government, its tourism promoters, and its neighbor the United States bolstered efforts to promote tourism as a form of cultural relations. In large part, this became viable because of what the historian Osgood Hardy described to the Los Angeles Publicity Club as the rise of a "new Pan-Americanism."[52] On the occasion of the fiftieth anniversary of the Pan-American Union, Dr. Osgood argued that the Good Neighbor Policy and war in Europe gave rise to this new sense of Pan-Americanism based on the need to create a moral union in the Western Hemisphere. By 1941, Mexican tourist promoters increasingly used to their advantage this cooperative atmosphere caused by war. One way in which the

Mexican government and tourist interests, namely, the Mexican Tourist Association, played on these sentiments was by organizing what came to be called the "Presidential Tour," which was a great spectacle of goodwill.

Hardly a tour of political leaders, it brought together presidents of U.S. motor clubs, heads of travel agencies, and, of course, journalists to the "real" Mexico beyond its border towns. The Mexican Tourist Association and the government's Department of Tourism organized this two-week Presidential Tour from March 30 to April 13, 1941, as a way to draw attention to and create publicity for the upcoming Inter-American Travel Congress to be held April 14–19 in Mexico City. Moreover, as one contemporary journalist pointed out, it served to foster friendship between two democratic nations as well as to convince participants that Mexico was "an ideal vacationland."[53] With funding from the Mexican government and a host of travel-related companies and civic groups, a nineteen-car caravan composed of U.S. and Mexican delegates as well as journalists from *Time, Fortune, Life*, and the *Christian Science Monitor* set off on April 1 from San Antonio to Mexico after an opening ceremony at which Alejandro Buelna Jr. (head of the official Department of Tourism) welcomed the U.S. delegates to Mexico on behalf of President Manuel Ávila Camacho.

For two weeks, Mexico's representatives dazzled the U.S. delegation.[54] The Texas Highway Patrol escorted the caravan from San Antonio to the border, at which time the Mexican Highway Patrol guided it all the way to Monterrey. On the outskirts of Monterrey, the local Chamber of Commerce welcomed the party on the road to the Hotel Monterrey. After a luncheon, the caravan drove to the village of Valles, where Tamaulipas governor Magdaleno Aguilar met delegates too. On their way from Valles to Mexico City, they ate lunch at Ixmiquilpan while entertained by a mariachi band. They stopped once more to see the Monument of Good Friendship (el Monumento de Buena Amistad) located along the Pan-American Highway on the outskirts of the capital city; the monument was built in 1936 by members of the U.S. expatriate community in Mexico City known as the American Colony. At the gates of Mexico City, beside the Indios Verdes statue, Interior Ministry officials greeted the party on behalf of Governor Javier Rojo Gómez.[55] Officials escorted delegates to a reception at the Hotel Reforma where some stayed, while others retired to their rooms at the Hotel Geneve, Hotel Ritz, and Washington Apartments. The Presidential Tour was pure spectacle. When delegates arrived by train to Fortín de las Flores, Veracruz, for example, a town famous for its gardenias and orchids, one hundred schoolchildren with bouquets of local flowers greeted the delegates as they disembarked. Veracruz governor Lic. Jorge Cerdan and his staff met the delegates as they arrived at Antonio Ruíz Galindo's recently opened ultraresort, Hotel "Ruíz Galindo."[56] That evening, Ruíz Galindo organized a "Tropical Festival," held alongside the hotel's pool, on which floated 2,000 gardenias. Behind the governor's table was a sign that read "Welcome," which was surrounded by both the Mexican and U.S. flags made entirely of flowers. Broadcast over the radio were speeches given by the governor, the *Christian Science Monitor* representative, Efraín Buenrostro of PEMEX and the AMT, and Lic. Horacio Casasus of the Mexican Automobile Association (AMA). Delegates enjoyed traditional Mexican music played by Veracruz's official, eighteen-piece orchestra, a marimba and dance band from Orizaba, Veracruz. Finally, friends, wives, and girlfriends of the local hosts dressed in regional costumes to give their guests a sense of colorful and diverse Mexico.[57]

Indeed, Mexico's government officials and private entrepreneurs went to great lengths to please invited guests from the United States. The Presidential Tour served to transform Mexico's image from the unruly to good neighbor in an effort to attract U.S. tourists to Mexico. But it also erased any doubts that Mexico was both dedicated to hosting American guests and a U.S. ally of economic development and democracy. In a farewell telegram to U.S. delegates as they passed through Monterrey on their way back to San Antonio, General Enrique Estrada (vice-president of the Mexican Tourist Association and manager of the FFCCN) reiterated the goals of Inter-American solidarity and travel: "Visits such as [this] of the Presidential Group serve the cause of Inter-American solidarity . . . since your honest interpretation of Mexico will bring about [an] interchange [of] spiritual values between our peoples through intensified large-scale travel."[58]

This same sentiment was only reiterated after Mexico declared war on Axis powers in May 1942. The common war effort brought the two countries even closer together and made even more real the objective of tourism and diplomacy. In 1944, the AMT teamed up with the government's Department of Tourism to produce and distribute a wartime tourist poster in which Mexico appears as a symbol of power and ingenuity. With a subtitle that reads "For the SAME Victory! MEXICO," the artist, Francisco Eppens, designed the personification of Mexico as an indigenous woman draped in the typical white tunic that is meant to symbolize "the nation" as well as freedom, liberation, and democracy—all principles on which the United States was established.[59]

2. Tourist poster produced by Mexico's Department of Tourism and the Mexican Tourist Association in the midst of World War II. Despite war, Mexico reminded the American public of her democratic solidarity and her modernity in the hopes that many would choose to spend their postwar holidays in Mexico. FRANCISCO EPPENS, MEXICAN TOURIST ASSOCIATION AND DEPARTMENT OF TOURISM, 1944, PRINTS AND PHOTOGRAPHS DIVISION [REPRODUCTION NUMBER, LC-USZC4-4357], LIBRARY OF CONGRESS, WASHINGTON.

An unlikely pair, wartime cooperation posed an ideal opportunity to promote travel to Mexico as patriotic and purposeful, especially given new shared values of sacrifice and democracy. The "same victory" alluded not just to the war but to the promise of a vacation spot that shared a similar future. Like the radio programs and other promotional materials, the spiritual purpose to which this advertisement alludes gave utilitarian-minded Americans a sense of mission on their holiday. They had an opportunity to not only spread American values and rest after their hard work but also to imbibe those values of their Mexican brothers who were on the road toward progress.

The success of this campaign to promote travel to Mexico as a form of diplomacy and as a way to complement the Good Neighbor Policy is hard to assess. Statistically, tourists seemed to have responded to efforts that linked travel to Mexico with Pan-Americanism and good neighborliness. There was a remarkable upsurge in entry numbers by 1941 (165,627) and again by the war's end in 1946 (254,844). More impressive than statistics, though, is the way in which tourists' language reflected the broader political message. One Ohio journalist who participated in the tour in 1941 stated: "We will not only tell the folks back home that Mexico is the ideal vacation land . . . we will tell them that here one breathes the same invigorating air which makes mankind instinctively understand the value of friendship and true democracy."[60] And, in one of my favorite letters, Dorothy Reinke, a young nurse from Oklahoma City, wrote about her trip to President Manuel Ávila Camacho, describing her experience in Mexico as transforming for her, "a sister from the north." Much to her surprise, she wrote, she found love and goodwill inside a package labeled "Mexican Vacation."[61]

Indeed, it appears that some tourists saw their role as ambassadors of goodwill on holiday. For most American tourists, Mexico likely became more commonplace and less unknown given the binational efforts to link travel there as something purposeful and to portray Mexico as the consummate good neighbor and ally during war. Without a doubt, though, the very nature of tourism—the heart of which is bringing faraway people together—advanced the cause of the Good Neighbor Policy by fostering mutual understanding and cooperation between Mexico and the United States.

There are more than a few questions raised here but the two most pressing relate to the underlying intention and consequences of promoting tourism as a form of diplomacy. The first is whether tourism as goodwill was merely fashionable sales rhetoric used to pay homage to the Good Neighbor Policy or whether people at the time really believed the concept. The second involves questions about power inherent in what seemed to be a one-way tourist exchange. Of the two questions, the first is difficult to quantify. Mexico's tourist promoters seemed to convey this concept more fervently than did American promoters at the time. At the same time, though, many American tourists recalled their experiences in Mexico along the same lines while others became outspoken advocates of building relations with Mexico through travel. It is safe to argue that this was not merely rhetoric or marketing but was seen as a new way of building transnational and transcultural bridges.

As for the second question, the seemingly benevolent cultural exchange through tourism was (and is today) not equitable.[62] It was unbalanced because Mexico had to prove itself worthy and familiar to prospective U.S. tourists who associated the country with banditry, backwardness, and tumult. Mexico's tourist promoters, with the help of public relations firms, government agencies, and "friends of Mexico," worked hard to change Mexico's image in the tourist imagination. Transforming its image was tantamount to asserting its national identity, or at least symbols of it. Most importantly, Mexico acted as the recipient of a one-way tourist flow originating from the United States. Whereas studies found that fewer Mexicans had the means with which to vacation abroad, Americans could guarantee the success of such a program given the expected boom in wealth and leisure time which would produce a mass tourism movement at the war's close. But if Americans were encouraged to perform democracy as tourists in Mexico, what values did their Mexican hosts impart? Herein lays the unevenness. As displayed by those who are simply hosts, with little to no economic power to travel abroad, those enduring travelogue qualities of hospitality and those guidebook images of the *indígena* remain the sticking points of Mexican tourism today. Mexico continues to receive tourists—from college spring breakers to wealthy yachters—while sending disproportionately fewer abroad.

That said, for both the Mexican and U.S. governments at the time, tourism served political, economic, and cultural purposes. For the U.S. government, profits meant hemispheric stability as well as a venue in which to export American values, especially wartime values, abroad. For Mexico, tourist interests did not just cooperate but they spearheaded efforts to promote tourism as an act of goodwill, knowing full well of the profits to be made in improved cultural relations. Thus, tourism's many faces: it fulfilled goals of Pan-Americanism, it provided a language within which to sell a holiday in Mexico, and it served economic goals of modernization and stability. On the eve of and during World War II, tourism complemented the work of government officials and, in fact, buffered the distrust and misunderstanding between the peoples of Mexico and the United States.

Notes

I would like to thank colleagues Suzanne Kaufman, Monica Rankin, and Andrew Wood for providing invaluable comments on earlier drafts of this chapter. I also want to thank the Tourism Working Group at the University of California, Berkeley, especially Alex Saragoza, for giving me an opportunity to present this chapter and for generously sharing their feedback. Funding from Loyola University Chicago, helped support travel to the National Archives and Records Administration in College Park, Maryland. Inspiration for this chapter was drawn from chapter 4 of my book *The Development and Promotion of Mexico's Tourism Industry: Pyramids by Day, Martinis by Night* (New York: Palgrave Macmillan, 2006).

1. Anonymous, "Mexican Travel Bureau Head Foresees Increased Tourist Move-

ment after the War," National Archives and Records Administration (hereafter NARA), College Park, Md., Record Group (RG) 229, E 40, Box 657 (n.d.).

2. Letter and report from Alejandro Buelna to Stanton Robbins of the OCIAA, February 14, 1944, NARA, RG 229, E 40, Box 657.

3. See Dina Berger, *The Development and Promotion of Mexico's Tourism Industry: Pyramids by Day, Martinis by Night* (New York: Palgrave Macmillan, 2006).

4. Particularly under the leadership of pioneers like Luis Montes de Oca, who founded organizations like the Mexican Automobile Association (AMA) and later the Mexican Tourist Association (AMT). See Alex Saragoza, "The Selling of Mexico: Tourism and the State, 1929–1952," *Fragments of a Golden Age: The Politics of Culture in Mexico since 1940*, ed. Gilbert M. Joseph et al. (Durham, N.C.: Duke University Press, 2001), 91–115.

5. See Berger, *Development and Promotion of Mexico's Tourist Industry*, chap. 1.

6. See various documents in NARA, RG 229, E 40, Box 656–657.

7. Kurt Weyland, "Critical Debates on Neoliberalism and Democracy: A Mixed Record," *Latin American Politics and Society* 46.1 (2004): 135–57.

8. "Mexico Makes Bid for Tourist Trade," *New York Times*, July 8, 1929.

9. María Emilia Paz, *Strategy, Security, and Spies: Mexico and the U.S. as Allies in World War II* (University Park: Pennsylvania State University, 1997), 11.

10. See Dina Berger, "A Drink between Friends: Mexican and American Pleasure Seekers in 1940s Mexico City," *Pleasure, Profit, and Refuge: American Adventures in Post-War Mexico*, ed. Nicholas Bloom (Lanham, Md.: Rowman and Littlefield, 2006), 13–34.

11. Christine M. Skwiot, "Itineraries of Empire: The Uses of U.S. Tourism in Cuba and Hawai'i, 1898–1959" (Ph.D. diss., Rutgers University, 2002).

12. Ibid., chap. 1.

13. Christopher Endy, *Cold War Holidays: American Tourism in France* (Chapel Hill: University of North Carolina Press, 2004).

14. Ibid., 33.

15. Delpar, *The Enormous Vogue of Things Mexican: Cultural Relations between the United States and Mexico, 1920–1935* (Tuscaloosa: University of Alabama Press, 1995).

16. On the Guggenheim Foundation, see ibid., 72–81. On Alma Reed, see ibid., chap. 4, and see her recently published memoir, *Peregrina: Love and Death in Mexico*, ed. Michael K. Schuessler (Austin: University of Texas Press, 2007). Alma Reed was an extraordinary woman. She was a journalist for the *New York Times* and the fiancée of Yucatecan governor Felipe Carrillo Puerto, who was assassinated in 1924. She was a longtime friend of Mexico who earned the name *La Peregrina* (the pilgrim).

17. Emily Rosenberg, *Spreading the American Dream: American Economic and Cultural Expansion, 1890–1945* (New York: Hill and Wang, 1982).

18. I am using the term "diplomacy" broadly but am drawing on the definition of "public diplomacy," a term commonly used in the field of communication studies. In "What Is Public Diplomacy?," University of Southern California Center on Public Diplomacy, http://uscpublicdiplomacy.com (visited July 11, 2006), public diplomacy is referred to as "soft" power diplomacy because it uses culture and education to promote ideas rather than "hard" power, or direct government-to-government communication. The obvious problem with the latter is that state officials cannot force citizens to accept new ideas; rather, they must be won over through their "hearts and minds." For this reason, forms of public diplomacy like cultural and educational exchange programs have been officially a part of foreign relations' strategies since the interwar years. See Frank A. Ninkovich, *The Diplomacy of Ideas: U.S. Foreign Policy and Cultural Relations, 1938–1950.* (Cambridge: Cambridge University Press, 1981), 8, and Ben D. Mor, "Public Diplomacy in Grand Strategy," *Foreign Policy Analysis* 2 (2006): 157–76. One of the best studies on public diplomacy is Gregg Wolper, "The Origins of Public Diplomacy: Woodrow Wilson, George Creel, and the Committee on Public Information" (Ph.D. diss., University of Chicago, 1991). Also see Geoffrey C. Middlebrook, "The Bureau of Educational and Cultural Affairs and American Public Diplomacy during the Reagan Years: Purpose, Policy, Program, and Performance" (Ph.D. diss., University of Hawaii, 1995).

19. See Wolper, "The Origins of Public Diplomacy."

20. "President Cárdenas' Proclamation Declaring 1940–41 Travel Years," January 29, 1940, Centro de Estudios Históricas Mexicanos: Luis Montes de Oca (hereafter CEHM: LMDO), 378/34756.

21. Letter from Inter-American Hotel Association secretary, Bennett E. Tousley, to Nelson Rockefeller, April 19, 1943, NARA, RG 229, E 40, Box 656.

22. For example, see the memorandum from Dorothy Lack to General Julian Schley dated November 19, 1944 in which Lack describes efforts made by U.S. government agencies to study tourism in Latin America: NARA, RG 229, E 40, Box 657. Also see Monica A. Rankin, "¡México, la Patria! Modernity, National Unity, and Propaganda during World War II" (Ph.D. diss., University of Arizona, 2004).

23. Delpar, *The Enormous Vogue of Things Mexican*; Julio Moreno, *Yankee Don't Go Home! Mexican Nationalism, American Business Culture, and the Shaping of Modern Mexico, 1920–1950* (Chapel Hill: University of North Carolina Press, 2003); Thomas O'Brien, *The Revolutionary Mission: American Enterprise in Latin America, 1900–1945* (Cambridge: Cambridge University Press, 1996); Naima Prevots, *Dance for Export: Cultural Diplomacy and the Cold War* (Hanover, N.H.: University Press of New England, 1998); Emily S. Rosenberg, *Financial Missionaries to the World: The Politics and Culture of Dollar Diplomacy, 1900–1930* (Durham, N.C.: Duke University Press, 2003); Penny M. Von Eschen, *Satchmo*

Blows Up the World: Jazz Ambassadors Play the Cold War (Cambridge, Mass.: Harvard University Press, 2004).

24. See Moreno, *Yankee Don't Go Home!*; O'Brien, *The Revolutionary Mission*; and Rosenberg, *Financial Missionaries to the World.*

25. From "What Is Public Diplomacy?" USC Center on Public Diplomacy, http://uscpublicdiplomacy.com (visited July 11, 2006), and Ninkovich, *The Diplomacy of Ideas*, 8.

26. See Middlebrook. In relation to Europe alone, see Amy C. Garrett, "Marketing America: Public Culture and Public Diplomacy in the Marshall Plan Era, 1947–54" (Ph.D. diss., University of Pennsylvania, 2004).

27. Von Eschen, *Satchmo Blows Up the World*, 82.

28. Ibid., 4.

29. *Morning Edition with Susan Stamberg*, Public Radio International, December 16, 2002.

30. U.S. Department of State, Bureau of Educational and Cultural Affairs, Citizen Exchanges: Cultural Programs Division. http://exchanges.state.gov/education/citizens/culture/envoys/index.htm (visited July 11, 2006).

31. Secretary of State Cordell Hull as quoted in J. Manuel Espinosa, *Inter-American Beginnings of U.S. Cultural Diplomacy: 1936–1948* (Washington: Department of State, 1976), 141.

32. Espinosa, *Inter-American Beginnings of U.S. Cultural Diplomacy*, 157.

33. Ibid., 165.

34. Ibid., 168–70.

35. Ibid., 172. For an in-depth examination of the OCIAA, see Rankin, "¡México, la Patria!"

36. J. M. Mitchell, *International Cultural Relations* (London: Allen and Unwin, 1986), 5.

37. V. Mc. Dunn, "Our Welcome," *La revista nacional de turismo* I:I (June 1, 1930), 37. Located in the Archivo Histórico "Genaro Estrada" de la Secretaría de Relaciones Exteriores, caja IV-300-I, exp. VI.

38. Colonel C. D. Hicks, "Tourist Business," *La revista*, 41 and 58.

39. Hubert C. Herring and Katharine Terrill, eds., *The Genius of Mexico: Lectures Delivered before the Fifth Seminar in Mexico, 1930* (New York: Committee on Cultural Relations with Latin America, 1931), v.

40. Transcribed speech by Dr. Lincoln Wirt sent to President Portes Gil in hopes of publication in Spanish by the official Press Department. Archivo General de la Nación (hereafter AGN), Emilio Portes Gil, caja 9, exp. 315/104, folio 14004 (September 6, 1929).

41. Texas Radio House was the "voice of University of Texas" whose studios were completed in 1939. UT's president appointed J. H. Lumpkin director of broadcasting, Alvan L. Chapman, director of radio research, and Elithe Hamilton Beal,

script editor. See pamphlet by Bernard Brister, *"Radio House": Forty Acres Gets an Airing* (July 1944), in the Texas Radio House collection at the Center for American History, University of Texas, Austin.

42. Report to the General Council of the AMT on July 7, 1941, AGN, Manuel Ávila Camacho (hereafter MAC), 704/170–1.

43. Monday programs offered American audiences information about Mexico, Wednesday programs offered listeners "dramatic shows" about Mexican people and culture, and Fridays offered Mexicans information about Americans.

44. See transcript from Monday, July 7, 1941, at 10:15–10:30 p.m. *Know Your Neighbor*, Radio House Collection, Center for American History, University of Texas, Austin.

45. *Know Your Neighbor*, Monday, July 7, 1941, Radio House Collection, Center for American History, University of Texas, Austin.

46. Ibid.

47. *Know Your Neighbor*, Monday, July 7, 1941, Radio House Collection, Center for American History, University of Texas, Austin.

48. *Know Your Neighbor*, July 21, 1941, Radio House Collection, Center for American History, University of Texas, Austin.

49. Ibid.

50. Lucas de Palacio, AMT press release, April 16, 1941 sent to travel agencies throughout the United States, AGN, MAC, 704/170–1.

51. Ibid.

52. Dr. Osgood Hardy, chair of the history department at Occidental College in Los Angeles, "El nuevo panamericanismo," speech given to the Los Angeles Publicity Club at the Biltmore Hotel on July 2, 1940, CEHM:LMDO, 376/34550.

53. "'Presidential Tour' Comes to Mexico," *Pemex Travel Club* 3, 118-A (March–April 1941).

54. Mexican delegates included the following: Alejandro Buelna Jr., William H. Furlong, Lucas de Palacio, José Rivera R., Francisco C. Lona, J. J. March, Ing. Carlos Bazan (Public Works or SCOP), Gral. Octavio de la Peña (owner of Washington Apartments in Mexico City), Antonio Pérez O., and Antonio Malo (Hotel Colonial and future owner of Tony's Bar in Mexico City). U.S. delegates include important members of the AAA and the delegate spokesperson, Clarence Werthan, secretary and manager of the Rocky Mountain Motorists, Inc., in Denver. For a description of the entire itinerary, see the report compiled by Pancho Scanlan and Jerry Ryan, "Presidential Tour to Mexico," *A.A.A. Travel News*, American Automobile Association, April 24, 1941, AGN, MAC, 704/701–1.

55. The two officials included Lic. Fernando Casas Alemán (Mexico City's next governor during Miguel Alemán's presidency) and Lic. Alejandro Gómez Maganda.

56. Antonio Ruíz Galindo had been a member of the revolutionary family since the early 1920s. Always a businessman, he turned hotelier in 1941 and eventually became president of the Mexican Hotel Association. In 1946, he was named

national economic minister, at which time he and Lucas de Palacio founded the Escuela Mexicana de Turismo (EMT), or Mexican Tourism School. Today, his son Antonio Jr. remains honorary president of the EMT in Mexico City.

57. This and other day-to-day activities planned for the delegates on the Presidential Tour can be found in Scanlan and Ryan, "Presidential Tour to Mexico."

58. Ibid.

59. Part of the Library of Congress Prints and Photographs Division, this poster can be viewed online at http://memory.loc.gov/pp/pphome.html. Also see James Oles, *South of the Border: Mexico in the American Imagination, 1914–1947* (Washington: Smithsonian Institution Press, 1993), 175.

60. AMT press release, April 16, 1941, sent to travel agencies throughout the United States, AGN, MAC, 704/170–1.

61. Dorothy Reinke to President Manuel Ávila Camacho, August 12, 1941, AGN, MAC, 548.3/4.

62. In particular, take a look at the school of anthropologists of tourism—Valene Smith, Nelson H. H. Graburn, and others—whose research shows how power and travel go hand in hand. Some like Dennison Nash argue that it is a form of imperialism. See chapters 1 and 2 in the path-breaking volume *Hosts and Guests: The Anthropology of Tourism*, ed. Valene Smith (Philadelphia: University of Pennsylvania Press, 1989).

ERIC M. SCHANTZ

BEHIND THE NOIR BORDER

Tourism, the Vice Racket, and Power Relations
in Baja California's Border Zone, 1938–65

One episode of the animated television comedy *The Simpsons* offers a clear idea of just how deeply interwoven associations of tourism are with Tijuana, in particular, and Mexico, in general. Speaking to the modern cultural value of organized recreation, Bart and Lisa Simpson exercise their American rite of youth by going to summer "Kamp Krusty." The experience proves to be bitter when the camp turns out to be more concentration camp than recreational escape. After thug counselors subject the campers to forced labor, Bart Simpson organizes an uprising, demanding that Krusty attend the camp in person as originally advertised. Meanwhile Krusty relaxes at Wimbledon, quaffing champagne, strawberries, and cream, until the mutiny forces his premature return to broker an armistice. The demented clown extends the olive branch, placating the insurgents with a sightseeing trip to "the happiest place on earth: Tijuana!!!"[1] The show's final sequence captures Krusty leading the merry band of rebels as they dart through a fictitious border arch that demarcates their passage across the international boundary.[2] We hear Frank Sinatra's version of "South of the Border," recalling a paradoxical association whereby tourists and cultural consumers transpose fragments of Iberian culture as properly Mexican: Spanish lace, mission bells . . . , *'Cause it was fiesta, and we were so gay*.[3] Postcard snapshots enshrine this as an archetypal vision of American touristic engagement in Tijuana: muted *charro*-clad mariachis, Bart and Lisa Simpson posed on the zebra-painted burrow, and the *tiro de gracia*, Krusty face first in the Tijuana muck, a bottle of tequila having delivered the k.o. punch.

Evoking Disneyland by way of Tijuana, and Mexico by way of Frank

Sinatra's version of "South of the Border," the show's writers have captured with trademark irony the iconography of twentieth-century leisure culture. The Kamp Krusty episode poignantly demonstrates what scholars of tourism have been arguing for the last fifty years: tourism is both recreational stress relief valve and cultural practice.[4] Moreover, economic growth generated in part by tourism helped transform otherwise unremarkable nineteenth-century backwater towns and *ranchos* such as Anaheim, Las Vegas, San Diego, and Tijuana into major cities that received daily injections of national and international visitors. Between the age of luxurious Pullman trains and the advent of the democratizing automobile, the California coastline, including Baja California's border zone, became a *pleasure periphery*.[5] Tracing the evolution of business and pleasure travel, we see the unmistakable signs of an emerging organized tourism industry in the American Southwest by the 1920s. Leisure culture and American consumerism, which begat organized tourism, cooled during the Depression but reemerged with marked intensity after the Second World War.[6]

American tourists visited Mexico's border cities expecting risqué entertainment, sizzling-hot floor shows, glitzy casinos, and colorful racing culture. Sightseers enthusiastically frequented Iberian cultural attractions such as bullfights and jai alai matches. Red-light tourism made Mexico's border cities magnets for bachelors and soldiers (after World War II), drawing a clientele that was predominantly foreign and male. Despite the coarse-grained, saloon milieu set, and well-publicized crimes that might dissuade them from Tijuana, women tourists frequented casinos and the horse and dog races, leading the consumerist charge in buying *curiosidades de lo mexicano*, as well as high-end imports. Mary Jane Brown often visited Agua Caliente as a part of regular trips to San Diego's Coronado Beach Hotel, referring to her dips below the border Mecca as the "proverbial cherry on the ice cream."[7] Alas, Hollywood's players continued to make Baja California a Mecca for freedom-loving hedonism. Tijuana's Agua Caliente had lost the brass luster from its original casino hotel complex but continued to attract a steady stream of aficionados and horsemen like Bing Crosby and Jack Warner.[8] Al Capone's patronage of the Agua Caliente resort set an early expectation for American mobsters, one that reflected a sense that there was a veritable gold mine of gullible gamblers to be extracted, and the introduction of telegraphed race results, pioneered at Tijuana's first hippodrome in 1919, created an opportunity to hedge wagering odds and thus manipulate payoffs. Also, the gangster element fused with the Hollywood set to create an atmosphere that tourists relished, especially at Tijuana's casinos and racetrack. Mafia chic and Hollywood star power fueled the Tijuana mystique and imbued it with ersatz glamour.

What follows is an analysis of policy, action, and perception by Mexico's officials (federal and state) and intellectuals, and by foreign gaming concessionaires and tourists. While the profile of American tourism changed little after the Depression, Mexico's border zone experienced a dramatic change as border tourism became largely controlled and employed by Mexicans. Meanwhile, international migration, fueled by immigration to the United States, transformed the long under-populated peninsula between 1940 and 1965.[9]

After a meteoric rise during the revolution and the Jazz Age, the border and the consumer market that fed the sightseeing industry faced new challenges triggered by the Depression. Specifically, comprehending the United States–Mexico border as a geographic site and arena of social conflict is essential to understand the asymmetric division of power revealed in the unequal flow of goods, services, and humans across the border. Mexico's proximity to the United States has given rise to unprecedented asymmetrical relations of power.[10]

Although delayed in its impact, ultimately the Depression created tremendous economic and political strains in Baja California's border zone that were exacerbated by three factors: the mass repatriation of Mexican immigrants (1929–33), the repeal of prohibition (1933), and President Lázaro Cárdenas's ban on casino gambling (1935). Tijuana's gaming industry became the primary target that Cárdenas attacked because it was a lucrative economic base of his rivals, Plutarco Elías Calles and Abelardo L. Rodríguez. By expropriating and nationalizing the Agua Caliente casino and resort (1935–37), Cárdenas struck out at Calles and the Northwest Group, eliminating their access to liquid wealth.[11] In addition to the strategic attack on Calles and Rodríguez, Cárdenas's developmentalist philosophy featured zero tolerance for the mechanized gaming industry and the nefarious nexus of revolutionary generals and crooked foreign capitalists who were exploiting Mexico through the casino-cabaret sector. He and others could not so easily stomach the Sonoran clique's duplicitous discourse that exhorted nationalist reformation of society through moralization and education campaigns even as it openly promoted gambling investments along the border (the Agua Caliente and Foreign Club) and even near the capital (Cuernavaca's Casino de la Selva).

Inter-elite political struggles revolved around competing camarillas, and the instrumental control, indeed, monopolistic control, of gaming reflects this process. Braulio Maldonado Sández received the nomination to be governor as Baja California Norte became Mexico's forty-ninth state to preempt General Rodríguez from making another attempt to seize power in Baja California. Nominated by Adolfo Ruíz Cortines and protected by Cárdenas after he left power in 1960, Maldonado Sández stood in his Michoacán exile in bitter defeat.[12] To understand the power relations that shaped Mexico's gaming industry after the Cárdenas ban, it is necessary to recall the legacy of foreign enclaves dating to the conquest but more recently fueling the nationalist policies of the institutionalizing stage of the Mexican Revolution. The casino-cabaret complex developed within the insular confines of the foreign enclave. Repatriating capital, disavowing federal labor policies, and segregating membership, no wonder Mexico has yet to fully restore the casino business that fueled its border economies during the first third of the twentieth century. Because the revolution stimulated a nationalist backlash against foreign investment, the Constitutionalist governments that came to power (1917–40) imposed increasing restrictions on foreign investors. In particular, foreign businesses had to recognize labor's legal right to organize (greatly strengthened after the passing of a federal labor law in 1929) and accept a national hiring quota of 50 percent (increased to 80 percent after 1929).[13] Adopting mixed partnerships of national and foreign capital was one way to placate Mexican officials and pass pesky labor inspections, especially if the principals wielded as much clout as General Rodríguez. Tourism projects often comprised mixed national and foreign investments, a favorite economic strategy that was pioneered in Sonora and adopted by Abelardo Rodríguez who employed this approach by forcing the casino-cabaret complex to open its doors to national workers as well as national elites who were seeking opportunities to invest in the border tourism economy. At once opportunistic and enabling, Governor Rodríguez's policies paved the way for Mexican officials to invest in Tijuana's premiere tourism resort, the Agua Caliente.[14]

Cárdenas's reforms attacked casino gambling but left untouched the gaming business that operated sporting wagers—horse races, jai alai, and American sporting events—through the Caliente Sports Book. President Miguel Alemán made the spirit of his policy law in 1947 as he introduced new restrictions on games and lotteries.[15] It is said that Cárdenas had spared the racing operation, largely through the influence of his secretary of defense and presidential successor, Manuel Ávila Camacho, who was a racing fanatic.

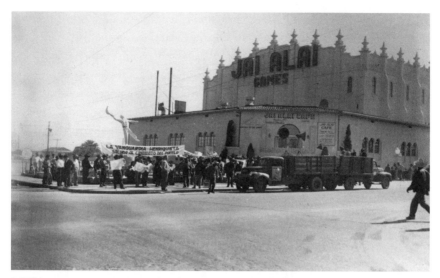

1. Militant unions representing workers from Tijuana's tourism sector protest in front of Tijuana's jai alai *frontón*, ca. 1950, against President Miguel Alemán and the PRI's hegemony in favor of one of Mexico's most impassioned opposition candidates to challenge the executive branch before 1988, General Miguel Henríquez Guzmán. This image speaks to the legacy of labor organizing in the Mexican North during and after the armed struggle, where camarilla politics and anticentrist antagonisms often pitted CROM affiliated locals in Baja California against the CTM and its official patronage by the PRI. OP 9866, PHO 04, 102. COURTESY OF SAN DIEGO HISTORICAL SOCIETY.

Moreover, the findings presented in this chapter indicate that Rodríguez recruited both presidents Ávila Camacho and Miguel Alemán as investors in the track business, but, perhaps more significantly, they also became absentee owners of nearby agricultural estates.[16] As landowners of the Tijuana hippodrome, Rodríguez and friends continued to reap substantial revenue from the gaming tourism sector. Gaming revenue enriched private wealth, but it also lightened the tax burdens on the dynamic economic sectors and subsidized public services.

The fact that Rodríguez and friends continued to operate Tijuana's Agua Caliente race track through an unsavory alliance with shady figures who were either once prominent officials of the old racing administration, such as James Nugent Crofton, or ascendant mafiosi, helped emboss the image of *Mexico negro*.[17] After internal volatility and high rate of turnover in track administrative teams, Tijuana's racing industry experienced a marked resurgence in status and stability after the arrival of John S. Alessio. Perhaps more alarming to his critics and reflective of noir history were Alessio's ties to organized crime. Such was his rapidly consolidating ring of influence and social grace that he earned the trust of General Rodríguez and was named manager of his own Banco del Pacífico in 1943. Later, through the lobbying efforts of Rodríguez and President Miguel Alemán, he was promoted to track manager at Tijuana's hippodrome.

Skepticism and dismay grew when the personal fortunes of public officials outpaced gains accrued to the public sector. An unsavory alliance between gangster elements and high-ranking officials generated symbiotic relations of political protection and economic plunder, which struck many Mexicans as patently unjust. The nefarious conduct of gangster elements and the degradation of state power by criminal syndicates generated legitimate political grounds for grievances.[18] These groups jeopardized Mexico's sovereignty, corrupting officials and resorting to violence when needed. President Alemán's chief of security was suspected of drug trafficking. Alemán received expensive gifts from foreign investors, among which figured gaming interests, helping to define his reputation for corruption.[19] Those who benefited most from gaming tourism were already power brokers of postrevolutionary Mexico. Less notice would have been taken had not the gaming industry rationalized gaming in terms of the functional benefits to civil society. Alessio himself fabricated his own myth of benevolent largesse by publicizing high-profile contributions made to schools, orphanages, and public hospitals. The newly recognized power of organized labor added another constituent force for a tourism industry fueled by regulated gaming. Some leaders even proposed restricting admission to wealthy foreigners in order to minimize the social ills of casinos and wagering.[20]

A Sure Bet: Tourism and the Politics of Gaming after Cárdenas, 1938–1965

Before Cárdenas's ban on casino gaming, the casino-cabaret-hippodrome complex stood at the center of Baja California's booming tourism economy. Its very enclave nature made it a natural target for nation- and state-building efforts of the revolutionary leadership. No sooner had the ink dried on the presidential decree when interested parties from diverse angles of the gaming sector began lobbying behind the scenes for the repeal if not rollback of Cárdenas's antigaming policies. Repeated scandals over clandestine gambling between 1938 and 1959 and the continuous debate over the relegalization of casino gaming underline just how central gaming has been for the tourism industry. The gaming industry produced tremendous wealth and hidden benefits for management as well as executive authority. Due to its seemingly boundless potential to generate revenue, the gaming sector actually subsidized public services and the productive economy by absorbing an extraordinary tax burden. Whether in the form of sortilege, sports wagering, horse racing, or underground Chinese casinos, the gaming business also served well-positioned officials and owners as a means of private enrichment. Inveterate gamblers and high-rolling Americans with no shortage of disposable income were anxious to play with their money. As the red-light and inebriant border functioned in the international imagination, the border of chance and action endowed Tijuana with a strategic if not comparative advantage that inspired and motivated American tourists to visit Baja California.

A look at the fate of the Agua Caliente racing complex and the sports book business it begat offers penetrating insight into the evolving relations of power that shaped Mexico's ruling party and Baja California's border economy. By way of conclusion I will discuss the Rosarito Beach Hotel casino and its closure to better understand the limits of "corruption" and extra-economic factors of doing business during the reign of the Partido Revolucionario Institucional (PRI). The fate of the Rosarito casino's widely suspected benefactor and patron, the populist maverick governor Braulio Maldonado Sández, speaks poignantly to intraparty power struggles that pitted left-leaning factions against the right wing of the PRI led by Abelardo L. Rodríguez. He became the inside candidate who spoiled General Rodríguez's attempt to name his own candidate when Baja California reached statehood in 1952.[21] Just as Maldonado Sández rose to power under the patronage of Adolfo Ruíz Cortines, with whom he shared "socialist ideals," he fell as Adolfo López Mateos took power. After nearly ten years of operating clandestinely, PRI party officials raided and closed the Rosarito Beach casino in 1959; many viewed this as a calculated indirect hit on Maldonado. Allowed to finish out his term, he fled to Michoacán, where Lázaro Cárdenas granted him a sort of internal exile.[22] The demise of Maldonado Sández and the closure of the Rosarito casino point to the monopoly that Tijuana's race and foreign book operation enjoyed.

Because of its strategic recruitment of presidential investors, Tijuana's racing complex was virtually immune to federal tampering. The distinguished lineage of high-ranking public officials who wielded economic interest in the Tijuana race track included Calles and Rodríguez and then broadened to include Manuel Ávila Camacho and Miguel Alemán. While most constitutionalist reformers who emerged with the revolution favored a strictly regulated gaming sector, General Cárdenas headed up a minority faction of reformers who favored abolishing casinos and most organized games of chance, including the sortilege or lottery. Cárdenas closed the complex despite pleas from workers who saw his anti-casino policies as attacks on their livelihood. After having won hard-fought battles to unionize workers across the border tourism sector including the Agua Caliente resort, track workers staged a lock-in protesting the loss of what had been a well-padd[ock]ed livelihood in 1935.[23] General Manuel Ávila Camacho, a racing devotee and fan of the Caliente track, allegedly persuaded Cárdenas to leave track management in the hands of the Alba Roja Union.[24] This ill-conceived and underfunded experiment with worker management soon floundered after only one year. It must have been a disappointment to the militant union. Having reminded Cárdenas that track operations had been handed over to Alba Roja by federal ruling in 1935, its leaders called on the president to intervene on their behalf a few weeks preceding the inaugural race.[25] After organized labor mounted a relatively successful campaign to desegregate the foreign casino-cabaret enclave, Alba Roja saw gaming as the key to attracting tourism to the border. Gaming tourism was fundamental for creating job security.[26]

For the next ten years, track management witnessed high turnover as rival racing camarillas jockeyed for position. What is noteworthy during this period is the reinsertion of old hippodrome racing interests, after which the shadowy presence of organized crime could soon be detected.

Jockeying for Power after Cárdenas: Inter-Camarilla Struggles and the Agua Caliente Race Track, 1937–47

After ten years of fitful starts, interrupted racing seasons, and the cross-border constrictions caused by World War II, Tijuana's racing complex was finally restored to a level of equestrian respectability. The first management team of Eugene Normile, the track manager at the hippodrome who had preceded Agua Caliente, purchased the track operation from Alba Roja for a discounted $132,000 in 1937.[27] Normile offered credible managerial experience that would rescue the Agua Caliente track from its Depression-era demise. The heavyweight pugilist Jack Dempsey even wrote President Cárdenas a letter of recommendation for Normile, his former manager and current business associate, emphasizing his unequaled honesty and ability to produce "high-class" racing events.[28] Racetrack scandals involving crooked management and mafia tampering were commonplace on both sides of the border. Caliente had its own tarnished reputation and Dempsey hoped that

Normile would be the polish.[29] Dempsey even included a word about Normile's symbolic respect for Mexican authority, noting that he had attended the funeral for General Álvaro Obregón at his house in Cájeme, Sonora.[30]

If the Depression made little impact on tourism and the border gaming industry between 1930 and 1934, the combined pressures of the repatriation and Cardenista casino policies effectively dampened the high life that Tijuana's tourism industry nourished.[31] One smart decision Normile made to help Caliente's flagging business was to invite his "old friend" C. S. Howard and Seabiscuit to race the Agua Caliente Handicap in 1938. If one thing spoke to the decline in wealth witnessed in the ten years of racing at Agua Caliente, it was the radical reduction of purse money offered in the Handicap—from $100,000 to $10,000. Attending Seabiscuit's victory were Baja California's top officials (Governor Rodolfo Sánchez Taoboada and Baja California's district military commander General Manuel J. Contreras), Tijuana's mayor and chief of police, as well as the usual Hollywood race milieu: turf fanatics Mickey Rooney and Louis B. Mayer.[32]

One of the first challenges that awaited Normile and the Tijuana hippodrome was restocking Caliente with quality horses. Tijuana's regional monopoly on horse racing had suffered when California began allowing parimutual racing and the Del Mar, Santa Anita (1934), and Hollywood Park (1938) tracks effectively cut into Caliente's market share. Agua Caliente responded by running on Sundays, a niche that Cuba's Oriental Park also carved.[33] However, consistent with what happened along the "red-light" and "inebriant border," World War II made its own pronounced impact on Tijuana's racing industry. First, the paucity of equestrian stock inverted as horses, trainers, and jockeys arrived at Tijuana en masse after being evicted from racetracks north of the border when they were converted to military purposes.[34] Then, U.S. security concerns in the wake of Pearl Harbor overrode border racing interests, and Mexico agreed to shut down border bookmaking and race operations. One such bookmaker, Eduardo Nealis Robles, protested to President Ávila Camacho that he had been given the president's very own assurance about running the business, not to mention prepayment of federal taxes to do so.[35] In a year Nealis Robles began managing the hippodrome, an indication that Ávila Camacho had listened and acted on his plea. An even deeper challenge to track business came when members of the Arguello-Olvera clan filed a lawsuit against General Rodríguez and the federal government's ownership of the land upon which the Agua Caliente resort was built.[36]

While the Supreme Court ruled in favor of the plaintiff in 1938, the feds waited to take decisive action until they received word of illegal gambling and swinging Hollywood soirees at the turf club and home of track manager Eduardo Nealis Robles. Apparently, much of the Agua Caliente casino's original gaming equipment had been relocated to the hippodrome grounds (the Turf Club) and Nealis's private cottage.[37] To execute the federal ruling in favor of the Arguello family, President Ávila Camacho sent federal troops to occupy the grounds on December 13, 1944. In addition to the gaming paraphernalia located in Nealis Robles's home, the government performed an audit that documented the annual losses racked by his racing administration.[38]

The strategic intervention by President Ávila Camacho points to the legacy of presidential participation in Tijuana's race business. With the federal ruling in favor of the Arguello family, the president sent a relative, Agustín Silveira Ávila, as the new track manager for the new hippodrome. Not all Arguello family members were happy with the way the litigation evolved. Alberto and Alejandro Arguello, for example, complained to the president that when they refused to consent to the new management team of Silveira and James Crofton, they were excluded from receiving the proceeds of the new lease. Moreover, Alejandro and Alberto Arguello claimed that they represented 90 percent of the landholders of their clan. Such blatant disregard of their rights was equaled by the strong-arm tactics of the government. For example, they found disquieting if not intimidating the overbearing imposition of General Rodrigo Quevedo, the top military official in Baja California Territory, who was more than likely protecting General Rodríguez's interests in the hippodrome.[39] While General Rodríguez's interest as owner of the race track land seemed threatened by the ruling, he continued to collect rent from it and arranged for advantageous provisioning contracts of forage for the track business and grains for the Cervecería Tecate.[40] Another maneuver designed to establish financial continuity amid the rapidly changing landscape was the reinsertion of James Crofton, the former manager of the Agua Caliente Jockey Club.[41] That Crofton had high-level access to the track's financial nerve center and was entrusted with monitoring accounting (*auditoria*) seemed to be an obvious step backward for the national autonomy. Retaining control over financial capital, however, was precisely the strategy that foreign investors would pursue after 1917, and especially after Cárdenas's expropriations of foreign property.[42] Crofton ultimately did not last but was replaced by another powerful outsider whose ties to General Rodríguez and incoming president Miguel Alemán further illustrate the operative strategy behind Tijuana racing business: recruiting presidents by inviting them to invest in the track business and the agricultural estates surrounding the Rodríguez-Calles holdings.

As World War II ended, President Manuel Ávila Camacho's secretary of interior (Gobernación) Miguel Alemán prepared to change the direction of Mexico's statist revolution. The *jarocho* president effectively tipped Mexico's postrevolutionary political equilibrium toward a more business-friendly government, one that was well received by General Rodríguez and the remnants of the enterprising Northwest Group. Alemán advanced the project of industrialization but dedicated special attention to tourism during his presidency. Not surprisingly, he would go on to lead Mexico's Department of Tourism after leaving office, setting down his thoughts about healthy recreation versus degrading leisure activities in *15 Lecciones sobre turismo*.[43]

Alemán was in office for no more than a year when congress amended federal gaming statutes. As Ávila Camacho's secretary of interior, Alemán was familiar with gaming statutes and Tijuana's hippodrome business. At the heart of legislative change was the ambiguously defined status of legal gaming, especially under the auspices of a private social club or through a sports book.[44] Anxious to stage a comeback, casino concessionaires sensed change in Mexico's gambling climate when the Alemán administration amended the gaming laws that had been passed during the Cárdenas era in 1938. Judging by the avalanche of letters directed to the president, either condemning or extolling the gaming industry, a notable shift in expectations regarding the return of the casino-tourism economy was evident. Mexico's officials at all levels illustrated an ambivalent attitude toward tourism policies or development plans that featured a prominent role for casino gaming. Mexico's congressional debate suggests that this ambivalence persists today.

Like past debates on Mexico's legal gaming, arguments divided into two camps whose distinctive positions, however, nourished similar concerns about working-class welfare and community development. Labor unions with vested interests in expanding the tourism service sector formed one major lobby group in favor of a more relaxed gaming policy. Alba Roja, representing many of the Agua Caliente workers since the Depression, wrote to Alemán, urging him to reestablish greyhound racing at the Agua Caliente, which would resuscitate tourism and generate badly needed employment for workers of the livery and taxi service sector.[45] By contrast, national merchants associations warned of the social dangers (the ills gaming posed to working-class welfare) that would revisit the border zone if Mexico City consented to organized gaming. A letter of endorsement from its Querétaro affiliate urged President Alemán to see through the hypocrisy of gaming "masquerading as sport." For even "if certain games of chance were permitted by law," these were still a parasitic drain on working-class wages.[46] A similar split over gaming policy between labor unions (pro) and commercial organizations (con) was evident during the 1920s and 1930s.

Various political groups took a position as well. The Partido Acción Nacional (National Action Party or PAN) roundly criticized Baja California's state and local governments for consenting to powerful Chinese syndicates who were running clandestine gambling and opium operations in Mexicali and Tijuana. If most of Mexico's public officials energetically repudiated casino gaming, evidence clearly links Governor Alberto V. Aldrete to employing a de-facto policy of using Chinese gaming and opium taxes to subsidize public works and other badly needed community services. *El Observador Objetivo* accused the Aldrete government of receiving hefty sums of money paid by the Chinese underground in exchange for continued gaming and opium businesses in Tijuana, Ensenada, and Mexicali.[47]

Aldrete happily reported to Alemán that the practice of collecting fees ($100,000 in Mexican pesos every quarter) from Chinese casinos and recreational centers, a euphemism used to describe opium dens, was an already established practice which his government eagerly accommodated. Most importantly, his government could meet budgetary expenses without raising taxes on so-called productive sectors.[48] Familiarity with the practice ran in the family. Aldrete's father had served as state treasurer when General Rodríguez was governor, and his duties included collecting taxes from the Chinese community.[49] Aldrete's report to Alemán detailed the Chinese exceptionalist formula that border officials used to exploit clandestine activities in order to subsidize their own interests in agriculture and manufacturing.

As founder of the Cervecería Tecate and one of a minority group of civilian executives to rule the federal territory of Baja California before it became a state in 1952, Aldrete possessed a business orientation that resonated with Alemán's rise to national power. In his pro-gaming policy, he further delineated the virtues of regulated gaming such as lotteries. Suppressed by Cárdenas's gaming statutes of 1938, Aldrete explained that the "lottery [was] not typical gambling." The sortilege or lottery was the oldest form of gaming to be systematically harnessed to the public weal.[50] Precedents date back to colonial New Spain where sortilege and bull and cock fighting were used to finance public expenditures.[51] Proceeds from the Caliente dog track (*galgódromo*) and jai alai wagers, according to Governor Aldrete, could effectively shoulder costs for operating hospitals, prisons, schools, orphanages, and other crucial public works. The issue was pressing due to an exploding population and the failure of the Ministry of Health and Welfare (SSA) to keep pace with such a demographic surge.

Aldrete's downfall came not from a casino scandal but rather from a different white collar crime that leads us back to General Rodríguez and his economic empire. Aldrete was run from office after a $4 million loan from Rodríguez's Banco del Pacífico to Tecate drew unwelcome scrutiny from federal officials.[52] The bank manager accused of having masterminded the shady loans was John S. Alessio, the Italian American, Horatio Alger–like figure who became manager of the Banco del Pacífico in 1943. Soon he became manager of the Tijuana race track, where he presided over Agua Caliente's most successful administration until he pleaded guilty to tax evasion in the United States in 1972. For his role in the Tecate loan fraud, Alessio and associates languished for six months in a Tijuana jail before President Alemán arranged for their release.[53] His tax-fraud conviction, for which he suspected Richard Nixon of exacting partisan vengeance, earned him two years at a Club Fed penitentiary for white-collar criminals.[54]

Alessio became the track manager of Agua Caliente with President Alemán's blessing, a move that coincided with the jarocho's ascension into the club of presidential privilege symbolized by investment in the track business.[55] Further evidence of this ascension came when he received the "gift" of Rancho El Florido, an estate that stood alongside the ranches of past presidents Calles, Rodríguez, and Ávila Camacho. Alemán's property had contracts for provisioning forage cereals to the Caliente racetrack as well as grains for the Tecate brewery. The region had given rise to an interlocking web of business interests, and the Calles-Rodríguez properties led the way by fusing agricultural, industrial, and commercial investments; their seafood processing plant at El Sauzal best exemplified this intersecting enterprise.[56] The president's trusted agents made sure that he received two new Lincoln Continentals and a hangar for his B-52 aircraft, gifts the president took painstaking care to dissimilate.[57] Graft was one of the hallmark expressions of what many saw as a very corrupt Alemán administration.[58]

Friendly relations with President Alemán proved key to the success of Alessio. It is also true that the Italian had the backing of San Diego's leading underworld figure and Alessio's godfather, C. Arnohlt Smith, not to mention

Benjamin "Bugsy" Siegel, the syndicate combination's West Coast point man until his murder in 1946.[59] It was Siegel who oversaw the extension of mafia businesses in California, none as lucrative as Caliente's wire service, which was essential for rigging the foreign book. Alfonse Capone's Chicago group had controlled the Tijuana racket dating to the prohibition years, and change in mafia control generated its expected violence.[60] Siegel and Alessio illustrated a fascination with Hollywood, and the feeling was mutual for many of tinsel town's leading players.

The nexus of mafia interests and Hollywood high-rollers endowed Tijuana with a noir flavor. Star-studded audiences traditionally gave Tijuana's racing crowds a qualitative punch from the track's opening in 1916. Such patronage by Hollywood reached its fullest expression in 1938 with the opening of Hollywood Park by Jack Warner. Hyping the presence of Hollywood players renewed the association of glitz and Tijuana's fast-paced racing action. John S. Alessio, Caliente racing concession holder, understood the marketing power that came with star power. The eldest and the clan leader, John especially enjoyed taking care of his favorite guests, personally escorting Elizabeth Taylor, Ben Gazzara, and Victor Mature to their reserved "viewing suites."[61] In fact, Caliente was just another stop on the leisure circuit, which headed south from Hollywood (including San Diego's Coronado Hotel, the fat farms of Baja California, the beach resorts of Acapulco) and eastward into the desert (starting with Palm Springs and ending with Siegel's novel experiment in Las Vegas). Siegel was himself obsessed with Hollywood star power.[62] Alessio's criminal background probably enhanced rather than tainted the Caliente mystique.[63]

Policing the Monopoly: Camarilla Politics and the Rosarito Beach Hotel Casino

Securing lucrative gaming concessions required arranging for the cooperation of important federal officials in Mexico City, and the case of the Rosarito Beach Hotel casino clearly illustrates this process. It also points to the powerful dynamic of patronage or camarilla politics; when regime change removed from power Adolfo Ruíz Cortines, Governor Braulio Maldonado Sández could no longer buy off federal officials and prevent federal police from raiding the open secret that was Rosarito's illegal casino. Two casino concession petitions for the Rosarito Hotel illustrate the corrupt nature of doing business under PRI rule.

The attempt to resurrect the prohibition-era Rosarito Beach Hotel Casino spoke to the continued demand by tourists for such entertainment as well as the degree to which these operations were protected by handsome kickbacks or special taxes to local officials in Baja California and Mexico City. Epitomized by the raid of the Rosarito Beach Hotel in 1959, clandestine gambling operations depended upon financial arrangements with local security and government.[64] Established in the 1920s, the Rosarito Beach Hotel featured a casino annex that had lain dormant since Cárdenas ordered the closure of gaming businesses. With Alemán as president who lent a sympathetic ear to casino tourism projects, gaming entrepreneur Pablo Sepúlveda wrote to his old friend, Rogerio de la Selva, who was Alemán's staff secretary. Sepúlveda stated up front that he hoped to obtain a gaming concession from gobernación, which was headed by Adolfo Ruíz Cortines, Alemán's successor. Once it was secured, he would establish a Mexican company with American partners, the standard for reintroducing foreign investment amid Mexico's nationalized capitalist development. They had selected the Rosarito Beach Hotel as the most promising site for such a casino. Perhaps this owed to proprietor Felipe Arce's aggressive campaign to restore the hotel to its prior splendor.[65] The casino would be operated as a private social club. Recalling the social clubs of the 1920s, it would comprise an exclusive membership. Sepúlveda stressed that it was the favorable publicity of the hotel's upscale guests that made it a popular getaway. Disclosing his personal stake in the casino at 25 percent of the profits, Sepúlveda hoped to persuade the right individual in gobernación with 15 percent of his cut if the concession was secured.[66] What is significant about the proposal is the clear understanding of the extra-economic factors for doing business.

Trying to massage the right contacts and grease the right palms could clearly become frustrating as evidenced in a similar letter written a decade later by a Los Angeles attorney, Max Gilford, to President Adolfo López Mateos. Gilford was married to the World War II pinup and horror film starlet Anne Gywnne in 1945,[67] and his Sunset Boulevard address epitomized the upscale Hollywood milieu referenced by Sepúlveda. Gilford articulated more clearly than Sepúlveda the restrictive social pact for the casino. It would be run as a "club" in order to save poor Mexicans from the suffering that gaming posed "to their families and . . . themselves." Here economic class trumped race/ethnic membership, as only Mexicans of "substantial wealth" would be allowed to participate.[68] López Mateos was unreceptive to Gilford's petition. This proved frustrating to the Hollywood player, who complained of having made several trips to Mexico City in order to wine and dine "Mexican nationals in their hotels . . . for the purpose of obtaining a license to gamble under the specific conditions in the Country of Mexico." An air of dejection is detected in his petition when he states that he has been taken by *coyotes*—a trusted government intermediary who managed to acquire gaming permits, among other things, despite the daunting requirements of the Mexican bureaucratic state.[69] In fact, his desperate tone is readily understandable, considering that the final raid that would close the casino and send Maldonado Sández packing for Michoacán was less than two months away. From exile he echoed the popular belief that Las Vegas gaming interests were behind the move to close the hotel, as a way of protecting market share with the resurgence of casino gaming in Baja California.[70] A social club, whether agreed upon contractually or verbally with a wink and a nod, could not withstand the whims of change emanating from Mexico City.

During the span of time between Sepúlveda's and Gilford's letters, regime change had left Governor Braulio Maldonado Sández without his benefactor Ruíz Cortines. A combined force of federal agents and military raided the Rosarito Beach Hotel casino in January 1959. Consider the observation that Mexico's renowned geographer Ángel Bassols Batalla made in his exhaustive study of the Northwest. Leaving El Sauzal, the cornerstone of the Calles-Rodríguez seafood-packing business, Bassols notes in his diary inscription for December 25, 1958: "Today is Christmas and at the Rosarito Beach Hotel Americans suck down copious amounts of liquor, before going to the gaming parlor (closed days after our visit). Rosarito has a bit of everything . . . to entertain bored millionaires."[71]

Two letters written by aggrieved tourists to López Mateos protest the raid and unfair treatment of American gamers.

> A word in reference to 25 or more of our Americans, in a Dirty Jail in Tijuana Mex. For Gambling! Now I will advise you of one thing. After all the good, American Dollars that have been spent in your country for years, by the Americans, and You allow this thing to Happen! To allow Mex. Judge the Right to Jail Decent Americans to be Robbed and then Thrown, into a rotten hole, that you People, call a Jail.[72]

Threatening to organize a border closure, American tourists followed the diplomatic cues from John and Allen Foster Dulles by staking notions of unbounded freedom for Americans pursuing business or leisure. The following letter draws the analogy more closely by comparing Mexico to authoritarian Guatemala:

Dear Sir,

I must strongly protest the arrest and imprisonment of the American tourists in Tijuana, BC. This is nothing short of an atrocity!

What a miserable way to treat friends who come to visit. What a blow to the Good Neighbor Policy. I am particularly alarmed because I make many trips to Mexico to enjoy your famous hospitality. I have always been treated kindly but now I fear to return, as but for the Grace of God. I would be rotting in a Tijuana jail, for I visited that very hotel just two days before it was raided.

Because this gambling casino was operating openly for many months it appeared to people that it was operating with the approval of the authorities. This is a fair assumption, otherwise why should it be allowed to operate?

Should the unsuspecting gringos then be arrested for gambling (some of them were only watching) and carted off to jail in a cattle truck, herded into a filthy jail without even a blanket to keep from catching cold or possibly pneumonia and then having an atrocious bail set at $1,600 . . . How would you like to visit a foreign country and be treated like these people are being treated in Tijuana? This is a terrible injustice!!

Do you approve of this? Are you not going to be embarrassed when our president visits you and your country is holding American prisoners in a manner similar to tactics of the Communist and Fascist? . . . This whole mess has shocked American and civilized people everywhere. It is worthy only of Guatemalans.

Please give it your immediate attention and justify my faith in a just and gracious Mexico.[73]

López Mateos's presidency was expected to renovate and moralize the border zone, but as with many moralization campaigns before and since, much of it came down to the art of public relations maneuvers such as reinvention and symbolic law enforcement. Before concluding, let us examine the language of desire and imagination that reflected tourists' perceptions and experiences in Tijuana.

The Agua Caliente Hippodrome: An Island of Wealth amid a Sea of Poverty

From its turn-of-the-century inception, Baja California's border tourism industry was largely developed around the model of casino and racetrack gambling, combined with the hotel-spa resort. Even before the construction of the Agua Caliente Casino and Spa (1927–29), Tijuana's short-lived luxury resort of international fame, Baja California's attractions were deliberately promoted as Old World, continental in their orientation, and liberal in their offering of gaming and entertainment services. Juxtaposed against the social conservatism that Midwestern migrants legislated in Southern California, Baja California's border created a hand-in-glove escape valve for hustlers, gangsters, and rounders. Evoked in the vernacular, the liberty Americans themselves searched for in Mexico was often cast in the disparaging moral geography of south of the border, "below the belt line." Whether it was a more relaxed attitude toward rye, sex, or roulette, most promotional writing hinted at the open-closed character with cultural codes that referred to a relaxed Old World (European) environment and an attitude free of judgment and censure. Borrowing a page from early promotional writing about Tijuana and its hippodrome, one piece in 1943 boasted the continental sophistication and gaming thrill that attracted well-heeled tourists to Baja California:

> Nourished by North American tourism that grows each day, and by the impulse of its own inhabitants that have been attracted by the comforts and business opportunities they offer. . . . A center of first class tourism, Tijuana resembles the upscale resorts of Deauville and Biarritz, with its up-tempo pulse beating with affluent visitors; with its sumptuous sights and scenery, like the Hippodrome, with wealthy guests enjoying its luxurious installations and services.[74]

This type of promotional writing effectively concealed the central tension that bedeviled border tourism planners; despite the projected clientele of upscale tourists, most customers did not meet the idealized line of status and prestige. In fact, sustaining the illusion of upscale tourism became a challenge for industry promoters. With the A-list of Hollywood players, the presence of organized crime and the usual set of hustlers effectively gave the Caliente race track the glamour that endowed Tijuana with a deliciously cheap yet titillating ambience. Much apart from the glitz embodied by Caliente patrons like Al Capone or Dolores del Río, serious race fans lent a much more solemn air to the track environment. Neither blue-blooded nor threadbare, most casino and horse-racing tourists tended toward the middle-income bracket. Agua Caliente had a well-established reputation among racing circles for quality horse racing, exotic betting, and innovative safety procedures. However, its tourist appeal lies in its ability to generate racing excitement infused with a casual, anything-goes tenor.

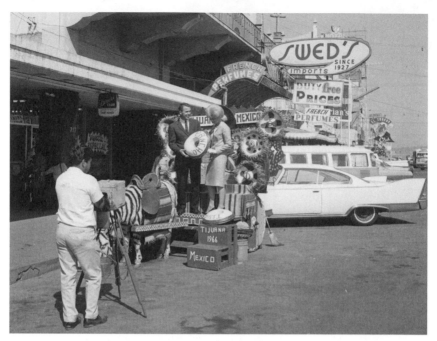

2. American couple visiting Tijuana. The painted burro snapshot spectacle becomes a central framing mechanism used to create an ahistoric tourism landscape in Tijuana, curiously suggesting a half-hearted attempt to distance sightseeing from pornographic spectacles like the donkey show. This couple posed in 1965, when a federally directed moralization campaign once again reformed Tijuana's image as a major destination for middle-class family tourism. OP 16552. COURTESY OF SAN DIEGO HISTORICAL SOCIETY.

Gaming space has traditionally been segregated and the Tijuana race track was no different.[75] In the same way wealth and power determined seating in the *plaza de toros*, race-track audiences, largely foreign, sat divided in the sun and shade.[76] Gradually racing's aristocratic tradition as the sport of kings begrudgingly gave way to the democratizing spirit and liberal ethos of leisure culture. While the wagering business did not discriminate, perceptions of class and race mattered when it came to organizing social space. Old money mingled with Hollywood parvenu, and plebeian onlookers tried not to show their envy. Recalling the social mix at Tijuana's Caliente track, one hard-core race fan recalled it as racist if not classist.

> The Clubhouse was occupied primarily by Americans and a few wealthy Mexican nationals. Locals were confined to the grandstand. At the cross-over, no one ever questioned you if you were American. But, Mexicans were regularly turned away and told that the Clubhouse was private. It

wasn't until the evening, when dog racing took over, that the two crowds would mingle together—the action being confined to the Clubhouse.[77]

The Sport of Queens—dog racing—was less pretentious and more inclusive. The notion that private space could effectively bar Mexicans was also with precedent. Mexican officials and foreign gaming operators resorted to the private social club to prevent objectionable clients from entering casinos. By making membership a private affair, the social club could insulate wealthy clientele, simultaneously reinforcing the sensation of privilege for those on the A-list while excluding those looking in from the outside. Racing tourism produced prodigious concentrations of wealth and attracted a cast of Hollywood stars, mafia thugs, and leisure travelers. The message it sent was decidedly contrary to what Cardenista Mexico had imagined. As the pace and volume accelerated, migrating peasants who clustered around Tijuana and other border cities in their passage to *el norte* became situational participants in the larger political economy of border tourism.

Tourists were profoundly affected by the double movement of wealthy tourists and wealth-seeking migrants with whom they crossed paths at the border. The illusive search for a wildly adventurous experience at the border created an unusual predicament for them like race aficionado Ron Hale, who described the social contradictions of border tourism. "Pulling at your pant leg and yelling 'chick-lay, one penny,'" roving gangs of child *chiclé* vendors surrounded American tourists once they crossed the border.[78] Their tattered clothing and forlorn eyes melted the hardened disposition with which tourists typically inured themselves on trips to the third world. Passing on the piñatas, the velvet Elvis, or later, the ceramic Bart Simpson, Hale would typically hand over a nickel or dime for the worthless knockoffs of Adams gum. Displaying telltale signs of squatting and irregular housing, Tijuana was full of shacks, smoke from burning rubbish, drying clothes flapping from improvised clotheslines, and cemeteries of decrepit cars. The grandiose hippodrome set the juxtaposition of wealth to a heightened symbolism. "All of a sudden, you would turn a corner, and there would rise the huge grandstand of Agua Caliente," Hale notes. He started attending Sunday races because California tracks were closed on the reinstitutionalized Sabbath. This landscape of stark contrasts engendered in Americans like Hale a bewildering mixture of curiosity, affection, and repugnance.

My experience with different racetracks was extremely limited at the time but over the years, I came to find that Caliente was not quite like anywhere else. Sure, much had to do with the fact that it was located in another country, but there was something strangely romantic about the place—even with its poor quality of racing. Here was kind of an oasis plopped down in the middle of miles of wooden shacks. . . . Just getting to Caliente was like an *E* ride at Disneyland.[79]

Where the track stood out in an equestrian bettor's mind was the loose, casual, typically Mexican ambience of Agua Caliente. An informant, Richard Rossman, echoed this sentiment, having spent a considerable amount of time at the Caliente complex as a boy. He remembers the Caliente track not so much for the renowned horses or racing innovations that popularized it but for its extensive gaming parlor with wall-to-wall slot machines. In comparison to the freedom and loose enforcement that characterized Tijuana's Caliente, Las Vegas seemed overly conservative.[80] Caliente offered illegal games of chance.[81] Loose enforcement, if not noncompliance, reflected multiple cultural, political, and social variables that made the border exceptionally popular for tourists. Rossman's father would load the family station wagon for monthly trips to Caliente, often returning noticeably lighter in the wallet and heavier in the spirit.[82] Spent, hung-over, and penniless, tourists depict their return to the United States as a begrudging step out of the desacralized play of Mexico and back into the normative calendar of production that awaited them at home.[83]

Next to loose enforcement stood Caliente's cosmopolitan nightlife to enhance its consumer appeal. Still considered "the pride of Tijuana," Caliente's Turf Club offered three shows daily:[84] The svelte Ruth Dieppe performed visually exciting dance routines while the Trio Tropicana offered a scorching blend of Caribbean rumba with flourishes of contemporary, "modern song." In addition, Amapolita sang *rancheras*, a reminder of how much border culture had transformed over the half century as well as bearing the unmistakable sign of opium and its migratory path north from Sinaloa.[85] Erudite *fronterizos* such as Frederico Campbell or Paul Vanderwood grasped the magnitude of change that had transformed the old Agua Caliente into a "laboratory of the *cardenista* revolution."[86]

Discussions of Tijuana ignore its contribution to the formation of modern leisure and tourism. Like an illegitimate child, Tijuana is often disregarded as an aberration resulting from the penetration of foreign capital and enterprising national elites.[87] Not unlike the rise of Las Vegas as "sin city," Tijuana's black legend owed in part to the gangster-Hollywood nexus. A red line of diversionary leisure stretched from Tijuana to Vegas with Hollywood at its base. These depraved cities were forever set against a related development in the tourism economy—Southern California's amusement park business (Disneyland's Magic Kingdom or the Knott's Berry Farm). Much as in Vegas in the 1990s, Tijuana's commercial boosters reinvented their image by deploying tourism police and public relations campaigns to promote family tourism. Tourists could imbibe admittedly contrived attractions, often representing American visions of old Mexico—where they shop for curios, watch bullfights, or eat Mexican cuisine.[88] A visit today to Tijuana's aging Agua Caliente race track to see the greyhounds may not entirely be a shock but it nevertheless brings home three salient points about the political economy of the border and the power play by PRIsta scions like Mayor Jorge Hank Rhon: slot machines have been installed to prop up the flagging track business, which by all signs has experienced a secular decline measured in both attendance and wagers; side-show entertainment ranging from zoo exhibits (some of rare and nearly extinct animals) to motocross shows has revived interest in a dying tourist complex; and access to the hippodrome is the direct result of powerful connections in the federal government.[89] Racing attendance has dropped across the United States as the number of Indian casinos opened, suggesting a decline in the popularity of horse culture. Tourism to the border, however, shows little signs of decline other than the border-crossing delays associated with U.S. security policies after the attacks of September 11, 2001.

Notes

1. David M. Stern, "Kamp Krusty," *The Simpsons* (20th Century Fox Film Corporation, 1992), http://www.snpp.com.
2. Reading the border as liminal space owes to the following scholarship on play, performance, and ritualized leisure: Kerwin Klein, "The Last Resort: Tourism, Growth, and Values in Twentieth-Century Arizona" (master's thesis, University of Arizona, 1990), 10, and "Frontier Products: Tourism, Consumerism, and the Southwestern Public Lands, 1890–1990," *Pacific Historical Review* 62.1 (February 1993): 39–71; William H. Beezley, *Judas at the Jockey Club: and Other Episodes of Porfirian Mexico* (Lincoln: University of Nebraska Press, 1987), 89–124; Daniel D. Arreola and James R. Curtis, *The Mexican Border Cities: Landscape Anatomy and Place Personality* (Tucson: University of Arizona Press,

1993) 90–92; Victor Turner, *The Ritual Process: Structure and Anti-Structure* (1969; reprint, Ithaca, N.Y.: Cornell University Press, 1977), and *Dramas, Fields, and Metaphors: Symbolic Action in Human Society* (Ithaca, N.Y.: Cornell University Press, 1976); J. B. Jackson, "Other-Directed Houses," *Landscapes: Selected Writings of J. B. Jackson*, ed. Ervin H. Zube (Amherst: University of Massachusetts Press, 1970), 55–72.

3. Frank Sinatra, *This Is Sinatra* (1957) (A) *The Capitol Years*, disc 1, "South of the Border (Down Mexico Way)," arr. Nelson Riddle. By the show's end, Bart delivers a parting *olé!*, not the trademark Grammercy *shhh.*

4. For a particularly poignant example of tourism as escape valve for modern angst, see Ben Hunter, *The Baja Feeling* (Ontario, Calif.: Brasch and Brasch, 1978), 20. "The Watts riot, the concerns of the nation and the world, our own personal problems . . . and all other concerns seemed to belong to another world, another place in time. They were no longer part of us. Neither was the future." Dean MacCannell, *The Tourist: A New Theory of the Leisure Class* (New York: Schocken Books, 1989), 40–44. For a detailed review and analysis of MacCannell's theoretical framework, see Georges Van den Abeele, "Sightseers: The Tourist as Theorist," *Diacritics* 10 (winter 1980): 2–14.

5. Louis Turner and John Ash, *The Golden Hordes* (London: Constable, 1975), cited in Peter Wollen, "Into the Future: Tourism, Language and Art," *Raiding the Icebox* (London: Verso Press, 1993), 190–212; Eric Schantz, "All Night at the Owl: The Social and Political Relations of Mexicali's Red-Light District, 1913–1925," *Journal of the Southwest* 43.4 (winter 2001), 91–143; John Jakle, *The Tourist: Travel in Twentieth-Century North America* (Lincoln: University of Nebraska Press, 1985). Klein, "Frontier Products," 39–71.

6. Hunter, *The Baja Feeling.* See Dina Berger's analysis of the private and public forces that developed modern tourism in Mexico: *The Development of Mexico's Tourism Industry: Pyramids by Day, Martinis by Night* (New York: Palgrave MacMillan, 2006), 45–53; 71–73.

7. Interview with Mary Jane Brown by Eric Schantz, Laguna Beach, California, July 12, 2005. See Mary Simon, *Racing through the Century: The Story of Thoroughbred Racing in America* (Irvine, Calif.: Bow Tie Press, 2002), 113–15. Paul Vanderwood's *Juan Soldado: Rapist, Murderer, Martyr, Saint* (Durham, N.C.: Duke University Press, 2004) offers a valuable contribution to the rapidly growing body of border studies, criminality, and the particularly rich crossroads of popular religiosity and the nation-state building process of the Mexican Revolution. Cf. Vincent Cabeza de Baca and Juan Cabeza de Baca, "The Shame Suicides and Tijuana," *Journal of the Southwest* 43. 4 (winter 2001). Even with alternative attractions such as Tijuana's Centro Cultural de Tijuana, founded in 1932 to strengthen ties between Baja California and interior Mexico, foreigners cling to

attractions along the Avenida Revolución. In the last quarter century, Americans have begun to discover cosmopolitan Tijuana, engaging in upper-end culinary tourism, art exhibits, or the modern mall development at the Zona del Río.

8. Confirming its special role as country club to the stars, Agua Caliente was the backdrop for Depression-era comedy in 1935. See *In Caliente*, dir. Loyd Bacon, starring Dolores del Río, Leo Carrillo, Pat O'Brien, and Edward Everett Horton. American tourism to Cuba suggests similar parallels as Mexico's red-light border. See Rosalie Schwartz's fascinating study *Pleasure Island: Tourism and Temptation in Cuba* (Lincoln: University of Nebraska, Bison Books, 1999).

9. Herzog, *Where North Meets South: Cities, Space, and Politics on the US–Mexico Border* (Austin: Center for Mexican American Studies, University of Texas, 1990), 47, 95, 115, 47, 95, 99, 115; David E. Lorey, *The U.S.–Mexican Border in the Twentieth Century: A History of Economic and Social Transformation* (Wilmington, Del.: SR Books, 1999), 262; Stephen Niblo, *War, Diplomacy, and Development: The United States and Mexico, 1938–1954* (Wilmington, Del.: Scholarly Resources Press, 1999), 100–101; Proffit, "Symbiotic Frontier," 321; Raul Fernández, *La frontera Mexico–Estados Unidos: Un estudio socioeconómico*; and "The Economic Evolution of the Imperial (USA) and Mexicali (Mexico) Valleys," *Journal of Borderlands Studies* 6.2 (fall 1991): 1–21; Jerry Ladman, *The Development of the Mexicali Economy* (Tempe: Bureau of Business and Economic Research, Arizona State University, 1975).

10. For interpretations of vice tourism as imperialist, see Hector Benjamín Trujillo Rodríguez, *Las prostitutas de Baja California* (Mexicali: UNAM, 1975); Braulio Maldonado Sández, *Baja California. Comentarios políticos* (Mexico City: SEP, 1993), 108–10; Malcom Crick, "Representations of International Tourism in the Social Sciences: Sun, Sex, Sights, Savings, and Servility," *Annual Review of Anthropology* 18 (1989): 307–44; Ecumenical Coalition of Third World Tourism, *Tourism Prostitution Development* (Bangkok: ECTWT, 1983); R. O'Grady, ed., *Third World Tourism* (Singapore: Christian Conference Asia, 1980).

11. Juan Platt to Abelardo L. Rodríguez, May 9, 1933; Abelardo Rodríguez to Plutarco Elías Calles, October 19, 1927; Abelardo Rodríguez to Pascual Ortiz Rubio, February 26, 1931, in Plutarco Elías Calles, *Correspondencia personal (1941–1945)* (Mexico City: Fondo de Cultura Económica, 1991), 281, 282, 199, 244. José Alfredo Gómez Estrada, *Gobierno y casinos: El origien de la riqueza de Ableardo L. Rodríguez* (Mexicali: UABC, Instituto Mora, 2002), 120–26; Angel Bassols Batalla, *El noroeste de México: Un estudio geográfico-económico* (Mexico City: Instituto de Investigaciones Económicas, UNAM, 1972) 66, 67, 90, 91. Carlos Martínez Assad, "El imperio económico de Abelardo L. Rodríguez," *Revolucionarios fueron todos*, ed. Carlos Martínez Assad and Ricardo Pozas Horcaditas (Mexico City: SEP/80, Fondo de Cultura Económica, 1982), 288–340. Roderic

Ai Camp, *Political Recruitment across Two Centuries: Mexico, 1884–1992* (Austin: University of Texas Press, 1995); "The Camarilla in Mexican Politics: The Case of the Salinas Cabinet," *Journal of Mexican Studies* (winter 1990): 85–108; "Education and Political Recruitment in Mexico: The Alemán Generation," *Journal of Inter-American Studies and World Affairs* 18.3 (August 1976): 295–321.

12. The best treatment of this remains Gabriel Trujillo Muñoz's "prólogo" to Braulio Maldonado Sández's *Baja California*, 7–62. These political divisions emerge with clarity in the published interviews of "Manuel Gómez Morín, Fundador del Partido Acción Nacional," 143–231, 217–27, and "Vicente Lombardo Toledano, Teórico y Militante Marxista," 235–409, both in *México visto en el siglo XX*, ed. James Wilkie and Edna Monzón de Wilkie (Mexico City: Instituto de Investigaciones Económicas, 1969). Also see Gabriel Trujillo Muñoz, introduction to Braulio Maldonado Sández, *Baja California*, 16 and 23.

13. Schantz, "All Night at the Owl."

14. Keith Haynes, "Dependency, Postimperialism, and the Mexican Revolution: An Historiographic Review," *Mexican Studies/Estudios Mexicanos* 7.2 (1991): 225–51; Niblo, *War, Diplomacy, and Development*.

15. Dirección General de Asuntos Jurídicos, Ley Federal de Juegos y Sorteos, *Diario Official de la Federación (DOF)*, December 31, 1947.

16. On the El Sauzal property, see Juan Platt to President Abelardo L. Rodríguez, May 29, 1933, in Calles, *Correspondencia personal*, 281, 282. Regarding the properties held by ex-presidents, as well as the business and maintenance issues surrounding the Alemán property, see José Navarro Elizondo to President Miguel Alemán Valdés, January 12, 1949; Rogerio de la Selva to President Alemán, February 13, 1948; Miguel Alemán to José Navarro Elizondo, July 23, 1949; José Navarro Elizondo (San Diego) to President Alemán, August 5, 1949, all in Archivo General de la Nación (AGN). fondo Miguel Alemán Valdés (MAV), exp. 101/11.

17. Francisco Martín Moreno, *México Negro*, 3rd ed. (Mexico City: Editorial Joaquín Mortiz, 1986), 525–614.

18. Notions of the shadow state, state-within-a-state, or metastate are well-developed concepts in Joaquín Aguilar Robles, *La guerra del opio* (Mexico City: Costa Amic, 1988), and Paco Ignacio Taibo II, *Sombra de la sombra* and *Cuatro manos* (Buenos Aires: Colihue, 1997).

19. Stephen R. Niblo, *Mexico in the 1940s: Modernity, Politics, and Corruption* (Wilmington, Del.: Scholarly Resources, 1999), 253–309, and *War, Diplomacy, and Development*, 100–101, 154–56; James Wilkie, "Review of Stephen R. Niblo, *Mexico in the 1940s: Modernity, Politics, and Corruption*," *American Historical Review* 107.2 (April 2002): 581; Enrique Ochoa, *Feeding Mexico: The Political Uses of Food since 1910* (Wilmington., Del.: Scholarly Resources, 2000), 81.

20. Ignacio Gutiérrez Argil (President of the Cooperativa Permisionarios Transportes de Pasajeros) to President Miguel Alemán Valdés, February 24, 1947, AGN, MAV, vol. 605, exp. 549.3/14.

21. Trujillo Muñoz, introduction to Braulio Maldonado Sández, *Baja California*, 16.

22. Ibid., 13–34.

23. At a time when the border labor markets was stretched thinly due to the forced repatriation, Cárdenas's policies added to the secular loss of employment. Vincente Cabeza de Baca, "Moral Renovation of the Californias: Tijuana's Political and Economic Role in American-Mexican Relations, 1920–1935" (Ph.D. diss., University of California, San Diego, 1991), 127, 147; Paul Vanderwood, *Juan Soldado*, 140–69; David Jiménez Beltrán, *The Agua Caliente Story: Remembering Mexico's Legendary Racetrack* (Lexington, Ky.: Blood Horse Publications, 2004), 79.

24. Indeed, President Ávila Camacho lent his hand to the opening of Mexico City's Hipódromo de las Américas, as influenced by his positive track experience at Tijuana during the 1930s. Jiménez Beltrán, *The Agua Caliente Story*, 83.

25. Alberto Peralta (Alba Roja) to President Lázaro Cárdenas, April 23, 1937, AGN, fondo: Lázaro Cárdenas (LC), exp. 549.3/38.

26. Petitions from union officials seeking to establish games of chance at Tijuana's jai alai frontón clearly reflect labor's vested interest in a tourism industry based upon attractions such as gaming. Ramón Alvarez (Sindicato de medicos y profesiones varias) to Presidente de la República, April 30, 1935, AGN, LC, exp. 549.3/38.

27. Lic. Ángel Carvajal to Secretario Personal del Presidente de la Republica, "Relativo al Sindicato de Trabajadores Hipódromo de Tijuana," December 2, 1937, AGN, LC, exp. 432/381, 6/300/11649; Jiménez Beltrán, *The Agua Caliente Story*, 83.

28. Jack Dempsey to President Lázaro Cárdenas, March 8, 1937, AGN, LC, exp. 549.3/5.

29. A veteran Tijuana racing personality and president of the Agua Caliente Jockey Club, Baron Long was involved with manipulating the odds in what became known as the Linden Tree scandal in 1932, pointing to the subsequent mafia handling of wire bets (comeback money), permitted by off-site gambling. Jiménez Beltrán, *The Agua Caliente Story*, 65–67.

30. Jack Dempsey to President Lázaro Cárdenas, April 14, 1937, AGN, LC, exp. 549.3/38 and 549.3/5.

31. Berger, *The Development of Mexico's Tourism Industry*, illustrates this point. Mary Simon, *Racing through the Century*, 118, likened Agua Caliente in 1932 to a surreal oasis in a landscape of economic horror.

32. Jiménez Beltrán, *The Agua Caliente Story*, 85–90.

33. Ron Hale, "Reminiscing about Old Agua Caliente," 1997, http://horseracing .about.com/library/blcaliente.htm; Jiménez Beltrán, *The Agua Caliente Story*, 93–95.

34. The U.S. military began making tracks supply centers or, in the case of Santa Anita, a distibution center for Japanese internment camps. Jiménez Beltrán, *The Agua Caliente Story*, 93–95.

35. Eduardo Nealis Robles to Presidente de la República, March 4, 1942, AGN, LC, exp. 549.3/4.

36. For the concession requests and detailed accounts of labor unrest, see AGN, LC, 549.3/38 Conflicto Obrero trabajadores de Tijuana, September 19, 1938; Manuel Ávila Camacho, Ed Nealis, 549.3/4 Carreras Caballos, February 11, 1941; Hipódromo Tijuana, March 10, 1943; Susana Lucero de Regnier (1942–44) 404.11/ 459, Tijuana BC. Ejidos "Rancho Tijuana: 11–26–43 exp. Relativo, 432/85, Amparo 11–1941. Lucero de Regnier was the heiress who had successfully and controversially sued for restitution in 1938. When the Supreme Court finalized its decision in 1943, de Regnier died of a heart attack at the age of sixty-four. Jiménez Beltrán, *The Agua Caliente Story*, 98, 99.

37. Quality liquor, a sumptuously supplied kitchen, massage tables, and sauna endowed Nealis with a well-rounded diversionary service for special clients. Jiménez Beltrán, *The Agua Caliente Story*, 100.

38. Ibid., 99, 100.

39. Alberto Arguello and Alejandro Arguello to Presidente de la República, December 14, 1944; Agustín Silveira to Presidente de la República, December 18, 1944; and José Escudero Andrade (Inspr. Gral. De Policia, Tte. Corl Inf.) to Presidente de la República, December 13, 1944. All in AGN, MAC, exp. 432/85, vol. C392, Manuel Ávila Camacho (MAC), galería 3.

40. For the forage arrangements, see José Navarro Elizondo to President Alemán, January 12, 1949; Rogerio de la Selva to President Alemán, February 13, 1948; Miguel Alemán to José Navarro Elizondo, July 23, 1949; José Navarro Elizondo (San Diego) to President Alemán, August 5, 1949, AGN, MAV, exp. 101/11. Of the 277 hectares composing the Agua Caliente property, General Rodríguez retained the grounds of the hippodrome measuring 39 hectares. "Expropriación de los bienes de la Cia Agua Caliente," Archivo Histórico del Estados (AHE) (Mexicali, Baja California), exp. 310/2664, Expropriación de Bienes e Inmuebles, 1938–1974, Gobierno del Territorio y del Estado, sección Adminstración de Bienes Muebles y Inmuebles, serie Bienes Inmuebles, caja 241.

41. Alberto Arguello and Alejandro Arguello to Presidente de la República, December 14, 1944, AGN, MAC, exp. 432/85, vol. C392.

42. According to Eduardo Robles Aguinaldo, son of Tijuana's police chief and an intern apprentice in charge of Caliente's bookkeeping department, Crofton retained exclusive access to Caliente's financial (*auditoria*) operations. Interview by Eric M. Schantz with Eduardo Aguilar Robles Maldonado, August 22, 1997, Mexicali, Baja California. Pointing to similar foreign influence in retaining economic power after cardenista nationalization, Clayton Anderson was able to

control much of the postharvest ginning and financing of Mexicali's cotton crop. Ángel Bassol Batalla, *El noroeste de México: Un estudio geográfico económico* (Mexico City: Instituto de Investigaciones Económicas, 1972), 58–61.

43. Under Alemán, Mexico witnessed a frenzy of transportation development, and a new coastal resort in Acapulco. Miguel Alemán, *15 Lecciones de turismo* (Mexico City: Consejo Nacional de Turismo, 1966).

44. Dirección General de Asuntos Jurídicos. Ley Federal de Juegos y Sorteos, DOF, 31 de diciembre, 1947.

45. Ignacio Gutiérrez Argil (President of the Cooperativa Permisionarios Transportes de Pasajeros) to President Miguel Alemán Valdés, February 24, 1947, AGN, MAV, vol. 605, exp. 549.3/14.

46. Aurelio Ramírez H. and J. Ventura Blanco L. (Cámara Nacional de Comercio en Pequeño de Querétaro) to Miguel Alemán Valdés, October 15, 1947, AGN, MAV, vol. 605, exp. 549.3/32.

47. "El Juego y Alcohol Aparecen en Baja California," *El Observador Objetivo*, May 28, 1947, AGN, MAV, exp. 549.3/32, vol. 605.

48. Governor Alberto V. Aldrete to MAV, May 20, 1947, AGN, MAV, exp. 101/11.

49. Enrique Aldrete, Alberto's father, acted as tax collector for the state treasury. See Marco Antonio Samaniego López, "El desarrollo económico durante el gobierno de Abelardo L. Rodríguez," 24.

50. Jackson Lears, *Something for Nothing: Luck in America* (New York: Penguin, 2003), 56.

51. Governor Alberto V. Aldrete to Miguel Alemán, May 20, 1947, AGN, MAV; exp. 101/11. For Novo Hispano precedents, see Juan Pedro Viqueira Albán, *Relajados o reprimidos? Diversiones públicas y vida social en la Ciudad de México durante el siglo de las Luces*, 2nd ed. (Mexico City: Fondo de Cultura Económica, 1995).

52. Myrna Oliver, "Obituaries; John S. Alessio; Influential Cross-Border Businessman," *Los Angeles Times*, March 26, 1998, 10; Matt Potter, "The Mr. San Diego Follies," *San Diego Reader*, September 30, 1999; Niblo, *Mexico in the 1940s*, 268.

53. Dr. Carroll Quigley (Professor, Foreign Service School, Georgetown University) to President Miguel Alemán Valdés, October 18, 1948, AGN, MAV, exp. 542.2/183, vol. 549; . Oliver, "Obituaries; John S. Alessio," 10.

54. Potter, "The Mr. San Diego Follies." John Alessio blamed Richard Nixon, who was "vengeful . . . for supporting Pat Brown against Nixon in the 1962 California gubernatorial race."

55. Jiménez Beltrán, *The Agua Caliente Story*, 100–101.

56. José Navarro Elizondo to President, January 12, 1949; Rogerio de la Selva to President Alemán, February 13, 1948; Miguel Alemán to José Navarro Elizondo, July 23, 1949; José Navarro Elizondo (San Diego) to President Alemán, August 5, 1949; all in AGN, MAV, exp. 101/11. In addition to taking a cut of the track wagering receipts, Alemán received the "gift" of Rancho El Florido. Alemán's

intermediary, his personal agent, was identified by oral sources as Col. Serrano. Bassols Batalla, *El noreoeste de México*, 66, 67. "Juan Platt to Abelardo L. Rodríguez, May 29, 1933," in Plutarco Elías Calles, *Correspondencia personal*, 281, 282.

57. On the Lincoln Continentals, see Miguel Alemán to José Navarro Elizondo, July 23, 1949; José Navarro Elizondo to President Alemán, August 5, 1949. Regarding the B-52 hangars, "Francisco Villagrán to Miguel Alemán," December 3, 1947, AGN, MAV, exp. 101/11; Niblo, *Mexico in the 1940s*, 259–61; Eric M. Schantz interview with Eduardo Aguilar Robles Maldonado, August 22, 1997; Potter, "The Mr. San Diego Follies."

58. Wilkie, "Review of Stephen R. Niblo," 581.

59. Bill Ritter, "Resort has had Ups and Downs since its more Prestigious Days," *Los Angeles Times*, August 20, 1985, 2. For a discussion of Benjamin ("Bugsy") Siegel's involvement with the Caliente track business, as well as narcotics, see Ed Reid and Ovid Demaris, *The Green Felt Jungle: The Truth about Las Vegas* (New York: Trident Press, 1963), 20–23.

60. Reid and Demaris, *The Green Felt Jungle*, 20–23. For the importance of telegraph communications for offsite sports wagering, see Schantz, "All Night at the Owl."

61. "Caliente 42 Year History Conflict," *Unión*, October 5, 1971. SDHS, Vertical file 4, Agua Caliente and William Staciem, "Foreign Affairs," *LA Magazine* (June 2000), 103–6.

62. Ritter, "Resort Has Had Ups and Downs since Its More Prestigious Days"; Reid and Demaris, *The Green Felt Jungle*, 20–23.

63. MacCannell, *The Tourist*, 25–27.

64. Los Angeles's clandestine gambling operations witnessed a sudden setback following investigations exposing police protection. Mayor Frank Shaw was forced to resign, and his graft-laden administration was riddled with improprieties. State Attorney Earl Warren ordered a raid of the clandestine offshore gambling barge, the *Rex*. See David Fine, *Imagining Los Angeles: A City in Fiction* (Reno: University of Nevada Press, 2000), 85, 110.

65. Proffit, "The Symbiotic Frontier," 331–32.

66. Pablo Sepúlveda to Srio. Lic. Rogerio de la Selva, September 22, 1949; Pablo Sepúlveda to Lic. Rogerio de la Selva, September 9, 1949, AGN, MAV, vol. 605, exp. 549.3/32.

67. Myrna Oliver, "Obituaries: Anne Gwynne, 84; World War II Pinup Played Spunky All American Girl in Horror Movies," *Los Angeles Times*, April 8, 2003, B11.

68. Max Gilford to Adolfo López Mateos, December 5, 1958, AGN, Presidentes, Adolfo López Mateos (ALM), vol. 727, exp. 549.3/2.

69. Ibid.

70. Maldonado Sández, *Baja California*, 110–14; Proffit, "Symbiotic Frontier," 322, 331–32; Richard Rossman, telephone interview by Eric M. Schantz. April 17, 2001.

71. Bassols Batalla, *El noreoeste de México*, 67.

72. Joseph Lowitz (Beverly Hills, Calif.) to Hon. Adolfo López Mateos, February 6, 1959, AGN, ALM, caja/vol. 727, exp. 549.3/2.

73. James Victor (Venice, California) to Adolfo López Mateos, AGN, ALM, vol. 727, exp. 549.3/2.

74. This promotional piece reveals a broader argument often made by the pioneering border scholar Ulises Irigoyen as to the specificity of the Mexican border economy. Enjoying favored status, the U.S. dollar ran rough-shod. Elías Alvarez del Castillo, "Tiene usted una idea de como es el Territorio Norte de la Baja California," *El Universal*, November 22, 1941, reprinted in Ulises Irigoyen, *Carretera transpeninsular de la Baja California*, vols. 3 and 4 (Mexico City: Editorial Donceles, 1943), 140.

75. For insightful commentaries on the social borders at hippodromes in the United States, see Lears, *Something for Nothing*, 56; Austin Coats, *China Races* (Oxford: Oxford University Press, 1983), 12, 36. The social division of Shanghai's racing milieu was organized around colonial divisions: race, nationality, gender, and class relations segregated the public space at the track.

76. Beezley, *Judas at the Jockey Club.*

77. Hale, "Reminiscing about Old Agua Caliente." Similar charges of racism were leveled against John Alessio's restaurant in La Jolla for attempting to limit the number of Mexican waitstaff.

78. Ibid.

79. Ibid.

80. Rossman, telephone interview by Eric M. Schantz.

81. Dirección General de Asuntos Jurídicos, Ley Federal de Juegos y Sorteos, DOF, 31 de diciembre, 1947.

82. Rossman, telephone interview by Eric M. Schantz.

83. Lears, *Something for Nothing*, 56. The gambling spirit has been described as conscientiously masculine, capitalistic in its pursuit of riches that rise and fall with magical if not maddening irregularity. If gaming's intense search for lady luck was a calling card for macho adventures, gaming tourism tended to produce a greater number of women tourists, helping to check the border's ambience of hypertestosterone. Genteel and steely stoicism were proper qualities with which gamers faced vertiginous losses or gains.

84. "El Hipódromo de Tijuana: El orgullo de Tijuana," Sindicato de Empleados de Cantinas, Hoteles y Restaurantes, December 23, 1950, December 30, 1950 (Tijuana), AHE, fondo: Gobierno del Territorio, sección: Salubridad, caja 186, serie: Generalidades, Erogaciones Normales de Administración, 200/9679.

85. AHE, fondo: Gobierno del Territorio, sección: Obras y Trabajos, caja 176, enclosure: advertisement, in *Nuevo Mundo*, August 15, 1956.

86. Frederico Campbell, *Tijuanenses* (Mexico City: Joaquín Mortiz, 1989). Between

aviation, pachucos, and the Agua Caliente motifs, this author truly expresses Baja California's iconographic existentialism. I want to thank the brilliant painter and cultural broker Victor Salomon for the tip on *Tijuanenses*. See also Vanderwood, *Juan Soldado*, 104–69.

87. Eric M. Schantz, "Meretricious Mexicali: Exalted Masculinities and the Crafting of Male Desire in a Border Red-Light District, 1908–1925," *Mexican Masculinities*, ed. Anne Rubenstein and Victor Macías González (Albuquerque: University of New Mexico Press, forthcoming 2009). The notion of vagination may be controversial but offers a corrective both perceptively and syntactically to the overwrought meanings of penetration by foreign capital (or phallus), reemphasizing the combination of courtship and recruitment, nurturing and netting, that Mexican officials used to attract and retain foreign investors and business.

88. A good example of native craft inspiring American visions of curios is found in Terry's discussion of traditional Huichol dress: "The hair is worn long and flowing, confined at the brow with handsome, woven head-bands (desirable curios)." T. Philip Terry, *Terry's Mexico: Handbook for Travellers* (Boston: Houghton Mifflin, 1909), 94.

89. José Martínez M., "Negocios sucios de Jorge Hank Rhon investiga comisión de la Cámara de Diputados. La prórroga por 25 años en la concesión para operar el Hipódromo de Agua Caliente, en Tijuana Se vio envuelto en el asesinato del periodista Héctor Félix Miranda, El Gato." Columna Contrapunto, *La Crisis*, October 15, 2005. Patrick McDonnell, "The Assassination of El Gato: Renewed Call for Answers Fallout Yet to Settle in Death of Popular Tijuana Journalist," *Los Angeles Times*, April 17, 1989. Dora Elena Cortés, "Tijuana, laboratorio electoral de las viejas dinastías del PRI," *Notiver*, October 7, 2004.

ANDREW SACKETT

FUN IN ACAPULCO?

The Politics of Development on the Mexican Riviera

> I can think of no place on the face of the earth that can surpass Acapulco.
> I have heard world-travelers liken it to the Italian Riviera and one say
> reverently, "Heaven is only a suburb of Acapulco."
> **MEXICAN NATIONAL AUTOMOBILE ASSOCIATION, *TRAVEL GUIDE FOR MEXICO*, 1947**

> People without scruples who are trying to enrich themselves . . . are
> developing projects to throw us out from our community, from our plots,
> from the homes of our families, because we are poor.
> **TELEGRAM FROM RUPERTO RODRÍGUEZ, SECRETARY OF THE COMISARIO EJIDAL DE SANTA
> CRUZ, ACAPULCO, TO PRESIDENT MIGUEL ALEMÁN, JUNE 24, 1947**

The year 1947 marks a watershed in the history of Acapulco. As postwar tourism began to boom, the Mexican state became heavily involved in the town's development. This development, which changed Acapulco from a dilapidated port town to a modern resort, could not have occurred without the intervention of the state. Throughout this process, the interests of hotel developers and tourists were paramount, and those of the people of Acapulco were secondary. This was not an accident—the state carefully planned and controlled the development of Acapulco. One of Mexico's premier architects designed the urban plan; the state placed control over all aspects of urban development, from zoning to commerce on the beaches, in the hands of a federal agency called the Junta Federal de Mejoras Materiales de Acapulco (Acapulco Federal Board for Material Improvements, hereafter JFMM or Junta Federal), and the Agrarian Department, under orders from President Miguel Alemán himself, expropriated the required land from *ejidita-*

rios.[1] Meanwhile, every year more tourists came, drawn by travel guides, such as the one quoted in the first epigraph to this chapter, that attributed a certain international image to Acapulco. At the same time, the people displaced by the development often challenged the growth of the "Mexican Riviera."

This challenge to Acapulco's growth took many forms. It was not as simple as merely rejecting tourism. Some people fought for their land, others to preserve their place in the tourism industry as better-funded competition emerged, backed up by the power of the state. And some turned the challenges of growth to their own advantage. Take Commissioner Ruperto Rodríguez, whom I quote in the second epigraph, writing to the government to complain about the expropriation of the ejido he managed. It turned out that Santa Cruz was not expropriated for another twenty-five years. Meanwhile, as migrants from rural Guerrero poured into Acapulco looking for work, Rodríguez, who remained commissioner through the 1950s, began selling land on the open market with the connivance (indeed, the active surveying services) of federal authorities, taking advantage of the burgeoning population brought to the city looking for work.[2]

In this chapter I weave together these stories: the state-driven development of Acapulco into a tourist resort, and the human cost of that project, while arguing that it was the active role of the state that made the development possible. Understanding the history of tourism involves more than just analyzing and recounting the tourist experience. The development displaced local residents and forced changes in their behavior. I look at these changes, equally as important a part of the history of tourism as Acapulco's growth as a resort.

The history of Mexico's most important, groundbreaking beach resort is impossible to reduce to the length of a chapter. Instead, I focus on certain episodes as these narratives develop, including the first expropriations of ejidal land, struggles over commercial activity on the beaches, and the changing geography of tourism and hotel location around Acapulco Bay.

Historical Background

Acapulco lies on the Pacific coast of Mexico, less than 500 kilometers directly south of Mexico City. It is located on a large, deep, crescent-shaped bay that is sheltered from the open ocean, making it an excellent natural harbor. Spanish conquistadors founded the city in 1521, and it was the only port on the

Mexican Pacific coast open to maritime trade during the period of Spanish colonial rule, when galleons from the Philippine trade docked there.[3]

After Mexican independence in 1821 and the end of the galleon trade, Acapulco sank into a long commercial decline. For the next hundred years, its only regular connection to Mexico City was by mule train. The coastal steamship system in the mid-nineteenth century provided the only regular contact with the outside world, as ships traveling up and down the coast stopped in Acapulco for coal and water.[4] Passengers on these ships bought fruit and souvenirs from the locals or went ashore for the day.[5] One observer commented that the only products worth purchasing were cigars and strings of seashells.[6] These were the only tourists.

As the Mexican economy grew during the Porfiriato, Acapulco was over-shadowed as a Pacific port by places such as Manzanillo, connected by rail to Mexico City.[7] Attempts to build a railway connecting Acapulco with the capital in the late nineteenth century were never completed.[8] In fact, Acapulqueño commercial elites resisted the construction of better transportation networks, fearing an end to their monopoly over economic activities such as mule transport, the import-export trade, wholesale purchasing of agricultural goods from outside Acapulco, and manufacturing. The predominant commercial firms, Alzuyeta y Compañía and B. Fernández y Compañía, which owned the majority of the mule transport services and harbor barges, actively impeded the construction of a Mexico City–Acapulco road by, among other things, bribing engineers and technicians commissioned by the federal government to issue negative reports on the possibility of construction.[9]

After the Mexican Revolution, Acapulco's isolation came to an end. The socialists briefly took power in Acapulco in the early 1920s. With the support of President Alvaro Obregón, they prioritized the completion of the Mexico City–Acapulco highway, partly in an attempt to overcome the economic power of local elites. Although the socialist leader Juan Ranulfo Escudero was killed in 1923, the highway was completed four years later, in 1927.[10]

The Beginnings of Tourism

The early tourism marketing of Mexico did not feature Acapulco as a destination. The railway companies did most of this marketing, and there was no value for them in promoting Acapulco, regardless of its natural attractions, since it was not connected to their rail networks.[11] Almost immediately following the completion of the Mexico City–Acapulco highway, however, both state and private writers thought differently about Acapulco. The city's attractions did not immediately change after the road opened, but writers no longer described Acapulco as a decaying port. After 1927, travel writers portrayed Acapulco as the crowning experience of a new tourist route, one that passed from Mexico City through the colonial cities of Cuernavaca and Taxco (both established tourist destinations) and then through the mountains to Acapulco.[12] The new highway, dubbed the "Ruta de los Galeones" (Route of the Galleons) by the Comisión Nacional de Caminos (National Highway Commission), was part of a growing road network accessible from the Texas border.[13] The state expected these connections to "develop international tourism, from which Mexico expects an intense social interchange that will bring about a better understanding and closer relationship with its neighboring countries."[14] Travel writers as well as government literature soon began to recommend drives to Acapulco as part of a Mexican vacation.[15]

By the early 1930s, Acapulco was a popular tourist resort for both Americans and Mexicans. More than 10,000 tourists came to the city in peak periods such as Christmas and especially Semana Santa (Holy Week), far outnumbering the town's population.[16] Nearly all camped on the beaches or in their cars, and those unable to afford their own cars took the regular bus service from Mexico City.[17] Acapulco's natural beauty was its main attraction. There were limited services, and the town's tourism infrastructure was undeveloped. There were only four small hotels in 1933, though investors planned a large, modern hotel. Visitors generally spent their time at the beach, deep-sea fishing, or simply admiring the "unparalleled view of the Pacific."[18] One guidebook claimed that "some one in a burst of enthusiasm said that Acapulco is a place of blue waters, white sand, green fish, and red parrots. Probably all this is true but there is more to the story than that. It is hot, moist and dirty, and yet there is a charm in the harbor and the fringe that surrounds it."[19]

Not only private writers were waxing poetic about Acapulco. By 1940 Acapulco, formally a seaport in name only, had been redefined as a tropical seaside resort by the producers of state tourism materials. This description from a Petróleos Mexicanos (PEMEX, the national oil company) travel guide for American motorists in Mexico encapsulates the modern Acapulco:

> Acapulco, at the end of the same highway which leads to Taxco, is a Pacific Coast seaport on the edge of a dramatically beautiful sheltered bay. Swimming at Acapulco in its sapphire blue waters—and always just

the right temperature—is a delightful privilege. Splendid beaches of clean, golden sand stretch for almost the entire length of the bay. . . . Fishing at Acapulco is grand sport, where the larger varieties put up a battle to gladden the heart of the most sophisticated fisherman. The town is quaint and charming, and includes several excellent hotels. Put Acapulco on your "must" list; you will not be disappointed. And when you arrive, wait for one of those fantastic sunsets which can happen only in Acapulco.[20]

What was important for PEMEX—the "privilege" of swimming, the beaches, fishing, charm, hotels, and sunsets of Acapulco—contrasts dramatically with the Acapulco that writers had presented before.

In an article published in 1939, "To the Aztec Land Where Fiesta Rules," the *New York Times* directed readers to both Acapulco and Mazatlán as "havens of extreme beauty" on Mexico's Pacific coast. The *Times* described Acapulco as having excellent beaches, which made it an "alluring resort," and noted how visitors could fish for dolphin, shark, mackerel, sailfish, blue marlin, ray, and fighting rooster fish.[21] Mexico's tourist importance to Americans skyrocketed at this time, which is why the *New York Times* featured it as a vacation destination. The outbreak of World War II in 1939 closed off Europe, including the French Riviera, to American tourists. During the war years, Mexico and Central America experienced a boom in tourism, beginning with an increase of approximately seven percent in the first half of 1940.[22]

Activating Development

From these early days, national-level political elites involved themselves in Acapulco development projects. In 1932, the Federal Secretary of Communications and future presidential candidate Juan Andrew Almazán joined with President Pascual Ortíz Rubio to form the Compañía Impulsora de Acapulco. They planned to build a hotel on coastal land acquired through expropriations carried out by the state of Guerrero. However, it was not until the late 1930s and early 1940s that the Mexican state officially began to develop Acapulco.[23] This process occurred simultaneously and is often synonymous with the political ascent of Miguel Alemán Valdés. Alemán was Secretario de Gobernación (Secretary of the Interior) during the presidency of Manuel Ávila Camacho from 1940 to 1946, and president of the Republic from 1946 through 1952. The Department of Tourism was part of the Secretaría de

Gobernación (Department of the Interior) during Alemán's tenure there, and it was then that Alemán became interested in the tourist industry.[24]

While Alemán was president, the Mexican state took control of much of Acapulco's land and transformed its urban geography. It expropriated the remaining *ejidos* closest to the water, which blocked the re-creation of Acapulco, and placed the beaches, already federal territory, under its direct control. Then it reoriented development from the Peninsula de las Playas (Peninsula of the Beaches, located southwest of downtown) and the center of the city into an arc along the entire bay. As part of the expropriation process, the government reorganized some of the most fertile land as a completely serviced subdivision of farms. This land was then sold to wealthy Mexico City investors, who used it to build second homes.[25] From the point of view of the state, Acapulco changed from a space whose primary function was residential, with tourism as a secondary concern, to the reverse.

The agency responsible for almost all development activity was the Junta Federal, which the federal government created in Acapulco in 1934. As with other Juntas Federales in frontier and port towns, the federal government organized it to use import-export taxes to supply potable water, drainage, and electricity; pave streets; and build hospitals, schools, and municipal buildings.[26] Alemán assigned the Acapulco JFMM a different task. He charged it with overseeing the transformation of Acapulco from a small port, with an informal tourist industry, into a resort centered on tourism. The Junta Federal focused on improvements with an eye on tourism, rather than those that merely improved the salubrity of the urban environment for residents. To implement this change of focus, Alemán altered both the Junta Federal's official assignment and its composition. He gave the JFMM blanket authority over nearly every aspect of the port's development.[27] Its responsibilities now included controlling newly expanded federal land; improving beaches and swimming places; extending existing and opening new streets; financing of works; and regulating planning, zoning, and contracts for the coastal road around the bay, parks, gardens, markets, schools, hospitals, parking lots, intersections, airports, a pier, and subdivisions.[28] Normally, municipalities controlled these planning and zoning functions. At the same time as he expanded its jurisdiction, Alemán revised the composition of the JFMM. With tighter federal control over appointments, he ensured that control over the development process remained in his hands.[29]

The Junta Federal based this development on an urban plan drawn up by an architect named Carlos Contreras.[30] Contreras was an important urban planner who had a lasting legacy on the landscape of Mexico City. He followed a general modernist formula.[31] Contreras was concerned with traffic and the efficient operation of the city and redrew Acapulco to focus on the road network and zoning. He planned the amplification and prolongation of streets; the construction of large boulevards; and the destruction of buildings between those boulevards to create grand parks. He wanted to physically move neighborhoods that blocked unifying development into larger residential zones and to create separate commercial, industrial, and governmental zones.

The Junta Federal began implementing the Contreras plan in August 1945. Its first step was to build a network to distribute potable water, to be immediately followed by a drainage system and street paving. These were all projects that, theoretically, would benefit the entire population. The Junta Federal and the agencies it directed, though, delayed or failed to complete many of the works. Instead, they initiated the construction of a wide coastal boulevard, running the length of the city, for the specific purpose of tourism development outside the old downtown. This road became the Costera Miguel Alemán. They concurrently began work on a new public park at Caleta, where the beautiful, sheltered beach was already a significant tourist attraction.[32] This construction embodied the changes wrought in the tourist industry as the state's involvement grew, displacing local businesses and altering the tourist experience.

On the Beach

The beaches of Caleta and Caletilla are located on the Peninsula de las Playas, which forms the west end of the crescent that encircles Acapulco Bay. They were the first beaches developed for tourism, and the site of the first *fraccionamientos* (subdivisions) aimed at the vacation market.[33] Travel writers focused on how "Mexican" the beach at Caleta was, highlighting how people engaged in activities the writers perceived as typically Mexican. In *Let's Visit Mexico*, for example, Bryon Steel suggested that Caleta was "an ideal beach dotted with gay umbrellas . . . a lovely place in which to lounge over a cup of coconut milk, and watch the natives dive for corals and seashells."[34]

Before the Junta Federal took over the beach, tourists bought their coconut milk and rented their umbrellas from a series of at least fifteen *puestos* (kiosks or stalls), some of which had been operating since the early 1930s.[35] These, too, underscored the *mexicanidad* of the beach, both in their mode of operation and their names. Some had regional Mexican monikers such as *El Popo* (the volcano outside Mexico City) or *El Bajío* (a region in the central part of the country), while others reflected local themes like *El Pez-Vela* (the sailfish) and *La Sirena* (the mermaid). For Mexicans, some of these names would have signified Acapulco, and some would have indicated that they could find food in the style of their home region. Owned mainly, although not exclusively, by women, the puestos filled an essential, though unregulated, role in the tourist experience by providing important services in an informal manner. When threatened by the Junta Federal, the *puesteros* (proprietors of the stalls) pointed to the reasons why their presence was important:

> In these stalls we provide tourists, who give life to our town of Acapulco, all the comforts and services which they need for their rest on Playa Caletilla. For these services, which include savoring the Acapulqueño snacks of ceviche and seafood, using the changing rooms and watching their valuable belongings with a guarantee for those owners who don't leave them confidently, because they know we're honorable, for all these services, we charge moderate prices which enable us to support our families.[36]

As the dynamics of tourism changed, so did the status of the puestos. By the mid-1940s, the puesteros could see already that their way of life was changing. Developers built hotels and villas above the beach, and a new road connected the area to the downtown.[37] The Contreras Plan called for the construction of commercial buildings to lodge the small businesses providing services to tourists on the beaches. Melchor Perusquía, president of the Junta Federal, explained that the government wanted to remove the "anti-aesthetic and unhygienic aspects of the booths which were provisionally installed in Caletilla. . . . They lack the most elementary sanitary services. No water, nor drainage, nothing which might have guaranteed the health of the business person or the tourist."[38] The state wanted to replace this supposed disorganization and insalubrity with a modern building containing showers, bathrooms, and changing rooms. Plus, they would monitor the hygiene of the seafood and meals that were served. These measures were paradigmatic of the planned commercialism that lay at the heart of the Junta Federal's vision of Acapulco and demonstrate the multiple overlapping motives. By regulating commercial activity on the beach, the Junta Federal could control access to the market. It could also earn rents from the businesses that were established and, if it wanted, collect taxes.[39]

Ironically, the puesteros indicated a clear awareness of the aesthetics of their presence when the state first threatened them with ejection in 1941:

> We understand that Acapulco, as a center of international tourism, represents a key aspect of our beloved *patria* and have the duty to present it aesthetically. In order to materialize the previous idea, we request you order by the proper channels the model and materials to us so that we can carry out the reconstruction of our kiosks and the uniformity that we must maintain.[40]

That they recognized the necessity of rebuilding their stalls—as well as the coherent and conscious links they made between international tourism, Acapulco, and aesthetics—indicates a sophisticated understanding of the modern ideal that the state, through the Junta Federal, would attempt to create later in the decade. Yet the puesteros lacked the resources to participate in the changes they saw sweeping Acapulco.

The Junta Federal completed the new, concrete commercial building by 1949, and although it granted some of the preexisting small businesses leases within it, they faced serious obstacles in continuing success. The rents were high. The JFMM forbid tenants from running changing rooms, which had been the base of their business before. Although it did authorize them to sell beer and promised them bathrooms, it did not build any in their locales. The Junta Federal gave the best locations, including bathrooms and changing rooms, to outsiders who had not previously run stalls on the beach. These tenants, unlike the former puesteros, paid even higher rents (six times) but had both a monopoly on these key resources and a second-floor terrace restaurant.[41]

The puesteros had two options—moving to locations they could not afford or staying in their old locations despite threats from the Junta Federal. They chose the latter. The chief of public health threatened them with closure in October 1949, and although the merchants tried to resist, the Junta Federal sent mounted police to close their stalls the next month, just before the peak tourist season began in December. The use of violence accomplished what regulation and economic pressure did not. A local newspaper, *Acapulco: Revista Illustrada Quinceneal*, commenting on the plight of the puesteros, criticized the Junta Federal for charging them "the pearls of the virgin for a stable made of concrete, that . . . had been paid for by the federal government" and then protecting it "with armed soldiers, like in the days of the Revolution, and as if they were dealing with assassins."[42]

The Junta's replacement of the individual stalls with the concrete building did not, in itself, improve hygienic conditions or the salubrity of the beach area. The state could do no more than enforce the physical location of the food services. The area appeared to be orderly and organized when the beach and the parking lot were empty, but there was nowhere for the businesses to place their trash, and garbage collection was irregular at best.[43] The septic discharge from nearby hotels and the unregulated food preparation practices contributed to an unhygienic recreational environment.[44] Other unplanned results of Caleta's commercial transformation emerged shortly thereafter, such as the appearance of prostitution in the cantinas.[45]

Taking Control of the Land: The Expropriation of the Ejidos

Similar changes occurred throughout Acapulco at this time. The Junta Federal began implementing the expropriation of the ejidos closest to downtown and the shore, forcing both the registered ejiditarios and other residents off to find new housing.

The ejido of El Progreso, for example, bordered on the urbanized part of Acapulco Viejo. When the Junta Federal expropriated it in 1947, there was opposition from multiple parties: the ejiditarios themselves; people who rented land from them and had already built houses in the urban zone of the ejido; community organizations like the Unión de Colonos de Acapulco, who wanted a *colonia popular* (affordable working-class neighborhood) to be built on the site and tried negotiating with the state to buy the land at reduced rates; and poor people and activists who wanted a colonia popular and invaded the land after it was expropriated, without attempting to cooperate with the state. The ejiditarios organized to avoid the disintegration of their homes—lobbying politicians, holding public demonstrations, marching down Acapulco's main streets with banners reading "The People of El Progreso have the right to live like people and among people," and calling for justice and respect for their homes. But they were unsuccessful.[46] The JFMM could not settle the expropriation disputes peacefully, and just as on the beaches, it resorted to force. The police burned houses and crops, and the army guarded the razed plots of land to ensure that people stayed off.[47] The state's incarceration of their leaders and continued use of violence forced the ejiditarios to accept the inadequate compensation offered by the state. Most remained in Acapulco, moving to the new workers' neighborhoods in the urbanized section of what had been their land.[48]

The idea of building neighborhoods with affordable housing on this land was not new. In his original plan, Contreras had set aside land for a Ciudad Obrera (Workers' City), a residential neighborhood for the employees who worked in the rapidly growing tourist industry.[49] The Junta Federal, however, moved slowly in creating neighborhoods with affordable housing, and Acapulqueños took it upon themselves to build them, seizing vacant land. On February 28, 1948, the Unión de Colonos de El Progreso invaded a piece of the former ejido El Progreso and demanded that the JFMM agree to urbanize it as a colonia popular. Within a week of the invasion, there were a thousand people living there.[50] The federal government eventually legalized their title to the land. As the city grew and the housing crisis worsened, Acapulqueños invaded land again and again.[51]

Next to the Colonia Progreso, 681 families lived in a neighborhood called Lázaro Cárdenas. They had seized land belonging to the Hernández family, who owned multiple properties in Acapulco. They demanded title to the land and insisted that the federal government amend the Contreras Plan to include their neighborhood. Recognizing that planned development could not be stopped, they accepted the understanding of Acapulco as a place for tourism but simultaneously insisted on a space where they could dwell.[52] As in the case of the puesteros on Caleta, Acapulqueños recognized and articulated how they could accommodate and participate in the state's plans. In this case, the state responded favorably.

The Costera

Through the Junta Federal the state undertook other large projects at this time. One key project was the construction of the Calzada Costera, a road that ringed the bay and became the axis off of which much future development would occur. In the early 1940s, Acapulco's center was located at the west end of the bay, while developers built vacation homes and hotels near Caleta, on the Peninsula de las Playas. Aside from El Papagayo and Hotel Las Hamacas, there were very few structures and no hotels around the arc of the bay. Contreras and the Junta Federal planned the Costera from the beginning as the "spine" of the city and the base of its future development.[53] Twelve kilometers long, it travels the entire length of the bay, and its construction opened up the rest of the amphitheater to subdivisions and hotels. Building the Costera was a critical step in realizing the transformation of Acapulco from a small port town on one end of the bay to a city surrounding it. The road was named the Costera Miguel Alemán after the president, in what was described by the former mayor, *priista* journalist, and chronicler

Carlos E. Adame as a spontaneous "display of gratitude for the physical and economic transformation of the port."[54] Although the naming is often held as evidence of Alemán's generosity to Acapulco, it can also be read as a reminder of the destruction of Acapulco Viejo and its replacement by tourist Acapulco. Other local writers were more hostile than Adame; one included it among the "capricious and insulting names" that the "parasitic and arriviste fauna" had bestowed on Acapulco as part of their "cultural destruction of the port's heritage."[55]

Although its net effect may have benefited Acapulqueños—if for no other reason than it reduced the traffic that previously plagued downtown during peak tourist times—the key result of the Costera's completion was that it opened up the rest of the bay for development. The building process, like so many of the changes that occurred in Acapulco, had immediate effects in that it displaced residents and forced changes in their behavior. One of the clearest examples of how the development project reshaped both the cultural and physical landscape of Acapulco involves the Costera's effect on local fishermen. Fishing was, not surprisingly, an important activity in Acapulco, and fishermen lived close to the water. They and other small boat owners used a beach called La Playa de Rincón (The Corner Beach) as a dry dock to haul out and repair their boats. However, the construction of the Costera, which was up to forty meters wide in places, required that both the beach and the area directly behind it be filled in. As a result, the state forced fishermen to move to new houses and to find new places to repair their boats.[56]

Hotel Development

After the government completed the Mexico City–Acapulco highway in 1927, tourism grew so rapidly that, just four years later, the eponymous *Terry's Guide* called Acapulco "a popular seaside resort" and referred to several hotels in town—even choosing one, the Miramar, as the most popular. The number of hotels skyrocketed in the next twenty years, and by 1954 there were 130 hotels in Acapulco under construction.[57]

The parts of the city where Acapulco's hotels were located changed during this period. The first modest guesthouses were downtown, in the area now known as Acapulco Tradicional, while the first hotels directed specifically and primarily at international tourists (including the famous El Mirador at La Quebrada, where the cliff divers jump) were located on the Peninsula de las Playas. After the construction of the Costera Miguel Alemán, however, the locus of hotel development shifted to the broad sweep of sandy beaches that stretched around Acapulco Bay, and away from the geographically cramped parts of the city. In the 1950s, large hotels like the Acapulco Hilton and El Presidente began to appear around the entire length of the bay, a process of development that continued through the 1960s and 1970s. By the 1980s, the primary locus of development had shifted to the area around Revolcadero Beach, now commonly known as Acapulco Diamante (Diamond Acapulco).

Many of the new hotels that opened up in the late 1920s and beyond were luxurious, at least in comparison with the preexisting ones, and were out of the price range of most Mexican tourists. The Miramar was located on what is now Calle Benito Juárez, two blocks southwest of the Zócalo, and opened in 1928 with twenty-four rooms, one of which even had a private bath. Prominent Mexican politicians such as Presidents Emilio Portes Gil and Pascual Ortíz Rubio stayed there.[58] The number of hotels in Acapulco continued to increase through the 1930s, with the major works of construction, like that of El Mirador, on the Peninsula de las Playas. By 1944 hotels were "everywhere," and El Mirador was now accompanied by Los Flamingos on the highest point of the peninsula.

Two separate hotel markets developed in Acapulco. In March 1934, the federal Department of Tourism released a list of the approved prices for lodging in various cities in Mexico, including Acapulco.[59] The best rooms at El Mirador cost twice as much as those at a guesthouse in the center of the city, an indication that the fragmentation of the market had already begun. In 1944, rooms at El Mirador cost thirty-five pesos for one person and sixty for two, while the smaller hotels aimed at middle-class Mexicans—also on the Peninsula, but down near Caleta Beach—charged rates like the Costa Verde's ten pesos for a room without private bath or the Eugenia's thirteen for a room with a bath.[60]

Compared to both the preexisting hotels and the standard of living of ordinary Acapulqueños, El Mirador was paradise. The owner/manager, Carlos Barnard Maldonado, had worked for a foreign oil company in his hometown of Minatitlán, Veracruz, and had retired with enough money to build a hotel in Acapulco.[61] He built the original hotel, consisting of a series of bungalows clustered around a main building, on cliffs overlooking the Pacific Ocean. The bungalows were placed to get the prevailing westerly sea breezes, and stone paths descended to beaches 120 feet below. As important for guests as the location, though, were the services the hotel offered. The hotel also had its own private source of drinking water, a nearby mountain spring.[62] Not just a luxury, the spring was required to provide potable water in an era when even the most expensive hotels experienced regular water shortages.

For American visitors, the hotels cushioned the foreignness of the experience by recreating the United States as much as possible. Thus, on his six-month tour of Mexico, the poet Selden Rodman stayed at El Mirador, noting that it was "a hotel where the rooms, the swimming pool, and the prices are American." He noticed the appearance of "monster hotels" including the Hilton, where construction had ceased for the moment, leaving a honeycomb of poured concrete ten stories high. The Hilton and other high-rise hotels like it soon formed the heart of Acapulco's hotel zone, as the area of the landscape devoted to hotels and tourism expanded around the bay.[63]

Although the beachside hotels on the bay supplemented most of the older hotels, El Mirador maintained its status, primarily because of the iconic cliff divers, or *clavadistas*, who dived from a platform outside the hotel more than forty meters into the water below. The image of cliff divers in Acapulco is a classic one, and they still dive today. It was immortalized in American popular culture by the film *Fun in Acapulco* (1963), in which Elvis Presley plays a former acrobat, down on his luck and stranded in Acapulco. His character overcomes his fear of heights diving off La Quebrada.

In spite of the increase in tourism, all was not perfect in Acapulco. The serious gaps in Acapulco's infrastructure were public knowledge even outside the city. In 1944, the tourism commission of the federal senate heard testimony about the abuses and neglect of local authorities in Acapulco. People complained that electricity was available for only a few hours each day, the streets were unpaved, only hotels with diesel pumps and artesian wells had a regular supply of potable water, and the price of fish and seafood skyrocketed during the high season to the point that locals could not afford them.[64] On top of the poor infrastructure, the local government failed to ensure that Acapulqueños did not commit abuses against tourists, such as overcharging and rudeness. Notably, these issues received national attention just before the Junta Federal became much more active in Acapulco's development. By focusing on the inability of the local government to create infrastructure and maintain the correct attitude toward tourists, the Mexican state justified its intervention and the federalization of development.

In spite of increased efforts on the part of the Junta Federal, the state was unable to address the problems. Eighteen months later, the owners of the principal hotels in Acapulco again began publicly complaining about the obstacles to the city's development: lack of electrical service; deficient water service; and the need to import meat, vegetables, and often even fish and seafood from Mexico City. Despite all the government promises, they complained, any hotel that wanted electricity had to implement costly private installations.[65]

A decade later, the situation had not improved, even with the considerable resources the federal government poured into the city. There was enough negative publicity about Acapulco in 1953 that Melchor Perusquía, former president of the Junta Federal de Mejoras Materiales de Acapulco, requested that *Excélsior* publish his response to their series "Acapulco en Quiebra" (Acapulco in Crisis).[66] In a thinly veiled defense of the Alemán regime, Perusquía explained that Acapulco's water system worked, the electric plant produced sufficient electricity to meet the city's needs, and the Junta Federal had the equipment to clear fallen rocks off the highway. According to Perusquía, the only reason for the recent decline in tourism in Acapulco was, ironically, the Junta Federal's work to improve the highway from Mexico City, along which eighty percent of the visitors to Acapulco normally traveled.[67]

The city continued to grow rapidly, and the federal government planned to invest more money into its beautification. In January 1955, the Junta Federal announced a plan to clean the beaches, add lights for evening use, construct a boat launch to protect swimmers, and repave and replant the entire Costera.[68] It also planned to fix the Carretera Escenica (Scenic Highway), an extension of the Costera which was in poor condition. In spite of the rhetoric about creating conditions for tourism and the violence used to bend local residents to its will, the Junta Federal was inefficient and ineffective. For example, more than ten years after the Junta Federal began the work, it was still laying tubing along the length of the Costera for the potable water system. The Costera and the Scenic Highway were constantly in need of repair, and the sewage treatment plant did not function.[69]

Many foreign tourists did not notice that the city was a mess because they ignored everything off the tourist path. The map in Byron Steel's *Let's Visit Mexico* (1946) demonstrates various ways in which tourist Acapulco was separated from the actual city. First, the map names the city "Mexico's Tourist Paradise"—not an official name nor a translation of "Acapulco" but the author's idea of what the city should be to his readers. Second, only those landmarks and physical features of the landscape that are relevant to tourism are mentioned, such as the major tourist beaches, the roads to recre-

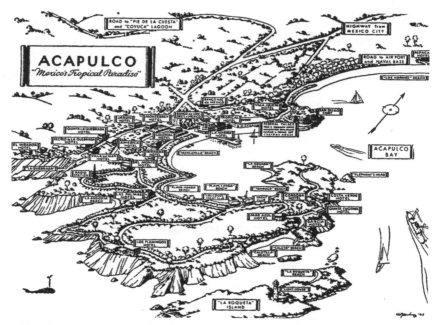

1. Map of Acapulco, Mexico's Tropical Paradise. FROM BYRON STEEL, *LET'S VISIT MEXICO* (NEW YORK: ROBERT M. MCBRIDE AND CO., 1946).

ational destinations, and the roads required to enter and leave Acapulco. Third, the only buildings on the map are those related to tourism: of the twenty-nine buildings featured, twenty-one are hotels, two are yacht clubs, two are landmarks (radio tower, lighthouse), two are banks, one is a tourist attraction (the fort), and one is the federal building (useful for post office, telegraph, and fishing licenses). This reinforced the perception that Acapulco existed solely for tourists and that the hotels constituted the most important part of the city, and it helped visitors ignore the poverty and the crises facing Acapulqueños.

Steel's text reinforces the idea that tourism existed without relevance for or reference to Acapulqueños. He wrote, "The recent tourist invasion of the town does not seem to have affected the way of life among the native residents. They still fish with ancestral spears and nets." While his words in part reflect the tourist gaze of a Western observer, the more profound implication is that the creation of multiple hotels and the arrival of thousands of pleasure-seekers would not have any impact on the city, nor would the city change to better take advantage of these visitors. Paradoxically, the seeds of change are visible in the text, as someone is serving the coconut milk, staffing the hotels, and skillfully operating the deep-sea fishing boats that the author recommends.[70]

Other observers gushed about Acapulco's merits and growth, such as Sydney Clark, a prolific travel writer and world traveler whose *All the Best . . .* travel series included a volume in 1952 on Mexico. Clark's general comments about tourism in the city, however, are perhaps the most interesting part of his analysis. Clark called Acapulco "as beautiful as any of her most favored rivals in the old or new world" and said that "in winter, when Acapulco's magnetism is at its strongest, all the hotels are full, and this despite the enormous recent increase—it is a phenomenon of the first travel magnitude—in accommodations of every type." The guide listed sixty hotels, a dozen more than in Mexico City.[71]

Clark saw Acapulco through a lens of privilege, primarily from the self-contained luxury hotels where he stayed. When his impressions are contrasted with Sybille Bedford's *Mexican Journey* (1953), it becomes apparent that there were multiple tourist experiences in Acapulco. Although Bedford had gone searching for the "Saint Moritz of the tropics where Americans fast and rich are supposed to go for big game fishing as well as dancing," she instead found an unpaved town, baking in its own mud. "Imagine a major resort, imagine Cannes, consisting solely of the Carlton, the Majestic and the Martínez, some acres of churned mud and fly-blown stands, and a strip of boarding houses," she griped. Bedford had arrived before the tourist season began, and the other guests at her hotel consisted of a Mexican family and four "Saxonians"—long-term residents of Mexico City who "sat in the dining room in their underwear, drinking whiskey and eating plum-cake."[72]

Bedford, an English writer, was just as biased as Clark by her perceptions of what a correct resort should entail and she probably overstated the decrepit nature of Acapulco. It is accurate to say that in the early 1950s Acapulco was already developing the mixture of luxurious hotels and poverty that characterized its existence through the century. The visitors who came in the early 1950s were, as today, divided among foreign tourists, weekend visitors from Mexico City, and property owners.

While most external observers applauded the replacement of undeveloped Acapulco with hotels, restaurants, and roads, some preferred the "primitive aspects" of the old Acapulco and questioned the development process. "Thousands of tons of cement and iron wrapped its traditional beauty," lamented one Mexican writer. "It took the appearance of a savage queen, who, quickly, by the imperatives of civilization, covered her nudity with an aristocratic, silken cloak." According to this observer, at the same time that this first, "wild" Acapulco was being covered with a modern city, people's behavior was becoming more motivated by greed and profit—indeed, the physical and cultural changes went hand in hand.[73]

Erna Fergusson, in her *Mexico Revisited*, was more perceptive than most foreign observers. Although she did not comment on the land invasions, the political unrest, or the growing numbers of landless Mexicans who populated the poorer neighborhoods, she did note the divisions between the experiences of Mexicans and foreign tourists. Fergusson also pointed out the connections between the wealth of Alemanistas and Acapulco: "Ex-President Alemán maintains a yacht in the bay which has been the scene of many political conferences that are whispered about but not reported in the press. Other political figures, enriched by office, make Acapulco their home."[74]

By the late 1950s, a visit to tourist Acapulco resembled the modern resort experience. Developers built all-inclusive high-rise hotels along the Costera, there were international restaurants and nightclubs, and American Airlines advertised it as a destination. The experience of tourists in Acapulco, though, and the creation of this experience required a series of changes and disruptions. The state had taken control of land and development in Acapulco, displacing the old Acapulco with something different. The Junta Federal sanitized the beaches and expropriated the ejidos, and investors shifted the locus of development and entertainment to the Costera. Meanwhile, more and more migrants seeking work and housing poured into the city. For these hundreds of thousands of poor Mexicans, their time in Acapulco was a daily struggle, a dramatic disjuncture from ideas of paradise on the Pacific.

Notes

1. The word *ejido* refers to a system of communal or cooperative farming in Mexico. An ejiditario is a member of such a cooperative farm.
2. Pablo Bailon Mendoza, Presidente de la Sociedad de Padres de Familia, et al., to Adolfo López Mateos (hereafter ALM) et al., September 21, 1959, Archivo General de la Nación (hereafter AGN), ALM, 404.1/1418.
3. See, e.g., William Lytle Schurz, "Mexico, Peru, and the Manila Galleon," *Hispanic American Historical Review* 1 (November 1918): 389–402.
4. See, e.g., John C. Simmons, *Journal* (1852), 44, Beinecke Library, Yale University,

WA MSS S-1434; Demas Barnes, *From the Atlantic to the Pacific, Overland: A Series of Letters* (New York: D. Van Nostrand, 1866), 128–29; Lillie I. Well, *My Journey to California*, n.p., Beinecke Library, WA MSS S-1669.

5. Anonymous, *Diary of a Voyage from New York to California, 1874–1875*. See also Simmons, *Journal*, and Well, *My Journey to California*.

6. Barnes, *From the Atlantic to the Pacific*, 129.

7. See, e.g., Great Britain Admiralty, *Geographical Section of the Naval Intelligence Division, Naval Staff: A Handbook of Mexico* (London: His Majesty's Stationery Office, n.d.), 222.

8. On June 7, 1880, the Mexican federal government granted a charter to the State of Guerrero to construct a railroad from Mexico City to Acapulco, a distance of some 456 km. See Lorenzo Castro, *The Republic of Mexico in 1882* (New York: Thompson and Moreau, 1882), 158; National Railways of Mexico, "Map of National Railways of Mexico and Operated Lines," 1911 and 1923, Seeley G. Mudd Library, Yale University, Latin American Collection, Mexico Eha1 Miscellaneous Pamphlets, Folders, etc. Descriptive of Mexico.

9. Rogelio Vizcaino and Paco Ignacio Taibo II, *El socialismo en un solo puerto* (Mexico City: Editoral Galache, 1983), 17.

10. Ibid., passim. See José R. Benítez, *Guía histórica y descriptiva de la carretera México-Acapulco* (Chilpancingo: Gobierno del Estado de Guerrero, 1991).

11. On early Mexican tourism and the railways, see Douglas A. Murphy, "Mexican Tourism, 1876–1940: The Socio-Economic, Political, and Infrastructural Effects of a Developing Leisure Industry" (M.A. thesis, University of North Carolina, 1988). Examples of promotional literature that exclude Acapulco can be found in publications such as *Grafton's Winter Tours through Mexico*, 1889, and *Mexico: A Foreign Land a Step Away*, 1909, Mudd Documents Library, Latin American Collection, Mexico Eha1 Miscellaneous Pamphlets, Folders, etc. Descriptive of Mexico.

12. Comisión Nacional de Caminos, *Caminos* (Mexico City: Banco de México, S.A.: April 1930), n.p.

13. Ibid. For a detailed description of the road and trail to Mexico City, see Great Britain Admiralty, *Geographical Section of the Naval Intelligence Division, Naval Staff*, 353–56.

14. See Secretaría de Comunicaciones y Obras Públicas, *Los caminos de México/The Roads of Mexico* (Mexico City: Comision Nacional de Caminos, 1931), 79–87.

15. See Marian Storm, *Prologue to Mexico: The Story of a Search for a Place* (New York: Knopf, 1931), 51; Michael Scully and Virginia Scully, *Motorists' Guide to Mexico* (Dallas: South-West Press, 1933), 156; Harry A. Franck, *Trailing Cortez through Mexico* (New York: Frederick A. Stokes, 1935), 303; Leone and Alice-Leone Moats, *Off to Mexico* (New York: Charles Scribner's Sons, 1935), 98; Louis H. Warner, *Mexico's Progress Demands Its Price* (Boston: Chapman and Grimes, 1937), 265.

16. Scully and Scully, *Motorists' Guide to Mexico*, 156.

17. Warner, *Mexico's Progress Demands Its Price*, 265. He saw bus travel as the way to "mingle with the common people and their belongings."

18. See Anita Brenner, *Your Mexican Holiday: A Modern Guide* (New York: G. P. Putnam's Sons, 1932), 174; Scully and Scully, *Motorists' Guide to Mexico*, 156; Franck, *Trailing Cortez through Mexico*, 303–11; and Moats, *Off to Mexico*, 98.

19. Warner, *Mexico's Progress Demands Its Price*, 287–88.

20. PEMEX Travel Club, *Driving down to Mexico* (Mexico City: 1940), n.p., Mudd Documents Library, Latin American Collection. The PEMEX Travel Club was founded to guarantee safety and ease travel for U.S. tourists after the petroleum expropriation. See Murphy, "Mexican Tourism, 1876–1940," 113.

21. *New York Times*, December 31, 1939.

22. *New York Times*, October 6, 1940.

23. See Francisco A. Gomezjara, *Bonapartismo y lucha campesina en la Costa Grande de Guerrero* (Mexico City: Editorial Posada, 1979), 188–89; *Palpitaciones porteñas*, July 1945, and Alejandro Gómez Maganda, *Acapulco en mi vida y en el tiempo* (Mexico City: Libro Mex, 1960), 42–43. Gómez Maganda was a local journalist who became a close friend of Miguel Alemán, which led to his election to major government posts for the state of Guerrero.

24. On Alemán's political career, see Enrique Krauze, *Mexico: Biography of Power*, trans. Hank Heifetz (1997; reprint, New York: HarperPerennial, 1998), 526–600. On his early interest in tourism, see pp. 521 and 545. For more detail on the permutations of organizational structure for the government agency in charge of tourism, see Munir Chalela Solano, *Una Secretaría de Turismo en México* (tesis profesional, UNAM Facultad de Derecho, 1973), Jorge C. Carmona Patiño, *Evolución de los organismos de turismo en México* (Mexico City: SECTUR, 1986).

25. Comisión Administradora de Terrenos de Acapulco, *Informe de trabajos realizados*, October 1950, and Eva Padilla Vda. de Dalgadillo y Francisco Vásquez to Miguel Alemán Valdés (hereafter MAV), August 9, 1952, both in AGN, MAV, 741.1/345. Alejandro Martínez Carbajal adds that they also built barracks.

26. *Diario Oficial*, August 8, 1934. There were Juntas Federales de Mejoras Materiales in most border and port cities, as they were expected to use a tax on imports and exports to finance infrastructure development.

27. Ibid., January 28, 1947.

28. Ibid., February 13, 1945.

29. Ibid., March 20, 1947. This occurred shortly after Alemán ordered the expropriation of the *ejidos*, their land to be sold *only* to the Junta Federal de Mejoras Materiales de Acapulco. There were seven members, a clear majority of whom were to be directly appointed by the federal government, including the president. There were representatives from the Secretaría de Bienes Nacionales e Inspección Administrativa (Federal Property and Administrative Inspection), the Secretaría de Comunicaciones y Obras Públicas (Communications and Public

Works), the Secretaría de Recursos Hidráulicos (Hydraulic Resources), the Secretaría de Salubridad y Asistencia (Public Health and Welfare); and, in a port like Acapulco, also the Secretaría de Marina (Navy), the mayor, and someone from business or industry in the locality. The state of Guerrero was excluded. The tight federal control was even more apparent in the body responsible for the disposition of the lands once they had been expropriated, the Comisión Administrativa de Terrenos, which had only three members, all federally appointed.

30. Andrew Sackett, interview with Marta Contreras (daughter of Carlos Contreras, author of the *Plano Regulador de Acapulco*), July 3, 2000, Pedregal de San Ángel, México; Carlos Contreras to Manuel Ávila Camacho (hereafter MAC), July 15, 1943, AGN, MAC, 545.21/21; Carlos Contreras to MAC, December 15, 1945, AGN, MAC, 545.21/21; *Trópico*, May 27, 1945.

31. See, e.g., Carlos Contreras, *El plano regulador del Distrito Federal 1933*, Biblioteca Justíno Fernández, UNAM.

32. *Trópico*, August 12, 1945.

33. The advertisement for Fraccionamiento Caleta in the February 27, 1944, issue of *Trópico*, for example, indicates that almost all the lots had been sold.

34. Bryon Steel, *Let's Visit Mexico* (New York: Robert M. McBride and Co., 1946), 291.

35. Paula García de Díaz et al. to MAC, April 4, 1941, AGN, MAC, 509/5.

36. Juana Quiróz et al. to MAV, January 25, 1947, AGN, MAV, 418.5/8.

37. Ibid.

38. Carlos E. Adame, *Obra y semblanza de un hombre: Acapulco y Melchor Perusquía* [1952], 56.

39. Why would a well-funded government agency want to increase revenues? Partially, at least, to fuel the accumulation of wealth by those in charge. After Perusquía, for example, left Acapulco (a place he had arrived with few resources), he privately developed large suburbs of Mexico City in the 1950s. The *puesteros* were not the only ones forced to leave Caleta; Maximino Ávila Camacho, brother of the ex-president, had had a mansion on the beach and his widow was forced to give it up.

40. Paula García de Díaz et al. to MAC, April 4, 1941, AGN, MAC, 509/5.

41. Juana Quiróz et al. to MAV, September 20, 1949, AGN, MAV, 418.5/8.

42. *Acapulco: Revista Illustrada*, November 16, 1949.

43. See, e.g., *Trópico*, May 8, 1952.

44. See, e.g., *Trópico*, November 2, 1956, and November 24, 1956.

45. See *Trópico*, April 18, 1956, and November 27, 1957.

46. AGN, MAV, 404.1/1188, May 24, 1947; *Palpitaciones Porteñas*, June 14, 1947.

47. Melchor Perusquía, Presidente de la Junta Federal de Mejoras Materiales de Acapulco, to Roberto Amoros, Oficial Mayor de la Presidencia de la República, August 7, 1948, AGN, MAV, 404.1/1188.

48. Liga Central de Comunidades Agrarias de la República, March 11, 1950, AGN, MAV, 404.1/1188.

49. Andrew Sackett, interview with Marta Contreras, July 3, 2000, and internal memorandum from Melchor Perrusquía to the Secretario de Bienes Nacionales e Inspección Administrativa (his most senior supervisor aside from the president), March 22, 1947, AGN, MAV, 545.22/30.

50. Interview with Nicolás Román Benítez, June 8, 2000.

51. Comité ejecutivo de Unión de Colonos de "El Progreso" (Nicolás Román B., President, Macario Mora, Srio.) to Adolfo Ruíz Cortines (hereafter ARC), January 19, 1954, and July 6, 1954, AGN, ARC, 111/445.

52. Unión de Colonos "Lázaro Cárdenas" to MAV, October 4, 1949, AGN, MAV, 503.11/315.

53. Melchor Perusquía, quoted in *Trópico*, November 25, 1945.

54. Adame, *Obra y semblanza de un hombre*, 29.

55. Ruben H. Luz Castillo, *Recuerdos de Acapulco* (Acapulco, n.d.), 103.

56. AGN, MAV, 609/197, April 16, 1947.

57. *El Universal*, August 16, 1954.

58. Franciso R. Escudero, *Origen y evolución del turismo en Acapulco* (Acapulco: H. Ayuntamiento Constitucional de Acapulco/Universidad Americana de Acapulco, 1997), 60, 106−7.

59. *El Universal*, March 22, 1934.

60. Frances Toor, *New Guide to Mexico* (Mexico City: Frances Toor Studios, 1944), 146−47.

61. Escudero, *Origen y evolución del turismo en Acapulco*, 90.

62. T. Philip Terry, *Terry's Guide to Mexico: The New Standard Guidebook to the Mexican Republic* (Boston: Houghton Mifflin, 1935), 461b−461e.

63. Selden Rodman, *Mexican Journal: The Conquerors Conquered* (New York: Devlin Adair, 1958), 182.

64. *Novedades*, January 8, 1944.

65. *Excélsior*, June 14, 1945.

66. *Excélsior*, January 8, 9, and 10, 1954.

67. Melchor Perrusquía, "Melchor Perrusquía habla acerca de las inversiones hechas en Acapulco," *Excélsior*, January 15, 1954.

68. *Excélsior*, January 26, 1955.

69. A. Gutiérrez et al. to Srio. de salubridad y asistencia, June 1, 1953, Archivo del Secretaría de Salubridad y Asistencia, 01/172.9(727.1)/1.

70. Steel, *Let's Visit Mexico*, 290−95.

71. Sydney Clark, *All the Best in Mexico* (New York: Dodd, Mead, 1952), 213−14.

72. Sybille Bedford, *The Sudden View: A Mexican Journey* (London: Victor Gollancz, 1953), 224−26.

73. Rafael Alvarez Dávalos, "Decadencia de Acapulco," *El Universal*, May 18, 1953.

74. Erna Fergusson, *Mexico Revisited* (New York: Knopf, 1955), 257−60.

LISA PINLEY COVERT

COLONIAL OUTPOST TO ARTISTS' MECCA

Conflict and Collaboration in the Development
of San Miguel de Allende's Tourist Industry

In 1960 a journalist from *El Vocero del Norte*, a newspaper published in San Miguel de Allende, Guanajuato, urged his fellow citizens to set aside their differences and support the tourist industry in their town, "the true Cradle of Mexican Independence."[1] Unlike other destinations where tourists merely pass through, he argued, San Miguel makes visitors "feel more Mexican" because of its important contributions to the nation. Indeed, as municipal officials had reminded the president of Mexico only a few years earlier, San Miguel was the home of Mexico's first soldier, first diplomat, and first municipal government, not to mention the "purest architectural inheritance of the colonial period."[2] The *El Vocero del Norte* article appeared in the midst of a heated debate over the future of San Miguel's tourist industry, and skeptics were right to challenge the writer's central premise. Ironically, the very industry that supposedly made visitors "feel Mexican" emerged largely from the efforts of a Hollywood film star, a Peruvian intellectual, and an artist from Chicago.

This essay explores the historical development of the tourist industry in San Miguel de Allende. Whereas many histories of the Mexican tourist industry suggest top-down strategies to capitalize on Mexico's heritage and attract foreign visitors, in San Miguel local elites sought out an international solution—in the form of tourism—to solve local economic problems. The tourist industry in San Miguel was not a state-led endeavor but rather a result of the efforts of a multinational cast of characters, international events such as the Great Depression and World War II, and even the legislation of foreign governments, thus demonstrating the importance of placing local histories within international and transnational contexts. The central component of this international approach to tourist development was the establishment of an art school that would bring artists from around the globe to San Miguel. Despite the multinational collaboration in the development of this industry, its early successes relied upon the extent to which prospective visitors perceived San Miguel to be a typical Mexican town.

The lack of a state-led strategy for tourist development in San Miguel does not suggest the absence of the federal government or national tourist organizations altogether. This essay contends that their involvement existed primarily on a discursive level rather than a material one. In other words, government discourse about national progress and unity fundamentally shaped the possibilities for the successful development of tourism in San Miguel, even in the absence of government financial support or direct participation. By presenting San Miguel as a typical Mexican town, early tourist promoters attempted to insert San Miguel into the national narrative posited by postrevolutionary government officials and reproduced by government agencies, tourist organizations, and guidebooks. This narrative emphasized the success of the revolution and juxtaposed certain destinations in a way that denoted the teleological progress of the nation, from the grandeur of the ancient pyramids to the modern cosmopolitan capital.[3] As San Miguel's tourist industry developed over time, locally or internationally produced narratives about San Miguel emerged that often contradicted this national narrative.[4] It was then that federal officials attempted to intervene more directly in the development of San Miguel's tourist industry. Ultimately, the story of San Miguel's tourist industry reveals the power of the Mexican government to shape patterns of development, tourist and otherwise, discursively even when it did not directly participate; however, it also reveals the limits of government discourse and the threats that alternative narratives posed.

The Mexican Revolution and the subsequent conflicts between the Catholic Church and the postrevolutionary state provided the context for the development of San Miguel's tourist industry. Since the colonial period the local economy had been linked to the silver mining industry in nearby Guanajuato, supplying the mines with textiles, leather goods, and tallow. The Guanajuato mines experienced an almost constant decline in production after Mexican independence, however, and despite a brief resurgence at the turn of the twentieth century the artisanal industries in San Miguel and other communities in the region struggled to remain relevant.[5] The diminution of these industries did not signal an inevitable economic collapse in San Miguel; indeed, the local agricultural industry was expanding. The violence and chaos of the Mexican Revolution and its aftermath resulted in a dramatic demographic decline, however, and extremely limited economic options in 1920s San Miguel.

Although San Miguel was not the site of major armed conflicts during the revolution, the population suffered nonetheless. The agricultural industry waned as workers joined the various revolutionary factions or immigrated to other parts of Mexico and the United States. Droughts, floods, and frost contributed to the hardship, with the state of Guanajuato losing approximately 75 percent of its corn crop in 1917 alone.[6] Last, typhus and other diseases spread rapidly, acting as both a cause and effect of migration. These dire conditions led to rampant banditry in San Miguel and many of the town's elite families left for Mexico City or Guadalajara. By 1920 the population had ebbed. Aside from the negative effects of war, the revolution brought few tangible changes to San Miguel. The large landholders in the countryside mitigated early attempts at agrarian reform by turning to a sharecropping system where the workers received plots of land and contracts guaranteeing daily wage labor and access to other resources. Almost half of San Miguel's rural adult male population held sharecropping contracts by 1930.[7] Elite families in the urban center of San Miguel retained a tenuous hold on local politics, but the unceasing threat of political and economic instability in the region eroded their grip.

A sense of normalcy descended on San Miguel after the revolution, but it was short-lived. By the mid-1920s President Plutarco Elías Calles, under siege on diplomatic and domestic political fronts, attempted to reassert his authority through enforcement of the anticlerical provisions of the Constitution of 1917. The promulgation of the Calles Law in July 1926 involved the confiscation of church property, the prohibition of public worship, the expulsion of foreign priests, and the closure of parochial schools, convents, and monasteries. The effects of the Calles Law were extensive and devastating in San Miguel because of the local religious tradition and the centrality of Catholicism in the daily lives of many in the community. The Catholic Church had a strong institutional presence in San Miguel where churches, seminaries, convents, chapels, and other religious buildings occupied practically every block of the city center. The majority of these buildings date to the colonial period, when wealth from the regional silver mining industry overflowed into San Miguel and the local elites offered thanks and attempted to ensure their salvation through generous contributions to the parish and the religious orders. At different points in its history, San Miguel, and specifically the Sanctuary at Atotonilco just outside of town, has been the destination for innumerable religious pilgrims from across Mexico. In fact Atotonilco is the site where Miguel Hidalgo y Costilla, widely recognized as the father of Mexican independence, obtained the famous banner of the Virgin of Guadalupe which he used to rally followers against Spanish colonial rule in 1810.

The unanticipated armed response of Mexican Catholics between 1926 and 1929, known as the *Cristiada*, delayed the enforcement of many provisions of the Calles Law. The majority of San Miguel residents were sympathetic to, or even outright supportive of the Cristiada. As soon as the Calles Law went into effect, the local branches of the Knights of Columbus and the Catholic Association of Mexican Youth began distributing flyers announcing a national economic boycott. Groups met clandestinely to celebrate the Catholic sacraments and to plan an armed rebellion and by September 1926 approximately 4,000 men in San Miguel were prepared to join others across the region to fight the federal government in the name of Christ the King.[8] The government stationed federal troops in San Miguel's principal plaza, converting a convent called Las Monjas into barracks and stables. This presence provoked attacks from the rebels, known as *Cristeros*, who would descend from their strongholds in the surrounding hills and engage the federal troops in the main square. The troops hanged the mutilated bodies of captured Cristeros from trees in the city center as a warning to their supporters, an image that continued to haunt eyewitnesses decades later.[9]

The federal government did confiscate some church property in San Miguel during the Cristiada. Nearly a year after the Calles Law went into effect, in July of 1927, the municipal government in San Miguel assigned people to monitor eleven of the main church buildings including chapels, convents, seminaries, and schools, and reported to the office of the governor that several others were closed permanently.[10] The process of officially nationalizing actual buildings took several years and did not originate from the desire to preserve them as part of the national heritage.[11] Rather, it reflected the drive to secularize the religious spaces by converting them into schools, military quarters, and government offices. For example, upon inspecting the contents and layout of the Parroquia, the main parish church on San Miguel's central plaza, the agent of the Federal Property Office noted that the government could potentially use the annex of the building for a school. The government nationalized the annex and placed it under the jurisdiction of the Ministry of Public Education in 1929.[12]

Government rhetoric about church property in San Miguel shifted following the peace accords of 1929 as part of a new strategy for unifying the nation and consolidating federal power. The Mexican government and the Catholic hierarchy ostensibly agreed to coexist peacefully; the government offered amnesty to the Cristeros and the churches opened their doors once again. This peace settlement meant that Mexican government officials could no longer nationalize church property with the explicit purpose of secularizing it, and thus a new logic emerged. Memoranda from federal and state officials to the municipal government legitimized continued surveillance of church property and activities in San Miguel by arguing that the buildings were "monuments of great artistic and historic value" and, moreover, emblematic of Mexican identity.[13] Catholics used the buildings under the condition that they conserved them, which meant that they could not post announcements on the walls and that they must avoid well-intentioned but historically inaccurate renovations.[14] These poorly enforced and highly subjective restrictions were less about actually preserving these structures than they were about building a national consciousness that superseded local and religious identities. In other words, by continuing to exert some control over religious spaces and by referring to the buildings as part of the nation's heritage, the federal government was attempting to consolidate authority culturally at a time when it was still too weak to do so politically in provincial towns like San Miguel.

The legacy of the church-state conflict and the onset of global economic depression intensified federal government attempts to create a sense of national unity. With plans underway to celebrate the twentieth anniversary of the beginning of the Mexican Revolution, the Ministry of the Interior urged citizens to set aside personal pride and old grudges and instead unite to celebrate the accomplishments of the nation. Because the "triumph of the Revolution [was] definitive and evident," the ministry argued, Mexico could embark on a mission of reconstruction and reconciliation.[15] Moreover, in acknowledging the successes of the revolution, Mexicans would legitimize the attempts of the federal government to consolidate power. The depression added urgency to the calls for nationalism. Through economic nationalism and commercial development, Mexico could moderate the effects of the Great Depression while simultaneously bolstering national pride and unity. The local implications of these national questions were enormous for San Miguel.

Because the majority of San Miguel residents resisted such revolutionary aims as anticlericalism and agrarian reform, there was no place for San Miguel in the emerging national narrative that hailed the revolution's achievements. This narrative portrayed a nation liberated from the tyranny of Porfirio Díaz and the Catholic Church where all people, including formerly marginalized indigenous communities, would stand as equals and share in the fruits of the revolutionary government's programs. Clearly, this narrative would have little resonance in a community that largely viewed the revolution in negative terms. While the national government declared the struggle a success and a *fait accompli*, in San Miguel *agraristas* and former Cristeros continued to battle over rights to land, socialist education, and religious freedom, in what is known as the Second Cristiada, with no clear resolution in sight.[16] Meanwhile, the local economy lagged. The revolution did not bring peace and prosperity to the residents of San Miguel, so they would have to seek out other avenues of change and economic development.

The Arrival of the Hollywood Star: José Mojica

Several newcomers to San Miguel, both Mexican and foreign, catalyzed local economic growth by developing a tourist industry and reintegrating San Miguel into the national narrative. Among these, the international opera and film star José Mojica played a central role. Born in San Gabriel, Jalisco, Mojica moved with his mother to Mexico City at the age of eight where he eventually studied music at the Academy of San Carlos. A series of minor theater roles and lucky breaks eventually led him to Chicago, where he performed with the Metropolitan and Chicago Civic Opera companies and received contracts for larger roles during the 1920s. His reputation grew, especially among female opera fans, and in 1929 Fox Films sought him out to star in films. Over a ten-year period he starred in sixteen films and had lesser roles in many others. Mojica first visited San Miguel in 1934 to attend the wedding of his friend, the Mexican bullfighter Pepe Ortíz. He enjoyed the town so much that in 1935, near the pinnacle of his fame, he decided to purchase and renovate an estate facing the Benito Juárez Park in San Miguel for himself and his ailing mother.[17]

Mojica was a cosmopolitan figure accustomed to the cultural milieu of large cities and he led the revitalization of cultural and intellectual life in San Miguel. He quickly earned a reputation for hosting lively parties at his new home, which he named Granja Santa Monica. Many long-time residents nostalgically look back on those gatherings as the center of social life in San Miguel.[18] Nationally and internationally renowned film stars, artists, composers, singers, and intellectuals made frequent appearances at these soirees, among them the singer Pedro Vargas, the comedian Cantinflas, the actress Dolores del Río, the great Mexican artists of the time, and a host of others from Latin America and Europe including the Chilean intellectual Pablo Neruda and the Russian ballerina Xenia Zarina. Beyond throwing memorable parties, Mojica played an integral role in the creation of a theater group called Companía de Aficionados de San Miguel and a lecture series which brought in speakers such as the writer Gabriela Mistral and the historian Manuel Toussaint.[19] Although these activities injected a certain vibrancy and excitement into the town, the relationship that Mojica formed with Toussaint set San Miguel on an entirely new path altogether.

Mojica and Toussaint led a coalition of local political leaders, intellectuals, and artists (Mexican and foreign) in an effort to obtain government recognition of San Miguel's historic value to the nation, preserve its ambiance, and develop a tourist industry. Government recognition was an essential component because it would legitimize San Miguel's claim to historic and aesthetic importance for outsiders, particularly tourists. Toussaint, a prominent Mexican specialist in colonial art and architecture, drew from his background in historic preservation and promotion in the town of Taxco to assist Mojica and others in the development of a similar program for San Miguel. In 1928, the Guerrero state legislature declared Taxco the first Mexican town protected under conservation law. The law aimed to preserve Taxco's architecture, particularly buildings like the Santa Prisca church which dated to the colonial era. Toussaint led the efforts behind this legislation and made a series of arguments for the preservation of Taxco, later published as *Tasco: Su historia, sus monumentos, características actuales y posibilidades turísticas.*[20] While the majority of the book emphasizes the importance of preserving Taxco's historic sites, as the title suggests Toussaint also viewed preservation and tourist development as the primary vehicles for reviving its local economy. Toussaint's program for Taxco was quite successful, placing it on the regular circuit for artists and other tourists by the mid-1930s.[21]

Toussaint outlined six recommendations for the preservation and development of the town, which became a blueprint for San Miguel. First, he emphasized the need to demonstrate why the town was worthy of preservation by enumerating its attractive natural characteristics and resurrecting its historical significance. The second stage involved the preservation of those natural and historical characteristics so that the town would maintain its ambience. This stage included the creation of building codes so that new developments would conform to their historic surroundings. Third, the community should have these codes protected under state or federal law. Whereas the first three guidelines addressed the physical appearance of the town, the last three highlighted the importance of social and cultural life. Toussaint's fourth recommendation was to foster local traditions such as festivals, artisanal industries, and folkloric music. Fifth, he suggested that the town develop artistic, literary, and historic activities and awareness. Finally, he underscored the importance of providing other recreational activities for tourists such as horseback riding, swimming, and excursions to other nearby attractions.[22] Mojica's coalition addressed all six recommendations within four years of his arrival in San Miguel, culminating in San Miguel's designation as a Typical Town by the Guanajuato state legislature in 1939.

The first step toward achieving this goal was the initiation of San Miguel's annual patriotic festivals in 1936. Cities and towns across the nation celebrate Mexico's independence from Spain on the fifteenth and sixteenth of September to commemorate Miguel Hidalgo y Costilla's call to arms in 1810. The festivals in San Miguel went beyond the simple performance of patriotism that occurred in many other areas, however. The committee in charge of these festivals—which comprised members of San Miguel's most prominent families such as the Malos and Sauttos, as well as Mojica—highlighted San Miguel's unique contribution to Mexican independence in the person of Ignacio Allende in order to mark San Miguel as a significant site deserving of additional government recognition and resources.[23]

Allende, a San Miguel native, was one of the chief conspirators in the early struggles for Mexican independence. The Spanish captured and executed him for treason along with other leaders Hidalgo, Juan Aldama (also of San Miguel), and Mariano Jiménez in 1811. When Mexico gained independence San Miguel honored Allende's sacrifice by taking his name. Although he played a major role in the independence movement, nationalist mythology never elevated Allende to the same status of Hidalgo, who is widely referred to as the Father of Mexican Independence or the Father of the Nation. Indeed, by 1934 the Ministry of Public Education was already undertaking efforts to preserve Hidalgo's home in the nearby city of Dolores

Hidalgo.[24] Thus, through their evocation of Allende in a letter requesting funds from the governor of Guanajuato, San Miguel's patriotic festival committee reminded the governor of their town's distinguished place in the history of the nation: "The historic place where our Nation's Independence almost began" and the birthplace of Allende, "one of the first to embrace the cause of independence."[25] Although the festival was a success, the committee failed to procure substantive support from the state government.

Mojica formalized the efforts of the festival committee by founding the Friends of San Miguel society in 1937. The society, modeled after the successful Friends of Taxco, represented a more serious commitment to historic preservation by the leaders of the community in the absence of material governmental support. Whereas men with historic familial ties to San Miguel dominated the old committee, relative newcomers such as Mojica and Leobino Zavala ran the new society.[26] The most significant difference between the society and the old committee, however, was that the society shifted the emphasis from Allende to San Miguel's architecture. This allowed the society to seek government support for historic preservation by adopting the same rhetoric the federal government used to justify the expropriation of church property only a few years earlier. Additionally, it positioned San Miguel as a likely candidate for protection under recent federal legislation aimed specifically at the preservation of historic or "typical" towns (*poblaciones típicas*).[27]

The criteria for determining whether a specific building or the zone of a town was worthy of protection under the law was somewhat vague. The law decreed that it was in the public interest to protect monuments linked to the nation's social or political history and towns that maintained their picturesque and typical ambience. The Friends of San Miguel therefore stated that their primary purpose would be to do the work necessary so that the government would declare San Miguel a national monument and provide for the preservation of its "typical character." Other goals of the society included the preservation and restoration of San Miguel's architectural and historical "gems," training and support for local artisans, the promotion and diffusion of local culture, collaboration with local charitable organizations, and the development of recreational activities that would benefit all classes of society.[28]

The task of demonstrating that San Miguel was a población típica proved quite complicated because a town or building's typicalness under federal law actually laid in its atypicality in comparison with other towns. The law implied that for a town to be typical or picturesque it needed to be free of the trappings of modernity; signs, flyers, parking lots, garages, automobile service stations, telephone and telegraph lines, electrical transformers, and vendor's stalls were either prohibited outright or subject to the approval of the Ministry of Public Education. Moreover, the law required that all new construction and any restoration of older buildings conform to the general architectural style of the town. In short, the place in question must retain an aesthetic that appears timeless and unchanging in a rapidly changing world. Ironically, state and federal governments pursued the opposite policy in other towns and cities across Mexico where drastic modernization projects altered rapidly urbanizing landscapes.[29] The Friends of San Miguel had to demonstrate that San Miguel preserved some essential, authentic quality that other Mexican towns had lost.

The Friends of San Miguel emphasized the town's claims to a colonial heritage in order to place it within the national narrative. As Taxco's growing popularity demonstrated, visitors in Mexico sought both the modern comforts of the capital and towns untainted by that modernity. The postrevolutionary impulse to valorize the indigenous cultures of Mexico while integrating them under a common mestizo identity piqued the interest of foreign travelers who wanted to see these cultures before they succumbed to commercialization.[30] Furthermore, publications such as *Mexican Folkways* mapped out the folk cultures of Mexico for pedagogical and tourist purposes. The marginalization of the indigenous community in San Miguel meant that the Friends of San Miguel would have to rely on the colonial architecture as its primary distinguishing feature. Although the postrevolutionary valorization of indigeneity appeared to be in direct conflict with the celebration of Mexico's colonial heritage, they were actually two sides of the same coin. According to the national narrative, the colonial missionaries tamed the barbaric, often nomadic indigenous people in the northern parts of Mexico, taught them the sedentary lifestyle, and encouraged the agricultural and artistic production the postrevolutionary government celebrated as folkloric. Thus, San Miguel's architecture—which the government already deemed politically significant during the Cristiada—played a culturally significant role in government attempts to develop a narrative of national progress. Consequently, the colonial town became another typical type on the map of Mexico's diverse cultures.[31]

The Friends of San Miguel therefore recognized the need to demonstrate San Miguel's important colonial and early-nineteenth-century past and emphasize that its essence had not changed since. Whereas buildings were the primary focus of the federal legislation, there was an implicit need to demonstrate that the people also stayed the same—that in a sense, there was no history since Allende's involvement in the independence movement. This was especially crucial in San Miguel because the recent history, riddled with violence, instability, and economic decline, contradicted the official national narrative of progress and unity. It was necessary, then, to develop a narrative about the history of San Miguel that elided recent conflicts and placed the town within the trajectory of the developing official national history.

This narrative materialized in a book written by Francisco de la Maza, Mexican historian and Toussaint's protégé.[32] De la Maza's book, published in 1939, portrays a linear history of San Miguel's progress and contributions until the twentieth century when, according to de la Maza, the city practically went dormant. This sequence of an upward trajectory followed by a period of latency reproduced the structure of Toussaint's work on Taxco and served as the basis for the argument in favor of San Miguel's protection under federal law. The history begins with the arrival of the Franciscans in 1542, who de la Maza depicted, from his reading of the Spanish chroniclers, as selfless, benevolent individuals who came to civilize the wandering nomads of the region.[33] De la Maza then traced the development of San Miguel's urban center and its industries, including the large-scale production of textiles and leather goods, to demonstrate San Miguel's crucial role in the colonial economy. Next, de la Maza provided the background of many of San Miguel's religious and civic buildings, fountains, and plazas, emphasizing their artistic value and colonial roots. Finally, he detailed the lives of prominent citizens from San Miguel including those involved in the independence movement, nineteenth-century religious figures, architects, and intellectuals, and even the Friends of San Miguel. Significantly, he glossed over the revolution and avoided mention of the Cristiada and local conflicts over agrarian reforms altogether. Instead, the people of San Miguel simply went about their daily lives as the rest of the country experienced violence and chaos. By eliding the conflicts and developments in twentieth-century San Miguel—the movement of people, the failing economy, the corpses hanging in the plaza—de la Maza contributed to the perception that San Miguel avoided being tainted by them and thus maintained its typical character.

The Ministry of Public Education did not approve San Miguel for protection under federal law, but the Guanajuato state legislature did. In 1939 the legislature declared the urban area of San Miguel de Allende a "typical" town. The provisions of the decree were practically the same as the provisions of the federal law: new construction and restorations, signage, gas stations, garages, parking lots, vendors' stalls, telephone, telegraph and electrical lines were subject to the approval of a local vigilance committee. Political appointees and elected members would compose the committee, with the condition that at least one member was a licensed architect. The decree placed the financial burden on the municipal government, stating that the local officials must provide the committee the support necessary to carry out its functions.[34]

Prior to the promulgation of the decree some officials expressed concern over the authenticity of San Miguel's buildings and the intentions of local leaders. A report to the governor's office written by Manuel Leal assured the governor that San Miguel remained one of the few cities in Mexico, along with Puebla and Querétaro, that had conserved their colonial heritage among the majority that had been "stupidly modernized."[35] Leal opined that San Miguel was worthy of preservation, but he cautioned that the success of the endeavor depended on the competency of the vigilance committee. He feared that the committee would cave in to personal tastes and contemporaneous trends when establishing aesthetic standards for San Miguel rather than preserve its authenticity. More specifically, he warned against the "Chulavistazation" of San Miguel, or the adoption of the artificial colonial style prevalent in California, for the sole purpose of attracting Texan tourists. Although Leal acknowledged that authentic Spanish colonial architecture existed in California, he insisted that the "humble missions lost in immense deserts" did not reflect the grand achievements of Spanish civilization.[36]

Leal's fears may have been well-founded. Mojica, the main force behind the preservation efforts in San Miguel, lived in Southern California while working in Hollywood and he was quite familiar with the Franciscan missions that inspired California's turn-of-the-century architectural and cultural movement known as the Mission Revival.[37] Indeed, his San Miguel home bears the name of the town where he lived in California—Santa Monica—and friends described it as a California-style ranch house.[38] It is quite possible that California's Mission Revival inspired Mojica's projects in San Miguel, but ultimately the matter is irrelevant when it comes to Leal's arguments for authenticity. Leal should have been more concerned with the fact that many San Miguel features he recognized as colonial had been renovated in the late nineteenth century. Notably the most recognizable of San Miguel's "colonial" landmarks, the Parroquia and the plaza it faces, which is commonly referred to as El Jardín, had been completely refashioned only a

1. San Miguel's Parroquia and Fray Juan, 2008. PHOTO BY LISA PINLEY COVERT.

few decades earlier to imitate European styles en vogue during the Porfiriato. A local architect, Zeferino Gutiérrez, under the direction of the regional Catholic hierarchy, constructed a pink sandstone neo-Gothic façade for the Parroquia unlike anything else in Mexico. Uniformly pruned laurels, benches, and a bandstand filled in the previously open plaza. Leal and others were willing to overlook certain inconsistencies in San Miguel's architectural milieu as long as they could continue to claim that it was more authentic than that of California.

A Peruvian Intellectual, an American Artist, and the Art School

The Guanajuato state legislature certainly considered San Miguel's potential for tourism when it passed the preservation law in 1939. What Leal and the legislators did not consider was the extent to which they would be able to control the development of a tourist industry in San Miguel beyond the regulation of its architecture. Two years earlier, foreign artists and intellectuals worked through the Friends of San Miguel and Mexican political channels to establish an art school in San Miguel. Although the school's early success relied upon the narrative cultivated by the national government and the efforts of the Friends, ultimately the directors of the school would set the terms for defining San Miguel for an international audience.

The Peruvian artist and intellectual Felipe Cossío del Pomar moved to San Miguel as a political exile in 1937. He originally visited the town several years earlier and returned as Mojica's guest because he thought it would be an ideal location for aspiring artists to escape the responsibilities of daily life and to paint.[39] He, along with Friends of San Miguel leaders Mojica and Zavala, met with the governor of the state of Guanajuato, Luis I. Rodríguez, to discuss the establishment of an art school. The governor enthusiastically supported their endeavors, just as he would later support San Miguel's designation as a "typical" town; financial support, however, would be minimal. After Cossío del Pomar located a building for his school—Las Monjas, the former convent converted into barracks—a mutual acquaintance arranged a meeting with Mexican president Lázaro Cárdenas so that Cossío del Pomar could ask permission to use the building. Cárdenas agreed to let Cossío del Pomar convert the building but offered no financial support. Cossío del Pomar assured him that the enrollment of foreign students would create enough revenue for the school to support itself.[40]

In the case of Guanajuato, the Cárdenas administration linked the processes of secularization and tourist development more astutely and intentionally than previous administrations. Determined to avoid the widespread violence of the first Cristiada, Cárdenas sought out other means of neutralizing opposition to his agrarian and educational policies. The state of Guanajuato—where in 1937 the discontented sectors of the Second Cristiada formally organized into a political movement called the National Synarchist Union or UNS—proved particularly problematic for Cárdenas. The UNS aimed to unite Mexicans and save them from the so-called dangers of the revolution, specifically Cárdenas himself, socialist education, Bolsheviks, Freemasons, Protestants, North Americans, and Jews. This counterrevolutionary, religiously conservative group brought together diverse sectors of the populace from the urban working class to professionals, sharecroppers, and students.[41] Although Guanajuato's governors during the Cárdenas administration, Enrique Fernández Martínez and Luis I. Rodríguez, were among his most loyal supporters, they were in extremely hostile territory and often reacted accordingly. The UNS faced particularly harsh repression under Rodríguez between 1939 and 1941 when over a hundred UNS supporters were killed at the hands of the government; many more were imprisoned.[42] Therefore the Cardenistas balanced traditional military methods of political control with more creative programs like tourist development. They found proponents of their revolutionary program among San Miguel's growing colony of foreign artists and intellectuals. By supporting their desire to open an art school the Cardenistas not only offered an economic alternative to the community; they also created an opportunity to swell the ranks of their sympathizers.

That art school, called the University School of Fine Arts or Bellas Artes, was Cossío del Pomar's brainchild. As a political exile, he was well aware of the Mexican government's relative tolerance of artistic expression and envisioned the school as a Mexican Bauhaus. Indeed, many prominent artists and intellectuals passed through its halls during the early years, including Rufino Tamayo, Federico Cantú, Carlos Mérida, Pablo O'Higgins, and José Chávez Morado.[43] It was an American named Stirling Dickinson, however, who was principally responsible for Bellas Artes's early economic success. Dickinson, an artist from Chicago, moved to San Miguel in 1937 after spending time in Mexico doing research for a book he illustrated, *Death is Incidental.*[44] He too initially visited San Miguel as Mojica's guest. They first met in Oaxaca, but Dickinson had seen Mojica in films and operas in Chicago several years earlier. Before the school opened its doors, Cossío del Pomar sought Dickinson's assistance. Dickinson became an associate director of Bellas Artes and designed its first catalog in both English and Spanish. Together they distributed ten thousand catalogs to universities and art institutes throughout the United States, Canada, and Latin America. Twelve students attended the school's first summer session in 1938, and the enrollment grew to over one hundred by 1939.[45]

Dickinson's advertising campaign targeted a very specific audience of art students by placing San Miguel within the narrative constructed by de la Maza and the Friends of San Miguel. Early publicity efforts targeted Dickinson's social circles in Chicago and defined the way that San Miguel would be imagined in the United States before it was widely visited. A travel feature in the *Chicago Daily Tribune* in 1937 quoted Dickinson describing San Miguel as "one of those 'undiscovered' towns you read about," a "typically Mexican" place where "life moves slowly after the fashion of long ago."[46] In these articles, Dickinson cast himself as an intrepid explorer and discoverer of a Mexican village that time forgot. Although it is possible that he actually believed this rhetoric, it is more likely that Dickinson sought to pique the interests of artists and intellectuals on the lookout for the next bohemian cultural center. By the mid-1930s, the most famous art colonies in the United States, such as those in Santa Fe and Taos, were becoming increasingly commercialized and popular as mainstream tourist destinations—and, therefore, less attractive to highbrow art circles.[47]

The art school's gestures toward these artists became quite explicit in 1938. Dickinson returned to Chicago to visit his parents and most likely to recruit students. Shortly after his visit, the columnist Judith Cass placed a story about San Miguel and the art school front and center in the *Chicago Daily Tribune* society pages. "San Miguel," Cass wrote, "undoubtedly will be included in the itineraries of many Americans who go to Mexico this summer, for the new art school there is attracting much attention." She also mentioned San Miguel's favorable summer climate and its location, much closer to the U.S. border than Mexico City. Finally, she mentioned the names of two Chicagoans who had already left for the school.[48] With this article, Cass (and Dickinson) wove a narrative about a San Miguel somewhat different from the undiscovered town that appeared in the paper the year before. Now it was a "cultural and tourist center" as well as a destination for well-known Chicago artists. Dickinson cleverly created a destination to appeal to both the bold traveler and the sophisticated artist.

In subsequent years Dickinson placed San Miguel within the context of the Mexican tourist industry. In 1940 the travel columnist for the *Chicago Daily Tribune* Frederick Babcock wrote two articles after visiting Dickinson in San Miguel. Babcock contrasted Taxco with San Miguel, which, he wrote, was quite similar to Taxco but "ha[d] not been spoiled by 'invaders' from north of the border." Babcock also suggested that the readers (Chicagoans) had a special opportunity to discover San Miguel while it was "still unknown to most of the tourists."[49] Babcock's second article in 1940 on San Miguel likewise framed the town as an opportunity for people to set themselves apart from average tourists and venture off the beaten path. Although San Miguel would surely "be discovered by the tourists" one day, in 1940, Babcock claimed, "the average American tourist [was] in too big a hurry to get to Mexico City" to explore places like San Miguel.[50]

The success of Cossío del Pomar's and Dickinson's promotional strategies became evident as the number of San Miguel's visitors steadily increased. The following years brought several changes to the city to accommodate the new art students, changes that laid the foundation of the tourist infrastructure in San Miguel. In order to keep and increase the numbers of these visitors, the art school's founders had to meet numerous challenges, such as the lack of restaurants and limited housing options. During the first year, Mojica offered meals for the students at his home for a small fee. By the second year, renovations at the school were complete, and the new building included a fully staffed dining hall as well as better art studios with room for more students. Of the one hundred students enrolled at Bellas Artes during 1939, thirty stayed in the brand new hotel Posada de San Francisco, owned by a local entrepreneur, Ramón Zavala Camarena, brother of Leobino Zavala. Cossío del Pomar converted the former ranch of Pepe Ortíz, bullfighter, into a guesthouse with an Olympic-sized swimming pool and fronton facilities. Many other students stayed with local families.[51]

Dickinson, the Friends of San Miguel, and de la Maza succeeded in eliding the social, political, and economic realities that residents of San Miguel faced on a daily basis. In so doing, they remade San Miguel into a typical, timeless town that represented an important stage in the national narrative. This rhetorical success did not alleviate tensions within the community. The enormous jump in enrollment at Bellas Artes from the first year to the second presented challenges and opportunities for all of San Miguel's residents. Within one year, they were exposed to both an influx of foreigners and several renovation projects around their city. Much-needed employment opportunities arose at the hotel and school, while other residents earned additional income by taking in student boarders. However, even as many locals viewed the foreign presence during these early years as relatively benign and even beneficial, the economic advantages did not always compensate for the challenges to the social order and moral values of the very religious community. Indeed, the leisurely lifestyles of the unchaperoned youth—especially the women—who increasingly frequented the local cantinas and loitered in the town square concerned many of San Miguel's residents. The most potent source of hostility toward foreigners in San Miguel was likely the Synarchist movement. Cardenistas were instrumental in bringing large numbers of foreigners, specifically those from the United States, to a community generally sympathetic to the UNS. This context undoubtedly colored the reception of Bellas Artes in San Miguel.

Consequently, while some of the city's residents, such as the Zavala family, welcomed the new economic opportunities, others linked the new foreign presence to the revolutionary government and reacted, often with violence. As early as 1940, the art students began to face resistance from certain residents of San Miguel. In 1941 Cossío del Pomar sought help from Enrique

Fernández Martínez, governor of Guanajuato and strong ally of Cárdenas, who sent extra police forces to guard the students against attack as they painted outside. The dissidents targeted property as well. In one incident, some residents vandalized a granite bust of Ignacio Allende donated to the town by the school, an attack on both the artists and the revolutionary government's centralizing project.[52] These incidents only prefigured a growing resentment over foreign visitors that would divide the community in the years to come.

Beyond violence against the art students, San Miguel's tourist industry suffered its most considerable setback at the end of 1941 with the attack on Pearl Harbor. Fewer Americans were willing to travel as a result, and several American instructors at Bellas Artes including Dickinson temporarily returned to the United States to enlist in the military. Cossío del Pomar kept the school open and continued to offer regular classes despite declining enrollment figures. He intensified recruitment of students and professors from Latin American countries such as Colombia, Peru, and Cuba, as well as from nearby Mexican universities in Guanajuato, Querétaro, and Morelia.[53] Cossío del Pomar abruptly abandoned his attempts to save Bellas Artes when the changing political climate in his home country, Peru, allowed him to return from exile. He sold the school in 1946 to a lawyer from Mexico City, Alfredo Campanella.

Despite these setbacks, the tourist infrastructure in San Miguel continued to grow and articles about the town still appeared in U.S. newspapers, a testament to its potential as an alternative to war-torn Europe. Three *Chicago Daily Tribune* readers wrote the travel editor with questions about San Miguel in the year after the attack on Pearl Harbor.[54] Diana Rice's *New York Times* column contained another article about the "well-known art center" in 1942 and included one of the first photographs of San Miguel in a major U.S. newspaper.[55] San Miguel also continued to make its way into Cass's *Chicago Daily Tribune* society pages, reinforcing the notion that San Miguel was a regular stop in the travel itineraries of the who's who in Chicago. Meanwhile, San Miguel celebrated its fourth centennial in 1942. The Friends of San Miguel erected a statue of the town's founder in front of the Parroquia and renovated La Plaza de Oriente, a dilapidated bullring, just in time for the festivities.[56] Also during the forties, the U.S. writer Hudson Strode visited San Miguel and published several articles about his travels throughout Mexico in *Holiday* and *Harper's Bazaar*. Collected into a single volume, his essays were published in 1947 as *Now in Mexico*.[57] Strode dedicated an entire chapter of his book to San Miguel, beginning with a description of the difficulties he faced visiting the city. With roads that were "virtually impassable during the wet season," "no airplane service," and trains that arrived at the station "at doleful hours between two and four in the morning," Strode concluded that San Miguel was "the least visited of all the lovely places in Mexico."[58] This description is in stark contrast to his portrayals of other Mexican towns like Taxco, Cuernavaca, or Acapulco as very accessible tourist destinations.

Strode provided a brief explanation of the historical significance of San Miguel, which he referred to as the "Cradle of [Mexican] Independence," demonstrating the success of the Friends' efforts to foreground San Miguel's historical contributions.[59] An unnamed Mexican senator took him to see Allende's house, next to the Parroquia, which was then owned by a local man who had converted the first floor into a drugstore. Strode, surprised that the Mexican government had not converted the house into a museum, mused over the possibilities for restoring it to its nineteenth-century grandeur. Unlike many other visitors, Strode was not fooled by San Miguel's pseudo-colonial architecture. "The town's exterior," Strode claimed, "had not remained wholly a museum piece, any more than Allende's drawing-room." He continued to discuss condescendingly the façade of the Parroquia: "The plaza church had had its face done over in a Gothic approximation by a celebrated Indian architect. . . . His genius for folk architecture, however, was not up to the advanced culture of a Gothic cathedral; hence the strangeness of the design. The façade was not right, but it was interesting, and in no sense offensive."[60] Here, Strode made a distinction between Mexican aesthetic standards and the more "advanced" standards of European architectural design but did not suggest that San Miguel's architecture was intentionally contrived by the Mexican government, the town's promoters, or anyone else, thus opening the possibility of interpreting the façade as authentic folk art.

Fortunately for those at the art school attempting to promote the colonial heritage of San Miguel, Strode's criticisms did not overwhelm his praise for the city. He spoke highly of Dickinson and Cossío del Pomar and his impressions of Bellas Artes were very positive. He noted that the students studied in a "gentle atmosphere of Old World beauty" and many stayed at the "two new pleasant hotels," which Strode predicted would provide accommodations for the many tourists who would visit San Miguel once better roads were constructed.[61] He closed by recounting a conversation he had with a traveling companion. "[San Miguel is] a charming place," Strode began, "I hope it doesn't change too much—too soon." His friend replied: "It seems like a supergood place to retire to . . . or to rest up in—or write a book in—or where a fellow might paint some pictures."[62] Strode's and his companion's ruminations over San Miguel, published and widely read in the United States, were practically self-fulfilling prophecies, especially since their publication coincided with America's postwar travel boom and the GI Bill.

San Miguel Becomes a "GI Paradise"

As the Second World War drew to a close, increased prosperity and leisure time allowed more and more people from the United States to travel abroad. While most American travelers preferred to visit sunny exotic beaches or take quick trips across the border in their new automobiles, others sought the experience that cities like San Miguel offered: quiet cobblestone streets, historic architecture, and a cultural, bohemian atmosphere, untainted by hordes of tourists and the consumerism emerging with the postwar boom. Given that many of these unconventional travelers came to San Miguel to enroll in classes at Bellas Artes, they usually stayed for longer periods than typical tourists did, often for a few weeks or even a few months. Many came with the intention of staying a few weeks but later chose to make San Miguel their permanent home.

Postwar San Miguel proved to be just as attractive to World War II veterans as it was to bohemian artists. In 1944, the U.S. Congress passed the Servicemen's Readjustment Act, more commonly known as the GI Bill, aimed at providing "Federal Government aid for the readjustment in civilian life of returning World War II veterans."[63] One of the major provisions of the bill was that the government would encourage veterans to attend college or vocational schools by covering tuition costs. The Canadian government passed similar legislation. While many veterans elected to study in the United States and Canada, Mexico was a popular choice for some because of the low cost of living. In the decade following the war hundreds of veterans took advantage of this opportunity to study at a number of schools in Mexico.[64]

One of the Mexican schools approved by the United States and Canadian governments was Bellas Artes in San Miguel. In June 1946 vice-consul of the United States in San Luis Potosí, Mexico, formally notified Dickinson that Bellas Artes could begin receiving war veterans.[65] News of the charming artists' colony quickly spread via word of mouth from one veteran to the next. The Canadian artist and war veteran W. J. B. Newcombe studied at

Bellas Artes in 1946 and recommended it to his friends Leonard and Reva Brooks. Leonard, who served as a war artist for the Canadian Navy, received approval in 1947 from Canada's Department of Veterans Affairs to study at Bellas Artes for eleven months. The Canadian government agreed to pay Leonard eighty dollars a month for living expenses, forty dollars a month for tuition, and sixty dollars for supplies.[66] The Brooks later invited the American author and naval veteran Charles Allen Smart to study art on the GI Bill in San Miguel; he arrived in 1949.[67] Dorothy (Dotty) Vidargas, another World War II veteran from Chicago, enrolled at Bellas Artes on the GI Bill in 1947 because a friend highly recommended it to her.[68] Several newspaper articles also mentioned Bellas Artes's new status.[69] In 1948, an article in *Life* magazine featured San Miguel as a "GI Paradise," a place where "veterans go to study art, live cheaply and have a good time."[70]

As the recollections of the veterans indicate, San Miguel lived up to its off-the-beaten-path reputation. Both Vidargas and Leonard Brooks recalled that there were few, if any, cars on the cobblestone streets of San Miguel when they first arrived in the late 1940s.[71] Leonard and Reva stayed at El Hotel San Miguel, where the monthly rate of forty-five dollars for room and board was well within the artists' budget, and the hot water in the communal bathroom was a luxury of which very few establishments in San Miguel could boast. They later rented a house for about ten dollars a month with no running water, electricity, or any other "modern" amenities.[72] The Posada de San Francisco, by this time nearly ten years old, had the only acceptable restaurant in San Miguel for women, Vidargas recalled, although many of the male art students spent time at La Cucaracha, a cantina in the center of town.[73] The cantinas were quite popular among the veterans, many of whom claimed that cheap alcohol was the only form of amusement in San Miguel.[74] Others, like Vidargas, spent their free time taking in new activities like watching bullfights.[75]

The presence of the war veterans had a significant impact on Bellas Artes and on the entire city of San Miguel. To accommodate the influx of students, the school began to offer classes throughout the entire year rather than only during the summer and winter months. The students' diversions at the cantinas and in the bullring, not to mention the nude models they used during art classes, continued to clash with the values of San Miguel's residents, causing many to rally around José Mercadillo Miranda, the parish priest who openly criticized the foreigners in pamphlets and from the pulpit.[76] The fact that many of the students dated and married Mexicans also disturbed some San Miguel locals because they viewed it as an intrusion into the private lives of Mexican families and a disruption of long-standing traditions of courtship and marriage.

Meanwhile, a conflict within Bellas Artes threatened the students' GI Bill funds, as well as San Miguel's future as a tourist destination. The students feared that the school's new owner, Alfredo Campanella, was more concerned with profits than with maintaining the art studios and attracting reputable instructors. In the spring of 1948, students and faculty pressed Campanella to meet a series of demands, ranging from improved studio space to an art supply store and drinking fountain. The director eventually conceded to some of the demands. He commissioned the renowed Mexican muralist David Alfaro Siqueiros to paint a mural at the school. The artist began work on the mural in June 1949 with the help of twenty students. Before long a power struggle ensued between Siqueiros and Campanella over the rapidly escalating costs of the mural. The struggle reached a climax when Siqueiros, the other instructors, and a vast majority of the students voted to boycott Bellas Artes on July 15, 1949, effectively closing its doors. Many of Mexico's most prominent artists and intellectuals, as well as San Miguel's leading businesspeople and politicians, supported their cause.[77]

The boycott escalated into an international dispute that revealed the growing importance of Mexico's tourist industry and highlighted tensions between the United States and Mexico over the threat of communism. Nathaniel Patterson, the attaché for veterans' affairs at the U.S. embassy in Mexico City, withdrew the Veterans Administration's recognition of Bellas Artes and encouraged the 125 U.S. veterans enrolled there to transfer to other approved Mexican institutions. Seventy-five of the veterans stayed behind with Siqueiros and the instructors, however, and reorganized the school in a new location in the hopes of regaining the Veterans Administration's approval. They even took their case to Mexican president Miguel Alemán at an inaugural event at the Palace of Fine Arts in Mexico City. In an attempt to placate the Mexican art community and in partial defiance of Patterson's decision, the Mexican secretary of education, Manuel Gual Vidal, agreed to incorporate the reorganized school under the auspices of the National Institute of Fine Arts. The school reopened within a month and Mexican inspectors verified that the new school was essentially the same institution as before, minus Campanella. Soon thereafter the Canadian government resumed support of the Canadian veterans studying in San Miguel.[78]

Campanella embarked on a campaign to discredit the new school by appealing to growing anticommunist sentiments in the United States and in Mexico. This multifaceted campaign involved direct threats against the students and instructors, as well as propaganda circulated through U.S. and Mexican government offices, Mexican newspapers, and local newsletters in San Miguel denouncing the school as a breeding ground for conspiratorial plots. In one flyer he accused them of training communist cells to infiltrate the United States.[79] The artists' affiliation with Siqueiros did not help their situation. The Mexican artistic community had many ties to the left, whether through direct involvement in the Communist Party, support for the Republican exiles from the Spanish Civil War, or merely an inclination toward socialist ideals. Diego Rivera's murals at the Detroit Institute of Arts and the Rockefeller Center in the 1930s led to controversy in the United States over their Marxist content.[80] In 1940 Siqueiros and Rivera found themselves in the middle of an international scandal after Siqueiros allegedly attempted to assassinate Leon Trotsky, whom Rivera and Frida Kahlo helped to harbor in Mexico City. These incidents underscored the communist activities in the Mexican artistic community, making the foreign artists associated with it an easy target in the early years of the Cold War. Finally, the UNS, still influential in the region, often equated foreigners with radical ideologies, which it considered in direct conflict with Catholic beliefs. Whatever the reason, many of the residents of San Miguel were convinced that spies infiltrated the art school; some proudly displayed signs on their doors that read "¡Católicas sí . . . Comunistas no!"[81] More than half a century later, Mexicans in San Miguel still talk about the scandal with the communist spies.[82]

Incidentally, because new legislation in the United States prevented the accreditation of any additional schools under the GI Bill, the full impact of the anticommunist campaign remains unclear. Whether directed by Washington or influenced by Campanella's efforts or motivated by a combination of these factors, Patterson refused to recognize the reorganized school, leaving the U.S. veterans in San Miguel without government support. Despite the veterans' appeals to the U.S. government invoking Good Neighbor sentiments by arguing that this incident could potentially damage the "good relations and cultural exchange" between Mexico and the United States, the Veterans Administration never renewed its support of veterans in San Miguel, forcing Dickinson and Cossío del Pomar to attract students from the United States by other means.[83]

A year later another incident occurred in San Miguel that could have been the final blow to its artist colony if not for the subsequent support of

Mexican government officials. On August 12, 1950, officials who purportedly worked for a Mexican intelligence agency deported eight instructors from the reorganized art school. Two of the faculty members were Canadians, Leonard and Reva Brooks. The other six were from the United States: Stirling Dickinson, Howard Jackson, Ruby Martin, Jack Baldwin, and James and Rushka Pinto. Conflicting stories abounded as to the true nature of the deportations. Some said that Campanella bribed Mexican officials to deport the instructors as revenge for the closure of his art school.[84] The explanation provided to the instructors was that they were not allowed to work in Mexico with tourist visas.[85] A *New York Times* article claimed that the instructors were expelled for allegedly opposing the United States military intervention in Korea.[86] After several failed attempts by the deported instructors to gain permission to return to Mexico, Leonard Brooks contacted General Ignacio Beteta, a former munitions officer to whom Brooks had once given painting advice. Beteta, remembering the favor, made the appropriate connections through his brother Ramón—an influential politician at the highest levels of the Mexican government—and the deported artists were permitted to return to San Miguel, proper working papers in hand.[87] Mexican government involvement in this scandal opened the door for increased federal attention to affairs in San Miguel and highlighted the government's growing interest in supporting foreign tourism and expatriates regardless of the larger policy goals of the United States.

The Revival of the Tourist Industry

Whereas the intervention of top government officials defied U.S. interests, it also signaled a growing concern over the way ordinary Americans viewed Mexico. By attracting international attention as a haven for communists, San Miguel once again diverted from the official narrative. When Cossío del Pomar returned to San Miguel in 1949, several key figures in the Mexican government hoped to renew the town's reputation among tourists by steering it back toward its role as an off-the-beaten-path, typical town. Adolfo Ruíz Cortines, a Mexican tourism official and future president of Mexico, sent a representative to San Miguel to encourage Cossío del Pomar to revive Bellas Artes. Around the same time, former president Lázaro Cárdenas approached Cossío del Pomar and suggested that he establish an art school in Pátzcuaro, Michoacán, instead. Although their attempts lacked the coherence of a concerted government effort, it is not merely coincidence that these officials expressed an interest in a new art school. San Miguel's reputation abroad as an art colony superseded its reputation as a typical Mexican town or as the birthplace of Allende, and therefore even government-led tourist development was constrained by this narrative.

In the fall of 1950 Cossío del Pomar and Enrique Fernández Martínez, former *cardenista* governor of Guanajuato, opened a new art school in San Miguel called the Instituto Allende. The school was incorporated with the University of Guanajuato, enabling students to earn a master's degree in fine arts. They welcomed Dickinson, the faculty, and students from the old art school with open arms. Occupying the newly renovated grounds of the historic Canal family estate on the outskirts of town,[88] the Instituto accommodated both serious artists and tourists. Cossío del Pomar, fearing that the integrity of the school would be compromised if it catered to the tourist trade, eventually allowed Fernández to buy him out.[89] With Dickinson and Fernández at the helm, the Instituto thrived and the tourist industry in San Miguel surpassed pre-boycott levels.

While some, like Cossío del Pomar, felt that San Miguel had reached its zenith in the years before the Second World War and the arrival of the GIs, others felt that the city was only beginning to realize its full potential as a tourist hotspot. The section of the Pan-American Highway that runs through Mexico was completed during the 1950s; the government constructed paved roads that branched off the main highway for direct access to San Miguel. Several travel features mentioned the newly paved roads to San Miguel, making it "off the beaten track yet easily accessible."[90] The city also began to appear on a number of sample Mexico travel itineraries and in travel agency advertisements.[91] Its growing tourist infrastructure and reputation as a picturesque Mexican town attracted Hollywood production crews that used the city as a backdrop for such films as *The Brave Bulls* and *The Littlest Outlaw*, thereby increasing San Miguel's publicity.[92] Finally, Dickinson created a buzz about the Instituto by advertising competitive art scholarships in major U.S. newspapers.[93]

By the late 1950s, the efforts of the directors of Instituto Allende to fashion San Miguel's identity as a cosmopolitan cultural center through newspaper and magazine articles and other art school publicity were clear. *Travel* magazine mentioned San Miguel in seven out of twelve issues in 1957 alone. This was due, in no small part, to *Travel*'s Mexico correspondent, Peter Olwyler, who moved to San Miguel in 1955 and at various times served as the Instituto's director of public relations and as a writing and photography instructor at the school. Short items in the magazine included the latest gossip on famous American authors, musicians, film producers, playwrights, and members of Mexican high society who visited San Miguel to take art and writing classes at Instituto Allende or to attend cultural events. Olwyler used carefully selected phrases to describe San Miguel as a "colony of literati," a "center for literati and artists," and the "old colonial culture-center."[94] Other aspects of San Miguel that he addressed in these brief articles were the nearby hot springs, a Canadian film festival, humanitarian efforts by Americans in San Miguel to aid Mexican flood victims, and the patriotic festivals in September, described as some of the best in Mexico. Aside from gossip, *Travel* also covered efforts by the Mexican government to promote tourism. Anticipating over 600,000 American tourists in 1957, the Mexican government, according to Olwyler, planned to continue expansion of the roadways.[95] The government issued over three million postcards in 1957 depicting different landscapes, paintings, and other "Mexican motifs" to promote tourism abroad.[96] Given Olwyler's affiliation with the Instituto Allende, his writings in *Travel* represented a conscious effort by the school's promoters to tap into a more mainstream group of travelers than before to compensate for the loss of the guaranteed GI funds enjoyed by the former school. In that spirit, Olwyler rewrote San Miguel into the national narrative, this time as a modern destination with an active, sophisticated social scene.

Although Olwyler's promotional efforts succeeded to a certain extent in attracting a more cosmopolitan crowd to San Miguel, the city's bohemian reputation still flourished. The American writer Wayne Greenhaw recalled several encounters with Allen Ginsberg, Neal Cassady, Jack Kerouac, and other beatniks in San Miguel during the 1950s while he was enrolled in writing courses at the Instituto.[97] The beatniks, "unofficial" tourists in search of an "authentic" version of Mexico, located it in San Miguel and other parts of the country.[98] Even though they considered themselves counterculturalists, to many Mexicans they represented all that was threatening and wrong with mainstream American culture. As was true of the bohemian artists who preceded them, the beatniks' lifestyles challenged the patriarchal values held by many Mexicans in the region.[99] According to Greenhaw's account, fears about them may have been well founded because Kerouac, Cassady, and Ginsberg spent nearly as much time drinking in La Cucaracha as they did writing at the Instituto.

Aside from the arrival of the beatniks, the late 1950s brought new accusations of communist activity that once again threatened the reputation of the foreign community in San Miguel. Articles in *Time* and the *Washington Post* and *Times-Herald* accused Stirling Dickinson of being a leader of the estimated one hundred "expatriate reds" in Mexico.[100] The *Washington Post* article by Bert Quint alleged that these American communists were plotting with the more than nine hundred Russians in Mexico, but that there was little to be done because the United States could not "impinge upon Mexican sovereignty."[101] The quote alluded to the desire of U.S. government officials to take on a larger role in curbing the perceived communist threat in Latin America, while Mexican officials, with the example of the alleged communist takeover and subsequent CIA-backed coup d'état in Guatemala fresh in their minds, insisted on policing their own nation.[102]

With the assistance of some family members in a prominent Chicago law firm, Dickinson managed to revive his reputation: he met with the House Un-American Activities Committee, which read a statement into the minutes clearing his name; he reached a monetary settlement with *Time*; and he arranged for the *New York Herald Tribune* news service to publish an article praising the Instituto and the entire artist community in San Miguel.[103] Titled "The 'Sorbonne' of Latin America," the article described in detail the low cost of living in San Miguel and the diversity of students studying at the Instituto—carefully noting, however, that "there is nothing Bohemian about the Instituto's group."[104] A significant portion of the article focused on Dickinson's service with naval intelligence during World War II and his contributions to the community in San Miguel. The reporter also noted that the news service had erred when it listed Dickinson as a communist leader and was pleased to correct that mistake.

As evidenced by continuing popularity of San Miguel as a tourist destination today, the damage control sufficiently preserved the city's reputation. A bilingual guidebook published in 1958 by the Instituto, *Guía de turista en San Miguel de Allende*, contained advertisements for at least ten hotels including "one of Mexico's finest," Hotel Instituto Allende, "on the grounds of the internationally famous arts, crafts, and writing center," demonstrating that San Miguel's tourist infrastructure was improving to meet the needs of the growing industry.[105] The late 1950s also brought more conscious efforts to attract domestic tourists to San Miguel. The rhetoric was slightly different from that used to attract foreign tourists. For example, the Spanish version of the above description of Hotel Instituto Allende did not mention the art school. Instead, the advertisement boasted "magnificent views, extensive gardens, attractive rooms, and excellent international cuisine."[106] This suggests that the Spanish-speaking population was not as likely to be drawn to

San Miguel for its artistic community, whereas the art scene was the main draw for foreign tourists who could find a good view, gardens, nice rooms, and haute cuisine in other parts of Mexico or even their own country.

The Mexican government participated in the trend of focusing on domestic tourists in yet another attempt to reincorporate San Miguel into the national narrative. This time government officials put a nationalist spin on the idea of an art school by opening its own cultural center under the auspices of the National Institute of Fine Arts (INBA) in 1962. They even used the site of Cossío del Pomar's original school, renaming it Centro Cultural Ignacio Ramírez, "El Nigromante." The school's namesake, Ignacio Ramírez, was a Mexican intellectual born in San Miguel in 1818. Although the center was one of many sponsored by INBA in cities across the country, officials singled it out as a model for future initiatives.[107] The center offered instruction in the fine arts for locals as well as tourists and sponsored many "cosmopolitan" events such as theatrical performances, ballets, and the Chamber Orchestra of Berlin.[108] Miguel Malo, director of the center, later wrote a tourist guidebook in Spanish to attract more Mexicans to San Miguel.[109] The guidebook, published by the National Institute of Anthropology and History (INAH), focused on the religious and civic architecture in San Miguel as well as the local fiestas rather than on cosmopolitan cultural events, an obvious return to the promotional strategies of Francisco de la Maza and the Friends of San Miguel in the 1930s. This guidebook became the authoritative text for many other Spanish-language guidebooks to follow: its images, captions, and often even its text have been copied and reproduced numerous times.

With the establishment of the Centro Cultural Ignacio Ramírez in 1962, the Mexican government had appropriated for its own goals of state formation the images and rhetoric that foreign artists and local residents created to describe San Miguel. The unfinished Siqueiros mural was the only tangible reminder of the events that transpired within the new cultural center's walls little more than a decade before; the decision to open a new art school there testified to the successful promotion in years past of San Miguel as an artist colony. Government officials hoped to attract Mexican and foreign artists to the new center in San Miguel by using the artist colony rhetoric, but it also infused a nationalistic aura into its promotion of the city by reminding Mexicans of the nineteenth-century Mexican intellectual Ignacio Ramírez and by eventually turning Ignacio Allende's home into a museum. The INAH guidebook written by Malo resurrected the histories of San Miguel's historic buildings and churches, which might have been forgotten if not for the individuals in the Friends of San Miguel. Similar to the early attempts to promote San Miguel as a tourist destination, the new government promotional materials carefully elided conflicts in the region, even as the state of Guanajuato continued to be a relative stronghold for oppositional politics.

While the Mexican government attempted to re-Mexicanize San Miguel, the city became home to an increasing number of expatriates as tourists became residents of the city that captivated them. As in previous years, many of the expatriates heard about San Miguel via word of mouth, but some also read about it in the proliferation of books and magazines that mentioned the city. This group comprised young artists, businesspeople, and retirees. San Miguel also became a destination for tourist families.[110] Foreigners rejected the government's name for the cultural center, continuing to call it Bellas Artes instead. Mexicans in San Miguel continued to debate options for San Miguel's economic future, particularly in the pages of *El Vocero del Norte*. Some advocated the path to industrialization pursued by many other cities in the region such as Celaya and Irapuato.[111] Regardless of their position on the issue, Mexicans increasingly had to negotiate that future on the expatriates' terms given their contributions to the city's economy and its image abroad. Many Mexicans continued to benefit from the foreign presence, including a veteran of World War II, Fortunato Maycotte, who moved his family from Mexico City to San Miguel in 1956 where they purchased Cossío del Pomar's dilapidated ranch and eventually converted it into a successful hotel. A vast majority of the town's residents were eventually linked to the tourist economy in one way or another.

The history of the tourist industry in San Miguel de Allende challenges the notion that postrevolutionary tourist development was simply a top-down phenomenon, directed by government or industry officials in Mexico City. The Mexican government did not lead tourist development in San Miguel for many reasons. The Cristiada created financial and political instability that forced government officials to focus tourist development efforts in other parts of the country. San Miguel lacked the infrastructure to support a substantial industry and required a tremendous amount of investment, a commitment that government agencies were not willing to make. Most importantly, however, San Miguel did not fit into the vision of Mexico that government officials, travel agencies, and guidebook authors cultivated: that of a unified, yet diverse Mexico, a Mexico that emerged from ancient civilizations to take its place among the modern nations of the world. The notion of diversity in this narrative was actually quite limited; it included many indigenous communities reborn as folk cultures, yet it excluded communities that chose not to participate in the revolutionary program.

The development of San Miguel's tourist industry was still constrained by this national narrative despite the initial indifference of government officials. Indeed, the multinational group of tourist promoters had to demonstrate that San Miguel was a typical Mexican town in order to attract tourists in the first place. However, as this essay demonstrates, the limitations imposed by the national narrative weakened with time. By ceding decision-making authority to individuals, and specifically to foreigners, government officials at all levels—local, state, and federal—as well as local citizens, relinquished the ability to control the future manifestations of San Miguel's tourist industry. The fickle demands of tourists and foreign residents, upon whom San Miguel's new economy relied, would impose new constraints, new narratives. But like the ones that preceded, these new narratives continued to hide the discord that the tourist industry emerged from as well as the conflicts and debates that it increasingly provoked. Given this history, can San Miguel really make tourists feel more Mexican? That is up to the visitors to decide for themselves.

Notes

The research for this essay was made possible through the Andrew W. Mellon Dissertation Fellowship in Latin American History, the Tinker Field Research Grant from the Council on Latin American and Iberian Studies at Yale University, and the Pre-Dissertation Grant from the Yale Center for International and Area Studies. This essay also builds on research completed at California State University, Long Beach, with the financial support of the McNair Scholars Program and the California State University Pre-Doctoral Program. I would like to thank Gilbert Joseph, Dina Berger, Seth Fein, Micol Seigel, Patricia Cleary, Jim Green, Julie Weise, Kate Unterman, Andrew Grant Wood, Gerry Cadava, and the anonymous readers for their comments and suggestions at various stages of this project.

1. "El Turismo, como industria bien organizada, ayudaría mucho a nuestra población," *El Vocero del Norte*, November 20, 1960, 1, 6.
2. Archivo General de la Nación (AGN), Miguel Alemán Valdés (MAV), exp. 741.5/ 28225, Martín Zavala Camarena to the Office of the President, November 17, 1952.

3. The use of the phrase "national narrative" in this essay is informed by the definition of "national memory" put forth in Mary Kay Vaughan's and Stephen E. Lewis's introduction to *The Eagle and the Virgin: Nation and Cultural Revolution in Mexico, 1920–1940*, ed. Mary Kay Vaughan and Stephen E. Lewis (Durham, N.C.: Duke University Press, 2006), 6. Although this analysis recognizes that the "postrevolutionary government" or the "state" is not a homogenous entity, it does assume a degree of continuity among the goals of various state actors in terms of consolidating political authority and achieving a degree of national integration, whether political, economic, or cultural. While acknowledging the participation of nonstate actors in the development of a national narrative, this work focuses on interactions with the "end result" at different historical junctures.

4. On the concept of multiple historical narratives, the development of historical narratives, and on the elision or "silencing" of histories, this essay draws from Michel-Rolph Trouillot, *Silencing the Past: Power and the Production of History* (Boston: Beacon Press, 1995). Some works challenge the inclusiveness of a national narrative, most notably Luis González y González, *San José de Gracia: Mexican Village in Transition*, trans. John Upton (Austin: University of Texas Press, 1974), and the tradition of microhistories that followed. This essay argues, however, that those works fail to acknowledge the constraints the national narrative imposes on their histories. For example, even though González asserts that certain events in Mexican history did not have an impact on San José de Gracia, the fact that he still addresses those events speaks to the discursive power of the national narrative.

5. Alan Knight, *The Mexican Revolution*, vol. 1: *Porfirians, Liberals and Peasants* (Cambridge: Cambridge University Press, 1986), 12.

6. Alan Knight, *The Mexican Revolution*, vol. 2: *Counter-revolution and Reconstruction* (Lincoln: University of Nebraska Press, 1986), 415.

7. Phyllis M. Correa, "Sharecropping and Agrarian Reform in the Township of Allende, Guanajuato," *Memorias: San Miguel de Allende, Cruce de Caminos*, ed. Jorge F. Hernández and Don Patterson (León, Gto: Impresas ABC, 2006), 159.

8. Alfonso Sánchez Díaz, ed., *La guerra cristera en Guanajuato* (Guanajuato: Ediciones La Rana, 2005), 19, 43–44.

9. Ibid., 136, n. 13; Felix Luna Romero, interview by Morton Stith and Katherine Walch, May 16, 2001, San Miguel History Archive (SMHA); Susan Beere, "Spotlight on People: Celia Hoyos de Téllez," *Atención*, October 31, 1978, 5.

10. Presidente Municipal to the Secretario General del Gobierno of Guanajuato, July 7, 1927, Archivo General del Municipio de San Miguel de Allende (AGMSMA), fondo Gobernación.

11. Article 27 of the 1917 Constitution technically nationalized the property of all religious institutions in Mexico, but similar to the rights of subsoil resources, the postrevolutionary state was too weak to enforce these rights in the 1920s. The

federal government, or more precisely agents of the Procuraduría General de la República (PGR), the rough equivalent of the Attorney General, had to apply to nationalize each specific building.

12. Notice from the Jefe de la Oficina Federal de Hacienda in León, Gto., Francisco Chávez Holguin, regarding the nationalization of the annex of the Parroquia, November 22, 1926, AGN, PGR, caja 125, leg. 132, exp. 10/422.1/244.

13. Circular from the Secretario General del Gobierno of Guanajuato to the Presidente Municipal, 1930, AGMSMA, Gobernación, Circulares, Gobierno Estatal, exp. 3.08.30, no. 93; Subsecretary of the Secretaría de Hacienda y Crédito Público to the person(s) in charge of various temples, May 7, 1930, AGMSMA, fondo Gobernación, sección Circulares, serie Gobierno Estatal, exp. 3.07.30, no. 87.

14. Ibid.

15. Secretario General del Gobierno to the Presidente Municipal, November 19, 1930, AGMSMA, fondo Gobernación, sección Circulares, serie Gobierno Estatal, exp. 1.011.30, no. 422.

16. On those who supported and benefited from agrarian reform in San Miguel, see Correa, "Sharecropping and Agrarian Reform," 158. Another analysis of agrarian reform in the municipality of San Miguel does not specify who the beneficiaries of agrarian reform were, using the more general terms "campesinos" or "agraristas" instead: Manola Sepúlveda Garza, "Historias rancheras: La lucha por la tierra en la hacienda Ciénega de Juana Ruiz, Municipio de San Miguel de Allende," *Guanajuato: Aportaciones recientes para su estudio*, ed. Patricia Moctezuma Yano, Juan Carlos Ruiz Guadalajara, and Jorge Uzeta Iturbide (Guanajuato: Universidad de Guanajuato, 2004), 243–60. On conflicts over agrarian reform in other parts of the state, see Jorge Uzeta Iturbide, "Ejidatarios y chichimecas: Identidad india a través de la formación de un ejido guanajuatense," *Guanajuato: Aportaciones recientes para su estudio*; Alfredo Guerrero Tarquín, *Memorias de un agrarista* (Mexico City: Instituto Nacional de Antropología e Historia, 1987), 207–42; and Manola Sepúlveda Garza, *Políticas agrarias y luchas sociales: San Diego de la Unión, Guanajuato, 1900–2000* (Mexico City: Procuraduría Agraria, Instituto Nacional de Antropología e Historia, 2000).

17. A variety of sources contributed to the biographical information on Mojica. His autobiography proved to be the most useful account of his life before his arrival in San Miguel, although his timeline occasionally conflicts with other better-documented sources. Fray José Francisco de Guadalupe Mojica, *I, a Sinner*, trans. Fanchon Royer (Chicago: Franciscan Herald Press, 1963). Some of the other helpful sources are Max Arthur, "The Padre Who Was Mojica," *Chicago Daily Tribune*, April 18, 1948, E5; and a series by Katherine Walch, "Remembering José Mojica," *El Independiente*, from the Betsey Davies Collection (BD). This privately held collection contains mostly newspaper clippings and most do not

include the date of publication, although most seem to have been published in the 1990s.

18. For example Bonifacio López Herrera y Ortega, interview by Elena Shoemaker and Katherine Walch, May 11, 2003, SMHA; Raquel Mojica and Maria Herrera D. Williams, interview by Katherine Walch, December 2002. Mojica's own autobiographical account, which emphasizes his journey to the priesthood, downplays his role in San Miguel social life but sufficient evidence exists to prove otherwise.

19. Walch, "Remembering José Mojica," BD.

20. Manuel Toussaint, *Tasco: Su historia, sus monumentos, características actuales y posibilidades turísticas* (Mexico City: Editorial Cultura, 1931).

21. On the development of Taxco as a tourist destination, see James Oles, "Walls to Paint On: American Muralists in Mexico, 1933–1936" (Ph.D. diss., Yale University, 1995), chap. 1.

22. Toussaint, *Tasco*, 211–15.

23. La Junta Patriótica de San Miguel de Allende to the Governor, August 7, 1936, Archivo General del Gobierno del Estado de Guanajuato (AGGEG), fondo Secretaría del Gobierno, Primer Departamento, 1.45.(3).1.

24. Summary of Projects planned for 1934, December 13, 1933, Secretaría de Educación Pública (SEP), Archivo Histórico, sección Departamento de Bellas Artes, serie Monumentos Artísticos e Históricos, 1931–1940, caja 5326. On the incorporation of Dolores Hidalgo into the national historical narrative, see Mario A. Vázquez Soriano, *Signos de identidad: los espacios simbólicos de Dolores Hidalgo* (Mexico: Instituto Mora, 1999). Although Dolores Hidalgo shares much of the same regional history as San Miguel (in fact Dolores was under the administrative authority of San Miguel until 1790) the national government singled out the figure of Hidalgo and the town of Dolores for recognition as early as the nineteenth century.

25. La Junta Patriótica de San Miguel de Allende to the Governor, AGGEG: "este histórico lugar fué donde casi se inició nuestra Independencia Nacional" and "fué de los primeros en abrazar la causa de la Independencia."

26. The Zavala family first arrived in San Miguel in 1899, whereas the "old" families traced their roots in San Miguel to the colonial period. On the Zavalas' arrival in San Miguel see Manuel Zavala Zavala, interview by Leonardo Rosen, October 9, 2002, SMHA.

27. "Poblaciones típicas," SEP, Departamento de Monumentos Artísticos, Arqueológicos e Históricos, Ley sobre protección y conservación de monumentos arqueológicos e históricos, poblaciones típicas y lugares de belleza natural, y su reglamento, January 19, 1934.

28. Francisco de la Maza, *San Miguel de Allende: Su historia, sus monumentos*, 2nd

ed. (Mexico City: Impresos Reforma, 1972), 134. The majority of the text in the first and second editions is identical with the exception of the introductions and the appendices in the second edition. In cases where the text is different I cite the first edition or specify why I cite the second.

29. For an example in the state of Guanajuato, see Daniel Newcomer, *Reconciling Modernity: Urban State Formation in 1940s León, Mexico* (Lincoln: University of Nebraska Press, 2004).

30. On the valorization of indigenous cultures and the ethnicization of the Mexican national identity, see Rick López, *"Lo más mexicano de México*: Popular Arts, Indians, and Urban Intellectuals in the Ethnicization of Postrevolutionary National Culture, 1920–1972" (Ph.D. diss., Yale University, 2001). For an example of a foreign traveler interested in indigenous cultures, see the Beinecke Rare Book and Manuscript Library, Yale Collection of American Literature, Mabel Dodge Luhan Papers, box 56, folder 1421, "Mexico in 1930," 82.

31. Oles argues that the twentieth-century interest in colonial architecture developed from a sense of nostalgia; however, this chapter argues that between the church-state conflicts and the ethnicization of national identity, interest in colonial architecture in San Miguel was more complicated. See Oles, "Walls to Paint On," 52.

32. Francisco de la Maza, *San Miguel de Allende: Su historia, sus monumentos*, 1st ed. (Mexico City: Instituto de Investigaciones Estéticas, Universidad Nacional Autónoma de México, 1939).

33. De la Maza, *San Miguel de Allende*, 9–10. The second edition offers a corrective to this version of history by including an appendix on the pre-Hispanic peoples who populated the region written by Miguel Malo.

34. Correspondence regarding Decree #292 of the Guanajuato State Legislature declaring San Miguel a Población Típica, May 27, 1939, AGGEG, fondo Secretaría del Gobierno, Primer Departamento, 1.24–3.9.

35. Ibid.

36. The term *Chulavistazos* refers to the community of Chula Vista in southern California.

37. On Mojica's recurrent interest in the Franciscans and Fray Junipero Serra, see Mojica, *I, a Sinner.*

38. Felipe Cossío del Pomar, *Cossío del Pomar en San Miguel de Allende* (Madrid, Spain: Playor, S.A., 1974), 26. There are actually two versions of this book, the second is titled *Iridescencia: Crónica de un centro de arte* (Guanajuato: Gobierno del Estado de Guanajuato, 1988).

39. Cossío del Pomar, *Cossío del Pomar*, 25–26.

40. Ibid., 38–41.

41. Guadalupe Valencia García, *Guanajuato: Sociedad, economía, política, cultura* (Mexico City: Centro de Investigaciones Interdisciplinarias en Ciencias y Humanidades, Universidad Nacional Autónoma de México, 1998), 36–37.

42. Ibid., 39. See also Guillermo Zermeño P. and Rubén Aguilar V., "Dos razones para el estudio y la investigación de la Unión Nacional Sinarquista—Partido Demócrata Mexicano en Guanajuato," *Guanajuato: Evolución social y política*, ed. José Arturo Salazar y García (León, Gto: El Colegio del Bajío, A.C., 1988), 281–98; and Jean Meyer, "An Idea of Mexico: Catholics in the Revolution," *The Eagle and the Virgin*, ed. Vaughn and Lewis, 281–96.

43. Cossío del Pomar, *Cossío del Pomar*, 45.

44. Heath Bowman, *Death is Incidental, a Story of Revolution* (Chicago: Willett, Clark and Company, 1937).

45. Cossío del Pomar, *Cossío del Pomar*, 46–47, 65.

46. Frederic Babcock, "Detour," *Chicago Daily Tribune*, October 17, 1937, E6.

47. On the appeal of places like Santa Fe and Taos to avant-garde artist circles, see Flannery Burke, "Finding What They Came for: The Mabel Dodge Luhan Circle and the Making of a Modern Place, 1912–1930" (Ph.D. diss., University of Wisconsin, Madison, 2002). For Santa Fe's transition to a middle-class tourist destination, see Charles H. Montgomery, *The Spanish Redemption: Heritage, Power, and Loss on New Mexico's Upper Rio Grande* (Berkeley: University of California Press, 2002), especially the conclusion.

48. Judith Cass, "The South Gets Full Share of Summer Trips," *Chicago Daily Tribune*, July 6, 1938, 13.

49. Frederic Babcock, "Another Taxco Discovered in North Mexico," *Chicago Daily Tribune*, March 31, 1940, F7.

50. Frederic Babcock, "Tourists in a Hurry Pass Up These Oases," *Chicago Daily Tribune*, April 7, 1940, J9.

51. Cossío del Pomar, *Cossío del Pomar*, 51.

52. Ibid., 94–96.

53. Ibid., 97, 142.

54. "Travel Queries Answered," *Chicago Daily Tribune*, December 31, 1941, 9; "Travel Queries Answered," *Chicago Daily Tribune*, April 8, 1942, 18; and "Travel Queries Answered," *Chicago Daily Tribune*, December 23, 1942, 12.

55. Diana Rice, "Two Mexican Summer Schools," *New York Times*, August 16, 1942, D8.

56. Cossío del Pomar, *Cossío del Pomar*, 55.

57. Hudson Strode, *Now in Mexico* (New York: Harcourt, Brace, and Co., 1947).

58. Ibid., 304.

59. Ibid., 306.

60. Ibid., 310–11.

61. Ibid., 314.

62. Ibid., 327.

63. U.S. Congress, Senate, *Servicemen's Readjustment Act of 1944*, 78th Cong., 2nd session, S.1767, June 22, 1944.

64. The State Department initially approved twenty Mexican schools and universities for GI Bill subsidies in 1946 (among them the school in San Miguel) and added many more in subsequent years. These Mexican schools were among hundreds of others approved worldwide. See Circular from the U.S. State Department to the American Diplomatic and Consular Officers, April 24, 1946, United States National Archives and Records Administration (hereafter NARA), State Department Record Group 84 (hereafter RG 84), Mexico City Embassy General Records, box 712.

65. Letter to the Secretary of State from Elías G. Garza, American Vice Consul of San Luis Potosí, June 4, 1946, NARA, RG 59, 103.9992/6–446, 1945–1949, box 397.

66. John Virtue, *Leonard and Reva Brooks: Artists in Exile in San Miguel de Allende* (Montreal: McGill-Queen's University Press, 2001), 99–100.

67. Ibid., 122.

68. Dorothy Vidargas, interview by the author, January 18, 2003. Her name at that time was Dorothy Birk.

69. "Education Notes," *New York Times*, May 12, 1946, 81; John Evans, "Minnesota Offers Hospital Administration Course," *Chicago Daily Tribune*, August 18, 1946, E6; "Education Notes," *New York Times*, August 18, 1946; W. Thetford LeViness, "Mexican Hill Town," *New York Times*, October 31, 1948, X18; Ernest L. Pratt, "Mexico Looks on Tourism as Big Business," *Chicago Daily Tribune*, January 9, 1949, E4; Frank Cipriani, "Ex-Chicagoans Re-Discover a Mexican Town," *Chicago Daily Tribune*, March 6, 1949, G1.

70. "GI Paradise," *Life*, January 5, 1948, 56–58, also quoted in Virtue, *Leonard and Reva Brooks*, 120.

71. Leonard Brooks, interview by author, July 15, 2004; Vidargas, interview by the author, January 18, 2003.

72. Virtue, *Leonard and Reva Brooks*, 105, 109.

73. Vidargas, interview by the author, January 18, 2003.

74. Virtue, *Leonard and Reva Brooks*, 121.

75. Vidargas, interview by the author, July 9, 2004.

76. Several sources, including "GI Paradise," and Cipriani, "Ex-Chicagoans Re-Discover a Mexican Town," mention the town priest's reactions to the students, although only a few mention Mercadillo by name, including Virtue, *Leonard and Reva Brooks*. He does not address this in his own memoirs of the same period, José Mercadillo Miranda, *Anecdotas sin importancia* (San Miguel de Allende: Impresa San Miguel, 1960).

77. AGN, MAV, exp. 11/1140. Also see Charles Allen Smart, *At Home in Mexico: How the Smarts Solved the Problem of Retiring on a Low Budget* (New York: Doubleday, 1957), 127–32; Cossío del Pomar, *Cossío del Pomar*, 159–62; Virtue, *Leonard and Reva Brooks*, 127–34; and Diana Anahalt, *A Gathering of Fugitives:*

American Political Expatriates in Mexico, 1948–1965 (Santa Maria: Archer Books, 2001), 108–9.

78. AGN, MAV, exp. 11/1140.

79. "Warning! Be Careful with the Deceitful Communists!," October 1949, NARA, RG 59, 103.9992/10–349, 1945–1949, box 407.

80. Helen Delpar, *The Enormous Vogue of Things Mexican: Cultural Relations between the United States and Mexico, 1920–1935* (Tuscaloosa: University of Alabama Press, 1992), 152–53.

81. Dorothy Vidargas, personal correspondence, March 29, 2003.

82. From a conversation between the author and some residents who were children in San Miguel at the time.

83. Quoted from a grievance letter signed by several veterans. AGN, MAV, exp. 11/1140.

84. Virtue, *Leonard and Reva Brooks*, 150.

85. "Artists Blame Mixup in Ouster from Mexico," *Chicago Daily Tribune*, August 15, 1950, 22.

86. "8 Deported by Mexico Linked to 'Peace' Aim," *New York Times*, August 15, 1950, 6. The author has been unable to locate documentation of these deportations in Mexican government archives.

87. Virtue, *Leonard and Reva Brooks*, 156.

88. Cossío del Pomar, *Cossío del Pomar*, 165–68.

89. Ibid., 167, 173–75.

90. For example, Stephanie Martin, "Mexican Town Pays Honor to Native Patriot," *Chicago Daily Tribune*, October 14, 1951, F17; and "Mexico City Road to Open," *Los Angeles Times*, November 16, 1952, D7.

91. For example, Roland A. Goodman, "Winter in Mexico," *New York Times*, December 9, 1951, 320.

92. Thomas F. Brady, "Mel Ferrer Gets Lead at Columbia," *New York Times*, February 14, 1950, 29; " 'The Brave Bulls' Is Moving Film," *Washington Post*, June 20, 1951, 17; Bosley Crowther, "Screen: Boy and a Horse," *New York Times*, December 27, 1955, 31; Arthur Pollock, " 'Serenade' South of the Border," *New York Times*, November 13, 1955, X5; and A.H. Weiler, "Screen: Lanza is Back," *New York Times*, March 23, 1956, 21.

93. For example, see "Scholarship Contest," *Washington Post*, September 30, 1951, L3; and Eleanor Jewett, "1954 Art Scholarship Available in Mexico," *Chicago Daily Tribune*, November 15, 1953, G8.

94. Peter Olwyler, "Dateline . . . Mexico City," *Travel*, January 1957, 9; ibid., August 1957, 7; and ibid., February 1958, 11.

95. Ibid., January 1957, 8.

96. Ibid., June 1957, 9.

97. Wayne Greenhaw, *My Heart is in the Earth* (Montgomery: River City Publishing, 2001).

98. Eric Zolov, "Discovering a Land 'Mysterious and Obvious': The Renarrativizing of Postrevolutionary Mexico," *Fragments of a Golden Age: The Politics of Culture in Mexico Since 1940*, ed. Gilbert Joseph, Anne Rubenstein and Eric Zolov (Durham, N.C.: Duke University Press, 2001), 253–57. See Eric Zolov, *Refried Elvis: The Rise of Mexican Counterculture* (Berkeley: University of California Press, 1999), for an overview of countercultural travelers in Mexico from the late 1950s to the late 1970s.

99. See Zolov, *Refried Elvis*, especially the introduction through chapter 3.

100. Bert Quint, "More Than 100 Expatriate Reds In Mexico Viewed as Peril to U.S.," *Washington Post and Times Herald*, August 30, 1957, A4; "Red Haven," *Time*, September 9, 1957, 46; both of these articles are quoted in Anahalt, *Gathering of Fugitives*, 160.

101. Quint, "More Than 100 Expatriate Reds in Mexico Viewed as Peril to U.S."

102. See Friedrich Katz, "La guerra fría en América Latina," *Espejos de la guerra fría: México, América Central y el Caribe*, ed. Daniela Spenser (Mexico City: Centro de Investigaciones y Estudios Superiores en Antropología Social, 2004), 11–28.

103. Anahalt, *Gathering of Fugitives*, 161–62.

104. Joe Hyams, "The 'Sorbonne' of Latin America," *Washington Post and Times Herald*, February 23, 1958, C12.

105. Miguel J. Malo Zozaya, *Guía turista en San Miguel de Allende* (San Miguel de Allende: Instituto Allende, 1958), advertisement section.

106. Translated from "magnífico panorama, extensos jardines, atractivos cuartos, [y una] excelente cocina internacional."

107. Report on the various facilities coordinated by INBA, 1964, SEP Archivo Histórico, INBA, Coordinación General, 1962–1972, caja 1.

108. Advertisement, Centro Cultural Ignacio Ramírez, summer of 1964.

109. Miguel Malo and F. León de Vivero, *San Miguel Allende* (Mexico City: Instituto Nacional de Antropología e Historia, 1963).

110. Mack Reynolds, "Vacation School for Tourist Families," *New York Times*, May 23, 1954, X23.

111. For example, "Se sabe que van a establecerse otras industrias en diversas lugares del Estado," *El Vocero del Norte*, March 1, 1970, 1; "Tal parece que otras ciudades como San Luis de la Paz, Dolores Hidalgo, y otras mas del Norte y Oriente del Estado, han recibido beneficios que a la nuestra se le han negado," *El Vocero del Norte*, May 31, 1964, 1, 6; and Antonio Ruíz Valenzuela, "San Miguel de Allende necesita industrias," *El Vocero del Norte*, March 20, 1966, 2.

JEFFREY M. PILCHER

JOSÉ CUERVO AND THE GENTRIFIED WORM

Food, Drink, and the Touristic Consumption of Mexico

The importance of food in human identity has long been recognized in the aphorism "we are what we eat," but recently scholars have also begun to consider the influence of our eating habits on others. The dinner table provides an arena for building community through two distinct processes, the physical act of sharing sustenance with insiders and the symbolic boundaries that exclude the food of outsiders as inedible.[1] Historically, those dividing lines are highly permeable, and groups often seek to assimilate alien foods, transforming them through the cultural act of cooking to render them safe for consumption. Yet people may also intentionally transgress the boundaries of edibility either as a form of domination or simply for thrill seeking.[2] Through food and drink, tourists from the United States have consumed their Mexican neighbors: alternately dominating, transforming, excluding, and embracing them according to an Orientalist logic that evolves with social relations in both countries.[3]

The demands of industrial provisioning have shaped mainstream notions of wholesome food in the United States since the 1880s, when tourists first encountered Mexican cuisine in the Southwest, but despite insistent advertising, many consumers have remained skeptical of the benefits of processed foods. Nineteenth-century urbanization made it impossible to provide fresh food from the surrounding countryside for millions of people, and the technologies of canning and refrigeration unquestionably improved the diets of poor city dwellers. Although industrial fast food has inspired growing discontent, there can be little doubt that the widespread provisioning of wholesome food and clean water contributed significantly to growing life expectancy in Europe and the United States.[4] Nevertheless, industrial supply systems required significant concessions from consumers, who could no longer trust their own sense of smell, taste, touch, and sight to judge quality. Forced to rely on brand-name goods of questionable purity, the working classes literally swallowed the alienation of industrial capitalism.[5] Under these circumstances, a counterculture emerged that rejected the benefits of Anglo-Saxon civilization, at least temporarily, and sought renewal through the exoticism of seemingly primitive lands like Mexico.[6] Primitive foods, in particular, offered a visceral thrill of transgression from overly processed factory fare. Anita Brenner, editor of the popular 1930s touristic magazine *Mexican Folklore*, recommended: *"Gusanos de maguey*, literally maguey worms, don't shudder, look like nothing you ever saw before. A highland delicacy."[7]

Both nations have embraced this culinary dichotomy, in which Mexican indigenous authenticity stands opposed to North American industrial efficiency, yet the reality is far more complicated. The United States has its own Creole cuisines, including New England dishes of native provenance and Southern foods shaped largely by African-American hands. Moreover, many contemporary icons of the U.S. industrial kitchen, including hamburgers and hot dogs, began as marginalized immigrant foods and gained mainstream acceptance, or "citizenship," through a process distinct from industrial rationalization.[8] Mexican entrepreneurs meanwhile applied modern technology to their own national cuisine, opening canneries for *frijoles refritos* (refried beans) and *mole poblano* (chile pepper sauce). As the staple tortilla came to be made overwhelmingly of *masa harina* (dehydrated maize flour), tourist restaurants achieved distinction by hiring women to make tortillas by hand. The fabled worm at the bottom of the tequila bottle was a completely invented tradition. According to legend, the pickled gusano provided a rustic indication of alcohol content (if too low, the worm would rot), but in fact it was added in the 1940s as a marketing gimmick by modernizing distillers seeking to enshrine tequila within a homespun national identity being staged by Mexican cinema.[9]

Although an enormous literature has documented the harmful effects of industrial food processing on both humans and the environment, the impact of tourists on the cultures they consume has not been defined so clearly.[10] The philosopher Lisa Heldke contends that food colonialism can have cultural as well as economic manifestations. Taco Bell certainly does violence to Mexican cuisine, but even the tourist's quest for authenticity proceeds from the imperial assumption that ethnic food is a resource available to North American consumers. "Food adventurers," as Heldke labels those who continually seek out novel cuisines, rarely acknowledge that their search depends on self-exploitation among migrant employees of ethnic restaurants in the United States as well as among tourism workers in developing countries. Feminists meanwhile connect such unequal power relations with the sexualization of social difference, whereby whites seek out ethnic experiences as a spice for the boredom of mainstream culture.[11] Yet critics of cultural food colonialism would not recommend a nativist rejection of foreign food either. Like all attempts to dictate food choices, the program for anti-imperial eating poses serious moral dilemmas.

This essay examines the different images of Mexico constructed by tourists through the foods and drinks they consumed. Visions of sexual contamination framed the initial Anglo encounters in the Southwest from the 1880s to the 1920s. Piquant chile pepper sauces and rough distilled alcohol were used as metaphors for the supposedly unquenchable passions of Mexican women. Ethnic culture posed a challenge for the expansion of Anglo civilization, to make the landscape safe for proper domesticity, including both pure foods and Victorian sexual control. A century later, by the 1980s, corporate, consumerist lifestyle was not only well established but had inspired its own countercultural revolutions, both gastronomic and sexual. For new generations, Mexican indigenous cooking and boutique tequilas offered an escape from the bland conformity of restaurant chains. Undocumented migrant workers had meanwhile become essential to middle-class domesticity—as cooks, cleaners, nannies, and gardeners—and their sexuality had to be erased from popular vision. Spring break in Cancún might still be a site of sex tourism, but in segregated enclaves for college students from the United States. Thus, each generation of North American tourists found a Mexico to fit its taste.

"Hot Tamales" in the Southwest

The tourist discovery of Mexico was in large part the story of internal colonialism in the Southwest, for the first sustained encounters between Anglos and Mexicans took place in lands conquered by the United States in 1848. Although the Treaty of Guadalupe Hidalgo guaranteed the property rights of former Mexican citizens, Anglo settlers claimed much of the best real estate through fraud and violence. To justify these swindles, Mexicans were stereotyped as lazy and duplicitous, hence unworthy of the land. Mexican women meanwhile gained a reputation as sexually available but racially threatening.[12] Some of the first Anglo migrants married into the local elite as an easy path to acquiring property, and when the land ran out, Mexican female sexuality was reduced to a tourist attraction. Two widely renowned symbols of Mexican womanhood, the "chili queens" of San Antonio and Prohibition-era border prostitutes, exemplified this alluring yet polluting focus of tourist consumption.

The chili queens were vendors who set up tables in city plazas to sell a variety of Mexican foods, not just chili con carne, to the diverse residents and tourists of San Antonio, Texas. The latter first appeared in large numbers with the arrival of the Southern Pacific Railroad in 1877, and shortly thereafter, San Antonio began to notice the importance of chili vendors as a tourist attraction. In 1879 the *Express* observed: "Strangers who visit San Antonio are frequently seen about these tables . . . tasting of this and that out of mere curiosity, and are often surprised to find that many nice things are served up."[13] Within a few years, they had become a fixture of tourist guidebooks. The 1882 edition of the *Alamo City Guide* described "lunch tables, where one can get a genuine Mexican breakfast with as good hot coffee as can be found in the city. Those who delight in the Mexican luxuries of tamales, chili con carne, and enchiladas, can find them here cooked in the open air in the rear of the tables and served by lineal descendants of the ancient Aztecs."[14]

Although one could savor a Mexican breakfast or lunch, the chili queens were most commonly associated with al fresco dining in the glow of brass lanterns. Because the vendors had been expelled from Alamo Plaza by urban renewal in 1893, tourists sauntered over to the Mexican side of town, west of the San Pedro Creek, for an evening of transgressive food and flirtation. With "various savory compounds, swimming in fiery pepper, which biteth like a serpent," chili con carne offered a satanic cauldron to Anglo palates accustomed to bland white sauces and suspicious of every possible adulteration.[15] In addition to challenging their physical bravery, masculine tourists also had an opportunity to test their virile charms through repartee with the chili vendors, "bright, bewitching creatures [who] put themselves to much trouble to please their too often rowdy customers."[16] Dusky and sharp-witted, they fit into the "hot tamale" stereotype of Mexican women waiting to be tamed in the imagination of Anglo men; not coincidentally, the chili vendors worked in Milam Plaza in the heart of San Antonio's West Side red-light district.

Contemporary illustrations published in the *San Antonio Express* made

1. "A Chili Queen," San Antonio, Texas, 1894. Portrait of a chili queen. COURTESY OF *SAN ANTONIO DAILY EXPRESS*, SUNDAY MORNING, JUNE 17, 1894.

this sexual connection clear. One drawing showed an attractive woman wearing a shawl and smoking a cigarette, an indication of her lack of propriety and hence sexual availability. An accompanying sketch depicted "some of the chili queen's friends," including a tourist from back east sporting a monocle and boat hat, an African American with outlandishly thick lips, and a "trans-San Pedro dude"—a diamond-studded gangster who crossed over to the Mexican side of town for his business dealings. Rounding out the quartet of "friends" was an aged crone, who served as procuress for the young woman according to artistic conventions dating back to medieval Europe and also reminded readers that her physical beauty would soon be ravaged by time.[17]

Much of the allure of the "chili queens" lay in their transgression of the boundaries of race and hygiene. Tourist advertisements highlighted the incongruity of finding Mexican vendors in a modern U.S. city. Just as their olive skin supposedly darkened the plazas of San Antonio, their foods threatened to pollute the bodies of those who dared to sample them. "Ignorance in the details of their manufacture is necessary to the complete enjoyment of tamales," wrote one journalist, who went on to explain that those

SOME OF THE CHILI QUEEN'S FRIENDS.

2. "Chili Friends," San Antonio, Texas, 1894. Composite representing types of people who visit chili stands in San Antonio, Texas. COURTESY OF *SAN ANTONIO DAILY EXPRESS*, SUNDAY MORNING, JUNE 17, 1894.

who have seen Mexican food being prepared in West Side *jacales* (shacks) "have been known to swear off on the seductive viands with surprising emphasis. The abstinence seldom lasts long, however, for tamales have too rare a deliciousness to be renounced on account of a trifle of dirt." His conclusion might have referred equally to the hygienic character of the tamales or to the supposed racial quality of the women who made them: "Since they can't be washed or disinfected it is well to take them as they are and thank heaven that they were ever made at all."[18]

The title of "queen," with its connotation of prostitute or transvestite, further emphasized the parody of Anglo standards of domesticity. For railroad travelers of the late nineteenth century, the Mexican vendors contrasted sharply with the prim waitresses working in Harvey House restaurants. This early restaurant chain set a standard for providing familiar and reliable New England–style cooking at stops along the transcontinental lines. Advertisements assured patrons that "Harvey girls" came from decent families back east and were carefully chaperoned by the company. Anglo "girls" thus promised to bring civilized dining to the "wild west," whereas

Mexican "queens" offered little more than a thrilling experience of a disappearing ethnic landscape.[19]

Drink was equally important in formulating stereotypes about Mexican culture. Historically, binge drinking has been no more common in Mexico than in the "alcoholic republic" to the north.[20] But the gradual spread of temperance sentiment, particularly in the U.S. South, left Mexican border towns as havens for tourist consumption, even before the Eighteenth Amendment took effect in 1920. For example, California's red-light abatement laws and similar local ordinances had outlawed alcohol in many parts of the Southwest since the late nineteenth century. During Prohibition, the bulk of rum-running came across the Great Lakes from Canada, where laws banned the consumption of alcohol but not its production and export. The national image of Canadians suffered little as a consequence because police and journalists focused on the Italian "menace," most notoriously, Al Capone. But the Mexican border emerged from the decade firmly established in the collective mentality as a "wide-open" place where "anything goes."[21]

Prohibitionists visiting the border were scandalized by the opportunities for tourist vice in the 1920s. Martha Bensley Bruère found "nothing that approaches decency or respectability in [Ciudad Juárez]; the streets are lined entirely and without exception with saloons, usually with American names above them—Jake's Place, Pete's Place, and the like—with gambling houses with gay Frenchified names, and with disorderly houses of the most blatant type."[22] Officials of the Methodist Church concurred, noting Tijuana's reputation as a "mecca of prostitutes, booze sellers, gamblers and other American vermin."[23] As these outraged moralists indicated, foreign businessmen and women dominated much of the vice trade along the border, but this did little to redeem the tourist's stereotype of Mexico.

Even those who crossed the border often had little actual experience with Mexican *aguardiente* (fire water) at this time. The first tequila exports, in 1873, consisted of three barrels shipped by Cenobio Sauza to El Paso, Texas, also the location of a presidential summit meeting in 1910 between William Howard Taft and Porfirio Díaz, which reputedly was celebrated with tequila. During Prohibition, smugglers carried some quantities of the Mexican drink across the border, although the greater part of both bootleg traffic and border-town sales came from British liquor transshipped through Mexico or U.S. manufacturers who relocated south of the line. The D&H and D&W distilleries of Kentucky, for example, transferred their plants to Ciudad Juárez for the duration.[24]

Regardless of its source, the connection between alcohol and prostitution was clear in the minds of both tourists and moral reformers. Eric Schantz has described the social and cultural geography of red-light districts on the border during Prohibition. Locations such as the Owl Café and Theater in Mexicali and the Aguascalientes Resort in Tijuana provided a full range of services to tourists. Visiting Hollywood celebrities could enjoy the race-tracks and the company of attractive women while sipping the finest Champagne; segregated bars offered the lower classes "vile alcohol disguised as whiskey" and prostitutes of all races.[25]

Women also participated in this border tourism, but even flappers did so at the risk of their reputations, and perhaps worse, as in the case of San Diego's notorious "shame suicides." In January 1926, the apparently upstanding family of Thomas Peteet, his wife Carrie, and daughters Audrey and Clyde visited Tijuana for a week of revelry. One evening, while Carrie rested in the hotel room, her husband and daughters went on a drinking spree that culminated with the alleged drugging and rape of the young women by the Tijuana chief of police and other assailants. After giving depositions to border authorities, the entire family returned home and committed suicide. During the subsequent trial, however, a variety of witnesses from both sides of the border testified to the scandalous drinking and immoral lifestyle of the Peteets, prompting a Mexican jury to acquit the suspects.[26]

Reform efforts dedicated to protecting society often started with the ethnic foods that supposedly nourished such delinquency. Health officials in San Antonio long worked to restrict the chili vendors, deeming them a public nuisance in the 1890s and eventually a threat to sanitation in the 1930s. But success in eliminating the ethnic cooks came only after chili had been domesticated for mainstream consumers through a process of industrialization. Already in the 1890s, D. C. Pendery of Fort Worth and William Gebhardt of New Braunfels had begun to market dried versions of chili powder as a pale imitation of the Mexican food cooked by San Antonio women. Eventually, they developed successful mail-order businesses shipping canned chili products throughout the country. Publicity photos of immaculate white-gowned workers in Gebhardt's factory reassured customers that the company maintained high standards of sanitation. Other nonethnic businessmen, such as Dave Pace and Elmer Doolin, likewise made fortunes selling Mexican-style products including bottled "Pace" picante sauce and "Fritos" corn chips.[27]

Restaurateurs also sought to capitalize on ethnic street foods by making them appear more hygienic and therefore acceptable to mainstream consumers. Otis Farnsworth, proprietor of the Original Mexican Restaurant, which opened in San Antonio around 1905, used only pristine tablecloths, napkins, and silverware that one would expect of continental cuisine. The menu had none of the combination plates that later came to distinguish Tex-Mex cuisine; waiters dressed in white coats presented each enchilada and tamale individually on fine china, according to a woman who dined there in the 1920s. "Ordinarily Father didn't want to eat anything unless Mother had cooked it because he didn't think anyone else could cook anything that was 'sanitary.' I think they had him fooled into thinking their food was sanitary by the immaculate manner in which an order was taken and served."[28] In Mexico City, William and Frank Sanborn offered a similar gold standard of tourist dining. Located in the renowned House of Tiles, formerly home of the elite Jockey Club, Sanborn's garnered the endorsement of *Terry's Guide to Mexico* as "the premier restaurante in the Mexican Republic" thanks to "certified pure water" and milk "from certified Jersey cows kept on the Sanborn Farm under scrupulously clean conditions."[29] Chefs greeted North American travelers with familiar hot cakes and ice cream sodas in addition to a nonthreatening selection of Mexican cuisine, including their signature dish, *enchiladas suizas* (Swiss enchiladas) topped with cream and cheese.

Notwithstanding the efforts of Otis Farnsworth and the Sanborn Brothers, Mexican foods had acquired a deeply plebeian image in the United States. The proliferation of taco shops and ethnic restaurants in the Southwest during the first half of the twentieth century, and their nationwide spread in the second half, only confirmed these lower-class associations. The adoption of the *china poblana* costume—an often low-cut peasant dress of red, white, and green—as an almost official uniform of waitresses in Mexican restaurants further cemented the connection between hot tamales and exotic sexuality that was already well established in San Antonio in the 1880s. The subsequent inversion of these stereotypes, and the discovery of a world-class cuisine among the indigenous peasantry of southern Mexico, are the subjects of the following section.

Gourmet Paradise in Deep Mexico

Even as Taco Bell and its rivals blanketed the United States with franchises in the 1970s and 1980s, more discriminating consumers set off in search of authentic Mexican cuisine and top-shelf tequilas. In doing so, they shunned the typical tourist locations along the border and in beach resorts and looked instead to a form of ethnic tourism in southern Mexico, particularly the state of Oaxaca. Their quest benefited from local developments, including the maturation of the national tourism industry and a growing appreciation among the Mexican elite for native cultures, which was reflected in the success of Guillermo Bonfil Batalla's bestselling indigenous manifesto, *México profundo* (Deep Mexico, 1987). Yet this new culinary tourism was just as commercialized as the rest of the vacation industry and likewise depended largely on fashions determined by the United States.

Perhaps the most important source of peasant gentrification came from the hippie counterculture appearing on college campuses in the 1960s, which questioned excessive consumerism, corporate bureaucracy, suburban lifestyles, and chemical pollution of the environment. In the hippie approach to eating, as the historian Warren Belasco has noted, "two guidelines proved handy: Don't eat anything you can't pronounce (i.e., no propylene glycol alginate, a stabilizer used in bottled salad dressing) and if worms, yeast, and bacteria grew on it, then it must be natural, for no self-respecting bug would eat plastic. Inverting established notions of spoilage, the countercuisine equated preservatives with contamination and microbes with health."[30]

This movement was matched in Mexico by youth who likewise began to question the single-party state and its ideology of assimilating Native Americans into a conformist mestizo "cosmic race." Indigenous symbols provided an alternative source of national identity for Mexicans who began calling themselves *xipitecas* (pronounced "hippy tecas," like the Aztecas). Some established groups to perform supposedly pre-Hispanic dances dressed in plumed costumes, while others followed the international hippies in creating a rock 'n' roll counterculture and searching out the hallucinogenic mushrooms of Mazatec folk healers in Oaxaca. Meanwhile, anthropologists went back to the countryside, doing fieldwork among indigenous communities and contributing to a new appreciation among the elite for rural food and drink.[31]

By the 1980s, the demand for authentic Mexican food on both sides of the border created a considerable potential market, which businessmen eagerly sought to exploit. The cookbook publishing industry was at the forefront of this movement, following the tone set by Diana Kennedy's *The Cuisines of Mexico* (1972). This landmark cookbook introduced readers to such classic recipes as *mole poblano*, snapper Veracruz, tamales from Michoacán, and Yucatecan pit-roasted pig. Kennedy subsequently published a number of sequels charting ever more exotic village foods, *Recipes from the Regional Cooks of Mexico* (1978), *The Art of Mexican Cooking* (1989), and *My Mexico* (1998). Kennedy and dozens of rivals blend the genres of cooking literature and travel writing, often including glossy photos of cooks, food vendors, and people celebrating local festivals in distinctive local costumes. The authors clearly mark the authenticity of their recipes, for example, assuring readers, "For local residents of Puerto Vallarta there is no *pozole* to compare with that of Señora Rafaela Villaseñor."[32] Such claims have become essential in the increasingly crowded Mexican cookbook market, as ever more exotic recipes offer a form of product differentiation.

Restaurants provided another venue for food adventurers to sample more authentic Mexican dishes. The appearance of Southwestern cuisine as part of a fascination with regional cooking in the 1980s contributed to this growth. A Los Angeles chef, John Rivera Sedlar, first revived Otis Farnsworth's approach of serving Mexican street foods as haute cuisine, and contemporaries including Robert Del Grande, Stephan Pyles, and Mark Miller soon followed suit. Although these upscale tamales and stuffed chile peppers were freely adapted using European cooking techniques, a number of more authentic restaurants opened in that decade, most notably the Frontera Grill in Chicago and Rosa Mexicano in New York. Mexicans proved equally savvy about commercializing their newly discovered culinary heritage. The city of Puebla refurbished as a tourist attraction the convent kitchen where, according to legend, *mole poblano* was invented. Restaurants such as Fonda Don Chon, in Mexico City, specialized in supposedly pre-Hispanic foods, while others began serving the *nueva cocina mexicana*, a nouvelle approach similar to Southwestern cuisine in the United States.

Starting in 1988, Kennedy's fans could experience the ultimate form of gastronomic tourism to Mexico by taking cooking classes with her through Culinary Adventures, a company organized by Marilyn Tausend. Oaxaca offered the natural focus for culinary tourism based on this pre-Hispanic past, and the state provided an important, although not exclusive, destination for Tausend's tours. Participants traveled first to Mexico City and began their experience with a visit to the world-renowned museum of anthropology, focusing not on the main pre-Hispanic displays but on the less frequently visited second-floor ethnographic exhibits. Having marked the objects of tourist interest, primarily cooking utensils and ethnic textiles, the group proceeded to the city of Oaxaca, where they met with Diana Kennedy, who shared her encyclopedic knowledge of Mexican cuisine. When not in class, students toured the monumental ruins of Monte Albán and went shopping in Oaxaca's numerous folk art galleries. The highlight of the trip for many was a visit to a private home in the Zapotec village of Teotitlán del Valle, known for its elaborate weavings. The local merchant family of Abigail Mendoza demonstrated the preparation of traditional wedding festival foods. Afterward, the indigenous cook and weaver accompanied the group to a rustic distillery of mescal, a Oaxacan version of tequila, then did a roaring business selling textiles to the tourists. For a final examination, the students were turned loose on the Saturday market in Oaxaca City to purchase dried chiles and herbs with the proviso that they had to pass through U.S. agricultural inspection to reproduce at home the dishes they had just learned.[33]

Tausend's success prompted a number of other culinary tour groups led by cooking schools and expatriate chefs living in Mexico. Culinary tourism also provided business opportunities for ethnic intermediaries. Abigail Mendoza parleyed her cooking skills and international connections into a successful tourist restaurant, and her exotic recipes soon found an appreciative audience far beyond the pueblo of Teotitlán del Valle. Diana Kennedy acknowledged her as "*the* star of the Zapotec kitchen," and both *Gourmet* and *Saveur* magazines ran feature articles on her.[34]

The gentrification of Mexican food in turn helped inspire a boom in top-shelf tequilas at the end of the twentieth century. The industry first began to transform itself in the 1930s, when Eladio Sauza, a prominent distiller and hacienda-owner in Tequila, Jalisco, anticipated the agrarian reform campaigns of revolutionary President Lázaro Cárdenas by diversifying into urban real estate in nearby Guadalajara, including the city's first commercial radio stations. Sauza's media connections, especially with regional mariachi musicians, proved highly useful in launching an advertising campaign to change the image of tequila from the drink of *albañiles* (bricklayers) to a national icon. Throughout the 1940s, a highly successful genre of *ranchero* movies featured an obligatory cantina scene, with paeans to tequila sung by the leading stars of the national cinema. Jorge Negrete and Pedro Infante even helped popularize the etiquette of licking salt, downing tequila shots, and sucking lime. Middle-class Mexicans, who previously would never have been seen with such a plebeian beverage, were soon emulating their favorite stars, so much so that to keep up with demand, producers began to dilute the traditional blue agave spirits, eventually reaching a legal minimum of 51 percent agave for *mixto* (blended) tequila, with the balance made up of other alcohols. Tequila soon became a truly national drink, consumed even in Yucatán, although many citizens of this distinctive southeastern state considered it an alien beverage and preferred their own local beers.[35]

Even as Mexican distillers updated their technological skills, social changes in the United States were crucial to the acceptance of Mexican alcohol. Although many have viewed Prohibition as a failure, the historian Catherine Gilbert Murdoch considered it a crucial turning point for gender relations in the United States. Prior to the 1920s, drinking was largely a public performance restricted to men in taverns. Women certainly drank, but they seldom did so in public for fear of moral condemnation. When alcohol consumption was driven underground, it paradoxically entered the domestic sphere, becoming a heterosocial activity. Fruity cocktails replaced the straight whiskey and beer of the saloons. Middle-class culture thus succeeded in taming the worst excesses of male boozing, in essence, "domesticating drink," although perhaps at the expense of growing rates of female alcoholism.[36]

Women drank increasing quantities as the century progressed, but it was seldom tequila, which retained a frat-house image of masculine excess until the 1990s. The sudden transformation of the drink's image was probably not a result of advertising; indeed, the boom came as something of a surprise to producers, who faced severe agave shortages as a result.[37] Instead of marketing, experts attributed the tequila boom to growing tourism, increased consumption by women in the United States, and renewed acceptance by the Mexican middle classes, for whom the drink had fallen out of fashion with the midcentury decline of ranchero movies.[38]

Regardless of the cause of the windfall, industry leaders sought to manage the boom by cultivating upscale consumers. Production focused on high-end *añejo* (aged for at least one year in oak casks) tequilas made from 100 percent blue agave, with particular attention to eye-catching bottle designs. Specialized forms of tourism likewise developed, including a Tequila Express train running from Guadalajara to the Herradura distillery, multiple tequila museums, and a theme park, Mundo Cuervo (Cuervo World), reputed to be a family-oriented attraction, complete with strolling musicians and local handicrafts. For travelers with other destinations, José Cuervo opened a chain of Tequilera restaurants in airport departure lounges throughout the United States and Mexico. New marketing campaigns adopted the rarified language of the sommelier: "Tequila is just as complicated as a fine wine when it comes to aromatic components," explained Ana María Romero, master taster for

Sauza. She continued: "The blue agave grown in the highlands of Jalisco contains more water while agave from the flatlands has more herbal notes and more fiber."[39] Advertisers even invented a new etiquette; after all, for tequilas selling at more than $200 a bottle, salt and lime were strictly passé. Journalist Matthew DeBord wrote: "Rather than swirling tequila, place your palm over the mouth of the glass and shake the liquid to release its aromas. One hundred percent blue agave tequila will smell of white pepper, pine needles and fresh herbs. Mixto tequila may exude an off aroma of burnt rubber."[40]

To prevent such quality-control problems, in 1994 Mexico joined the Lisbon Accord, granting tequila "denomination of origin" (DOC) status. A Tequila Regulatory Council thereafter determined standards for what could be sold as "tequila" in signatory nations. An obvious target for this regulation was the homebrewed alcohol made by small growers in the region. Council director Ramón González observed: "Having some of those drinks is like getting a cat shoved down your throat backwards."[41] Yet local moonshine was less of a problem than international competition. Mexican shortages encouraged South African companies to market an agave drink, although they could not call it tequila because of the DOC restrictions.[42] But no such constraints bound the United States, which has become the world's foremost consumer of tequila. By 2003, more than 80 percent of the tequila sold in the United States was shipped in bulk and bottled by local distillers. Although many believe that unauthorized sales of poor-quality tequila undermine the Mexican drink's reputation, industry leaders have profited from this cross-border wholesale trade. Sauza and Cuervo, struggling to compete for transnational markets, have forged strategic alliances and mergers with the conglomerates Allied Domecq and Heublein, who rationalize production between Mexican and North American subsidiaries. Without political support from leading producers, attempts to restrict tequila bottling to Mexico have been rejected as a form of trade protectionism.[43]

The two-tiered structure of tequila—with a relatively small market for estate-bottled añejos and mass sales of U.S.-blended mixtos—extends to the entire Mexican tourism industry. Culinary vacations to Oaxaca are limited to the elite, while most North Americans consider nachos and margaritas as the apex of Mexican gastronomy. Nevertheless, versions of authentic Mexican cuisine have staked a claim within the rapidly growing market for gourmet foods in the United States. In doing so, they have largely eschewed the sexuality, if not the contamination, that formerly defined Mexican culture.

But the question remains whether the ethnic and national community will benefit from this contemporary boom any more than did the chili vendors of San Antonio a century ago.

The original warnings of cultural imperialism, that local cultures would soon disappear before an onslaught of McDonald's restaurants, have gone out of fashion within academia, although that has not stopped populists such as the French burger Luddite José Bové. Rather than seek to bulldoze restaurants directly, scholars have focused on the subversion of American-ization by people who appropriate the global chain into local cultures and create hybrid versions of fast food. Anthropologists have also observed that the tourist consumption of culture runs both ways across the Rio Grande, with middle-class Mexicans eager to sample North American popular culture through McDonald's and even Taco Bell.[44] However reassuring such notions of subaltern resistance may sound, there remains a "fundamental difference between the flow of food northward to rich countries, and the flow of food southward." As Richard Wilk points out: "The average North American consumer never has to think of where their grapes, tomatoes, or cornflakes come from, but at the other end of the scale of global power, things look very different. This is partly a matter of being poorer and want-ing to spend money more carefully." Yet more important, he notes, was the preservation of class distinction within local societies: "Knowing about for-eign goods, how to consume and buy them, was one of the ways that colonial elites maintained their cultural power."[45]

The social contexts of consumption are of vital importance in determin-ing the outcome of market relationships. As the case of culinary tourism to Mexico illustrates, perhaps the most important advantages of the head start in industrialization by the global north has been the ability to create valuable brands. Corporations such as Taco Bell, like earlier entrepreneurs William Gebhardt and Elmer Doolin, have made fortunes mass-producing the ethnic foods of others. The French have taken a different approach, parlaying ro-mantic notions of the soil and of peasant cultivation through the cachet and legal protection of *terroir*. But regardless of its source, the image of northern power and modernity has underwritten their enduring profitability. Mexi-can products, by contrast, remain mired in the "perfect" competition of basic commodities. Even the legal protections of terroir for tequila have been largely undermined by the structure of global alcohol markets and the need to seek alliances with conglomerates based in the north. Ethnic inter-mediaries such as Abigail Mendoza face still greater disadvantages vis-à-vis multinational corporations. For her traditional dishes to retain their cachet within the local community, they must remain carefully guarded secrets and cannot leak out to magazines such as *Saveur*. Moreover, unlike such fabled secret formulas of the corporate world as KFC's eleven herbs and spices or Coca-Cola's syrup, it would be virtually impossible for Mendoza to profit from mass-producing Oaxacan peasant dishes. One even wonders about the long-term viability of the ethnic restaurant she operates as migration pat-terns and the inroads of capitalism increasingly distance village life from its former traditions.

Changing social relationships, particularly gender expectations, within the United States have had a tremendous impact on the nature of the tour-ism business in Mexico. In Victorian society, when the sexuality of Anglo women was supposed to be tightly constrained by patriarchal domination, fantasies of transgression were put off onto Mexicans and other exotics. The liberation of middle-class women, and their movement from the kitchen into the workplace, has caused a reconfiguration of the social contexts in which the labor and bodies of the "other" were consumed. Thus, hot tamales and chili queens have been replaced by new exotics—indigenous Oaxacan women—who provide gourmet food to women rather than sexual favors to men. The Zapotec chef has become an updated version of the late-nine-teenth-century brand "Aunt Jemima," an African American "Mammy" who was desexualized to sublimate the threat of domestic workers within white households. Such an image has become necessary as undocumented mi-grant workers from southern Mexico have taken over the work of mowing lawns and caring for children in middle-class families. True, Mexico has remained a source of sex tourism, but it has increasingly become a scenic background for frolicking college students in Cancún.[46] The sexuality of the Mexican "other" has been suppressed to facilitate the global realignment of labor, including the need for two-income families to maintain middle-class status in the United States.

Nevertheless, the gusanos consumed in upscale Oaxacan restaurants continue to mark a crucial boundary between a primitive Mexico and a modern United States. Peasants formerly grilled these worms fresh off the agave as a source of protein, but restaurants generally get a dried product, which they sauté in butter to reconstitute, and then sell for upwards of $10 a plate so that tourists can experience a moment of transgression from eating them on tacos. At the same time, contemporary debates about migration portray Mexican workers as a source of contamination, worms invading the nation. The exoticism surrounding ethnic foods and identities becomes another justification for excluding people from the body politic; their labor is consumed, however squeamishly, while their human rights are denied.

Notes

An earlier version of this essay was published as "From 'Montezuma's Revenge' to 'Mexican Truffles': Culinary Tourism across the Rio Grande," in *Culinary Tourism*, edited by Lucy M. Long (Lexington: University of Kentucky Press, 2004), 76–96.

1. Emiko Ohnuki-Tierney, *Rice as Self: Japanese Identities through Time* (Princeton, N.J.: Princeton University Press, 1993).
2. Lucy M. Long, "Culinary Tourism: A Folkloric Perspective on Eating and Otherness," *Culinary Tourism*, ed. Lucy M. Long (Lexington: University of Kentucky Press, 2004).
3. See Edward W. Said, *Orientalism* (New York: Random House, 1979), 20–50.
4. Jack Goody, *Cooking, Cuisine, and Class: A Study in Comparative Sociology* (Cambridge: Cambridge University Press, 1982), 154–74. For contemporary protests, see Wendell Berry, *The Unsettling of America: Culture and Agriculture* (San Francisco: Sierra Club Books, 1996); Carlo Petrini, *Slow Food: The Case for Taste*, trans. William McCuaig (New York: Columbia University Press, 2001).
5. On resistance to this trend in France, see Martin Bruegel, "How the French Learned to Eat Canned Food, 1809–1930s," *Food Nations: Selling Taste in Consumer Societies*, ed. Warren Belasco and Philip Scranton (New York: Routledge, 2002), 113–30.
6. Fredrick B. Pike, *The United States and Latin America: Myths and Stereotypes of Civilization and Nature* (Austin: University of Texas Press, 1992); Helen Delpar, *The Enormous Vogue of Things Mexican: Cultural Relations between the United States and Mexico, 1920–1935* (Tuscaloosa: University of Alabama Press, 1993).
7. Brenner later collected material from the magazine into a tour guide, *Your Mexican Holiday* (New York: G. P. Putnam's Sons, 1941), 281.
8. Donna R. Gabaccia, *We Are What We Eat: Ethnic Food and the Making of Americans* (Cambridge, Mass.: Harvard University Press, 1998). On the complexity of ethnic and national boundaries within the U.S. food processing industry, see idem, "As American as Budweiser and Pickles? Nation-Building in American Food Industries," *Food Nations: Selling Taste in Consumer Societies*, ed. Warren Belasco and Philip Scranton (New York: Routledge, 2002), 175–93. For the instructive early history of the hamburger, see David Gerard Hogan, *Selling 'em by the Sack: White Castle and the Creation of American Food* (New York: New York University Press, 1998).

9. Matthew DeBord, "Más Tequila!" *Wine Spectator* 28.2 (May 15, 2003), 86–90.

10. Upton Sinclair, *The Jungle* (New York: Doubleday, Page, 1906); Rachel Carson, *Silent Spring* (New York: Fawcett Crest, 1962); Jack Doyle, *Altered Harvest: Agriculture, Genetics, and the Fate of the World's Food Supply* (New York: Viking, 1985).

11. Lisa Heldke, *Exotic Appetites: Ruminations of a Food Adventurer* (New York: Routledge, 2003); bell hooks, "Eating the Other: Desire and Resistance," *Eating Culture*, ed. Ron Scapp and Brian Seitz (Albany: State University of New York Press, 1998), 181–200; Uma Narayan, "Eating Cultures: Incorporation, Identity, and Indian Food," *Social Identities* 1.1 (1995): 63–86.

12. Arnoldo de León, *They Called Them Greasers: Anglo Attitudes toward Mexicans in Texas, 1821–1900* (Austin: University of Texas Press, 1983).

13. Quoted in Donald E. Everett, *San Antonio: The Flavor of Its Past, 1845–1898* (San Antonio: Trinity University Press, 1975), 32.

14. Quoted in Andrew F. Smith, "Tacos, Enchiladas, and Refried Beans: The Invention of Mexican-American Cookery," *Cultural and Historical Aspects of Food*, ed. Mary Wallace Kelsey and ZoeAnn Holmes (Corvallis: Oregon State University Press, 1999), 183–203.

15. Edward King (1874) quoted in Gabaccia, *We Are What We Eat*, 108–9.

16. *San Antonio Express*, June 17, 1894.

17. Ibid.

18. *San Antonio Express*, August 25, 1897, quoted in Everett, *San Antonio*, 33.

19. Harvey A. Levenstein, *Revolution at the Table: The Transformation of the American Diet* (New York: Oxford University Press, 1988).

20. W. J. Rorabaugh, *The Alcoholic Republic: An American Tradition* (New York: Oxford University Press, 1981); Peter Thompson, *Rum Punch and Revolution: Taverngoing and Public Life in Eighteenth-Century Philadelphia* (Philadelphia: University of Pennsylvania Press, 1998). For Mexican comparisons, see William B. Taylor, *Drinking, Homicide, and Rebellion in Colonial Mexican Villages* (Stanford, Calif.: Stanford University Press, 1979).

21. Eric Schantz, "All Night at the Owl: The Social and Political Relations of Mexicali's Red-Light District, 1909–1925," *On the Border: Society and Culture between the United States and Mexico*, ed. Andrew Grant Wood (Lanham, Md.: SR Books, 2004), 114; Andrew Sinclair, *Prohibition: The Era of Excess* (Boston: Little, Brown, 1962); Gilman M. Ostrander, *The Prohibition Movement in California, 1848–1933* (Berkeley: University of California Press, 1957).

22. Martha Bensley Bruère, *Does Prohibition Work?* (New York: Harper and Brothers, 1927), 80.

23. Quoted in Oscar Martínez, *Border Boom Town: Ciudad Juárez since 1848* (Austin: University of Texas Press, 1978), 58.

24. Tim Mitchell, *Intoxicated Identities: Alcohol's Power in Mexican History and*

Culture (New York: Routledge, 2004), 94; Bob Emmons, *The Book of Tequila: A Complete Guide* (Chicago: Open Court, 2003); Martínez, *Border Boom Town*, 59; Sinclair, *Prohibition*, 198.

25. Schantz, "All Night at the Owl," 100, 106–11, 115–20; see also Paul Vanderwood, *Juan Soldado: Rapist, Murderer, Martyr, Saint* (Durham, N.C.: Duke University Press, 2004), 90–103.

26. Vincent Cabeza de Baca and Juan Cabeza de Baca, "The 'Shame Suicides' and Tijuana," *On the Border*, ed. Wood, 145–76.

27. Gabaccia, *We Are What We Eat*, 165, 219–20.

28. Mary E. Livingston, *San Antonio in the 1920s and 1930s* (Charleston, S.C.: Arcadia Publishing, 2000), 41–42.

29. T. Philip Terry, *Terry's Guide to Mexico* (Boston: Rapid Service Press, 1944), 243.

30. Warren J. Belasco, *Appetite for Change: How the Counterculture Took on the Food Industry* (Ithaca, N.Y.: Cornell University Press, 1993), 40.

31. Claudio Lomnitz-Adler, *Exits from the Labyrinth: Culture and Ideology in the Mexican National Space* (Berkeley: University of California Press, 1992), 255–56; Eric Zolov, *Refried Elvis: The Rise of the Mexican Counterculture* (Berkeley: University of California Press, 1999), 107–8.

32. Diana Kennedy, *My Mexico: A Culinary Odyssey with More than 300 Recipes* (New York: Clarkson-Potter, 1998), 56; see also 282.

33. This account is based on the author's experience of a Culinary Adventures tour to Oaxaca, January 4–13, 1992.

34. Kennedy, *My Mexico*, 390. *Gourmet*, February 1991; *Saveur*, Summer 1994.

35. José Orozco, "Gabriel Espíndola Martínez: Tequila Master," *The Human Tradition in Mexico*, ed. Jeffrey M. Pilcher (Wilmington, Del.: SR Books, 2003), 225–33; Mitchell, *Intoxicated Identities*, 153, 163; Steffan Igor Ayora-Díaz and Gabriela Vargas-Cetina, "Romantic Moods: Food, Beer, Music and the Yucatecan Soul," *Drinking Cultures: Alcohol and Identity*, ed. Thomas Wilson (London: Berg, 2005), 155–78.

36. Catherine Gilbert Murdoch, *Domesticating Drink: Women, Men, and Alcohol in America, 1870–1940* (Baltimore: Johns Hopkins University Press, 1998).

37. An industry-wide blight further depressed production; prices peaked in 2002 before beginning to stabilize. See Ana Guadalupe Valenzuela-Zapata and Gary Paul Nabham, *Tequila: A Natural and Cultural History* (Tucson: University of Arizona Press, 2004).

38. Ioan Grillo, "On the Tequila Express," *Latin Trade* 11.10 (October 2003): 68–69.

39. Quoted in Patricia Alisau, "Discovering Mexico's Liquid Treasure," *Business Mexico* 14.11 (November 2004): 56.

40. DeBord, "Más Tequila."

41. Grillo, "On the Tequila Express," 68.

42. Ibid.

43. "Storm in a Tequila Bottle," *Economist*, October 4, 2003, 38.

44. The case for cultural imperialism has been argued forcefully by George Ritzer, *The McDonaldization Thesis* (London: Sage, 1998). For countervailing arguments, see James L. Watson, ed., *Golden Arches East: McDonald's in East Asia* (Stanford, Calif.: Stanford University Press, 1997); Jeffrey M. Pilcher, "Taco Bell, Maseca, and Slow Food: A Postmodern Apocalypse for Mexico's Peasant Cuisine?" *Fast Food/Slow Food*, ed. Richard Wilk (Walnut Creek, Calif.: Altamira Press, 2006), 69–81.

45. Richard Wilk, *Home Cooking in the Global Village: Caribbean Food from Buccaneers to Ecotourists* (Oxford: Berg, 2006), 17.

46. This is not to deny the existence of border-town brothels or the more recent growth of "romance tourism" by middle-class women looking for sex with so-called beach boys. See Deborah Pruitt and Suzanne LaFont, "For Love and Money: Romance Tourism in Jamaica," *Annals of Tourism Research* 22.2 (1995): 422–40.

M. BIANET CASTELLANOS

CANCÚN AND THE CAMPO

Indigenous Migration and Tourism Development
in the Yucatán Peninsula

Studies that examine the cultural meanings of tourism concentrate on the tourist or the communities located in tourist centers.[1] Yet in light of tourism's regional impact, its value and significance are highly contested at the periphery of tourist zones.[2] Indeed, as a result of rural-urban migration, these debates make their way to tourist centers and become integrated into mainstream social conceptions of tourism. The international tourist resort of Cancún offers an example of this process. Cancún is well known for its white sandy beaches and turquoise waters. Advertisements of this tourist city depict expansive hotels full of modern amenities, such as air conditioning and swimming pools, nestled within the mysterious land of the Maya with its grand pyramids and exotic flora, fauna, and people. Local leaders suggest that these images display only one facet of Cancún. They argue that Cancún consists of three cities: the hotel strip where all the tourists congregate, the commercial center where the everyday business of selling tourism happens and the middle class lives, and the *colonias* (shantytowns), locally known as *regiones*, located on the periphery of the commercial center where the working class resides and the emerging middle class constructs large homes that represent their aspirations for social mobility.

Cancún is made up of more than just the images circulated internationally, the tourists who congregate annually, and the people who reside within its city boundaries. Rural indigenous communities on the margins of tourist sites also play a central role in the invention and development of and the local value attached to tourist projects like Cancún. What does tourism mean in terms of economic opportunities and cultural change to communities located on the periphery of tourist regions? What kinds of relationships develop between tourist resorts and the communities that may be somewhat distant from tourist sites but nevertheless provide the labor necessary for these sites to exist? Tourist encounters—whether face-to-face, via a satellite dish, or through storytelling—profoundly shape the lives of the people who inhabit these communities. It is through the circulation and discussion of these encounters that indigenous communities make sense of tourism development and of their place within it.

In order to understand native people's perspective of tourism, I employ the concept of the "native gaze"—the universalizing ways local people "see" tourism and tourists and construct them as other.[3] Tracing the permutations of these encounters, both positive and negative, through a case study of Kuchmil, a rural Maya community with a history of migration to Cancún, allows us to examine how indigenous communities in Mexico's Yucatán Peninsula make sense of, engage with, and gaze back at the products, services, and people that form part of the Cancún experience.[4] The mixed feelings generated by this relationship illustrate the far-reaching effects of tourism development and highlight local criticisms of the limitations of modernization projects.

I also rely on the theoretical concept of the "migrant circuit" derived from studies of transnationalism in order to engage with the local and global implications of tourism development in Mexico.[5] According to the anthropologist Roger Rouse, a migrant circuit represents a "*site* in which transnationally organized circuits of capital, labor, and communications intersect with one another and with local ways of life."[6] Within such a circuit, social constructions of meaning such as community, gender, and tourism are no longer limited to a specific locale but are defined by the social interactions and relations within multiple sites. Considering that Cancún is made up of transnational circuits of bodies, money, labor, and communications, the concept of the migrant circuit provides a way to think critically about the circulation of the social meanings of tourism within this space and about the *regional* affects of transnational capital and international tourism. The following discussion maps out the development of the Kuchmil-Cancún migrant circuit and provides a brief overview of the historical roots of Cancún's establishment.

Cancún: A National Tourist Project

Understanding what people make of tourism and the particular feelings generated by tourist encounters entails situating tourism within the wider political economy of global restructuring and projects of modernity.[7] In Yucatán, the state government considered tourism a way to generate revenue for state projects. In 1901, Yucatecan politicians lobbied the national government to build a railroad to the peninsula's isolated eastern region in order to facilitate the exploitation of its natural resources and archaeological sites.[8] Likewise, Governor Felipe Carrillo Puerto (1922–24) promoted tourism in order to fund his socialist revolutionary government and to foster a regional indigenous identity.[9] After liberalizing Yucatán's divorce law in 1923, Carrillo Puerto's administration circulated brochures abroad that advertised Yucatán as the ideal place for a quick divorce and an exciting vacation.[10] This publicity campaign attracted foreign visitors from North America, Europe, and Canada and created a new revenue source for the revolutionary government.[11] Carrillo Puerto also inaugurated the construction of a road to Chichén Ítza, one of the archaeological sites being excavated by the Carnegie Institute.[12] To foster pride in Maya culture and language, Carrillo Puerto sponsored weekly cultural programs and disseminated copies of the *Chilam Balam* and the *Popol Vuh*.[13] Thus, Yucatecan politicians primarily considered tourism a way to promote a regional identity and to improve their local economy.

For the federal government, however, tourism formed part of the postrevolutionary nationalist cultural project intended to unify a fractured nation and to modernize the nation-state.[14] This project involved creating a national Mexican identity rooted in Mexico's pre-Columbian and colonial past and folk culture. To showcase these national treasures, the Mexican government funded the excavation of archaeological zones and their conversion into open-air museums of Mexico's past. The presence of numerous archaeological sites, beautiful colonial cities, and "typical" indigenous villages eventually transformed the Yucatán Peninsula into a site for heritage tourism—tourism that promotes the consumption of a nation's cultural heritage (cultural traditions, archaeological sites, historical buildings, landscapes, and the like) by a domestic and foreign audience—and into an integral component of the nation-state's tourism plan.[15] Yet the success of tourism as a development model required more than the presence of antiquities. Beginning in 1927, the federal government invested heavily in its local infrastructure (roads, hotels, airports), changed its migration policies, and created ministries and associations to promote tourism abroad.[16] Unfortunately, insufficient funds, the Great Depression, World War II, and a lack of organization limited the growth of Mexico's tourism industry.[17]

To increase the number of tourists within Mexico, the administration of

President Miguel Alemán Váldes (1940–46) attempted to "modernize" tourism by shifting the focus from heritage tourism to beach tourism—a type of tourism that promotes "sand, sun and sea" activities.[18] Such a transformation was expected to increase foreign exchange, allow for the commodification of Mexico's natural beauty, and cater to the growing Mexican middle class. Nevertheless, Mexican tourism continued to be defined in part by heritage tourism because Mexico's archaeological sites and colonial cities remained popular tourist sites.[19]

The Cancún project continued this effort to modernize tourism and the nation through its blend of heritage and beach activities.[20] After World War II, improvement in transportation and communication technologies made tourism accessible to the expanding middle class of industrialized countries who could afford a holiday abroad. For Third World countries, tourism was considered a new way of attracting foreign exchange and developing peripheral zones and regions.[21] This development was intended to promote job growth in poor regions dominated by agriculture and fishing industries and thereby meant to curb rising migration flows to industrialized urban centers. Not surprisingly, by the late 1960s the Mexican government considered tourism as the most effective way to modernize the countryside and divert mass migration from Mexico's core to its periphery.[22] After years of planning, the construction of Cancún began in 1971.

Cancún served as a model for the future development of four other tourist cities in Mexico: Ixtapa-Zihuatenejo in Guerrero, Cabo San Lucas and Loreto in Baja California Sur, and Huatulco in Oaxaca.[23] Cancún was the first of these cities to be built because it was sparsely populated, easily accessed topographically, situated adjacent to the warm waters of the Caribbean Sea (an area with a history of successful tourist projects), and located near the famous archaeological sites of Chichén Ítza and Tulum. In addition to providing jobs, this tourist project served as a civilizing mission in which rural indigenous peasants would be transformed into good workers and modern citizens through contact with foreigners from industrialized countries.[24]

Since these tourist cities have emerged as international tourist sites within the last two decades, researchers have recently begun to examine their economic, political, and social significance for the surrounding region and nation, and for international relations. Studies of Cancún have focused on the growth and development of the city itself and its effect on neighboring cities.[25] Although these studies point out the increasing number of migrants, many of whom are indigenous, arriving daily in search of work, they do not dwell on the implications of establishing an international tourist center within a predominantly indigenous region.

The Kuchmil-Cancún Migrant Circuit

For rural indigenous Maya communities, tourism has not produced the advantages propagated by the national tourist plan. Ana Juárez's study of Tulum demonstrates that tourism reduces the natural resources available and essential to the survival of Maya communities.[26] Similarly, Quetzil Castañeda documents the struggle between the state, private capital, and the indigenous community of Pisté, which neighbors Chichén Ítza, over the benefits of tourism development.[27] Alicia Re Cruz's study of Chan Kom draws attention to tourism's impact on rural indigenous communities. Re Cruz suggests that migrant labor from Chan Kom to Cancún ruptures traditional forms of work and household organization and results in a power struggle between "modern capitalists" and "traditional peasants."[28] These studies provide a glimpse into the complex feelings generated by this modernization project.

But what does tourism mean to indigenous communities that are more geographically isolated and not as extensively studied by social scientists as the communities of Pisté and Chan Kom? The community of Kuchmil, which is located in the heart of the southeastern jungle of the state of Yucatán and is far away from the Maya tourist corridor, provides an example of a rural indigenous community's expectations of and reactions to tourism. In the late 1890s, a Maya peasant discovered the postclassic ruins and drinking well of Kuchmil during his search for land to cultivate corn. In 1930, the federal government recognized the land in and around Kuchmil as part of the *ejido* (communal land grant) of Chan Sahkay.[29] Ninety-two residents lived in Kuchmil at this time. By the 1960s, a federally recognized elementary school was established in Kuchmil, but the community was still too small to house a secondary school and a health clinic. Although all the residents were devout Catholics, local residents traveled to the neighboring town to attend mass in its colonial church. In the 1980s, after the community built a new church, a priest began visiting the community once a month to perform mass. In 1986, the establishment of a *secundaria* (equivalent to junior high school) in a neighboring town made it possible for the children of Kuchmil to study near their home.

Prior to 1990, an unpaved road provided the only route by which to access Kuchmil. Since this road was rocky, making it slippery and treacherous to cross during the rainy summer months, most people traveled by foot, horse, or bicycle, with the exception of the Coca-Cola sales representatives whose diesel trucks were powerful enough to traverse most landscapes. Leaving the village for the nearby city of Valladolid required at least a day's travel. This geographical isolation limited out-migration and ensured that village life remained rooted in traditional practices. By 2001, the local population had grown to 123 inhabitants. Kuchmil residents cultivated corn, built wood huts with thatched roofs, and spoke Maya as their primary language; the women continued to wear *hipiles*.[30] Not surprisingly, these social practices and customs made life in Kuchmil appear as if it were timeless.

While the villagers were cognizant of the heritage tourism that generated significant revenues in the region (even before the construction of Cancún), few villagers, predominantly men, worked directly in this industry due to the relative physical isolation of Kuchmil and the limited job opportunities made possible by this type of tourism. Of those who sought work in heritage tourism sites, a couple of men worked for archaeological excavations, while others worked as anthropological informants of "typical" Maya culture. Kuchmil women, in contrast, spent their days sewing hipiles for tourist consumption. Due to its seasonal nature and the geographical isolation of most archaeological sites, heritage tourism was never intended to substitute for farm work. Instead, local participation in heritage tourism supplemented farm work in Kuchmil.

In contrast, mass tourism, which generates tourist cities like Cancún, relies on large amounts of labor and thus attracts migrants. As Cancún became internationally renowned for its white sandy beaches, warm tropical waters, and lively nightlife, migration to this city radically increased, growing from 8,500 workers in 1975 to 419,815 inhabitants in 2000.[31] By the year 2002, 142 hotels had been built, serviced by 60 percent of the economically active residents living in the county.[32] Male migrants tend to work as waiters and bartenders in hotels, restaurants, and nightclubs, while female migrants are more apt to work as domestic servants in private homes and chambermaids and waitresses in hotels. Yet given the seasonal nature of tourism, mass tourism does not generate enough well-paying jobs to improve the economic status of most peninsula residents. Access to steady well-paying tourist jobs hinges on age, language use, and education, characteristics that exclude a significant portion of rural residents, as in the case of Kuchmil.

In spite of the distance between Cancún and Kuchmil, the residents of Kuchmil were quick to take advantage of the benefits generated by international tourism. Seasonal male migration to work in Cancún's construction industry quickly replaced previous forays to seek wage work in Valladolid. In the late 1970s and early 1980s, upon graduating from junior high and high school, Kuchmil youth, primarily boys who had spent most of their young lives in boarding schools, found work in Cancún as waiters, bellboys, and bartenders. Initially, only a few women worked as domestic servants in Cancún, but after the road was paved in 1990 and a bus route was established that reduced travel to Cancún from one day to a six-hour bus ride, young women from Kuchmil joined their brothers there. However, these unmarried women preferred domestic service work to hotel work because it offered a more flexible schedule and significantly higher daily wages. Today it is expected that the young men and women of Kuchmil will migrate to Cancún after finishing high school, if not before.

As a result of this participation, the community of Kuchmil was not immune to the changes brought on by mass tourism. As migrants travel between Kuchmil and Cancún, cultural practices and knowledge of these sites impinge on each other. Migrants' ideas about gender roles, work, space, and social relations were rooted in local customs and rural village life. Not surprisingly, as migrants spent time in Cancún, they adopted urban cultural practices and acquired knowledge about health and the legal system unavailable back home. Kuchmil migrants' encounters with foreigners and non-Yucatecan Mexicans influenced their ideas about their bodies, their culture, their country, and themselves. Upon returning home to Kuchmil, migrants brought with them these new ideas, feelings, and attitudes. This constant circulation of goods, knowledge, and behaviors within this migrant circuit produced a multitude of experiences and emotions in both communities.

To unearth the experiences and ideological tensions generated by tourism in Kuchmil, I first analyze the community's perceptions of Cancún and tourism—its native gaze. Considering that most migrants moved to Cancún between the ages of thirteen and sixteen, generational differences between those who leave and those who remain behind, along with shifting ideas about the meaning of work, deeply influence these perceptions. Additionally, I examine the local discourse on Cancún, because how people talk about tourism also shapes their perceptions of tourism. Frequent encounters with tourists coupled with the technological revolution, through satellite television, expose native people of tourist sites to universal images of the tourist. Not surprisingly, as result of these "encounters," native discourse about tourism centers on these universal images. Analyzing how these ideas circulate and gain salience sheds light on how tourism shapes Maya cultural ideologies and village life.

Pueblos and Peasants

At first glance, tourism does not appear to have had an impact on village life in Kuchmil. Even local residents, when asked about tourism and its effects, located tourism as happening elsewhere, such as in the city of Zací (named Valladolid by the Spanish conquistadores), a pre-Columbian city that is currently the commercial epicenter of southeastern Yucatán. Valladolid's colonial architecture, freshwater *cenotes* (sinkholes), and its proximity to the ruins of Chichén Itzá and Ek Balam and the sacred talking cross of Xocen have attracted thousands of tourists. According to local residents, tourists drove by Kuchmil in their quest for authentic archaeological "treasures," Indian *pueblos* (villages), and well-known sites of orchestrated adventure such as the eco-archaeological park Xcaret, where tourists explore Maya ruins, swim with dolphins, and snorkel in the park's underground river. Occasionally, tourists who veer off the main highway in search of "authentic" Indian villages "discover" Kuchmil. Since it is not located near a well-known tourist site, these encounters are few and far between.

Ironically, by maintaining particular cultural values and forms of expression that reinforce the idea that "tourism has passed us by," the community of Kuchmil represents itself as a harmonious Maya *pueblo* based on a communal landholding system, the very image that attracts tourists and anthropologists in search of authentic Maya people. I chose Kuchmil as a field site because of its "traditional" way of life, with its wood houses and thatched roofs, its continued use of the hipil by local women, its practice of swidden agriculture, its ejido, and its fluency in the Yucatec Maya language. As such, Kuchmil defined itself against that which it did not want to become, namely, the large, impersonal towns and cities that Kuchmil residents considered to be inhabited by people who do not respect one another and to be plagued by social problems such as alcoholism, political corruption, and extreme poverty. To attract tourism, anthropologists, and the dollars that they carry, indigenous communities like Kuchmil must stage their authenticity by remaining timeless and marginal on the surface.[33]

Yet during encounters with tourists and foreigners, Kuchmil residents depicted themselves not as the cultural inheritors of ancient Maya culture but as humble, poor *campesinos* (peasants or farmers) who were deeply invested in ideas about "progress." Although they acknowledged that they

1. Preparing for the Fiesta of the Santa Cruz. PHOTO BY M. BIANET CASTELLANOS.

were descended from *los antiguos* (the ancient Maya), Kuchmil residents did not claim an indigenous identity as Maya. Historians and anthropologists point out that "the Maya" is not a homogenous, stable ethnic identity but rather has been constituted over time by state policies, ethnopolitics, racial hierarchies, and the global economy.[34] Initially imposed by Spanish colonizers, this ethnic identity continues to be perpetuated by intellectuals and the international media. Some rural and urban Yucatecans adopted this term as a conscious form of self-identification following the internationalization of indigenous movements in the 1960s.[35] I use the term "Maya" because I wish to engage with the academic community. However, many "Maya" people today use self-referents based on class, dress, and linguistic markers rather than ethnicity. In Kuchmil, residents refer to themselves as *campesinos*, *óotsilo'ob'* (poor people), *macehaules* (workers), *mestizos*, and "de Kuchmil" (to be from Kuchmil).

As a result of their encounters with foreigners and Mexicans from other regions, such as Chiapas and Oaxaca, Kuchmil migrants in Cancún adopt the identity of *mayero*—someone who speaks Maya—to differentiate themselves from other ethnic groups and linguistic speakers and to create a sense of ethnic solidarity. According to the anthropologist Wolfgang Gabbert, in some regions, *mayero* can refer to "anyone who speaks Maya, irrespective of descent or social status."[36] Among Kuchmil migrants, this term did not hinge on speaking Maya but was used specifically to refer to a particular ethnic and class position and social experience within a particular setting, that is, a migrant of Maya descent who may or may not speak Yucatec Maya but who was raised by campesinos in the Yucatán Peninsula. When Mariela Can Tun explained to me the definition of a mayero, she jokingly commented, "Since you speak Maya, you are a mayera!" Of course, we both knew that this identification hinged not just on speaking Maya but on being "Maya," a social position rooted in "race/class distinctions."[37] During their first few years in Cancún, Kuchmil migrants' social networks consisted primarily of other mayeros who provided job information, emotional and social support, and resources (e.g., loans).

The legacy of colonialism also taints local perceptions of tourism and continues to affect social practices to the present day. After the Spanish conquest of Mexico, the Maya lost their land, were conscripted into indentured servitude, and suffered extreme poverty.[38] As a result, Maya cultural knowledge was lost, and cultural artifacts were stolen and in some instances destroyed by foreigners.[39] During my first visit to Kuchmil, local residents made evident their tense and fraught relationship with the ruins of this legacy. After being shown the ruins of the postclassic pyramids on which Kuchmil was built, an archaeology student, Pauline Sánchez,[40] and I set out to examine the broken pottery shards lying at the bases of these pyramids. We were chased away by children who threw rocks at us and accused us of being "treasure hunters." Kuchmil residents have purposely kept these ruins hidden from tourists and foreigners because they fear that the legacy of their ancestors will be stolen or purchased with American dollars. On a few occasions, local residents offered to sell me archaeological artifacts they discovered in their *solares* (house plots) because it was assumed that as a foreigner I would be interested in buying such items.[41] This type of exchange, both commercial and social, bred a distrust of foreigners and at the same time generated a desire for the purchasing power of American dollars.

The Work of Tourism

Kuchmil's ambivalence toward tourism also stemmed from the conflicting outcomes associated with tourism development. While mass tourism created jobs that paid better salaries than local sources of employment, these jobs did not necessarily meet local expectations of social and economic mobility. These expectations arose in the 1960s before the construction of

Cancún as a result of the ecological degradation of local farmland and declining government subsidies for small farmers. At this point, residents of Kuchmil realized that wage work had become a necessity for the reproduction of village life. Not surprisingly, many residents came to believe that wage work would improve the quality of their lives and thus increase their children's social mobility.

Kuchmil parents encouraged their children, in particular boys, to participate in wage labor after finishing school. To improve their children's access to well-paying jobs, Kuchmil families sent their sons, and in some instances daughters, to regional boarding schools (both elementary and secondary) in the late 1960s; these families believed that an education would provide their children with the essential skills for steady wage employment. By the time these children graduated from boarding school in the early 1980s, the construction of Cancún had already begun. Tales of a dollar-based economy and an abundant source of jobs motivated these youth to try their luck in Cancún.

The first cohort of migrants reaped the benefits of a booming and developing international tourist city. The hotel industry's interest in developing loyal, long-term, skilled employees allowed these migrants to quickly move up the hotel industry's job hierarchy and settle in Cancún. Eventually, these young men married and brought their wives and sisters to Cancún. By the 1990s, single women had become equal participants in this migrant circuit. As a result of this steady out-migration, Kuchmil residents gained access to a wide social network to facilitate the job search. Consequently, Cancún became known first and foremost as a source of steady employment for Kuchmil youth and secondarily as a source of seasonal employment for the community's married men. Most importantly, tourism appeared to be capable of fulfilling Kuchmil parents' expectations of social and economic mobility.

The community of Kuchmil discussed tourism using metaphors previously employed to describe corn cultivation. In Kuchmil, 'iši'im (corn) was life. Also called *gracia* (meaning both thanks and grace of God), corn was considered both sacred and sustenance.[42] Thus, corn was work and work meant corn. For the youth of Kuchmil, the decline in the productivity of agriculture made tourism synonymous with work and life. Juan, a young male migrant, explained: "Sin el turismo, no hay trabajo. Sin el turismo, no comemos." [Without tourism, there is no work. Without tourism, we don't eat.] Since few employment opportunities exist beyond the service industry for recipients of a high school diploma or a vocational degree, Kuchmil youth have become dependent on tourism for work. Horacio, a Kuchmil migrant, emphasized this dependency when he told me, "Vivimos del turismo. [We live off of tourism.]" Thus, for today's youth, tourism was work and work meant tourism.

Unlike corn cultivation, whose bounty was considered to be dependent on divine providence, tourism as a relatively new phenomenon was not considered sacred. Tourist jobs could not be conjured through prayer or feasts to the saints. The residents of the countryside had little control over tourist flows and transnational hotel corporations' hiring practices. Yet they depended on the fickle tastes of tourists and their willingness to tip. Kuchmil migrants criticized this dependency, especially as the model of tourism development changed over time. Initially, the construction of Cancún generated jobs, but they were primarily low-skilled jobs in construction and services (hotels, shops, restaurants) that were filled by Maya farmers. As hotels expanded and more hotels were built, the small labor pool forced developers to recruit workers from the surrounding countryside and neighboring state of Yucatán. The labor shortage ensured that businesses invested time and money to train these workers. Gustavo, the first Kuchmil migrant to arrive in Cancún in 1980, recalled how the hotels sent recruiters directly to the shantytowns to recruit workers with high salaries for menial labor. He remembered, "Como de antes no había problema para conseguir trabajo. . . . Un día dejas de trabajar y al otro día ya tienes empleo. [It wasn't a problem to get work back then . . . You could leave your job on one day and the next day you could find another one.]" Between 1974 and 1977, however, low-skilled jobs (e.g., janitors, construction assistants, and dishwashers) decreased, while skilled jobs in services and construction (e.g., construction workers, waiters, receptionists, and tour guides) increased.[43] More experienced workers from other parts of Mexico migrated to Cancún to fill these positions.[44] By 1985, 35,000 residents, most of them from the neighboring state of Yucatán and the central states of Mexico, inhabited the "support city."[45]

In the mid-1980s, however, a shift in the classic tourism model challenged the conviction that tourist jobs improved regional economies. Previously, Cancún was designed to attract tourists who were willing to pay top dollar for exclusive access to its beaches and turquoise waters. This type of tourism was premised on a sharp separation between work and leisure, requiring the construction of a tourist city in which workers and clients rarely interacted, with the exception of the workers who serviced the tourists in the hotels.[46] In order to sustain its growth, tourism manufactured

2. Hotel mimics Palapa designs of Maya homes.
PHOTO BY M. BIANET CASTELLANOS.

more low-wage jobs than professional jobs.[47] Accordingly, migration to Cancún multiplied exponentially. But by the mid-1980s, mass tourism required a shift in these practices, transforming the classic model of tourism through a demand for a variety of services and experiences.[48] Activities oriented around the sun and the sea no longer satisfied tourists. New sites for consumption, like shopping centers, outdoor water activities, lagoon activities, and *mercados* (outdoor markets), were established or revitalized. To address these changing tastes, the Fondo Nacional de Fomiento del Turismo (FONATUR or the National Tourism Development Trust) no longer built massive hotels. Rather, new hotel projects were intentionally kept small to blend in with the local environment and were located along the underdeveloped coastal area between Cancún and the Belizean border.[49] Regardless of the push to develop tourism south of Cancún, migrants continue to arrive daily in Cancún.

In light of this labor surplus and following global trends, hotel corporations are no longer willing to invest in their workers. Employees are offered

short-term contracts rather than the previously common long-term contracts, are expected to work longer shifts, and must forgo vacation time
during the high tourist season. As a result of this shift in labor practices,
Kuchmil residents have come to equate tourist work with slave labor during
the colonial period—as conveyed to them by their grandparents' experiences—due to the long work hours, double shifts that left them sleep-
deprived, low wages, limited vacation time, and, in some instances, haz-
ardous work conditions. Consequently, migrants who were replaced with
unskilled short-term contract employees sought jobs south of Cancún,
along the Mexican Riviera, while a few have returned to the more flexible
schedule and independent life of farm work in Kuchmil.[50]

For those who remained behind in Kuchmil, tourism was likened to the
legendary *štáab'ay*,[51] a beautiful, seductive woman who attracts men away
from their communities. The štáab'ay, a mythical and ghostly female figure in
Yucatec Maya culture, represents the downfall or social death of man. She
appears to men at night or while they are away from their communities, for
example, working in the *milpa* (cornfield). Like the štáab'ay, the beauty of
Cancún attracts foreigners and locals alike. The money, however, motivates
migrants to settle and raise their families in Cancún.[52] The residents of
Kuchmil argued that the migration of their youth resulted in the declining
vitality of their local leadership and sense of community. Adela, a prominent
young woman in Kuchmil, exclaimed, "No nos ayuda el turismo. Se lleva a la
gente. Si no, fueramos muchos. [Tourism doesn't help us. It takes people
away. If not (for tourism), there would be many of us (here).]" Migrants also
echoed this fear. Leonardo, a Kuchmil migrant, lamented, "Para mi, el pueblo
se está desapareciendo. Ya no hay gente. La gente se va. Cuando regresó a mi
pueblo, no hay nadie. [To me, *el pueblo* is disappearing. The people are gone.
All of the people leave. When I return to my pueblo, there is no one.]"

For the community of Kuchmil, Cancún represents the phantasmic effects of modernization. As a metanarrative of progress and development
based on scientific reason and capitalist discipline, modernization projects
like Cancún were intended to transform rural subsistence farmers into disci-
plined workers. This process, however, did not benefit all members of rural
communities and thus produced casualties.[53] Many Kuchmil residents and
migrants feared that their desire for "progress"—for jobs—would result in
the loss of local customary practices and resources and in the process would
eradicate the Maya community. Not surprisingly, Kuchmil's native gaze
highlights the contradictions inherent in tourism development.

The Excess of Tourism

Part of this anxiety over cultural loss derives from what migrants in Cancún and residents in Kuchmil perceive as tourism's excess. The opulent nature and massive scale of tourist resorts contrast sharply with rural life and the simple architecture of Maya villages. Not surprisingly, Maya residents considered tourist behavior, through its excess of consumption, violence, and vulgar behavior, as a threat to their way of life. Oscar, a youth in Kuchmil, clearly articulated the culture of tourism. "[Los turistas] enseñan otro tipo de cultura . . . son más libres . . . en que toman, fuman, se drogan, en que usan lentes de lujo, se pintan el cabello . . . no tienen pena. [(The tourists) teach about another type of culture . . . they are more free . . . in that they drink, smoke, take drugs, in that they use sunglasses, paint their hair . . . they have no shame.]" Locals were exposed to these performances not only through tourist encounters in Kuchmil and in Cancún but also through satellite television, where shows filmed in Cancún, like MTV's *Spring Break* and E!'s *Wild On*, depict this excess.

John Urry suggests that "acting as a tourist is one of the defining characteristics of being 'modern' and is bound up with major transformations of paid work."[54] As a result, at the heart of the tourist experience are activities that focus on "re-creation," that is, the process by which tourists engage in relaxing, recreational activities that incorporate reenactments of "traditional" native rituals.[55] In the case of Cancún, these activities include sexual exploits, sunbathing (for some in the nude), binge drinking, dancing at nightclubs, shopping, jungle trekking, cave diving, and visiting museums and archaeological sites. Therefore being a tourist in resorts like Cancún implies being at leisure in a "sensuous geography," in which the built environment is created to overstimulate the senses and the body and thus create a new sensory orientation to a particular place.[56] As a result of this universal portrayal of the tourist and such marketing approaches to tourism, Urry notes that the tourist, like tourism, is perceived as a contradictory figure.[57]

Likewise, contradictions abound in the native gaze. Through discussions of this excess, Kuchmil residents and migrants defined themselves against what they were not and criticized modernization projects like Cancún. Kuchmil residents desired "progress" for their village and the jobs and improved infrastructure the government peddled in the form of tourism development. But they did not unquestioningly embrace all the trappings of modernization projects, including many of the attitudes and behaviors migrants adopted from tourists and urbanites, in particular when they resulted in a lack of respect for local cultural practices and beliefs. Oscar's summary of tourist characteristics encapsulated many of these new social practices. For example, migrants who drank excessively were not able to save money and thus did not send remittances to their families in Kuchmil. Locals claimed that migrants who did not return to Kuchmil to help with village fiestas and failed to fulfill social and labor obligations to their families became too individualistic and too modern because they placed their own progress ahead of everyone else's. Hence these migrants neglected to maintain intragenerational relationships based on mutual respect and social obligation.

Attached to this excess was the feeling of desolation and danger, exacerbated by the city's segregation by ethnicity and class. The elite lived in expensive condos in the Zona Hotelera (hotel zone) or in gated communities in the commercial center. The middle class initially built their modest homes in the commercial center, but as land became scarce and expensive, they settled in the regiones, where the working class and poor struggled to survive and local gangs thrived. For the residents of Kuchmil, Cancún was synonymous with the regiones. The lush tropical jungle had been consumed by housing developments, and the cool ocean breeze did not blow so far inland. Few palm trees dotted the landscape of these shantytowns. The regiones of Cancún could be compared to a desert, one made up of unpaved streets and covered in trash. This image of Cancún contrasted sharply with the images of Cancún advertised to foreigners.

Among rural communities, Cancún was also well known for its thugs, gangs, and crime. The juxtaposition of poor shantytowns filled with a seasonal labor force and the Zona Hotelera's constant and obscene exchange of high-priced goods, elaborate meals, and American dollars resulted in rising gang activity and the illicit trade of bodies, drugs, and commodities. Migrants lived in the shantytowns controlled by gangs. As a result, the community of Kuchmil described regiones of Cancún as the "Zona de Peligro" (danger zone), a play on words with reference to the Zona Hotelera. Community members feared for the safety of their family members, particularly male migrants who worked evening shifts as bartenders, stewards, and waiters. Francisco's experience substantiates the everyday feeling of dread that is associated with life in Cancún. On his way home from work in the early morning after payday, Francisco was attacked by a gang; his head was sliced open by the blows of the gang's machete, and his money and watch were stolen. The gang nearly killed Francisco. Another moment of violence occurred in broad daylight. Jovana, the wife of a Kuchmil migrant, was robbed in front of a church. She was on her way home from the grocery store when a young man shoved her to the ground and yanked the gold chains off her neck. These stories of assault and battery made Kuchmil families wary of sending their children to work in Cancún.

The constant threat of assault on one's person and home translated into the need for constant vigilance. Migrant men learned to maneuver the city's danger zones at night and constantly switched homes in search of neighborhoods with minimal gang activity. Migrant women sent their gold jewelry to Kuchmil for safekeeping and spent their days inside their homes in order to guard their property, their children, and themselves. In many instances, children were sent to Kuchmil to be taken care of by grandparents because parents wanted their children to experience what it felt to be "free" from fear and from the confinement of cramped rented rooms. This apprehension over Cancún served to perpetuate the image of the countryside as a safe haven from the dangers of tourism and thereby fostered an interdependent relationship between Cancún and Kuchmil. Kuchmil became the repository of goods, children, and money, while Cancún became known not only as a site of pleasure but also as a site of exploitative labor conditions and danger.

For the communities that provided the labor that made possible its existence, Cancún was an ambivalent presence. At first envisioned as a city of economic opportunities where class mobility was possible, the brilliance of Cancún has worn down, only to be replaced by a global city facing increasing inequalities between the rich and the poor, escalating violence within its shantytowns, and a surplus of low-wage, short-term contract jobs. Regarded by the nation-state as the solution to the economic crisis of the countryside, the tourist project of Cancún has failed to fulfill its promise, especially after Hurricane Wilma hit the coastline in October 2005. Instead of transforming rural communities of farm workers into full-time wage workers, tourism's lack of economic stability for the working class ensured that migrants maintained their ties with communities of origin and that communities like Kuchmil continued to rely on farm work to supplement wage work. For example, rural families sent corn and beans to enhance migrants' diets during lean times, while migrants sent money to help their rural families cultivate larger cornfields in order to increase their families' economic security.

Indeed, these communities provide the labor essential for the service industry and serve as sites for the social reproduction of this labor.[58] As a result, Cancún and the countryside have become dependent on each other.

As people move back and forth between Kuchmil and Cancún, they must negotiate the inherent contradictions of tourism development and figure out their place within such modernization projects. In order to do so, Kuchmil migrants and residents actively engage with tourism, not only by participating as laborers but also by creating their own native gaze of tourism. The complex imaginary that makes up the native gaze is informed by universal tropes (e.g., the tourist as foreign and always at play), local conceptions of work and play, and the racial and structural inequalities incorporated into tourist cities. Not surprisingly, these images and ideas circulate throughout the region, funneled via migrant circuits such as the one connecting Kuchmil and Cancún. Consequently, the dialogic process that creates the native gaze shapes how locals interpret and participate in tourism development and construct their own meaning of the value of modernization projects like tourism.

Through this process, rural indigenous communities also influence regional and international perceptions of tourism. They produce the background of quintessential rural villages that attract foreign tourists and yet at the same time resist this depiction by representing themselves as workers, as a specific class and racial subject, within the tourist economy. By examining the regional effects of tourism development, we can gaze back on tourism from its margins. In doing so, we make central what is considered marginal and insert rural communities located at the margins of tourist sites, like Kuchmil, into the contemporary discourse of tourism.

With the continued expansion of the Riviera Maya (located south along Quintana Roo's coast) and the construction of FONATUR's new Costa Maya project (located along Mexico's border with Belize and projected to be completed by the year 2020), encounters between tourists, workers, and rural communities will continue to alter the meanings of tourism. In contrast to Cancún, these tourist sites, along with all of FONATUR's new projects (Barrancas de Cobre, Palenque, Nayarit, and Sea of Cortés), promote ecotourism —tourism that is environmentally friendly and respectful of local cultural practices—as the new model for tourism development. This type of tourism encourages—and in a sense is based upon—respectful interaction with "natural" environments and the people who inhabit them. Yet whether this interaction will generate respect between native people and tourists and the tourism industry (both state-driven projects and transnational corporations) remains to be answered.

Notes

1. For a discussion of the cultural significance of the tourist, see Dean MacCannell, *The Tourist: A New Theory of the Leisure Class* (Berkeley: University of California Press, 1999); Victor Turner and E. Turner, *Image and Pilgrimage in Christian Culture: Anthropological Perspectives* (Oxford: Basil Blackwell, 1978); and John Urry, *The Tourist Gaze: Leisure and Travel in Contemporary Societies* (London: Sage Publications, 1990). For studies of communities located in tourist centers, see Quetzil Castañeda, *In the Museum of Maya Culture: Touring Chichén Ítza* (Minneapolis: University of Minnesota Press, 1996), and Ana M. Juárez, "Ecological Degradation, Global Tourism, and Inequality: Maya Interpretations of the Changing Environment in Quintana Roo, Mexico." *Human Organization* 61 (2002): 113–24.

2. See Daniel Hiernaux-Nicolas and Manuel Rodríguez Woog, "Tourism and Absorption of the Labor Force in Mexico," *Regional and Sectoral Development in Mexico as Alternatives to Migration*, ed. Sergio Díaz-Briquets and Sidney Weintraub (Boulder, Colo.: Westview Press, 1991), 313–29.

3. This gaze is in part a reproduction, a copy, of the tourist gaze because it constructs difference based on universal tropes of tourism, tourists, foreigners, and capital gleaned from television, photographs, and encounters. Cf. Walter Benjamin, *Illuminations*, trans. Harry Zohn (New York: Schocken Books, 1968 [1955]). The tourist gaze is an adaptation of Michel Foucault's medical gaze. According to John Urry, the tourist gaze is a "socially organised and systematized" view of difference, of "the other" and the exotic that is "constructed through difference." See Urry, *The Tourist Gaze*, 1. This gaze has become universalized as a result of the revolution in technology and communications that has disseminated images representing and thereby defining people from far off places and non-Western societies as different and exotic—as "the other"—for Western audiences. In the case of Cancún, these images overwhelmingly focus on azure ocean waters, white sandy beaches, ancient pyramids, expansive tropical jungle, and dark exotic faces. Just as in the tourist gaze, issues of authenticity and essentialism serve as tropes for the native gaze. In spite of these limitations, the native gaze offers insight into a perspective on tourism development that has been understudied. For example, A. LaVonne Brown Ruoff provides a rich analysis of the depictions of foreigners in early Native American oral history and texts. Ruoff concludes that these depictions portray foreigners as lacking a sense of justice and humanity. See A. LaVonne Brown Ruoff, "Reversing the Gaze: Early Native American Images of Europeans and Euro-Americans," *Native American Representations: First En-*

counters, Distorted Images, and Literary Appropriations, ed. Gretchen M. Bataille (Lincoln: University of Nebraska Press, 2001), 198–221.

4. To protect the privacy of the people I met, I use pseudonyms for the names of villages, e.g., Kuchmil. I do not use pseudonyms for cities such as Cancún. This analysis is based on an ethnographic study conducted during twenty-eight months over a twelve-year period (1991–2002).

5. See Roger Rouse, "Mexican Migration and the Social Space of Postmodernism," *Diaspora* 1 (1991): 8–23.

6. Ibid., 18.

7. MacCannell, *The Tourist*.

8. Gil Joseph, *Revolution from Without: Yucatán, Mexico, and the United States, 1880–1924* (Durham, N.C.: Duke University Press, 1995 [1982]).

9. According to Gil Joseph, Carrillo Puerto considered ethnic pride as a way to develop class consciousness and solidarity among peasants and the working class. See Joseph, *Revolution from Without.*

10. Stephanie Smith, "If Love Enslaves . . . Love Be Damned!" Divorce and Revolutionary State Formation in Yucatán, Mexico," *Sex in Revolution: Gender, the State, and Everyday Life in Twentieth-Century Mexico*, ed. Jocelyn Olcott, Mary Kay Vaughan, and Gabriela Cano (Durham, N.C.: Duke University Press, 2006), 99–111.

11. Smith, "If Love Enslaves . . . Love Be Damned!"; and Thomas Gann, *Ancient Cities and Modern Tribes: Exploration and Adventure in Maya Lands* (New York: Charles Scribner's Sons, 1926), 72–74.

12. Gann, *Ancient Cities and Modern Tribes*, 79. In 1923, the Carnegie Institute was contracted by the Mexican government to conduct a series of investigations on the culture, history, ecology, and economy of the Yucatán Peninsula. This project included the excavation of the archaeological site of Chichén Itzá, which became one of three archaeological sites promoted by the Mexican Tourism Board in 1939. See Alex Saragoza, "The Selling of Mexico: Tourism and the State, 1929–1952," *Fragments of a Golden Age: The Politics of Culture in Mexico since 1940*, ed. Gilbert M. Joseph, Anne Rubenstein, and Eric Zolov (Durham, N.C.: Duke University Press, 2001), 91–115.

13. Joseph, *Revolution from Without.*

14. For a discussion of tourism as a nationalist cultural project, see Saragoza, "The Selling of Mexico," 91–92. For a discussion of tourism as a state-led modernization project, see Dina Berger, *The Development of Mexico's Tourism Industry: Pyramids by Day, Martinis by Night* (New York: Palgrave Macmillan, 2006).

15. Heritage tourism may be initially deployed toward a domestic audience. But in the case of Mexico, the promotion of *indigenismo* and *lo mexicano* was directed at both domestic and international audiences. See Berger, *The Development of Mexico's Tourism Industry*, and Saragoza, "The Selling of Mexico." Linda K.

Richter points out that heritage tourism can be imbued with multiple meanings. It can be used to represent a local or national identity or to promote political socialization. See Richter, "The Politics of Heritage Tourism Development: Emerging Issues for the New Millenium," *Contemporary Issues in Tourism Development*, ed. Douglas G. Pearce and Richard W. Butler, 108–26 (New York: Routledge, 1997). For a discussion of the folklorization of Maya culture by the nation-state and scientists, see Quetzil Castañeda, "The Aura of Ruins," *Fragments of a Golden Age*, ed. Joseph, Rubenstein, and Zolov, 452–67.

16. Berger, *The Development of Mexico's Tourism Industry.*

17. Ibid.

18. Saragoza, "The Selling of Mexico."

19. Ibid.

20. Although the Mexican government and a few private Mexican banks were the primary financiers of Cancún's construction, the Inter-American Development Bank joined this venture in 1972. Playa Blanca was the first hotel to open for business in 1974. In 1989, the Mexican government relaxed its laws to permit the privatization of the tourist industry. For a more detailed discussion of Cancún's development, see Fernando Martí, *Cancún, Fantasy of Bankers: The Construction of a Tourism City from Base Zero*, trans. Jule Siegel (Mexico City: Litho Offset Andina, 1991).

21. See Michael J. Clancy, "Export-Led Growth Strategies, the Internationalization of Services, and Third World Development: The Political Economy of Mexican Tourism, 1967–1992" (Ph.D. diss., University of Wisconsin-Madison, 1996), and Martin Mowforth and Ian Munt, *Tourism and Sustainability: Development and New Tourism in the Third World* (London: Routledge, 2003 [1998]).

22. The construction of Cancún in the marginalized eastern region of the Yucatán Peninsula was the result of the nation-state's long involvement with tourism. In contrast to the densely populated western region of the peninsula, the eastern region was sparsely populated due to its rocky terrain, great distance from the government seat, and the ravages of civil war. The Maya in this area spent fifty years fighting for autonomy from the Mexican government (1847–97). For a history of the Caste War, see Nelson Reed, *The Caste War of Yucatán* (Stanford, Calif.: Stanford University Press, 1964), and Terry Rugeley, *Yucatán's Maya Peasantry and the Origins of the Caste War* (Austin: University of Texas Press, 1996). In 1901, the state of Yucatán lobbied the national government to build a railroad that would connect both these regions and thereby facilitate the state's exploitation of the natural resources in the east. One year later, however, the Díaz administration severed the eastern region from Yucatán by creating the territory of Quintana Roo. Establishing this new territory served as the national government's attempt to weaken the economy of and further politically marginalize the state of Yucatán. See Joseph, *Revolution from Without*, 213–27. During

the twentieth century, the federal government allocated *ejidos* from Quintana Roo's dense forests, which increased this territory's population. The population boom that resulted from the establishment of Cancún in Quintana Roo made it possible for this territory to become a state in 1974.

23. See Clancy, "Export-Led Growth Strategies, the Internationalization of Services, and Third World Development," and Michelle Madsen Camacho, "The Politics of Progress: Constructing Paradise in Huatulco, Oaxaca" (Ph.D. diss., University of California at Irvine, 2000).

24. The Mexican government promoted other civilizing missions through the Cultural Missions program and the education curriculum in rural boarding schools established by the Secretary for Public Education. See Mary Kay Vaughan, *The State, Education, and Social Class in Mexico, 1880–1928* (Dekalb: Northern Illinois University Press, 1982); Augusto Santiago Sierra, *Las misiones culturales, 1923–1973* (Mexico City: Secretaría de Educación Pública, Setentas, 1973); Paul Eiss, "Redemption's Archive: Revolutionary Figures and Indian Work in Yucatán, Mexico" (Ph.D. diss., University of Michigan, 2000); and María Bianet Castellanos, "Gustos and Gender: Yucatec Maya Migration to the Mexican Riviera" (Ph.D. diss., University of Michigan, 2003).

25. See Hiernaux-Nicolas and Rodríguez Woog, "Tourism and Absorption of the Labor Force in Mexico"; Cuahtémoc Cardiel Coronel, "Cancún: Turismo, sub-desarrollo social y expansión sectario religiosa," *Cuadernos de la Casa Chata, Centro de Investigaciones y Estudios Superiores en Antropología Social* 6 (1989): 1–143; Michael J. Clancy, "Tourism and Development: Evidence from Mexico," *Annals of Tourism Research* 26 (1999): 1–20; and Michael J. Clancy, *Exporting Paradise: Tourism and Development in Mexico* (New York: Pergamon, 2001).

26. Juárez, "Ecological Degradation, Global Tourism, and Inequality."

27. Castañeda, *In the Museum of Maya Culture.*

28. Alicia Re Cruz, *The Two Milpas of Chan Kom: A Study of Socioeconomic and Political Transformation in a Maya Community* (Albany: State University of New York Press, 1996).

29. Kuchmil was designated a *parcela* (parcel) of the ejido of Chan Sahkay.

30. Both *hipil* and *huipil* represent the ethnic dress worn by indigenous women. *Hipil* is the spelling used in the Yucatán, while *huipil* is the spelling used in central Mexico.

31. For the 1975 population statistics, see Martí, *Cancún, Fantasy of Bankers.* For the 2000 population statistics, see Instituto Nacional Estadístico, Geográfico e Informático (INEGI), *XII Censo General de Población y Vivienda* (Mexico, 2001), 41.

32. For the number of hotels in Cancún, see H. Ayuntamiento Benito Juárez, *Memorias 1999–2002* (Cancún: Pixel Press, 2002), 65. For the number of economically active residents in the county, see INEGI, *Cuaderno Estadístico Municipal, Edición 1999: Benito Juárez, Estado de Quintana Roo* (Mexico City, 2000), 58.

33. Dean MacCannell refers to the process of creating the everyday part of the tourist experience as a "staged authenticity." See MacCannell, *The Tourist*, 91–107.

34. See Terry Rugeley, *Yucatán's Maya Peasantry and the Origins of the Caste War* (Austin: University of Texas Press, 1996); Matthew Restall, "Maya Ethnogenesis," *Journal of Latin American Anthropology* 9 (2004): 64–89; Quetzil Castañeda, "We Are *Not* Indigenous! An Introduction to the Maya Identity of Yucatán," *Journal of Latin American Anthropology* 9 (2004): 36–63; Wolfgang Gabbert, "Of Friends and Foes: The Caste War and Ethnicity in Yucatán," *Journal of Latin American Anthropology* 9 (2004): 90–118; Paul Eiss, "Deconstructing Indians, Reconstructing Patria: Indigenous Education in Yucatán from the Porfiriato to the Mexican Revolution," *Journal of Latin American Anthropology* 9 (2004): 119–50; Juan Castillo Cocom, "Lost in Mayaland," *Journal of Latin American Anthropology* 9 (2004): 179–98; and Wolfgang Gabbert, *Becoming Maya: Ethnicity and Social Inequality in Yucatán since 1500* (Tucson: University of Arizona Press, 2004).

35. See Peter Hervik, *Mayan People within and beyond Boundaries: Social Categories and Lived Identity in Yucatán* (Amsterdam: Harwood Press, 1999). For a discussion of Maya identity politics in Guatemala, see Kay B. Warren, *Indigenous Movements and their Critics* (Princeton, N.J.: Princeton University Press, 1998), and Edward F. Fischer, *Cultural Logics and Global Economies: Maya Identity in Thought and in Practice* (Austin: University of Texas Press, 2002).

36. Gabbert, *Becoming Maya*, 111.

37. Ruth Behar, "Rage and Redemption: Reading the Life Story of a Mexican Marketing Woman," *Feminist Studies* 16 (1990): 236.

38. For a discussion of Maya life under colonial rule, see Nancy Farriss, *Maya Society under Colonial Rule: The Collective Enterprise of Survival* (Princeton, N.J.: Princeton University Press, 1984).

39. See Diego de Landa, *Relaciones de las cosas de Yucatán* (Mexico City: Editorial Porrua, 1978), and John Lloyd Stephens, *Incidents of Travel in Central America, Chiapas, and Yucatán* (New Brunswick, N.J.: Rutgers University Press, 1949).

40. In 1991, Pauline Sánchez accompanied me on my first field visit to Kuchmil.

41. The majority of the families in Kuchmil showed me the archaeological artifacts they possessed only after they confirmed my lack of interest in purchasing these artifacts. I was informed of other pyramids in the nearby area years after I first visited Kuchmil.

42. Farriss, *Maya Society under Colonial Rule*, 19, 324.

43. Fred P. Bosselman, *In the Wake of the Tourist: Managing Special Places in Eight Countries* (Washington, D.C.: Conservation Foundation, 1978).

44. Ibid.

45. Robert J. Dunphy, "Why the Computer Chose Cancún," *New York Times*, March 5, 1972, sec. 10.

46. Daniel Hiernaux-Nicolas, "Cancún Bliss," *The Tourist City*, ed. Dennis R. Judd and Susan S. Fainstein (New Haven, Conn.: Yale University Press, 1999), 124–39.

47. See Cynthia Enloe, *Bananas, Beaches, and Bases: Making Feminist Sense of International Politics* (Berkeley: University of California Press, 1989); Hiernaux and Rodríguez, "Tourism and Absorption of the Labor Force in Mexico"; and Sylvia Chant, "Tourism in Latin America: Perspectives from Mexico and Costa Rica," *Tourism and Less Developed Countries*, ed. David Harrison (London: John Wiley, 1992), 85–101.

48. Urry, *The Tourist Gaze*.

49. M. Bianet Castellanos interview with Lic. José A. Bayon Ríos, director of FONATUR, July 30, 2002. According to Lic. Bayon Ríos, FONATUR was no longer trying to attract American tourists but instead was focusing on European tourists and wealthy elite tourists because they were more interested in adventure tourism.

50. The Mexican Riviera refers to the area of coastline sandwiched between the tourist sites of Cancún and Tulum.

51. Also spelled *x-táabay*.

52. Female migration was not discussed in the same way in Kuchmil. While the community was concerned with protecting young women's sexuality, the settlement of women in Cancún was not a big concern for the community because, given that women participate in exogamous marriages, they are expected to eventually leave their community. More importantly, their presence in Cancún solidified kin networks in this city and strengthened ties within the migrant circuit. See Castellanos, "Gustos and Gender."

53. James Ferguson, *Expectations of Modernity: Myths and Meanings of Urban Life on the Zambian Copperbelt* (Berkeley: University of California Press, 1999).

54. Ibid., 3.

55. Nelson Graburn defines the "re-creation" aspect of tourism as "the renewal of life, the recharging of run-down elements." See Graburn, "The Anthropology of Tourism," *Annals of Tourism Research* 10 (1983): 11. However, the concept of "re-creation" also invokes the practice of re-creating native rituals for tourist consumption. I use "re-creation" to refer to both processes.

56. Paul Rodaway quoted in John Urry, "Sensing the City," *The Tourist City*, ed. Judd and Fainstein, 71–72.

57. Urry, *The Tourist Gaze*.

58. Michael Buroway, "The Functions and Reproduction of Migrant Labor: Comparative Material from Southern Africa and the United States," *American Journal of Sociology* 81 (1976): 1050–87.

MARY K. COFFEY

MARKETING MEXICO'S GREAT MASTERS

Folk Art Tourism and the Neoliberal Politics of Exhibition

In the summer of 2001 newly elected president Vicente Fox unveiled what would be an economic cornerstone of his administration: a comprehensive development campaign to convert Mexico into a "full service tourist destination."[1] As part of this campaign his administration pledged $1.6 billion dollars to invest in more than 200 different projects aimed at, among other things, "incorporating local communities into the tourism industry."[2] To date some of these initiatives include a massive promotional campaign aimed at developing eco-tourism, convention and trade-show tourism, as well as the more conventional "sand-and-sun" variety, the easing of border bureaucracy and elimination of value-added tax on tourist purchases, and the development of a tourism corridor from Central Mexico to Panama, known as the Puebla to Panama Plan.

While many of these initiatives were already in place, after the terrorist attacks on the World Trade Center and the Pentagon on September 11, 2001, the Fox administration sought an extra $40 million from the Mexican legislature to redouble its efforts on this front.[3] As is often noted, tourism accounts for more than nine percent of Mexico's annual GDP (recently bumped to third place after oil exports and remittances sent by migrated labor north of the border) and approximately 10.2 percent of Mexican workers are employed in this labor sector.[4] For destinations like Cancún, nearly the entire local population and much of the region depend directly or indirectly on tourism. As a consequence, the precipitous drop in tourism occasioned by the terrorism-induced fear of flying and a global economic recession severely threatened Mexico's economic growth as well as the Fox administration's development agenda, one heavily dependent upon the mobility of labor, goods, and bodies enabled by NAFTA.[5]

In addition to direct advertisement and legal reforms, "cultural diplomacy" has been a key tactic in Fox's economic plan. Alongside ads announcing "Mexico, closer than ever," blockbuster exhibitions of Mexican art, organized in part by the Ministry of Tourism but also by private agencies with a vested interest in this economic sector, were developed for travel to museums in the United States, as well as European nations of strategic import (namely, England, France, and Germany).[6] In this essay, I focus on one such blockbuster—the Great Masters of Mexican Folk Art—a traveling exhibition organized by Banamex-Citigroup from the collection generated by its subsidiary, Fomento Cultural Banamex, A.C. The exhibition showcased the work of "master artisans" identified and promoted by Banamex's Programa de Apoyo al Arte Popular (Folk Art Support Program) which has been operating since 1996. It began at the Dallas Museum of Fine Arts in 2001, traveled to the Mexican Fine Arts Center Museum (MFACM) in Chicago in 2002, and culminated at the Smithsonian's National Museum of the American Indian, located in the George Gustav Heye Center in the Financial District of Lower Manhattan, in 2002–2003.[7]

Great Masters was ostensibly organized and traveled to assuage national anxieties about the Citigroup buyout of Banamex, Mexico's largest private bank, in 2001.[8] However, when the exhibition arrived at its New York venue, its role in the transnational tourist economy became more apparent. Here, near the environmentally and economically devastated environs of ground zero, the colorful exhibition helped to draw large crowds to an undervisited museum and a part of the city devastated after the 9/11 terrorist attacks. Simultaneously, it promoted different forms of folk art tourism through its showy presentation of authentic "masterpieces" easily acquired through high-end Internet outlets or on a south-of-the-border shopping trip.[9]

Great Masters of Mexican Folk Art represented "the largest exhibition of Mexican folk art ever displayed outside of Mexico."[10] However, unlike exhibitions in the past, within the exhibitionary didactics folk art was presented as individually authored fine art rather than as an anonymously produced expression of the mestizo nation's indigenous soul. Its organizers continued to employ the naturalizing rhetoric of authenticity rooted in the essential being of the nation's popular classes. However, they downplayed the purported indigenism of folk art in favor of a deracinated lexicon of "community."[11] For example, the wall text and promotional materials that introduced the exhibition listed "indigenous" groups as but one of the many "communities" engaged in handcrafts production:

> The artisan's activity is part of the social, economic and cultural groups of the rural environment, of the popular areas in the city and obviously of the many indigenous groups in the country. . . . This handcrafts production . . . [has] either an aesthetic objective linked with its everyday use, or a ritual purpose that immerses them into a system of symbols that make up the identity of the community.[12]

Yet despite this rhetorical gesturing toward the communal roots of popular art, the exhibition obscured any understanding of the regional or social context out of which these traditions emerged.

Rather than illuminating local economies, social rituals, or the historical contexts for Mexico's different folk art traditions, the exhibition organized objects by material: clay, wood, stone, textiles, metals, paper, leather, vegetable fibers, and mixed media. By emphasizing the material and formal qualities of folk art, Great Masters constructed them as objects of art, not as artifacts of sociality, and attempted to provide basic instruction to visitors and consumers in the aesthetic appreciation of this art form. Discussion of process, detailed in the catalog and in video monitors throughout the exhibition, did not include *in situ* or ritual use but rather explanations about how the objects were manufactured: the preparation of materials, aesthetic choices, and creative intentions of individually named artists. Artists were identified by city and state, but because they were dispersed throughout the exhibition, visitors could not make meaningful connections between particular crafts, materials, or traditions and their regional provenance.

Further, the exhibition's English title—Great Masters of Mexican Folk Art—also indicated its organizers' desire to deemphasize social function in favor of aesthetic quality. In Mexico "folk art" is most often referred to as either "artesanía" or "arte popular." While terms like "folk art," "handcrafts," "manual arts," "industrial arts," and "popular art" are treated as synonyms and used interchangeably in English translation, none fully captures the complete scope of the category. The Spanish term "arte popular" is conventionally translated as "folk art" in U.S. exhibitions. However, by appending "Great Masters" to this term, the exhibition's organizers signaled their desire to construct what has historically been valued for its associations with anonymous labor, as a "fine," albeit traditional, art.

These rhetorical and display strategies promoted folk art as high art, as fetishized objects divorced from the social relations that give them meaning and proffered instead as collectibles for the global market of high-end crafts. And critics of the show were quick to point out the uncomfortable proximity between these exhibition strategies and department store displays. For example, the *Wall Street Journal* reporter Willard Spiegelman objected to the show's "slick marketing," arguing that the exhibit "performs an artistic version of a NAFTA maneuver."[13] Likewise, the *New York Times* art critic Ken Johnson lamented the impact of "global market forces" on the sanctity of authentic Mexican folk production, writing:

> The problem [with the exhibition] is that the kind of local, rural or regional cultures from which folk art traditionally emerges and in which it thrives are everywhere being—or already have been—overtaken by global capitalism. This is a crisis for folk art: whereas it was once produced in small communities for the use of their own people, folk artists now produce hand-made luxury goods for high-end trade.[14]

Suspicious of the "fat, glossy exhibition catalog, with a text that reads like advertising copy," Johnson correctly inferred that Banamex's promotion of Mexican folk art was part of a broader desire to commercialize its production and to develop markets for its sale worldwide. However, the vision of holistic communities being infiltrated by the forces of "global capitalism" that he conjures is not only naive but also historically inaccurate. Likewise, his assertion that the crisis of folk art can be discerned in the physical transformation of useful objects into "hand-made luxury goods for high-end trade" reflects his own ignorance of the genealogy of the very category itself, not to mention the long history of artisanal participation in the global market for "luxury goods."

Critiques like those by Spiegelman and Johnson conjured well-worn clichés about folk art that locate authenticity in the formal integrity of the objects themselves and the supposed purity of communal roots. This analogy between the authenticity of the folk object and the folk community implies that any changes in the appearance of folk culture or any direct engagement with the market represents the corruption of both art and artisan. However, the history of folk art development in Mexico reveals, to the contrary, that the folk canon itself was constituted within a nexus of market considerations, from international economic and cultural exchange to national development initiatives to local attempts to negotiate the impact of these forces.

The sociologist Néstor García Canclini argues that the "starting point" for an analysis of folk art should not be the identification of its authentic formal properties and their discrimination from mass or commercial forms but rather the "system that gives rise" to particular categories of culture "in order to fulfill economic, political, and psychosocial functions necessary for its reproduction."[15] Thus he suggests that we "consider which functions are fulfilled by arts and crafts, not in opposition to, but as part of, capitalist logic, within the present-day cycle of reproduction of economic and cultural capital in dependent countries."[16] Rather than lament the effects of globalization on local craft production, Canclini insists we examine the "entire cycle of capitalism," so as to understand and analyze "changes in production, circulation, and consumption."[17] Following Canclini's lead, I argue that the effects and dangers of corporate sponsorship today pertain not to the objects themselves, or even to the authenticity of their traditions, but rather to how their production, dissemination, and consumption structure the relationship between citizens, the economy, and the state.

What follows is a history of Mexican folk art initiatives and exhibitions in order to demonstrate the extent to which this field of objects is always already structured by commercial concerns in which the shaping of national and tourist consumption has been an essential component. Since the Revolution of 1910, folk art has been enlisted by the modernizing nation-state as an agent of popular citizenship and economic development. What is new, however, is the supranational dimension of citizenship that Banamex-Citigroup is targeting through its support program for local artisans and through the agency of transnational exhibition. Appeals to "Greater Mexico" evident in the timing, promotion, and display strategies of Great Masters is consistent with the Fox administration's attempts to capitalize on migrated Mexican labor and to induce small business owners to enter into the export economy enabled by NAFTA as a form of individual rather than state subvention of the national economy.

Folk art has always been enlisted in foreign exhibition as an agent of political and economic diplomacy; however, as the Mexican state shifts from a state-sponsored capitalism and social welfarism to a privatized form of "social liberalism," the production and subsidization of folk art is being privatized as well. Through its collecting practices and exhibition program Banamex-Citigroup's Folk Art Support Program works to move artisans into the global marketplace and off the state's welfare rolls. Similarly, through exhibitions like Great Masters, the privatizing state and its corporate partners work to cultivate folk art tourism by promoting folk art consumption as a form of ethical tourism, whether virtual or actual. Thus, Great Masters induced producers and consumers on either side of the border to participate in the Mexican economy through an ethos of personal responsibility and cultural expression that lines up with and is indeed dependent upon the neoliberal restructuring of state and society over the last three decades. In the current conjuncture of global capitalism, state privatization, and transnational culture, what is at stake is not the authenticity of Mexican folk art but rather the ways in which its producers and consumers are located within the economic networks of the tourist economy and the political risks of privatization for artisanal labor. In the final section of the essay I explore in greater detail the exhibition's didactic strategies and the promotional activities that surrounded it, in order to clarify how and in what ways it appealed to a transnational citizenry of Mexican-identified consumers and promoted folk art tourism as a form of ethical consumption.

Folk Art, Exhibition, and the Postrevolutionary State

Folk art has been a pillar of Mexican nationalism, modernization, and popular governance since the turn of the twentieth century. While intellectuals demonstrated an interest in what had been known as "ethnic" or "manual" industries prior to the Revolution of 1910, the cultural reforms inaugurated by President Álvaro Obregón's (1920–24) Minister of Public Education, José Vasconcelos, enlisted folk art in a host of nation-building projects aimed at consolidating a society fragmented by regional, racial, and class differences, as well as ten years of civil war. One of the Obregón administration's first acts was the organization, in 1921, of an elaborate festival to celebrate the centennial of the culmination of Mexican independence (1821). As part of these festivities Vasconcelos commissioned the artist Dr. Atl (the Nahuatl pseudonym for Gerardo Murillo) to curate an exhibition of popular art.

In the first edition of his catalog for the exhibition of popular arts (1921), Dr. Atl established the technical accomplishment of Mexican craftsmen through a comparison with other cultures and then provided a survey of objects culled from different eras, regions, traditions, and uses. While his list of objects derived from native as well as foreign techniques, rural as well as urban producers, and quotidian as well as luxury goods, they were all homogenized as *lo popular* and credited to the "Indian" whose "innate" manual abilities provided the modern nation with a redemptive and authentic cultural essence.[18] The ensuing exhibition initiated multiple projects for delimiting the field of folk art to only those traditions (dead or alive) deemed authentically Mexican. These initiatives concerned not only the creation of an official canon but also the eventual integration of disenfranchised populations and their labor into a federally subsidized tourist industry, and the development of export markets for Mexican goods. Part of a profound revaluation of folk art, these early public overtures also established a canon and aesthetic hierarchy that persists to this day.

In the first decade after the revolution, the project of revaluing traditional Mexican crafts was largely undertaken by Mexican intellectuals and foreign advocates working autonomously but in conjunction with a government still unsure about how best to exploit this social resource. Artists like Dr. Atl and Roberto Montenegro, anthropologists such as Manuel Gamio and Alfonso Caso, and foreign promoters such as Frances Toor and René d'Harnoncourt lobbied the government on behalf of craftspersons, arguing that federal support would strengthen rural communities by providing a means for their entry into the international economy as cultural producers for domestic and foreign markets. To develop these markets promoters argued that Mexico needed to research authentic craft traditions, perhaps even rescue them by reviving select traditions and retraining artisans in their manufacture, and then publicizing this information through catalogs, almanacs, and exhibitions at home and abroad.

In 1922, when Dr. Atl published the second edition of his catalog for the Popular Arts Exhibition, he revised the text from a mere survey of Mexico's craft traditions to a sociohistorical analysis of the current state of Mexico's folk art. In this text he lamented the effects of industrialization and identified those forms he felt were prospering as well as those that were in decadence. And while he worked tirelessly to safeguard their quality and intensify their production, he also sought to promote folk art as a source of economic development through the opening of new markets for these products in Europe and the United States.[19] Despite Atl's growing fears about the negative effects of commercialization and the taste of foreign tourists on Mexico's "vernacular arts," he nonetheless pushed hard for federal funding to participate in international expositions of popular art so as to improve Mexico's image abroad and foment the development of export markets. For this reason, he convened the National Committee of Popular Arts in 1920 (composed of Atl, Jorge Enciso, Roberto Montenegro, Diego Rivera, and

Adolfo Best Maugard), a quasi-governmental organization that formed the precedent for a plethora of future agencies responsible for defending and diffusing the nation's folk heritage.

Alberto J. Pani, Secretary of Foreign Relations during the Obregón administration, charged the National Committee with organizing exhibitions and monographs for travel to the world's fair in Rio de Janeiro (1922), an exhibition in Los Angeles (1922), and another in New York City (1930) at the Metropolitan Museum of Art.[20] These exhibitions of Mexican popular arts in turn created a "vogue for things Mexican" at home and abroad.[21] U.S. department stores exhibited Mexican crafts in their window displays at the same time that prestigious galleries and museums hosted exhibitions.[22] Prominent politicians and capitalists also turned to culture during this period to ease political and economic relations between the two nations (and thus setting a precedent for the more interventionist Cold War period). Most notably, U.S. ambassador Dwight Morrow and John D. Rockefeller used their patronage of Mexican folk art to great effect in protecting U.S. interests in Mexico throughout the 1930s and 1940s.

The success of these efforts also spurred tourism to Mexico as they coincided with a folk revival in the United States prompted by industrialization on the one hand and, on the other, a growing desire to codify an autochthonous national identity equal to but distinct from European pedigrees. Mexican tourism had suffered enormously during the turmoil of the revolution and in its aftermath as a result of political tensions over the status of U.S.-owned assets and diplomatic recognition for the new political regime. However, by the 1930s travel to the region was reinvigorated by Prohibition as U.S. citizens sought refuge in the luxury casinos developing along the border. Subsequently, the closing of the Western European market to U.S. travelers on the eve of World War II proved an added boon, propelling the tourist sector to fourth place, as a contributor to economic growth, behind mining, food, and textile production.[23]

Between 1938 and 1946, foreign tourism, predominantly from the United States, increased from 90,000 to over 300,000, a number that would double again by 1960.[24] As scholars of Mexican tourism have pointed out, during this period the industry developed in a piecemeal fashion as the state did not directly invest in it until the 1960s.[25] Thus the phenomenal growth in foreign tourism from 1930 through the 1960s has been attributed in part to "a fortuitous combination of historical, geographic, and socio-political factors," not the least of which was Mexico's close proximity to the United States and its increasingly affluent population.[26] While certain improvements in transportation networks and infrastructure, such as highways and clean water, were accomplished by the state during this period, it was largely the public relations generated through cultural activities abroad that drummed up international interest in Mexico as a tourist destination. Despite the unsystematic nature of state development of tourism prior to the 1960s, the historian Alex Saragoza argues that the state was active in the "selective appropriation of cultural forms to 'image' the country."[27] He traces the representation of Mexican culture and heritage, in particular in terms of race and gender, through advertisements funded by its tourist agency for foreign newspapers. These strategies were legible, in part, because of the exhibitions mounted simultaneously.

The blockbuster exhibitions of Mexican art held in New York at the Met in 1930 and at the Museum of Modern Art (MOMA) in 1940 demonstrate the diplomatic and commercial dimensions of the vogue for Mexican crafts throughout this period as well as the imaging of the country for tourist consumption. Supported by the Ministry of Industry and Commerce and the National Committee for Popular Art, these exhibitions were nonetheless coproductions between Mexican intellectuals, U.S. capitalists, and a coterie of cosmopolitan cultural brokers with economic, political, and professional interests in the promotion of Mexican art. For example, the Mexican Arts show of 1930 was reportedly instigated by U.S. ambassador to Mexico Dwight Morrow with funds from the Carnegie Corporation, the American Federation of the Arts, and additional support from the newly formed Mexican Arts Association, an organization founded by Frances Flynn Paine, Abby Rockefeller, Elizabeth Morrow, Emily DeForest, and Frank Crowninshield (the editor of *Vanity Fair*) to "promote friendship between the people of Mexico and the US by encouraging cultural relations and the interchange of Fine and Applied Arts."[28]

Like earlier exhibitions held in Mexico, the installation at the Met owed as much to nineteenth-century museum display as it did to the curio shop.[29] The curator, René d'Harnoncourt, placed a wide variety of objects, ranging from ceramics and lacquerware to textiles and oil paintings, on the walls, floor, and low display counters in a large open gallery with little regard for categorization by material, genre, or period. In his folk art selections, d'Harnoncourt cleaved closely to the canon devised by Atl, Montenegro, and Enciso in 1921. Further, this exhibition reiterated and helped to solidify a set of truths about Mexican folk art and its political significance, namely, that folk objects are a mestizo expression of an essentially indigenous character, representing, in d'Harnoncourt's words, a fusion of "foreign ideas and Indian psychology."[30] And further, that through exhibiting its national culture, Mexico was declaring itself "freed from foreign rule, influence and censorship" and "ready to take its place as a unit of importance in the great world of art."[31] Like Atl, d'Harnoncourt also strove to walk a fine line between lambasting the effects of tourism on Mexico's vernacular arts and soliciting cultural commerce as a mode of economic development for the postrevolutionary state. "In the end," writes the art historian James Oles, "rather than elevate Mexico to the rank of modern nations, [the exhibition] helped cement an image of the country as timeless and rural, as peaceful and colorful."[32]

The exhibition Twenty Centuries of Mexican Art held in 1940 at MOMA, which was motivated by Rockefeller interests in Mexico, modernized its design by eschewing the curio display style that characterized earlier exhibitions in favor of the modern day art display style pioneered at the MOMA. Rather than mixing genres and periods, the curators established a linear and progressive narrative of cultural development that positioned folk art as the cultural glue unifying centuries of artistic development and political change. As Roberto Montenegro explained in his catalog essay on the topic, Mexico's popular art provided a living link with Mexico's preconquest past, despite centuries of foreign domination and economic imperialism. Further, "primitive popular arts," he claimed, demonstrated a "good taste" that had persevered despite the "bewildering" pressures of modernization and a voracious tourist trade that rewarded kitsch. "It should be noted," Montenegro concludes, "that the objects which the Indian keeps for his own daily use are very different from the articles of commerce whose low quality turns a pure and exquisite art into tourist curios of no great importance. That is the reason why our folk art, in every period, has served as a true symbol of the artistic instincts of the Mexican people."[33]

As Montenegro's remarks make clear, the exhibition of Mexican folk art was as much about promoting Mexican culture as it was about cultivating an informed taste-culture among foreign consumers. And despite his derogatory remarks about the negative effects of commercialization, the MOMA exhibition recreated an outdoor Mexican market in its sculpture garden where visitors could buy examples of the craft traditions they had just seen on display. These two early exhibitions set the rhetorical and display strategies for exhibitions of Mexican folk art, establishing the agency of exhibition for negotiating everything from economic relations between producers and the international craft market to political negotiations between nations and the private interests of corporations.

From Producer Collectives to Corporate Grants:
Converting Artisans into Entrepreneurs

Despite the plethora of exhibitions devoted to Mexican arts and crafts throughout the 1920s and 1930s, the Mexican government remained somewhat tentative in its outlays of cash and commitment of state resources to subsidization until the late 1930s, when economists began to view folk art as a potential source for national economic development and profit (largely in response to the success of the Met exhibition). The historian Rick López argues this prompted a schism between folk art promoters in the 1940s and 1950s, as some began to push for the industrialization and rationalization of craft production and the elimination of high-end labor-intensive genres in favor of low-end novelty items that could compete within an international market for cheap souvenirs.[34] Throughout this period, the prior concern for aesthetic integrity and rural welfare waned as artisans became increasingly impoverished and subject to exploitation by local loan sharks and commercial intermediaries who bought in bulk and brokered deals with foreign commercial outlets that diverted profits from the producers to federally subsidized wholesalers.

Opponents of industrialization agitated for a federal plan to rescue folk art and artisans from commercialization. In 1951 the National Museum of Popular Arts and Industries was inaugurated under the auspices of the National Indigenist Institute (INI) and the National Institute of Anthropology and History (INAH) to research, collect, and promote the folk art traditions under threat by commercialization.[35] By 1951, López reports, the National Museum of Popular Arts and Industries was providing technical and marketing assistance to over 3,500 artisans and purchasing 1,400,000 pesos worth of art from them.[36] With five museums across the country, the organization was able to broker cooperative arrangements with various states and, by coordinating local efforts with government agencies, to establish regional markets. Additionally, the museum initiated studies of the economic and technical aspects of craft production for the purposes of generating legal protections as well as publishing a national atlas to facilitate foreign exhibitions and tourism.[37]

These efforts resulted in a craft revival in the late 1960s that sought to combat the effects of commercialization, bringing about a renewed federal commitment to rural welfare. In 1960, a senatorial commission working with the museum and several federal financial institutions (including the National Banks of Foreign Commerce and Cooperative Development [Banfoco], and a Fund for Small Loan Guarantees) convened a study and determined that artisans needed access to low-interest credit and assistance in marketing their goods themselves.[38] In 1961 President Adolfo López Mateos (1958–64) endowed the Fondo de Fideicomiso para el Fomento de las Artesanías to be managed by Banfoco. The Fund coordinated a consortium of lenders who could provide low-interest loans to artisanal cooperatives who would in turn manage accounts of revolving credit so as to eliminate loan sharks and help folk artists regain some control over the production and sale of their goods.[39]

President Luis Echeverría (1970–76) reformed the Fund in 1970 with the creation of the autonomous Fondo Nacional para el Fomento de las Artesanías (FONART). As one of the many neopopulist policies Echeverría enacted in the wake of the state massacre of protesting students in Tlatelolco in 1968, FONART not only redirected funds that had been diverted to urban producers back to rural artisanal communities but also extended credit on faith, ending the collateral system and guaranteeing low-interest credit lines following the timely repayment of initial loans.[40] Further, FONART created wholesale retail outlets throughout the country for medium and high-end crafts. With FONART buying in bulk and returning a percentage of the commission on sales, artisans could work in more resource intensive genres and indulge in aesthetic experimentation without risking the marketability of their wares. López argues that these reforms enabled artisans to take control of the production and sale of their goods, leading eventually toward sustainable forms of collective mobilization through which they successfully negotiated with local, state, and commercial entities on their own behalf.[41]

Historically, Mexico's support of artisanal labor has resulted in the largest producing sector in the world—approximately six million craftspersons. Yet this sector has never contributed more than 0.1 percent to the gross national product. Clearly its value for the state lies elsewhere. Néstor García Canclini has long argued that under Mexico's state-directed capitalism, folk art "solved" the problem of rural unemployment, revitalized consumption through the production of difference, "reconcile[d] backwardness with beauty" for the purposes of tourism, and did ideological work for the nation-state.[42] However, in the era of neoliberal economic reform, the financial burden of maintaining this vital labor has been partially privatized.

In 1996 the Fomento Cultural Banamex entered into the field of folk art production with the creation of its Programa de Apoyo al Arte Popular (Folk Art Support Program). A civil association, owned and funded by Banamex, Fomento Cultural Banamex was created in 1971 to take over the administration and conservation activities of the National Bank of Mexico's collection of national patrimony.[43] For most of that time the Fomento devoted its activities to the conservation of colonial buildings, purchasing colonial, academic, and modern Mexican art, and organizing exhibitions of what became the largest private collection of national art in the country. While popular art was not initially a collecting priority, with the advent of its Folk Art Support Program in 1996, Fomento Banamex quickly amassed one of the largest collections of folk art as well.

The Folk Art Support Program underwrites grants for artisans it has identified as "masters" in the field of folk art production. Fomento Banamex not only supplements the incomes of the artists it selects but also purchases their work for its collection, which it then promotes through publications and exhibitions at home and abroad. By fostering self-support among the workshops it consolidates, the initiative hopes "to stimulate their transformation into micro and small enterprises with better bonds to the market."[44] In short, it attempts to convert traditional craftsmen into entrepreneurs, so that they might in turn minister to the needs of their own communities and thereby move artisans away from welfare toward greater personal responsibility for their own economic and social development.

The ethics of autonomy promoted by Banamex corresponds with the neoliberal ideology of "solidarity" instantiated by President Carlos Salinas de Gortari in his National Solidarity Program (PRONASOL) launched when he took office in 1988. An attempt to soften the social burden of his neoliberal reforms, PRONASOL instituted a move away from what Salinas derided as state "paternalism" toward social "solidarity" with four main objectives: "Respect for the will, initiatives, and organizational forms of individuals and communities . . . full and effective participation and organization by the communities[, and] . . . co-responsibility [in project management] and transparency [in the handling of resources]."[45] PRONASOL successfully married liberal economics with the neopopulist rhetoric of "solidarity," creating a new policy paradigm that the historian Alan Knight has dubbed "social liberalism."[46]

By asserting that individuals and communities were coresponsible for their own social welfare and that of others, the rhetoric of solidarity crafted privatization as a pragmatic adjustment to the new global economy, a democratic check on the political and cultural hegemony of the Federal District, and an acknowledgment of Mexico's pluralism. Within this context, the Banamex Folk Art Support Program represents the first stage in privatizing craft production, and therefore an important component of the "dismantling of the Mexican welfare state" under neoliberalism. The implication of Banamex in this process exceeds its efforts with the nation's "master" artisans, as its folk art collection has been instrumental in plugging both producers and consumers into the global markets and flows that neoliberalism exalts.

The Splendors of Neoliberalism: NAFTA and the "Will for Form"

Mexico's neoliberal transformation began in 1982 when it defaulted on its international loans after the bottom fell out of the oil market (the source of Mexican prosperity and speculative investment throughout the preceding decade). President Miguel de la Madrid (1982–88) initiated macroeconomic stabilization measures through trade liberalization. De la Madrid's successor, Carlos Salinas de Gortari (1988–94), deepened the state's commitment to neoliberalism by championing free-market reforms and negotiating Mexico's entry into the North American Free Trade Agreement (NAFTA).[47] Salinas's promotion of trade integration with the United States and Canada not only upended the postrevolutionary state's ideological commitment to the rhetoric of national sovereignty but also put an end to four decades of state-led development through import-substitution industrialization. This betrayal of the political and economic orthodoxies of the postrevolutionary period was necessitated in part by the debt crisis which brought International Monetary Fund (IMF) austerity measures to bear upon the national economy. However, it was also enabled by the slow dissolution of state authority following 1968 and exacerbated by the Mexico City earthquake in 1985, which further exposed the incompetence and corruption of the federal government and its ruling party. Paradoxically, it was the illegitimacy of the 1988 election results that pushed Salinas toward and eventually enabled his more radical neoliberal reforms.

Unlike de la Madrid, who reacted to Mexico's debt crisis by reaffirming state control over finance and industry (most evident in the nationalization of failing banks), Salinas began to court foreign investment in order to restore confidence in the Mexican economy and to stem the flight of capital. The political scientist Stephanie Golob argues that the economic recession, combined with Salinas's lack of popular support at home, made him overly sensitive to the esteem of an "external constituency" and more dependent upon the success of free market reforms "to provide results and forestall societal demands for political reform."[48] This shift in economic policy required a shift in symbolic rhetoric, as historically political sovereignty had been identified with Mexican control over national territory and resources (most powerfully dramatized by Lázaro Cárdenas's nationalization of the oil industry in 1938). Golob continues, "To reconcile liberalization with the Revolution," Salinas rearticulated national strength and values from autonomy and protectionism to a "strength through integration" argument, linking Mexico's future prosperity and security to its access to the global market and a new cosmopolitanism referred to again and again as "modernization."[49]

The Salinas administration cleverly crafted a historical genealogy for modernization that legitimated integration through an appeal to a "Mexican will" or common bond that had survived conquest, colonization, and the wars of independence, reform, and revolution. Just as Mexico had "reconquered" its "collective confidence" in the face of challenges past, it would face new threats with a similar "will."[50] This "ideological bridge" between the Mexican past and its free-market "destiny" was accomplished by changing the articulations of sovereignty from bounded, territorial metaphors to a dematerialized concept of culture and values, flowing effortlessly from the deep past toward an ordained future.

Speaking at his inauguration, Salinas explained:

> A nation is a community that shares a past and a future. *A past, that is, a history, a culture and values that are essential to its tradition; and a future, a historical project that brings together diverse wills into a common effort.* A pact between the past and the future, the nation is the memory of what we have been and the affirmation of what we will become.[51]

By shifting the terrain of identity and sovereignty from protected resources and bounded territory to a collective will embodied in memory and transmitted through cultural traditions, Salinas countered the common logic whereby U.S. economic investment threatened to "Americanize" Mexico. Now, Mexico's strength and sovereignty required economic integration rather than protectionism, and Mexican culture would serve as both prophylaxis and alibi for trade liberalization.

This "ideological bridge" whereby Salinas rhetorically recharacterized Mexico's past as prefiguration for an integrationist future was masterfully deployed during the negotiations of the North American Free Trade Agreement. As in Salinas's rhetoric, Mexican culture was enlisted to assuage anxieties about the loss of national sovereignty and to craft a marketable Mexico to the "external constituency" so essential to the success of his economic reforms. A major sticking point in the negotiations between Mexico, the United States, and Canada was the status of the culture industries. Opponents from across the political spectrum successfully raised the specter of the "Americanization" of national cultures as the imminent danger of bilateral trade agreements with the region's hegemon.

In Mexico these anxieties were anticipated by the government and corporate elites and addressed through a blockbuster spectacle that showcased a national culture so inviolate it had evolved over thirty centuries, persevering through a succession of interventions to arrive essentially unchanged in a breathtaking exhibition at New York's Metropolitan Museum of Art. Thus when Canadian journalists queried Jaime Serra Puche (Secretary of Industry and Commerce and Mexico's chief negotiator) on this point, he simply dismissed any implication of vulnerability stating, "This has little relevance for Mexico. If you have time, you should see the exhibition *Mexico, Thirty Centuries of Splendor* [sic] and you will realize there is no cause for concern."[52]

Mexico: Splendors of Thirty Centuries, the blockbuster exhibition to which he refers, presented a seamless linear narrative of Mexican culture that reiterated Salinas's inaugural address in which he argued that a "nation is a community that shares a past and a future . . . a historical project that brings together diverse wills into a common effort."[53] If we compare this exhibition with MOMA's Twenty Centuries of Mexican Art (1940), and in particular with respect to the role played by folk art traditions within the exhibition logic, instructive insights emerge as to how the Mexican past and its traditions were construed to serve the political exigencies of the two periods. Whereas in 1940 the Mexican nation-state laid claim to an impressive twenty centuries of art, by 1990 it could trace its cultural heritage an extra ten centuries further into the past. And while both shows divided this history into chronological epochs beginning in Mesoamerica, followed by the colonial period and culminating in the modern era, MOMA's exhibition parsed this material thematically as well, by adding "folk art/arte popular" as a fourth category.

In the Twenty Centuries exhibition, "folk art/arte popular" was treated ahistorically as a relatively static but nonetheless vital form of national expression that because of its links to native traditions could synthesize the discontinuities of Mexico's history, geography, and social classes. In his essay for the exhibition's catalog, Roberto Montenegro exclaimed, "All these show clearly that the contemporary craftsman still guards a tradition antedating the Conquest, which neither time nor foreign domination has been able to disturb."[54] Following a different strategy, the Splendors exhibition in 1990 integrated a highly selective set of folk objects into the flow of time with the preponderance of examples (silver, lacquered wood, *talavera*, and *rebozos*) concentrated in the galleries of colonial art and then again through their formal vestiges in modernist painting. This essentially Vasconcelian vision of cultural mestizaje was echoed in Octavio Paz's introductory essay wherein he pronounced "the synthesis of opposites" as the key to the Mexican "will for form."[55] Concluding his essay, Paz eulogizes the ultimate figure of "transcendent mediation"—the Virgin of Guadalupe—exalting, "She is mediation between the Old and New Worlds, between Christianity and the ancient religions . . . she is the bridge between the here and beyond."[56] If in 1940 popular art was the synthesizing agent of Mexico's oppositions, by 1990 it was a hybrid spirituality best exemplified by the syncretic, but fundamentally Catholic, *Guadalupana*.

An extremely conservative vision of *mexicanidad*, this exhibition narrative supplanted the traditional association between Mexican culture and a politicized indigenismo. It situated the revolution, and by extension mural art, into a longer history of continuity, a synthetic "will for form" that was an inviolable cultural, not political, impulse. On the one hand, the Splendors exhibition demonstrated to domestic and foreign audiences that Mexican culture was the most ancient and evolved in the region and thus strong enough to withstand the threats of MTV or Celine Dion. As Octavio Paz explained in the introduction to the catalog, "The theme of this exhibition of Mexican art unfolds before our eyes: the persistence of a single will through an incredible variety of forms, manners, and styles."[57] On the other hand, the "splendor" of Mexico's cultural wealth countered the stereotypes of Mexico as a land of poverty, corruption, and filth mobilized in the rhetoric of NAFTA's U.S. opposition. In response to Ross Perot's "giant sucking sound"—a metaphor that called up images of toilets, parasites, and sexual deviancy—Splendors offered evidence of meticulous craftsmanship, pristine landscapes, and spiritual order. Just as MOMA's Twenty Centuries of Mexican Art promoted "good neighborliness" after the chaos of the revolutionary war and the nationalization of Standard Oil's Mexican assets, Splendors helped to smooth over the obstacles to regional integration, once again creating a tourist- and consumption-friendly version of Mexican culture. However, this time, stripped almost entirely of its historical links to radical politics, Mexican art, folk or otherwise, was configured instead as a synthetic process or "will" toward national realization as form.

Despite its heavy emphasis on the spectacular remains of pre-Columbian cultures, the Splendors exhibition all but erased contemporary indigeneity from its picture of Mexican life and culture. More to the point, folk art was resignified as an emblem of Mexico's cultural hybridity rather than a sign of its essential Indianness. In this way the exhibition corroborated Salinas's depoliticized and deracinated "ideological bridge," making Splendors the first blockbuster to mobilize the cultural politics of neoliberalism. For the kinds of folk objects displayed in the Splendors exhibition, the hybrid account was actually more accurate than the essentialist narrative offered by Montenegro at midcentury. However, what matters here is not divining the truest genealogy of folk art, but rather the ideological uses to which its display has been put. This shift in emphasis, from the indigenous/national to the hybrid/global, helped to lay the groundwork for Banamex-Citigroup's agenda as well. In the Great Masters exhibition, "arte popular" was attributed the ethnically vague category of "community," not the Indian. Instead of being praised for their ability to resist the imposition of foreign culture, *artesanos* were credited for their innate ability to adapt and integrate multiple influences into their already syncretic traditions.

Collecting and Consuming Folk Art: Imaginative and Physical Tourism

Following from and building off these successful precedents, Great Masters once again put Mexican folk art on display for a U.S. audience, this time to reinvigorate tourism after the devastating effects of 9/11. The corporate sponsors for the Great Masters exhibition, which included the heavily marketed alcohol industries of Cerveza Corona and Herradura Tequila as well as Aeromexico, the national airline, make the tourism incentive behind this exhibition quite clear. Just as in the aftermath of the revolution, a folk art exhibition provides a colorful image of a tradition-bound Mexican culture, one stripped of any reminders of the problems introduced by NAFTA or a post-9/11 world. Additionally, the strategies employed through the Great Masters exhibition provide insight into recent efforts to craft the production and consumption of folk art into expressions of personal responsibility, a necessary component of the neoliberal tourist economy. Under this new logic, participation in the market (as an entrepreneurial artist, collector, or tourist) is encouraged as a mode of ethical behavior. The Great Masters exhibition articulated three interrelated processes toward this end through its exhibition practices and promotional activities: (1) it helped to create a particular kind of aesthetic and cultural distinction for folk art objects, a necessary condition for the entry of artisans into the export market as self-enterprising entrepreneurs; (2) it fostered the development of a twenty-first-century collectors market facilitated by the Internet through which local artesanos could go global; and (3) it promoted folk art tourism to Mexico as both economical and ethical.

This was, of course, the explicit intention of the Folk Art Support Program through which the collection on display was amassed and for which the exhibition's representational strategies were devised. To this end, the catalog and wall text elaborated in great detail the Folk Art Support Program of Fomento Cultural Banamex, A.C. This emphasis on Banamex-Citigroup's corporate philanthropy revealed the neoliberal dimensions of corporate sponsorship, collection, and exhibition within the Mexican context. As the text reproduced in the introductory panel to the exhibition as well as the take-away pamphlet explained:

> The [Folk Art Support] Program has three principal stages. Artisans representing the most important branches and specialties in the Mexican Republic were selected during the first phase. These artisans were awarded with a sum of money and Fomento Cultural Banamex, A.C. bought many of their pieces in order to make up the collection now presented to the public. . . . During the second stage, the needs to be satisfied were identified so that the workshops of such artisans were consolidated, with the main objective of passing on the knowledge and mastery of the great masters to others, in order to avoid its irreparable loss. . . . *Finally, the third stage is intended to make best use of the self-support of some of these consolidated workshops in order to stimulate their transformation into micro and small enterprises, with better bonds with the market.* (My emphasis)

While the first two stages of the Folk Art Support Program reiterate the commitments of promoters from the turn of the century to date, the third stage provides a new twist. Earlier calls for artisanal subsidization were undertaken in the interest of preservation and rural development, and as discussed earlier, with the development of FONART, state welfare did indeed transform the social and economic conditions of rural craftspersons, enabling collective mobilization and greater control over their livelihoods. The Banamex initiative, however, introduces the World Bank rhetoric of "micro and small enterprises," revealing the ultimate stakes of the Support Program to be not rural welfare but individual responsibility: the transformation of artisans into entrepreneurs with "greater links to the market." Thus, the first two stages—identifying masters and consolidating their workshops through grants and award monies—seek to enable the third. This is accomplished through economic and technical support but also through the promotional activities of honoring individuals with distinction-granting awards that boost their resumes and therefore the market value of their wares. Then, by promoting these "Great Masters" and their work in coffee-table publications and exhibitions that target an international market, Banamex-Citigroup raises their profile and creates the aura of fine art necessary for the entry of these artists into a more lucrative global market for high-end but "local" crafts.[58]

When Great Masters went on view at the Mexican Fine Arts Center Museum in Chicago the relationship between collecting and global markets was explicit in the public programming and press coverage related to the exhibition. Speaking to a *Chicago Tribune* reporter, Cesareo Moreno, the museum's Visual Arts Director, argued that the "adaptability" evident in the "fusion" of Native American, Asian, Moorish, and European styles in Talavera pottery had prepared artisans for the demands of the twenty-first-century marketplace. "Now the role of the artisan has gone international," Moreno explained without apparent irony, "the artesano has moved with the times and gone from local to global. It is part of this adaptive, creative quality that is so intrinsic to the Mexican. The pieces are more like works of art today and they now sell them to collectors."[59]

As if to facilitate this "adaptability," the museum sponsored a Collectors' Forum in which folk art experts and local collectors discussed their passion for Mexican crafts while also addressing modes of purchase. At this event, Norma García, a mental health worker and museum board member, described her collecting activities as a product of her "love" for her "own culture."[60] The prominent chef Rick Bayless enthused about the "whimsy" and "spontaneity" of the objects he displays at his two upscale restaurants, Frontera Grill and Topolobampo.[61] John Venator, president and CEO of the Computing Technology Industry Association, praised the exhibition catalog, calling it "a Bible for collecting," and noted that the MFACM's shop and Collector's Corner offered both "reasonably priced" and "high-end stuff."

However, the "ultimate" way to collect folk art, he exclaimed, was to take a trip to Mexico City or Oaxaca to commission pieces directly from artisans while touring their workshops.[62] For those who cannot travel, Susan Danly, curator of Casa Mañana, a concurrent exhibition of the Morrow collection of popular arts on view at Amherst College, explained to a *Tribune* staff reporter that there are a number of Internet outlets for folk art, citing Novica.com for its "above average quality at affordable prices."[63]

The sociologist John Urry argues that there has been a substantial increase in the "service class" as a result of changes in mass communications and the increasingly central position of culture in contemporary society.[64] This class is defined by its cultural rather than economic capital, involvement in symbolic work (media, advertising, design, or industries that "service" capital), commitment to fashion, and an ethic of pleasure that is caught up with forms of self- (often bodily) expression as a form of communication with others. The collectors of the kinds of midrange and high-end folk art promoted by Banamex-Citigroup fall into this category or class. Witness the occupations and description of motives cited at the Collectors Forum organized at the MFACM: a chef/restaurateur, Internet impresario, and a Latina social worker/museum board member.

Rapacious consumers of the new service class comprises what Urry calls "post-tourists" to describe their emphasis on playfulness, demand for variety, and self-conscious disposition toward the tourist performance and gaze.[65] As the primary demographic for the customized, flexible, and segmented markets of "new tourism," the post-tourist's consuming patterns are characterized by a demand for highly differentiated, often politicized, commodities that imply nonmass forms of production (that is, through the use of natural materials or handcrafted aesthetics).[66] These changes in consumption and tourism are related to the consonant emergence of cultural and eco-tourism as distinct product categories within mass tourism.[67]

Focusing on the tourist experience, the anthropologist Julia Harrison critiques Urry's emphasis on postmodern irony as well as Dean MacCannell's insistence on tourists' neocolonial search for "authenticity" in the places and peoples they encounter.[68] Harrison suggests, instead, that the contemporary tourist experience is much more complex, and that "service-class" tourism involves a search for the "authentic self" not the "authentic other."[69] Harrison's insights into the ethics of the self that motivate tourists help to explicate the emergence of both consumer and tourist desire for more meaningful forms of engaging difference. Using ethnographic data collected in interviews with Canadian tourists, Harrison concludes that one significant factor in contemporary tourists' perspective is a "moral thinking . . . grounded in a desire to fulfill their obligations to others, to show respect for others, to live a 'full life,' and to conduct their lives with dignity."[70] While Harrison notes that tourists are often blind to the "disjuncture" between the "assumed goodness of their moral position" and the "lived, social, cultural, political, and economic reality of local people," the experiential phenomenon she describes has been exploited by the industry in any number of ways, some ethical and some cynical.[71] Folk art tourism appeals in a very calculated way to the "moral" impulse and consuming habits of the post-tourist by linking purchases from local producers to forms of self-expression and cultural identity, ethical development, and the fulfillment of an obligation to others.

The representational practices of the Great Masters exhibition helped to produce the "imaginative pleasure" necessary for consumption. In the view of the sociologist Colin Campbell, the pleasure of consumption is not merely materialistic but also involves the "anticipation" of and "day dreaming" about the experience, the conjuring of a drama to be actualized through the purchase.[72] In this respect, the imaginative pleasure of consumption, in particular of objects associated with other places, peoples, and realities, is caught up in aspects of what Urry calls "virtual" and "imaginative" forms of travel.[73] As Urry notes, these modes of travel are necessary for physical travel.[74] Thus, the representational practices and promotion of consumption evident in the displays and programming of Great Masters can also be understood as inducements to travel, either virtually through Internet forays or physically. The emphasis on handcrafted processes and regional provenance suggested a shopping itinerary "south of the Border" that was promoted as a form of ethical tourism for its ability to help sustain traditions and contribute to the local economies of Mexico's picturesque but impoverished regions.

It comes as no surprise that over the three years that the exhibition traveled in the United States, a series of articles appeared in the nation's newspapers describing in breathless detail the joys and relative ease of folk art tourism, with an emphasis on shopping as a kind of individualized economic stimulus. For example, when the exhibition opened in Dallas, the *Washington Post* published two articles on shopping for folk treasures. One, a breezy travelogue penned by Susan Harb, charted the voracious path of "two longtime friends" with skills "honed by extensive travel in Third World countries" and weekend excursions to "Bloomies and the Sixth Avenue flea market" as they moved south from Guadalajara to Oaxaca seeking "friendly tokens reflecting everyday Mexican culture" on a $200 budget.[75] The second article struck a more scholarly pose as its author, Bruce Selcraig, endeavored to situate his "folk art buying forays" to Oaxaca within a history of foreign collecting and its impact on the local folk art economy.[76] Selcraig surveyed the regional traditions of Oaxaca's valley towns, discussing textile weavers from Teotitlan such as Arnulfo Mendoza, the master woodcarver Manuel Jiménez from Arrazola, and the Aguilar sisters, ceramicists from Ocotlán whose large ceramic female figures and Frida Kahlo figurines were featured prominently in the Great Masters exhibition along with the work of the other artists mentioned by name. Stressing "an undiluted authenticity" over bargain hunting, Selcraig nonetheless promoted folk art tourism as a form of ethical consumption, asking rhetorically, "What better way to directly pump money into one of Mexico's poorest states?"[77]

As these two articles demonstrate, folk art tourism appeals to the post-tourist in part because it offers the ludic pleasures of shopping and the moral pleasures of "doing good." It also provides a sense of adventure and differentiated products that distinguish it from the experience and souvenirs of mass tourism. Thus it would seem to offer the post-tourist consumer everything that she desires. But what of the cultural producers who manufacture the differentiated commodities that give folk art tourism its ethical cachet to begin with? The moral appeal to individual consumption as subsidy parallels the logic of personal responsibility that neoliberalism exalts and has its corollary in the privatization of folk art production. As the flip side of this ethic of consumption, the Fomento Banamex's Folk Art Support Program works to convert formerly collective forms of production into individual entrepreneurialism. Through this process, the artesano becomes an artist and his or her labor is redefined as a form of individual creative expression.

It is important to note that the Mexican government has always refused to define artisanal production as labor, thereby blocking unionization and other measures of political organization necessary for participating within the corporatist structure of the ruling party and state. Nonetheless, so long as folk art was subsidized through producer collectives and valued as an artifact of sociality, artisans could organize and negotiate for their needs through their symbolic status as a valued social class. The development of FONART and its mechanisms of support did provide artisans with a modicum of power as Rick López has demonstrated with respect to the laquerware producers in Olinalá.[78] Addressing the complexities of this history,

López writes, "Mexico's ethnicized national identity . . . enabled artisans to lift themselves out of the depths of poverty and powerlessness, but it has also marginalized them in relation to national politics. It has allowed them to be considered fine craftspeople, but never, independent, creative artists free to take their art in any direction they like."[79]

At first glance, the Folk Art Support Program would seem to provide the very means that López indicates would truly liberate folk artists from the marginalized space of the "ethnicized national." However, upon closer scrutiny, there are hidden costs to the "liberation" offered by "Master" status. The Folk Art Support Program not only atomizes the collective structure of folk art production but also creates a hierarchy among producers that enables some, but certainly not all, to enter into the more lucrative global export market.[80] And while this may, during periods of high demand and market growth, enable the "Masters" to climb the economic ladder, it further delimits their ability to organize as laborers in the export economy or as service providers within the tourist industry. The significance of this shift in status lies in its implications for how folk artists can engage politically with the impact of global tourism on their everyday lives. As individual artists, the Masters of Mexican folk art fall outside the categories of service and community, the two spaces of negotiation afforded "locals" within political struggles over tourist development and sustainability.

Rather than agonize over the commercialization of folk art *objects*, critics of Banamex-Citigroup would do better to concern themselves with how its support program is changing the relationship between producers, the market, and the state. The deleterious effects of globalization are not the commodification of authentic folk art, for from the moment they entered the canon as "folk art" these objects were constituted as both patrimony and commodities. Instead the more troubling concern is how privatization diminishes the state's role as a provider of services, and how this, in turn, redefines the relationship between folk artists and the market in ways that further limit their ability to negotiate on their own behalf. Ultimately, the Great Masters exhibition provides insight into the at times contingent but nonetheless crafty exploitation of these conditions for the purposes of corporate gain and further "dismantling" of the Mexican state.

By inducing individuals in the United States and Mexico to participate, as producers and consumers, in a folk art and tourist economy, Great Masters seeks to enlist us all in the recovery of Mexico's economy. It is in this way that we are all implicated in the processes of globalization and capitalist accumulation, no matter how unequally. And while tourists have the option of refusing to enter the game, folk art producers are compelled to play whether they want to or not. The foregoing analysis of the Great Masters exhibition demonstrates the hidden costs of cultural tourism for Mexico's most vulnerable populations, prompting us to ask who the "masters of the Mexican folk" really are.

Notes

1. Jeanie Casison, "Rediscovering Mexico," *Incentive* 175.11 (November 2001): 53.
2. Ibid.
3. Graham Gori, "Mexico Hopes to Lure Travelers with Its Close-to-Home Status," *New York Times*, September 28, 2001, sec. w, 1.
4. World Travel and Tourism Council, *Mexico Travel and Tourism: a World of Opportunity* (London: WTTC, 2003), 4.
5. Hale E. Sheppard, "Salvaging Trade, Economic and Political Relations with Mexico in the Aftermath of the Terrorist Attacks: A Call for a Reevaluation of U.S. Law and Policy," *Boston University International Law Journal* 20.1 (spring 2002): 33–72.
6. Roberto de la Cruz, "Mexico: Campaign in U.S., Europe to Overcome Slump in Tourism," *Global Information Network*, November 21, 2002, 1; Stephen Kinzer, "Mexico's Cultural Diplomacy Aims to Win Hearts in U.S.," *New York Times*, August 1, 2002, E1, late edition.
7. The complete international itinerary of the exhibition, including related exhibitions and statistical information on the number of visitors and works included, can be found at http://www.banamex.com/esp/filiales/fomento_cultural/exposiciones/exp_itinerantes21.htm (visited on May 21, 2009).
8. Ginger Thompson, "A Surge in Money Sent Home by Mexicans," *New York Times*, October 29, 2003, sec. A, 14.
9. See, for example, http://www.novica.com; http://www.livelyarts.com; http://www.mexicanfolkart.com; http://www.lafuente.com; http://www.farflungarts.com; http://www.dreamweavergiftgallery.com; http://www.oaxacawoodcarving.com; http://www.ebay.com; and http://www.collectorsessentails.com.
10. Eva Penar, "Grandes Maestros del Arte Popular Mexicano from the Collection of Fomento Cultural Banamex, A.C." *Dialogue* 25.2 (March/April 2002): 15.
11. I have analyzed the political dimensions of this shift from a nationalist discourse based in the *indigenismo/mestizaje* dialectic to the neoliberal rhetoric of "com-

munity" in greater detail in "From Nation to Community: Museums and the Reconfiguration of Mexican Society under Neo-Liberalism," *Foucault, Cultural Studies, and Governmentality*, ed. Jack Z. Bratich, Jeremy Packer, and Cameron McCarthy (Albany: State University of New York Press, 2003), 207–42.

12. Text quoted from an informational brochure dispensed at the exhibition.

13. Willard Spiegelman, "The Gallery: Mexican Folk Art, Sumptuous and Slickly Marketed," *Wall Street Journal*, November 28, 2001, sec. A, Eastern edition, 20.

14. Ken Johnson, "With the Folk Being Globalized, What Is Folk Art?" *New York Times*, August 16, 2002, sec. E, 30.

15. Néstor García Canclini, *Transforming Modernity: Popular Culture in Mexico*, trans. Lidia Lozano (Austin: University of Texas Press, 1993, 2000), 30.

16. Ibid., 37.

17. Ibid., 38.

18. Karen Cordero Reiman, "Constructing a Modern Mexican Art, 1910–1940," in James Oles, *South of the Border: Mexico in the American Imagination, 1914–1947*, exhibition catalog, Yale University Art Gallery (Washington, D.C.: Smithsonian Institution Press, 1993), 23.

19. Karen Cordero Reiman, "Fuentes para una historia social del 'Arte Popular' Mexicano: 1920–1950," *Memoria: Museo Nacional de Arte* 2 (spring-summer 1990): 31–56.

20. Dr. Atl, *La Historia del Comité Nacional de las Artes Populares* (Mexico City, October 27, 1932), reprinted in Cordero, "Fuentes para una historia social del 'Arte Popular' Mexicano," 40.

21. Helen Delpar, *The Enormous Vogue of Things Mexican: Cultural Relations between the United States and Mexico, 1920–1935* (Tuscaloosa: University of Alabama Press, 1992).

22. James Oles, "For Business or Pleasure: Exhibiting Mexican Folk Art, 1820–1930," *Casa Mañana: The Morrow Collection of Mexican Popular Arts*, ed. Susan Danly, exhibition catalog, Mead Art Museum, Amherst College (Albuquerque: University of New Mexico Press, 2002), 11–29.

23. *Annuario turístico de México* (Mexico City: Asociación Nacional Automovilística, 1947), 104.

24. Ibid., 101–2.

25. Michael Clancy contends that before the 1960s tourism was not recognized as an area of economic activity. Following a study conducted by the central bank at mid-decade, the government was encouraged to rapidly develop tourism as part of the export economy. Clancy argues that this shift resulted from the winding down of the "Mexican Miracle" as the policy of import substitution that had driven economic growth since the 1940s began to falter due to peso devaluations, balance of payments problems, population boom, and growing unemploy-

ment. The postwar boom in international tourism encouraged development officials and agencies to view tourism as a potential resource for Third World development. Thus, the government began to actively organize the industry in particular through the planning of resorts, building of hotels, and the creation of international commercial airlines. As a result of this policy of export promotion, by 1970 nearly two million foreigners visited Mexico, by 1980 the numbers approximated four million, and by 2000 the estimate was nearly twenty million per annum. See Michael Clancy, *Exporting Paradise: Tourism and Development in Mexico* (Oxford: Pergamon, 2001).

26. Mary Lee and Sidney Nolan describe these as a rich pre-Columbian and Spanish heritage, wide variety of landscapes and climates, large tracts of Pacific and Gulf shoreline, and a postrevolutionary government that invested in the creation of a unified national identity resulting in the restoration of ancient ruins, creation of museums, and preservation of colonial cities and architecture. Like Clancy, they note that the real boom in tourism occurred in the late 1960s as a result of planned development, especially in the creation of coastal resort areas. Nolan and Nolan, "The Evolution of Tourism in Twentieth-Century Mexico," *Journal of the West* 27.4 (October 1988): 14–25.

27. Alex Saragoza, "The Selling of Mexico: Tourism and the State, 1929–1952," *Fragments of a Golden Age: The Politics of Culture in Mexico Since 1940*, ed. Gilbert Joseph, Anne Rubenstein, and Eric Zolov (Durham, N.C.: Duke University Press, 2001), 91.

28. Oles, "For Business or Pleasure," 24.

29. Ibid., 26.

30. René d'Harnoncourt, *Mexican Arts* (New York: Southworth Press, 1930), xiii, quoted in Oles, "For Business or Pleasure," 26.

31. D'Harnoncourt, "The Exposition of Mexican Art," *International Studio* 97 (October 1930): 50, quoted in Oles, "For Business or Pleasure," 27.

32. Oles, "For Business or Pleasure," 27.

33. Roberto Montenegro, "Folk Art," *Twenty Centuries of Mexican Art* (New York: Museum of Modern Art/INAH, 1940), 110.

34. Rick Anthony López, "*Lo más mexicano de México*: Popular Arts, Indians, and Urban Intellectuals in the Ethnicization of Postrevolutionary National Culture, 1920–1972" (Ph.D. diss., Yale University, 2001), 277–302.

35. Ibid., 294–96.

36. Ibid., 302.

37. Ibid.

38. Ibid.

39. Ibid., 304.

40. Ibid.

41. López describes events in Olinalá wherein local artisans were able to create a road that allowed them access to regional markets without having to rely on local caciques to transport their products for heavy fees. Ibid., 309.

42. García Canclini, "Artisanal Production as a Capitalist Necessity," *Transforming Modernity*, 37–47.

43. For a self-produced history and survey of its activities, see Fomento Cultural Banamex's webpage at http://www.banamex.com/esp/filiales/fomento_cultural/.

44. Text quoted from take-away brochure for *Great Masters of Mexican Folk Art: From the Collection of Fomento Cultural Banamex*, n.p.

45. Carlos Salinas de Gortari, *Political Participation, Public Investment and Support for the System: A Comparative Study of Rural Communities in Mexico* (La Jolla: Center for U.S.–Mexican Studies, University of California, San Diego, 1982), quoted in Jonathan Fox, "Solidaridad, Programa Nacional de (PRONASOL)," *Mexico: History, Society and Culture*, ed. M. S. Werner, 2 vols. (Chicago: Fitzroy Dearborn Publishing, 1997), 1360.

46. Alan Knight, "Salinas and Social Liberalism in Historical Context," *Dismantling the Mexican State?* ed. Rob Aitken, Nikki Craske, Gareth A. Jones, and David E. Stansfield (London: Saint Martin's Press, 1996), 1–23.

47. Jorge G. Castañeda, *The Mexican Shock: Its Meaning for the U.S.* (New York: New Press, 1995), and Paul Lawrence Haber, "Neoliberalism," *Mexico: History, Society and Culture*, ed. Werner, 1014–19.

48. Stephanie R. Golob, "Beyond the Policy Frontier: Canada, Mexico and the Ideological Origins of NAFTA," *World Politics* 55 (April 2003): 377.

49. Ibid., 390.

50. Carlos Salinas de Gortari, "Primer informe de gobierno," *Comercio exterior* 39 (November 1989): 946; cited in Golob, "Beyond the Policy Frontier," 393.

51. Carlos Salinas de Gortari, "Discurso de toma de posesión," *Comercio exterior* 38 (December 1988): 1144, cited in Golob, "Beyond the Policy Frontier," 393. My emphasis.

52. Quoted in Néstor García Canclini, "North Americans or Latin Americans? The Redefinition of Mexican Identity and the Free Trade Agreements," *Mass Media and Free Trade: NAFTA and the Cultural Industries*, ed. Emile G. McAnany and Kenton T. Wilkinson (Austin: University of Texas Press, 1996), 143.

53. Salinas de Gortari, "Primer informe de gobierno," 946; cited in Golob, "Beyond the Policy Frontier," 393.

54. Montengro, "Folk Art," 109.

55. Octavio Paz, "Will for Form," *Mexico: Splendors of Thirty Centuries*, exhibition catalog (New York: Metropolitan Museum of Art, 1990), 37–38.

56. Ibid., 37–38.

57. Ibid., 4.

58. Art museums and cultural consumption have always performed the function of

creating distinction for the purposes of legitimating social differences, as Pierre Bordieu has explained at length in *Distinction* (London: Routledge, 1984). As the examples below reveal, the consumers for Mexican folk art cluster into two main groups, people who identify as Latino/a and members of the "service class" who, in John Urry's words, "do not own capital or land to any substantial degree . . . [who] 'service' capital; enjoy superior work and market situations generally resulting from the existence of well-defined careers" and, most importantly for the purposes of this essay, make up a large sector of the consumers of "new tourism." John Urry, *The Tourist Gaze*, 2nd ed. (London: Sage Publications, 2002), 80–81.

59. Quoted in Mary Daniels, "Art that Celebrates Life: Raw, Vital and Diverse Forms of Mexican Folk Art Capture Collectors' Hearts," *Chicago Tribune*, February 10, 2002, 15.

60. Ibid.

61. Ibid.

62. Ibid.

63. Ibid.

64. Urry is referring to Bourdieu, *Distinction*; see *The Tourist Gaze*, 80–81.

65. Urry, *The Tourist Gaze*, 84–93.

66. Ibid., 14.

67. While both cultural tourism and ecotourism began to be recognized in the 1970s, their profitability wasn't really exploited until the 1990s when the industry began to heavily promote these forms as specialized products within an increasingly segmented market. See Bob McKercher and Hilary du Cros, *Cultural Tourism: The Partnership between Tourism and Cultural Heritage Management* (New York: Haworth Hospitality Press, 2002), and Salah Wahab and Chris Cooper, eds. *Tourism in the Age of Globalisation* (London: Routledge, 2001).

68. Harrison is responding in particular to Dean MacCannell, *The Tourist: A New Theory of the Leisure Class* (New York: Schocken Books, 1976) and Urry, *The Tourist Gaze*.

69. Julia Harrison, *Being a Tourist: Finding Meaning in Pleasure Travel* (Vancouver: University of British Columbia Press, 2003), 34.

70. Ibid., 23.

71. Ibid.

72. Colin Campbell, *The Romantic Ethic and the Spirit of Modern Consumerism* (Oxford: Basil Blackwell, 1987).

73. Urry delineates "virtual" and "imaginative" travel basically along the digital/analog divide. However, the latter category also refers to books, museum exhibitions, etc., in addition to TV, radio, and film.

74. Urry argues that due to the advent of mobile technologies, the 1990s witnessed a "time-space compression" in which geographic space and time were overcome

by people's ability to come together through technologically assisted means. Urry, *Tourist Gaze*, 141.

75. Susan Harb, "To Market, to Market: Dos Señoras and $200," *Washington Post*, November 11, 2001, sec. E, 1.

76. Bruce Selcraig, "Change of Peso: Oaxaca is a Haven for Folk Arts and Crafts— And Smart Shoppers," *Washington Post*, November 11, 2001, E1.

77. Ibid.

78. López, "Artisans of Olinalá, 1875–1972," in *"Lo más mexicano de México,"* 324– 418.

79. Ibid., 413.

80. There were always hierarchies among folk art producers, particularly in terms of gender; nonetheless, the state's investment in folk art as a collective art form rendered all production, in theory, equal. Within an entirely commercial context, this formal equality disappears as some producers get nominated as "Masters" and others remain unnamed and invisible, their wares not particularly coveted or lucrative. I'm indebted to Wayne Modest for pointing this out.

ALEX M. SARAGOZA

GOLFING IN THE DESERT

Los Cabos and Post-PRI Tourism in Mexico

In June 2004, the Mexican government's tourist development agency, FONATUR (Fondo Nacional de Fomento al Turismo), quietly announced its intention to cut back by nearly half the agency's original plans for Baja California Sur and its adjacent areas. Unveiled with much fanfare in 2001, the project initially called for a budget of $1.3 billion for a multifaceted effort spanning a number of sites, primarily along the coastlines facing the Sea of Cortez, also known as the Gulf of California. Called the Escalera Náutica (Nautical Ladder, Stairway, or Staircase), the megaproject envisioned over twenty marinas, several beachside resort complexes, and transportation improvements that would attract a flow of tourists via boat, air, and vehicles, primarily from the United States, to the region. For Mexico, the project promised to produce thousands of jobs and to accelerate the economic development of that part of the country. But the enormously complex and costly plan soon floundered; three years later the initial grandiose scheme was reduced in scope and was renamed the Mar de Cortés project.[1]

Nonetheless, the story of the Escalera Náutica pointed to a distinctive shift in Mexican tourism consistent with the fundamental change implicated in the election of Vicente Fox to the presidency in 2000. The momentous victory by the right-of-center candidate marked the eclipse of the seventy-year reign and political dominance of Mexico by the Partido Revolucionario Institucional, or PRI.[2] Thus, the electoral defeat of the PRI also spelled the end of that party's virtual control over the making of Mexican tourist policy, leading to the displacement of *Priistas* as the main power brokers between private capital investment and the tourist industry in Mexico. As this essay suggests, the Escalera Náutica held a particular significance in the trajectory of the role of the state in the formation of tourist policy, as the megaproject affirmed the Fox administration's aim to deepen the economic relationship of Mexico to the United States and to further the neoliberal orientation of the Mexican state toward tourist policy. While Americans have always been the major market for Mexican tourism, the Escalera Náutica reflected a specific concern for drawing the wealthiest of American travelers, as exemplified by the resort complex of Los Cabos, notably the Cabo Real development controlled by the heir of one of Mexico's most prominent economic groups. Along this vein and the focal point of this essay, the project confirmed an important break in the representational imaginary of previous government-led tourist efforts, where luxury tourism and its corollaries became the overriding basis for large-scale tourist planning involving the state and its private-sector partners. The consequent representational move, with its concerted attention to the high-budget traveler by policymakers and their private capital allies, implicated the construction of tourist spaces that eschewed a deliberate cultural association with *mexicanidad*. Rather, Cabo Real strove to create a site of affluent placelessness, in which the amenities and aura of the resort could have been anywhere—the location in Mexico was essentially incidental to the resort's trappings and ambience.

The Escalera Náutica lavishly imagined wealthy boat owners cruising from one marina to the next, resort complexes generating lodging for thousands of visitors, and vehicles filled with tourists spending American dollars. The plan's ambitious outlook encompassed the tier of states along the U.S.–Mexico border, where various means of transport would link the coastlines on either side of the Sea of Cortez. In addition, FONATUR's planners called for a transpeninsular highway to facilitate the transport of yachts and the like from the Pacific side of the peninsula to the other. The road would lessen the time for boaters (presumably from the United States) to put into the warm waters of the Sea of Cortez from their home ports along the Pacific coast. It was a vision anchored in the economic expectations of closer ties with Mexico's northern neighbor, but the Nautical Ladder concept also involved the historical precedents that buoyed the Fox administration's hopes for the large-scale expansion of tourist development focused on Baja California Sur. Yet, like that history, it is a tale punctuated by political intrigue, dubious business dealings, and unanticipated reversals.

Tourism and the Presidency: The Politics of Policy

Vicente Fox was the not the first Mexican president to promote major tourist projects ostensibly to benefit his country's economy. The fact that the Escalera Náutica also held profits for the business allies of the occupant of Los Pinos (presidential residence) was also not a historical novelty. Indeed, much of the history of tourism in Mexico reveals the collusion between political and economic interests, as well as bloated profit projections, inept planning, social dislocation, and harm to the environment. In many respects, it is an old story, perhaps best captured in the presidential regimes of Miguel Alemán Valdés (1946–52) and Luis Echeverría (1970–76).

Early in his political career, Miguel Alemán witnessed the gains to be made from the promotion of tourism. The astute political operator from Veracruz was undoubtedly aware of the thriving bustle of Havana, Cuba, just across the Gulf of Mexico, given the cruise ships that periodically swung by the Mexican port city to and from the Cuban capital. When in 1940 Alemán became the campaign manager for the successful presidential bid of Manuel Ávila Camacho, the ambitious *veracruzano* joined the inner circle of party leaders. During the campaign, the crafty Alemán made alliances, brokered deals, and learned much of the intimate aspects of the lives and finances of the postrevolutionary elite.[3] As a consequence, he became well versed in the rewards of linking tourist activities with political influence, such as the case of Abelardo Rodríguez. A military revolutionary figure, Rodríguez had parlayed his posting to Baja California to build a sizable fortune through shrewd if not shady business deals, including the establishment of the Agua Caliente racetrack at Tijuana and later a gambling casino attached to the racing emporium, both of which drew droves of border tourists from southern California and beyond to "TJ" and its aura of ill-repute. Rodríguez would subsequently become an interim president of Mexico (1932–34). Although his successor to the office, Lázaro Cárdenas, largely suppressed such illicit tourism, the basis of Rodríguez's riches was well-known lore in Mexican political circles by the time Alemán ascended to the next step in his political career.[4]

In the meantime, Mexican government officials had moved to improve the country's tourist capability—an effort that came under the aegis of the cabinet position filled by Alemán once Manuel Ávila Camacho assumed the presidency in 1940. As secretary of the interior during that period, Alemán used his post to muscle himself and his cronies into the embryonic tourist development of a then rather sleepy port on the Pacific coast, Acapulco. Within a brief span, Acapulco was transformed into a premier site for both domestic and international tourists.[5] (Historical circumstances facilitated the rise and stature of the port city as a tourist destination, namely, World War II and its immediate aftermath, in which the Mexican beachside resort area offered a temporary substitute for the prewar Eurocentric international tourist circuit.)

The rapid development of Acapulco represented a decisive turn in Mexico's tourist-oriented policies. Previously, governmental promotions had largely focused on the country's monumentalist heritage ("pyramids and cathedrals") to encourage tourism, centered on Mexico City and its environs. In contrast, when he became president in 1946, Alemán exploited his executive authority to accelerate the pace of Acapulco's expansion for tourism. For foreign travelers, Acapulco became a renowned beachside playland, as its international reputation also made it attractive to Mexico's upper and middle classes. After his departure from the presidency, Alemán continued to have a highly influential hand over the government's tourist policies. For several years, he headed Mexico's national tourist commission, all the while making sure to channel state resources into his own tourist-related interests.[6] As a result, Alemán left behind an enduring though dubious legacy: the use of tourism as a vehicle for the aggrandizement of well-placed politicians and their private-sector allies within a dominant one-party regime.

In 1970, Luís Echeverría became president of Mexico, allegedly as a neopopulist and eager to regain some semblance of credibility for the ruling party in the wake of the student-led protests of 1968 and the debacle that followed. In that context, Echeverría attempted to distance himself from the influence of Alemán over tourist planning and to promote the profitability of the travel industry for Mexico. Toward that end, Echeverría revamped the infrastructure of the government's tourist operations that culminated in the formation of FONATUR in 1974. The newly organized government agency assured its place in Mexican economic history with its first major project: the development of a strip of oceanfront on the Yucatán Peninsula that became Cancún.[7]

The building of Cancún set a new course for Mexican tourism, as the axis of state-directed tourism moved further away from its original pyramids-and-cathedral orientation, and posed a direct challenge to the singular importance of Acapulco's "sea-and-sand" appeal. Pandering to international travelers who favored the Caribbean, Cancún's development signaled a desire for more tourists from Europe and the United States, especially from the latter's Northeast and upper Midwest. By implication if not design, Cancún's planners were basically unconcerned with drawing large numbers of Mexican tourists, given the site's location far from the country's largest cities. By this time, Acapulco, and to a lesser extent Veracruz, for instance, received much promotional attention from both state and federal tourist agencies aimed primarily at Mexican travelers. At its inception, the advertising campaign for Cancún clearly manifested a different orientation. The glitz and modern amenities of the area, with its obvious marketing toward well-heeled, youthful visitors, quickly made it an enormously popular foreign tourist attraction. Meanwhile, Alemán's Acapulco, already a tawdry shell of its glory days of the 1950s, withered by comparison. The former unrivaled star of beachside tourism in Mexico, Acapulco was displaced by the new development facing the aquamarine waters of the Caribbean. Cancún's near-instant success set in motion the implementation by FONATUR of two additional major resort areas on the Pacific coast, Huatulco and Ixtapa, which, in effect, confirmed the decline of Acapulco as a prime destination for international tourism. Still, despite the construction of the integrated complexes of Huatulco and Ixtapa and the subsequent emergence of Puerto Vallarta as yet another Pacific coast resort area, Cancún remained the crown jewel of Mexican tourism, easily outpacing its Mexican rivals for tourist dollars and the attention of investors, foreign and domestic.[8]

A major transition in Mexican tourism, however, was on the horizon, as in the early 1980s the country's leaders initiated a concerted move toward the privatization of its economy. As a consequence, the overarching role of the federal government in Mexican tourism, specifically the FONATUR agency, shifted to accommodate greater influence from private capital, both foreign and domestic.[9] Nonetheless, Cancún's popularity loomed large, as government officials selectively sanctioned tourist development along the Yucatán Peninsula's coastline, or what became known as the Mayan Riviera in the promotional literature of the travel industry. Though the presidential administration of Carlos Salinas de Gortari (1988–94) set limits of various sorts on the construction of tourist sites on the Mayan coastline, the neo-liberal turn failed to avoid timeworn corrupt practices. In the background of tourist development along the peninsula, for instance, stood key *políticos* of the then-ruling PRI party. Among them was the powerful figure of Carlos Hank González, whose influence shadowed the tourist corridor south of Cancún. In fact, at the outset of his presidential term, Salinas had appointed the notorious Hank González to the cabinet position of secretary of tourism, despite his well-deserved reputation for venality and corruption. Thus, the constraints imposed by Salinas on tourist development in the Yucatán served in effect to channel much of the area's tourist activity toward those sites already in the hands of investors, including those linked to Hank González and similarly positioned business insiders.[10]

To the Sea of Cortez: The Move toward *El norte*

By the year 2000, much of the Yucatán's prime tourist areas had been staked out by well-connected investors, and many of the best spots along the Pacific coast south of Puerto Vallarta had also been largely claimed. Predictably perhaps, and consistent with much of his political economic agenda, Vicente Fox and his business friends (dubbed Amigos de Fox) cast their lot northward. Among Fox supporters was the crusty, venerable Mexican businessman Juan Sánchez Navarro, key leader of Grupo Modelo, the dominant beer company of Mexico (maker of Corona Extra, among other brands). Grupo Modelo's growth strategy had encompassed the acquisition of smaller regional breweries, especially those that served the western and northwestern part of the country, including the region along the Sea of Cortez.[11] It was therefore not a great surprise when in 1986 Eduardo Sánchez Navarro, scion of the Modelo fortunes, began to invest in real estate along the southern tip of the Baja California Sur, including a coastal strip nestled between San José de Cabo and its more lustrous cousin, Cabo San Lucas, or simply, Los Cabos.[12]

The seaside real estate acquisition by Eduardo Sánchez Navarro paralleled the accelerated movement of other major Mexican business interests into the tourist industry that coincided with the privatization efforts of the de la Madrid and Salinas administrations. This policy shift signaled a change in the role of FONATUR, as the agency retreated from hotel construction and management, allowing well-financed Mexican businessmen to forcefully enter the tourist sector, at times in conjunction with foreign investors, and often with the connivance of Mexican political actors. In this policy move, FONATUR's oversight of tourist developments lessened, and with the end of PRI political domination, the resultant decentralization of authority led to local governments having much more influence over tourist-related projects outside of federally mandated efforts. Rather, the agency moved toward the building of infrastructure and to partner with private businessmen, such as Eduardo Sánchez Navarro, in the construction of new sites for international travelers.[13]

His plan for Los Cabos, titled Cabo Real, called for a vast real estate development to include hotels, golf courses, and timeshare properties. The Modelo heir expected to build lodging properties, for example, and to sell the operating licenses on an equity or franchise basis. He succeeded early on in making such agreements with "name brand" chains such as Hilton and Meliá, for example, to create a prestigious profile for his Cabo Real development within the high-budget travel industry; other well-known hotel chains soon followed. Thus, Cabo Real quickly evolved into a tourist zone clearly pitched toward a very wealthy clientele. As a capstone to the project, Sánchez Navarro also laid plans for the construction of a huge marina in San José de Cabo, with more than a hundred slips, and surrounded by upscale condominiums, timeshare properties, hotels, and a golf course.[14]

The inspiration for the Escalera Náutica was well underway before the electoral victory of Vicente Fox in 2000, whose candidacy was strongly supported by Juan Sánchez Navarro, among other luminaries of Mexico's private sector. Given the ties between the Grupo Modelo family fortunes and Fox, the proposed Nautical Ladder made solid political sense, and the economic rationale—virtually entirely based on the American tourist market—seemed more than plausible in the first few heady months following Fox's unprecedented presidential triumph. And other political allies of the newly elected president stood to gain from the budgeted expenditures, among them the head of Mexico's largest cement company (Cemex), Lorenzo Zambrano, as well as glass-making tycoon Federico Sada; not surprisingly, both men were members of the Amigos de Fox group along with the father of Eduardo Sánchez Navarro.

Escalera Náutica was an integrated regional plan centered on the southern portion of the peninsula, Los Cabos, but it also embraced other sites in Baja California Sur as well as the coastal areas of the states of Nayarit, Sonora, and Sinaloa. The plan by FONATUR envisioned three main flows of tourism via plane, boat, and vehicles. The improvement in airport facilities at San José de Cabo had taken place since the 1990s, including a short strip of a four-lane toll freeway to zip visitors from the airport to the resorts along the southern end of the peninsula between the edge of San José to the outskirts of Cabo San Lucas. The planning concept also took into account the vehicular tourist traffic from the southwestern United States to spots along both sides of the Sea of Cortez. Ferries would contribute to the project by making it possible for tourist traffic to go back and forth from places like Mazatlán on the coast to La Paz on the peninsula. Thus, the blueprint of

Escalera Náutica included improvements to key highways and the building and/or remodeling of roadside amenities, the renovation of ferry facilities, and the building of a land bridge across the peninsula.

The glamour of the plan was clearly the attention given to the construction and/or improvement of infrastructure and services for large boats, especially those based at California's marinas from San Francisco to San Diego. Over twenty docking sites were written into the plan, several of them in an arc from Loreto to Cabo San Lucas and around to the Pacific side of the peninsula. To ease the trip from the Pacific shore to the waters of the Sea of Cortez, trailer truck rigs would carry boats over a transpeninsular highway from one side of the peninsula to the other. And to mollify nature lovers, the plan boasted opportunities for eco-tourism through the availability of natural reserves and aquatic protected areas. The scheme anticipated that "Baja" would become the major pole of tourism originally imagined by FONATUR twenty years earlier, when Los Cabos was among the sites, along with Cancún, projected by the agency for future tourist development. Thus, the Baja California peninsular area would finally offer a counter to the preponderance of Cancún in the structure of the country's tourism,[15] while the vision of Escalera Náutica acknowledged the decisive proximity of the U.S. border, as it manifested the centrality of the tourist market literally next door—the source of about seventy-five percent of foreign tourists to Mexico.

On the face of it, the plan appeared well conceived, with its seamless linking of various types of transportation to ease the flow of visitors through the targeted region. In addition, the megaproject seemed to be on sound financial footing, given the populous Sunbelt areas on the other side of the border, punctuated by the burgeoning growth of cities like Las Vegas and Phoenix and the demographic boom inland from Los Angeles and San Diego. The projected growth of these population centers and their proximity meant relatively low airfares and/or short driving distances, which also spelled greater frequency of travel opportunities for U.S. tourists, and very importantly, for return visitors. Moreover, FONATUR's planners were apparently aware that large boat sales in the United States had increased substantially through much of the 1990s. Of particular significance, the calculations of Mexican tourist officials evidently took into account that a growing number of aging but affluent baby boomers across the border represented an upscale market for timeshares, retirement homes, and vacation rentals that were financially accessible, close to a beach, well-appointed, and within a brief flight to U.S. airports (and medical facilities, if needed). The

Escalera Náutica, bolstered by the optimism surrounding Vicente Fox's election, as well as the pre-9/11 warming of relations with the United States, seemingly had all of the makings of a tourist success.[16]

Ladder to Nowhere

Almost from the beginning, Escalera Náutica was beset with problems, as the initial enthusiasm for the plan ebbed due to faulty projections and ill-managed resources. To be fair, a large measure of the project's flawed start stemmed from a sluggish U.S. economy, the slow recovery of international tourism from the 9/11 attack on New York, and related factors. Still, even under the best of circumstances, the plan's complexity and multifaceted implementation would have been an enormous challenge for an easy launch. In this respect, the designers of Escalera Náutica underestimated the difficulties met by previous efforts to promote tourism in the region. The Fox administration's megaproject was not the first to conjure up dreams of dollars streaming into the peninsula from U.S. travelers. Indeed, the days of lumbering recreational vehicles, camper trucks, and station wagons making their way to "Baja" resonated with the Nautical Ladder's refashioned hope for SUVs to spearhead caravans of vehicles from the United States to destinations along the coastlines of the Sea of Cortez. Nonetheless, the planners at FONATUR seemed oblivious to the warning signs strewn along the highways of the peninsula, where neglected, weed-infested RV parks sat as grim reminders of former tourist endeavors and their inflated aspirations. A dark cloud soon shadowed the most luminous image of the Escalera Náutica.[17]

The number of boats needed to profitably fulfill FONATUR's projections became an embarrassing issue, as boating experts were quick to question the viability of the agency's estimates for the marina component of the project.[18] Furthermore, the design of the marinas left much to be desired. Ocean currents and tides created constant dredging problems, for instance, at the new Punta Santa Rosalillita marina, a surfing hotspot where the Nautical Ladder begins. This type of planning ineptitude by FONATUR extended to other aspects of the project. The transpeninsular highway, similarly dependent on faulty boating projections, became a near joke, as the roadway abruptly ended after a few miles from its starting point to become a rutted dirt track. Worse for Mexican tourist officials, the land bridge concept was greeted with staunch opposition from a bevy of environmental groups within and outside Mexico. And small landowners, pushed off their land to make way for the project, mounted a noisy campaign to recover their properties that added to the public embarrassment of Mexico's tourist planning office. In sum, the vaunted expectations of the Nautical Ladder, not unlike the euphoric start of the Fox administration, withered in the face of mounting criticism. The government of Vicente Fox essentially conceded its overblown goals for the project, when, three years after the launching of the Escalera Náutica, the Secretary of Tourism announced a drastically reduced version of the plan and renamed it Proyecto Mar de Cortés.[19]

To complicate matters for the beleaguered megaproject, another thorny issue arose, as legislation was proposed to permit gambling establishments in Mexico, including at or near the country's premier tourist sites. The question provoked rifts within the private sector and its political allies, where certain elements of Mexican capital opposed the juxtaposing of Las Vegas–type casinos with upscale resorts. Among the leading critics of the gambling initiative was Eduardo Sánchez Navarro. The Fox administration initially waffled on the matter, but the gambling licensing debate went forward without explicit opposition from the president. More importantly, Fox appointed a pro-casino Secretary of Tourism, who remained publicly in favor of the proposed legislation after his appointment. Yet Fox's own party announced its disapproval of the gambling casino proposal after much internal factional wrangling, while the rival left-of-center party declared its support for the pro-gaming measure. For businessmen like Sánchez Navarro, the issue strained relations with the Fox government and added to the gathering clouds over the Escalera Náutica project.[20] Still, despite the plan's problematic development, a telling shift had taken place in the imaging of Mexican tourism.

Golfing in the Desert: The Representational Move

The debate over casinos and tourism held a particular irony for Baja California, given the historic association of border tourism, as it was charitably called, with gambling and its attendant seamy activities. In Los Cabos, the exclusive resort La Palmilla (billed as the "one and only") stands today as testimony to the linkages between that past and the present in Baja California. According to local lore, La Palmilla began in 1956 as a getaway built by the son of Abelardo Rodríguez for his cronies and celebrity acquaintances from both sides of the border who flew in and fished during the day and caroused afterward late into the night. The profits of tourism had allowed the former revolutionary military governor of Baja California and his clan the means to enjoy their gains in relatively splendid isolation at the tip of the peninsula, far from the raucous Agua Caliente racetrack and the rowdy bars and brothels of Tijuana.

This vice-inflected imagery of border tourism, however, would be substantially attenuated in the late 1920s and 1930s by the efforts of Mexican government officials. In that period, the image-makers of Mexico, as the historian Dina Berger has shown, worked to disassociate "going south of the border" from the disreputable imaginary generated by Mexican "border towns" and their American visitors as well as the lingering negative views spawned by the instability of the revolution. That governmental campaign to ameliorate the image of Mexico for foreign travelers reflected the duality of "pyramids" (tradition, folkloric culture, and related themes) and "martinis" (modern conveniences, fashionable amenities, and chic locales)—to borrow Berger's metaphor for such efforts—that focused on Mexico City and its surrounding archeological ruins and "colonial" towns such as Guanajuato and San Miguel de Allende.[21] The rise of Acapulco in the post-1940 period introduced a third and distinctive "sea-and-sand" type of touristic imagery, with its romantic if not eroticized subtext, into the Mexican tourist representational index.[22]

Hence, by the 1960s three major elements basically composed the tourist imagery of Mexico targeting foreign travelers, two of which earned the bulk of the official support of the governmental apparatus to promote tourism: the "pyramids and martinis" dichotomy and Acapulco's beachside orientation. The border zone as tourist destination was generally marginalized by official circles, though it was obviously accommodated by the dominant one-party regime of the PRI; the political interests involved in such tourist activity and its economic gains sustained its sufferance by the government's policy makers. Regardless, these three aspects of international tourism in Mexico clearly banked on visitors overwhelmingly from the United States.

Consistent with international trends, the post–World War II American travel market diversified into more discrete segments, which pushed international tourist destinations to widen their representational repertoire in response for advertising purposes. The Mexican government followed suit and moved toward the concept of integrated resort complexes that were carefully selected and designed for the international travel market. This well-documented policy shift began in the late 1960s and became a watershed in Mexico's tourist history, including a reworking of the country's state-led bureaucratic apparatus that culminated with the debut of FONATUR in 1974. As a consequence, the rapid emergence in the 1970s of Cancún as a major attraction for foreigners added a fourth and distinctive aspect to the established framing of the Mexican tourist imaginary. The "sea-and-sand" orientation of Cancún acquired an unmistakably youthful, energetic, and playful inflection—a continuous beach party on groomed white sand along the aquamarine waters of the Caribbean. The subdued tinkle of martini glasses in the midst of hushed conversations over the day's trek to the pyramids of Teotihuacán, for instance, initially gave way in Cancún to thumping rock music, bikini-contests, and Corona-swilling college students and their would-be imitators. Indeed, the search for fun and adventure of a previous generation in Acapulco seemed tepid in comparison to the "party hardy" overtones of Cancún's image, especially in the United States.[23] More importantly, the selling of Cancún for tourist consumption underscored the diversifying dependence on American travelers to sustain the growth of Mexico's tourist industry.

Chasing tourist dollars, therefore, compelled Mexico's tourist policy-makers to adjust to an increasingly segmented and fluid market keyed to American tastes. Cancún served to demonstrate this point, which held important implications for the subsequent development of tourism in Mexico. In the midst of Cancún's early ascent as an international travel destination, the Mexican government touted other integrated resort destinations, notably Huatulco and Ixtapa. Yet none of these sites rivaled the spectacular success of Cancún, nor did they acquire the youthful notoriety of their Caribbean counterpart, punctuated by its association with the annual spring break revelry of American students.[24]

For Mexico's tourist-policy planners and private-sector partners, however, consistent success proved to be an elusive quest, given the travel market's evolving permutations. FONATUR and investors in Mexican tourism were continuously pressed to keep up with the multiplying tastes of travelers, particularly those from the United States.[25] Visiting parents, for instance, looked for more activities for their children, leading to the proliferation of theme parks, petting zoos, and the creation at most hotels of kids-activity centers to entertain the younger children of guests. Restless teens also found their needs addressed through the availability of jet skis, scooters, parasailing, kayaks, banana boats, and arcades, among other forms of entertainment. For well-heeled shoppers, who yearned for American-style malls as opposed to traditional Mexican markets, tourist sites offered shopping centers with boutique name-brand stores, while food services and sports bars plied the tastes of Americans seeking familiar surroundings while on vacation. On the other hand, there were still those who wanted some "culture" on their trips, including side visits to a conveniently located archaeological ruin. In this vein, FONATUR began to construct tourist circuits that connected historic sites with hotel zones. And over time the concerns of eco-tourists also needed to be acknowledged, as well as the growing desire for spas, and spa treatments, gym facilities, exotic massages, and gourmet cuisine.

Cancún tourist promoters, as a result, strove to offer an increasing array of extensions to the resort's original youth-charged, beach party inflection. Tour buses began to briskly transport travelers to Mayan archaeological sites from a large, organized transit center, not far from an aquatic park that allowed youngsters a diversion (and parents a measure of relief from nagging children to do something "fun"). Along the main hotel-studded roadway of Cancún, shoppers eventually had available a shopping mall, which boasted upscale stores surrounded with American-style eateries, bars, ice cream parlors, and commercial decor. While Cancún continued to retain its youthful tourist aura, with all its attendant nightlife and beach-related activities, the segmentation of the tourist market eventually led to an evident blurring of the site's former imaging.[26]

In effect, as exemplified in Cancún, the segmentation of the American tourist market drove the making of Mexican tourism policies. As a consequence, the Mexican tourist imaginary fragmented from its early "pyramids and martini" orientation, and the subsequent "sea-and-sand" dimension of Acapulco, into a growing collection of seemingly disparate pieces. By the 1990s, the imaging of Mexico for touristic purpose was increasingly complicated by changing demographics, tourist fads, and the shifting expectations of travelers in general, those from the United States most importantly. Thus, major tourist sites in Mexico, such as Cancún, presented a burgeoning buffet of activities and amenities to attract new foreign travelers and to entice former visitors to return.[27] In this context, the accelerated move to privatize the Mexican economy after 1982 served to intensify this tendency in the development of tourism with enduring consequences, such as the near frenetic building of tourist capacity in those areas most favored by American tourists, adding to the historic imbalance in the geographic distribution of tourist activity and investment in the country.

The controls of FONATUR over tourist development, never ironclad or consistently enforced, relaxed through the 1980s and into the subsequent decade, contributing to the rapid appearance of new sites dubiously planned and with questionable considerations for basic concerns like water usage, sanitation, ecological integrity, and housing for workers. The presence of well-connected politicos such as Carlos Hank González in these projects marked much of the process as the Cancún tourist corridor became a hotbed of rumored shady deals, money laundering, bureaucratic corruption, and political profiteering.[28]

Furthermore, the neoliberal tourist strategy evinced an obvious propensity to cultivate affluent adult and older visitors, an apparent move away from the youthful orientation associated with Cancún. As a result, the original tourist representational core of Cancún was essentially decentered. Strained by the desire to be more inclusive of tourists' diversifying desires, the shining star of post-1960s Mexican tourism lost a measure of its luster by the end of the 1990s. The building of an expanding number of exclusive upscale tourist resorts south of Cancún indicated a troubling fact for the country's tourist policy: the slippage of Cancún as a destination for high-budget travelers. The profitability of the high-budget tourist market evidently influenced the thinking of Mexican policymakers in the midst of the move toward privatization of the tourist industry. Powerful economic interests, often with ties to the dominant political elite, staked out those areas designated for tourist development with the wealthy traveler in mind. With luxury tourism at the forefront of the new Mayan Riviera development, the previous and privileged position of Cancún gradually sagged by comparison.[29]

In this light, the electoral victory of Vicente Fox heralded a new beginning for Mexico, and the announcement of the Escalera Náutica pointed to a fresh era for tourist policy, relatively free of corruption, backroom deals, fraudulent practices, and cronyism.[30] The project, however, also mirrored the greater reliance of the Fox presidency on its expectant relationship with the United States to energize the Mexican economy. Los Cabos, therefore, represented a distinct direction, as the heavy tourism investment along the Yucatán Peninsula, and the resultant asymmetries involved, would be counterbalanced by the development of the Baja California region. Tellingly, the tourist image envisioned by the promoters of the Nautical Ladder minimized the initial beach-party tenor of Cancún, and there was scant if any viable tourist circuit easily available in Baja for marketing purposes. The crumbling remnants of the peninsula's missions dating from Spain's colonial era, for instance, offered poor substitutes for the spectacle of the pyramids of Teotihuacán, Chichén Itzá, or Monte Albán.

Rather, the target demographic of Escalera Náutica was composed primarily of the growing numbers of rich retirees, older wealthy travelers and baby-boomer adults from the upper-income echelons of American society.[31] The previous signature symbol of Los Cabos, the rich sports fisherman, had been joined by the golfer, resplendent in name-brand attire, teeing off toward a fairway designed by the aristocrats of golf course design. Nowhere was this image more in evidence than the hotels and golf courses along the highway connecting the two Cabos, that is, the Cabo Real complex of Eduardo Sánchez Navarro. The representational move reflected in the Cabo Real development signified an emergent turn in Mexican tourist policy—an image far removed from tourist advertisements in the 1920s with comely Indian maidens or those of the 1940s featuring stylish modern women in Mexico City.

Instead, the Los Cabos of Sánchez Navarro and his counterparts particularly privileged a male-inflected imaginary. In contrast to the established reputation of Cancún, the prevailing image of Los Cabos is much more likely to be a middle-aged or older male, lining up for a putt on an immaculately manicured green bounded on one side by scrabble hills and cactus, and on the other, by the dark blue waters of the Sea of Cortez. Implicit in this picture is the golfer's partner lounging poolside or having a treatment at the hotel spa, as young children are very unlikely to be around. And there is scant chance to encounter a bevy of loud teenagers in the hotel's lobby, waiting for a cab to take them to a dance club for a night out. To the contrary, the imaging of Los Cabos is luxuriously sedate, sophisticated, and insulated, more reminiscent of a wealthy gated community or enclave than a beachside vacation getaway. Indeed, the upscale hotels along Cabo Real are usually separated by marked strips of land, extending from the highway to the shoreline. Security guards and bright plastic markers on the beachfronts keep unauthorized visitors from entering the spatial moat surrounding the resorts. A kiosk with a guard usually marks the formal entrance to most of the hotels, with checks for those leaving and entering the property. It is apparent that the planning of Cabo Real took into account American high-budget male tourists with corresponding consequences, such as the construction of golf courses in a desert setting—or as one publication put it, a "Scottsdale, Arizona by the sea."

In brief, Los Cabos, as represented in Cabo Real and similar properties, points to a turn away from salient elements in the prior history of Mexican tourism. First, the cultural association of traveling in Mexico, for example, visiting its iconic pyramids, has been basically cast aside in a setting that fails to lend itself easily to the celebration of the country's cultural patrimony and/or monumentalist heritage.[32] Second, and following on the previous point, the experiential aspect of the country has been minimized, if not erased, in the constructed tourist space of Los Cabos, where "going out" to a local Mexican supper club, for instance, has been replaced by a self-absorbed, exclusive atmosphere: the desires of tourists are virtually fulfilled within the multifaceted confines of the hotel and its amenities, facilities, and services. Third, Los Cabos projects a masculinist inflection, expressed by its manifest cultivation of a tourist image punctuated by golfing, sailing, and fishing, with an implied attendant sphere defined by the availability of specialized services clearly tilted toward a female clientele. Fourth, extravagant luxury and its trappings accentuate much of the marketing of Los Cabos, with particular attention given to the relaxed access to exotic, and usually very expensive, accoutrements. Indeed, there is a sense of placelessness in the posh resort complex of Cabo Real, as the guests within could be at almost any luxury tourist site and basically enjoy the same amenities.[33] The Mexican government's early tourist promotions, which underscored the unique setting of traveling "in Mexico," with its distinctively wrought "Mexican" fusion of modernity and tradition, has been essentially displaced in Los Cabos. To the contrary, the resort complex of Eduardo Sánchez Navarro revels in its ability to offer an Americanized notion of insulated and plush affluence for corporate captains and their mates.

The visual paradox of lush golf greens in the midst of a desert landscape suggests the enormous challenge of sustaining the contemporary appeal of developments like Cabo Real. In this respect, the tourist vision of Sánchez Navarro for Los Cabos reflects the trenchant inequality within Mexico's most important market for foreign visitors, that is, the United States.[34] It is beyond the scope of this essay to detail the trend toward increasing income inequity in the United States and its correlation with international luxury tourism, but Cabo Real clearly resonates with the enormous and disproportionate wealth of the highest ranks of American society. In this respect, the recent slippage in the popularity of Cancún among high-end tourists augurs well, at least in the short term, for Eduardo Sánchez Navarro and his partners, who have invested so lavishly in the touristic possibilities of Los Cabos for a very wealthy American clientele.

Yet the history of tourism demonstrates that the attraction of tourist destinations changes, as well as the composition of the visitors to those sites.[35] Consistent with what students of tourism refer to as the resort life cycle, Acapulco at one time boasted the presence of the world's jet set at its hotels and beaches. But those glory days of Mexico's first premier "sea-and-sand" tourist site faded and were eventually eclipsed by the glitz of its subsequent Caribbean rival, Cancún. The international jet set drifted away from Acapulco and basically never returned, as the one-time centerpiece of Miguel Alemán's vision for Mexican tourism sank as a high-end destination and became a site for cheap package tours, one-day cruise stops, and weekend beach getaways for the country's financially strapped middle class.[36] Recently, Mexican tourist officials have made efforts to rehabilitate Acapulco as an international tourist destination and to recenter attention to the country's monumentalist heritage, such as its "magical colonial" cities and archaeological wonders, that is, to animate cultural tourism. Questions remain, however, as to who will be the tourists that such renewed efforts will draw and with what consequences for the tourist spaces implicated by those measures. Thus, history will tell whether the original vision of the Escalera Náutica, as embedded in the tourist imagery of Cabo Real, will be able to avoid the pitfalls of Mexico's tourist past.[37] In brief, Mexico's international travel industry has pinned its future largely on a very affluent, discrete strata of American society, with a corresponding and historically distinctive representational move.

There was a certain irony in the new name bestowed by the Fox administration for the Nautical Ladder project. At the small regional museum of Baja California Sur at La Paz, an exhibit chronicles the attempts of men since the 1500s to exploit the pearl beds of the bay, including the notorious conquistador Hernán Cortés. A few years after the collapse of the Aztec empire, Cortés sent an expedition to search for the storied pearls to be found in the waters off La Paz. But the meager results failed to fulfill his expectations. Determined to find a trove of the fabled pearls, Cortés himself trekked to the arid peninsula to lead the enterprise. The waters of the bay failed, however, to yield the expected bounty, and Cortés soon returned to the mainland with his embittered hopes for quick wealth. The future of Mexican tourism in Baja California Sur would do well perhaps to heed the lessons of the past.

Notes

1. The basic information on the project is available from the website created by the Ministry of Tourism. The website can be found at http://www.escaleranautica .com/ubicacion.html. I am indebted to the research assistance of Sophia Luber

in the writing of this essay and to the helpful comments of Dina Berger and Andrew Wood.

2. The focus of this essay will be on foreign travel to Mexico, not domestic tourism. Foreign travelers to Mexico spend much more per day than domestic tourists, hence the attention given to foreign visitors as a source of foreign earnings for Mexico. Studies of Mexican tourism indicate that around 70 to 80 percent of all international tourists to Mexico come from the United States, taking into account the occasional fluctuations up or down in that figure. Tourism to Baja California Sur generally nears 90 percent from the United States. The definition of tourism here is based primarily on foreign visitors, though there is a debate over the precise definition of what is meant by "foreign visitor." In that respect, the growing trend toward second homes in Mexico, for example, begs the question as to whether such stays can be considered tourism, especially when such homes are used for vacation rentals by their foreign owners. Similarly, the expansion of retirement homes primarily for foreigners in Mexico also complicates the definition of tourism, particularly when residents go back and forth between such residential sites on both sides of the border. And the increase in timeshares in Mexico also adds to the complexity of the definition of tourism, especially when timeshare owners extend their visits by combining their timeshare stay with regular hotel lodging, for example. Furthermore, the case of Mexico is further complicated by the importance of border tourism and where the contiguous boundary with the United States facilitates cross-border flows, where the tourist may only stay in Mexico for a few hours, as opposed to the more typical tourist who travels a certain distance to get to the tourist destination. For an extended discussion on the definition of tourism, see Chris Rojek and John Urry, eds., *Touring Cultures: Transformations of Travel and Theory* (New York: Routledge, 1997).

3. On the background of Alemán, see Stephen R. Niblo, *Mexico in the 1940s: Modernity, Politics, and Corruption* (Wilmington, Del.: Scholarly Resources, 1999), esp. chap. 5.

4. On Abelardo Rodríguez and his early role on border tourism, see José Alfredo Gómez Estrada, *Gobierno y casinos: El origin de la riqueza de Abelardo L. Rodríguez* (Mexico City: Instituto Mora and Universidad Autonoma de Baja California, 2002), 118–30, 140–44, 176–86.

5. On this process, see Alex M. Saragoza, "The Selling of Mexico: Tourism and the State, 1929–1952," *Fragments of a Golden Age: The Politics of Culture in Mexico since 1940*, ed. Gilbert Joseph, Anne Rubenstein, and Eric Zolov (Durham, N.C.: Duke University Press, 2001), 91–115. See also Andrew Sackett's essay on Acapulco in this volume for a more detailed analysis of its tourist development.

6. See Paul Kennedy, "New Hotel Boon to Acapulco Tourism," *New York Times*, April 15, 1962. In this article, the reporter notes the decline of Acapulco due to the lack of sound planning during the city's boom years.

7. See Michael Clancy, *Exporting Paradise: Tourism and Development in Mexico* (Amsterdam: Pergamon, 2001). This is a detailed study emphasizing the institutional aspects of the development of tourism in Mexico, with particular attention to the formation of FONATUR and its consequences. Among the agency's charges was the construction and management of hotels, including the development of a chain of upscale properties, El Presidente hotels, in order to attract other foreign-based "name-brand" chains to FONATUR sites. The move toward privatizing the tourist industry facilitated the building of hotels by private capital and the eventual withdrawal of FONATUR from hotel management to focus on infrastructure development.

8. Cancún's dominance as a tourist destination has been underestimated in official statistics due to the inclusion of border tourists from the United States into the overall number of international tourists that visit Mexico. The dominance of sites of attraction for American tourists is reflected in the continuing investment and flow of tourists to those areas that continue to the present. Thus, the proximity of Americans to the coastal areas that rim the eastern side of Baja California peninsula and the northwestern states of Sonora, for example, and the continuing attraction of the Cancún corridor, has led to the dominance of those areas in terms of numbers of tourists and investment. On this point, see "Crece 34% en Mexico la inversión turística," July 26, 2007, http://grupoforma.com, and "Prefieren extranjeros 10 destinos de Mexico," May 14, 2007, http://grupo reforma.com (visited August 29, 2007).

9. It is beyond the scope of this essay to examine the concentration of economic power within the private sector of Mexico, but the main beneficiaries of the privatization process were often the same companies and/or individuals that dominated the private sector prior to the neoliberal turn.

10. For an overview of this period of time, such as the links among politicians and drug trafficking, see Julia Preston and Samuel Dillon, *Opening Mexico: The Making of a Democracy* (New York: Farrar, Straus and Giroux, 2004), 264–69, for events involving Carlos Hank González. On the limits on tourist development along the Yucatán Peninsula, see Anthony DePalma, "Mexico Moves to Limit Projects along Its Coast," *New York Times*, July 31, 1994.

11. The growth strategy of Modelo included the acquisition of two breweries in 1954: the first was in Guadalajara and the second in Torreón. Subsequent acquisitions also took place in the northeast and southwest of the country, in 1961 and 1981 respectively.

12. The administration of Miguel de la Madrid encouraged tourism in the midst of the severe economic crisis of the early 1980s as a means of boosting foreign earnings. On this point, see William Stockton, "Mexico Pushes Tourism Anew," *New York Times*, April 27, 1986.

13. For an overview of this process, see Clancy, *Exporting Paradise*, 71–92. This led

to the fact that a large proportion of the hotels, for example, in major tourist areas such as Cancún, were owned by Mexican business groups, but the hotels were often under franchise agreements with highly reputable hotel chains such as Marriott, Hyatt, Hilton, Melia, and the like. A major exception was the Posadas group that had its own chain of "name" hotels, i.e., Fiesta Americana, in addition to a franchise agreement with Holiday Inn. The move toward privatization under Fox also led to a greater decentralization of federal authority over tourist development. Unfortunately and probably unexpectedly, this post-PRI move has made it easier for local governments to violate with much greater and frequent impunity rules and regulations concerning tourist-related projects, thus producing a new wave of corruption within the tourist industry, particularly in the corridor south of Cancún, i.e., the Mayan Riviera. Clearly this was not the intent of the Fox administration and neoliberal policymakers, but the results point to obvious and frequent violations, ranging from building codes to the construction of beachside lodging sites ostensibly prohibited by federal laws. On this point, see "Busca SECTUR eliminar corrupción por playas," June 22, 2007, http:gruporeforma.com (visited August 29, 2007).

14. The building of the tourist complex of Sánchez Navarro in Los Cabos, and the change that it precipitated, caught the attention of many observers, including the travel writers of major newspapers in the United States. See, for example, Robert Reinhold, "A New Baja California," New York Times, February 16, 1992. The basic wealth of Eduardo Sánchez Navarro stems from his father's interest in the Modelo brewery; using that capital as leverage, he has amassed a real estate empire that includes upscale apartment complexes in Mexico City as well as his holdings in Los Cabos. He has also invested in airport facilities and airlines with an obvious eye toward using such assets to boost tourism to his properties in Baja California.

15. The information on the Escalera Náutica comes from a variety of sources, including the website of the project by the Secretariat of Tourism, http://www.esca leranautica.com/ubicacion.html (visited August 29, 2007). It should be noted that FONATUR's original foray into Baja California encompassed Los Cabos, but much of the original investment by the government agency was made in Loreto, further north on the peninsula. But Loreto has yet to achieve any of the popularity of Cancún, and it has failed to keep up with Los Cabos. On the fitful efforts to build tourism to Loreto, see Sandra Dibble, "A New Day Dawns in Sleepy Loreto," December 28, 2005, http://signonsandiego.com/uniontrib (visited August 29, 2007).

16. The election of Vicente Fox coincided with the election of George W. Bush in 2000, and both men quickly indicated an interest in a warming of relations between the two countries. The attack on New York in September 2001 and its consequences doomed Fox's hope to make Mexico a central concern of the Bush administration.

17. For an early critique of the project and its faulty projections, see Kenneth R. Weiss, "Uncertain Road for Baja Plan," *Los Angeles Times*, May 14, 2002. See also "Escalera Nautica: Mexico's Stairs to Nowhere," http://www.mexfish.com (visited August 27, 2007), which republished an article by Gene Kira that originally appeared in *Western Outdoor News*, June 15, 2002. On the problematic boating projections, see also the article by the *Los Angeles Times'* writers Chris Kraul and Kenneth R. Weiss of November 11, 2003, found in the online magazine website Ecowatch at http://www.bajalife.com/ecowatch/marina.html (visited August 28, 2007). Also see Kenneth R. Weiss, "Still Not Home Free," *Los Angeles Times*, March 23, 2005, for a description of the ecological problems generated by the Escalera Náutica project. On a similar critical note, see Sonya Angelica Diehn, "Escalera Nautica: Stairway from Heaven to Hell," Americas Program (Silver City, N.M.: Interhemispheric Resource Center, January 30, 2003). For a description of Baja California Sur before the onset of large-scale tourist efforts, see Susan Benner, "Where the Cactus Meets the Sea," *New York Times*, March 27, 1988. Luxury tourism also raises a more fundamental question over its ability to promote economic development. For an excellent critique of using luxury tourism for economic development purposes, see Ludger Brenner and Adrian Guillermo Aguilar, "Luxury Tourism and Regional Economic Development in Mexico," *Professional Geographer* 54.4 (2002): 500–520.

18. The issue of the boats to fill the slips of the marinas projected in the Escalera Náutica plan was raised by numerous sources. Ken Weiss in his article for the *Los Angeles Times* of May 2002 (see note 17) found that a sailing expert questioned the entire logic of the nautical aspect of the plan, highlighting the difficulty of getting to the planned transpeninsular highway, the unwillingness of boat owners to have their boats ferried across land, the lack of desire for boat owners to put into the marinas as opposed to natural anchorages, and the problematic calculations that were made by FONATUR. A report from the Center for Competitive Analysis at the University of Missouri noted the rise in big boat (those over $1M in cost) sales through 1998, but it cautioned that the unusual stock market boom accounted for much of that increase. See Center for Competitive Analysis, "The U.S. Boat Building and Repairing Industry: National Trends and Characteristics," College of Business Administration, University of Missouri, St. Louis, July 2000, 2.

19. The announcement of the reduction of the original plan for Escalera Náutica was in 2004. See Will Weissert, "Baja's 'Nautical Staircase' Stumbles," *Los Angeles Times*, January 25, 2004. For an update on the new Mar de Cortés plan and its still questionable elements, see Sandra Dibble, "Mexico's Bid to Lure Boaters a Tough Sale," October 30, 2005, http://www.signonsandiego.com/news (visited August 29, 2007).

20. On the gambling issue and the role of Sánchez Navarro, see *Reforma*, "Definen

futuro de casinos," December 19, 2004, http://www.reforma.com (visited August 29, 2007). Also *Reforma*, "Entrevista: Eduardo Sánchez Navarro," October 27, 2004, http://www.reforma.com. On the gambling controversy in Mexico, see Anna Cearley, "Slot-Like Machines May Skirt 1947 Law," August 14, 2006, http://www.signonsandiego.com/news (visited August 29, 2007).

21. See Dina Berger, *The Development of Mexico's Tourism Industry: Pyramids by Day, Martinis by Night* (New York: Palgrave Macmillan, 2006).

22. On the concept of representational index, see Chris Rojek, "Indexing, Dragging and the Social Construction of Tourist Sights," *Touring Cultures*, ed. Rojek and Urry, 53.

23. The appeal of Cancún has become commonplace among U.S. students. On this point, see the comments found in Corey Kilgannon, "Margaritas at 10 a.m.: City Kids on Break Pick New Party Spots," *New York Times*, March 28, 1999.

24. FONATUR's Huatulco project began with large expectations, but it has failed to become the premier site initially envisioned by its planners; see Larry Rohter, "Mexico Looks to a Second Acapulco," *New York Times*, December 20, 1988.

25. Note here the comments of reporter Larry Rohter on Cancún: "The continuing construction of hotels the length of the long stem of the island has forced a search for new markets. . . . Yes, the prevailing atmosphere as one cruises Kukulcan Boulevard, the busy strip where most of Cancún's 122 hotels are clustered, remains that of an Orlando or a Las Vegas dropped intact next to pellucid Caribbean waters." See Rohter, "What's Doing in: Cancún," *New York Times*, March 8, 1998.

26. Cancún tourist officials in 1996 asked spring-break visitors from the United States to tone down their behavior; see Edwin McDowell, "Cancún Tells its Spring-Break Visitors to Behave Themselves," *New York Times*, March 11, 1996.

27. This elaboration of tourist activity to meet proliferating demands from discrete segments of the tourist market soon led to the term "Cancúnization" in Mexico, with an evident pejorative connotation. See Rebecca Maria Torres and Janet D. Momsen, "Gringolandia: The Construction of a New Tourist Space in Mexico," *Annals of the Association of American Geographers* 95.2 (2005): 314–35. Recently, Cancún's travel industry professionals have attempted to do a "makeover" of the beach resort's former imagery, facilitated by the reconstruction necessitated by the impact of Hurricane Wilma in 2005; on this effort, see "Hoteliers Want to Refine Cancún's Image," *New York Times*, March 18, 2006.

28. There is an enormous literature on the corruption of tourist policy, such as the consequences of the connections between politicians and drug traffickers, including those involving Carlos Hank González. See, for example, "Murder, Money and Mexico: The Rise and Fall of the Salinas Brothers," which aired in April 1997 on the PBS series *Frontline*; see the readings link and the article by Peter Lupsha, "Transnational Narco-Corruption and Narco-Investment: A

Focus on Mexico," which was originally published in *Transnational Organized Crime Journal* in 1995. Lupsha argues that money laundering investment by Mexican drug draffickers has "always" used tourist projects for such purposes, including the Cancún-Tulum corridor as a site of "symbiosis" between "narco-power" and political elites in Mexico. The *Frontline* website includes a profile of the Hank family and its corrupt dealings, entitled "The Family Tree." See the website for the show at www.pbs.org/wgbh/pages/frontline/shows/Mexico. In this vein, and with reference to the shady dealings of the Hank family in such matters, see Sam Dillon, "A Mexican Official's Account of his Back-Door Escape," *New York Times*, February 15, 2000; also Douglas Farah, "Prominent Mexican Family Viewed as Threat to U.S., *Washington Post*, June 2, 1999, A1.

29. The intent to cultivate high-end tourism was clear in the publication of the book called *Mexico Chic* by the country's Tourism Promotion Board; see *Travel Weekly*, "Mexico Reveals Its Chic Side," November 3, 2003, 72. On the rise of Los Cabos in comparison with other Mexican tourist destinations, see *Reforma*, "Visita turismo Cabos y Vallarta," December 22, 2005, http.//www.reforma.com. For the decline of Cancún, see *Reforma*, "Pierde Cancún a la elite," May 14, 2006, http://www.reforma.com (visited August 29, 2007). A similar report appears in *Reforma*, "Opta el turismo por dos playas," May 16, 2006, http://www.reforma .com. As indicated in Saragoza, "The Selling of Mexico," the low-cost aspects of travel to Mexico represented a key element of the early promotions by the country's tourist agencies through the 1950s, but that changed to a large extent with Cancún. This trend has intensified so that the "affordability" of travel in Mexico has become nearly silent in the official promotional literature of Los Cabos.

30. See Tim Wiener, "On Tourism, Mexico Now Thinks Green," *New York Times*, August 31, 2001. In this article, Weiner notes the effort by Mexican governmental officials to rein in the abuses of the recent past. But the article also notes the questionable expectations of the Fox administration's regarding the Escalera Náutica project, especially its boat projections for the marinas.

31. On the affluent orientation of Los Cabos, see Christopher Reynolds, "Going High-Class in Cabo," *Los Angeles Times*, November 15, 1998; and *Reforma*, "El lujo en Los Cabos," October 9, 2005, http://www.reforma.com (visited August 29, 2007). For another early indication of the wealthy tourist orientation of Los Cabos, see Weiner, "What's Doing in: Cancún," where the writer warned readers to bring "plenty of cash" if they planned to visit the area. San José de Cabo is by far the more relaxed as compared to Cabo San Lucas. While both towns possess a night life, it fails to compare with the rowdiness and scale of Cancún, based on this author's observations.

32. Sánchez Navarro has included in his most recent development, Puerto Los Cabos, a museum that promises to include not only fine art but also exhibits on

the "rich history of Mexico," as well as access to an "authentic 17th century mission" on a nearby hill that overlooks the resort complex. See the website of the Puerto Los Cabos project, www.loscabosguide.com/puertoloscabos/index .html. The complex of Puerto Los Cabos also includes other marketing dimensions for retirees from the United States. For a general discussion of Baja California and the retirement segment of the market, see "Builders Bet on Mexico: Will U.S. Baby Boomers Cross the Border to Retire?" *Wall Street Journal*, January 18, 2006. Timeshares represent yet another aspect of tourist-related activities, including those at Los Cabos, such as the Casa Dorada complex of Sánchez Navarro; timeshares represent a major source of growth sector in Mexico. On this latter point, see *Reforma*, "Pierde hoteleria tradicional ante tiempos compartidos," October 21, 2005, http://www.reforma.com (visited August 29, 2007).

33. For a theoretically informed discussion of placelessness or nonplace, see *Diacritics* 33.3−4 (2003), particularly the essay by Robert Davidson, "Spaces of Immigration 'Prevention': Interdiction and the Nonplace," esp. 10−13. The notion of status and self-expression has been a key element in the development of luxury tourism; on this point, see Cailein Gillespie and Alison Morrison, "Elite Hotels: Painting a Self-Portrait," *International Journal of Tourism Research* 3 (2001): 115−21. See also Torres and Momsen, "Gringolandia." The luxury hotels of Cabo Real usually possess a "Mexican"−style eatery; but they are just as likely to also have a restaurant serving Japanese or Italian food. In many cases, the Mexican eatery is relegated to casual fare, often offered poolside and/or for breakfast. The "fancy" hotel restaurants are usually not based on Mexican cuisine.

34. On the historical background to growing income inequality in the United States, see Godfrey Hodgson, *More Equal than Others: America from Nixon to the New Century* (Princeton, N.J.: Princeton University Press, 2004). There is an enormous literature on this topic; see, e.g., David Cay Johnston, "Corporate Wealth Shares Rises for Top-Income Americans, *New York Times*, January 29, 2006. For a picture of income inequality and age (the richer tend to be older), see "Revising Our Ideas of 'Rich,'" *Dallas Morning News*, September 7, 2003. See also the newspaper series initiated by Janny Scott and David Leonhardt, "Class in America: Shadowy Lines that Still Divide," *New York Times*, May 15, 2005.

35. The literature on the resort life cycle is extensive. For a recent discussion of this concept as it relates to beach-oriented sites, see Sheela Agarwal, "The Resort Cycle and Seaside Tourism: An Assessment of Its Applicability and Validity," *Tourism Management* 18.2 (1997): 65−73. Also see Sheela Agarwal, "Restructuring Seaside Tourism: The Resort Life Cycle," *Annals of Tourism Research* 29.1 (2002): 25−55. On the issue of tourist segmentation, see Robert Inbakaran and Mervyn Jackson, "Understanding Resort Visitors through Segmentation," *Tourism and Hospitality Research* 6 (2005): 53−71. See also Sara Dolnicar, "Beyond 'Commonsense Segmentation': A Systematics of Segmentation Approaches in

Tourism," *Journal of Travel Research* 42.3 (2004): 244–50. The Mexican tourism promotional campaign of 2004 featured a clear case of segmentation in the advertisements, which included scenes involving "participatory" tourist activities (join the party), a golf-centered vignette, and a scene involving a kindly Mexican tour guide charming a traveling group of elderly women; see *Advertising Age*, August 16, 2004, 12. In a *New York Times* article published soon after the start of the Fox administration, the writer notes the effort by the new regime to avoid the mistakes of the past, including the apparent fading of Cancún and the "bust" of Acapulco. See Graham Gori, "Cancún Dreaming: Will a Sleepy Town be Next?" *New York Times*, November 18, 2001.

36. On this effort to animate tourism to Mexico's "magical towns" and to make over Acapulco for upmarket visitors, see *Travel Weekly*, "End of Mass Market in Acapulco," April 4, 2004, 21. Also on the Acapulco makeover, see James F. Smith, "Acapulco Mounts a Make-Over," *Los Angeles Times*, September 27, 1999. The rehabilitation of Acapulco is likely to be a hard sell in light of the current violence generated by the drugs and corruption that plague the city; see James C. McKinley Jr., "With Beheadings and Attacks, Drug Gangs Terrorize Mexico," *New York Times*, October 26, 2006. On the issue of cultural tourism, see "Buscan impulsar turismo cultural," August 13, 2007, http://gruporeform.com (visited August 29, 2007).

37. There are cautionary signs that Los Cabos may have already "peaked" as a high-end tourist destination; see Beverly Beyette, "The Cancúning of Cabo," *Los Angeles Times*, March 2, 2003.

THE BEACH AND BEYOND

Observations from a Travel Writer on Dreams,
Decadence, and Defense

As Mexico's first tourism development, North America's first tropical beach getaway, a magnet for Hollywood stars when they could no longer go to Europe, and playground for the international jet set well into the seventies, Acapulco is a full-fledged tourism legend. The "Queen of the Mexican Riviera" is a dame with a past and a conveniently selective memory, able to draw on the strength of her reputation and wealth of anecdotes to keep generating myths, regardless of their basis in hard, historic fact.

Acapulco: The Pulling Power of the Past

Some Mexicans deplore the port's decline since its golden days and conclude, with inimitable fatalism, that it has only a past and not a future. But this seventy-something-year-old resort in Guerrero state is still a major player in a country of 110 million where tourism is the third generator of income.[1] And its past is what helps keep it a sentimental favorite, over the relative newcomer Cancún—the only tourist destination in Mexico that receives more visitors than Acapulco.

Acapulco's decline is a well-kept secret abroad, as are its social divisions (about one third of its greater population of about two million people lives in slum conditions).[2] However, some of its problems came to light after a scandal in 2003 about water quality on Mexico's beaches, exposing not only severe pollution but also hostility to outside comment.[3] I asked some Acapulqueños—icons of the past, tourism professionals, and service workers—what they thought of their tourism history and the role of foreigners in their lives, hoping to probe that vibrant but often discordant relationship between myth and memory that I have noticed in Acapulco over the last ten years, and which I find fascinating.

Denial and contemporary mythmaking are powerful tools in Acapulco and still manage to pull the tricks abroad. In Tianguis 2004, the main Latin American tourism fair held in this Pacific resort every spring, I met an English journalist on her first visit to Mexico who had fought for a commission to write a travel article about the coastal city and was in a quandary once she'd seen a bit of the place. "At home, Acapulco still has a reputation as somewhere glamorous and exotic," she confided, a puzzled look on her face. Nobody in soggy Britain really imagines that Acapulco's perpetual sun shines down on a seedy and run-down resort that has seen far better days.

Any travel writer or tourism promoter recommending the erstwhile "Pearl of the Pacific" as a holiday destination has to grapple with this difficulty in some form: some call it dazzling, some call it a *basurero* (garbage dump), and both are right. What's more, a foreigner or first-timer cannot travel to Acapulco in the company of a Mexican without hearing "You should have seen it in the old days—it was so clean, so perfect, the most beautiful bay in *todo el mundo*."

Mexican children grow up with this misty-eyed patter, absorbing a lament for Acapulco's glorious epoch of the 1950s from their parents and grandparents, as though it were an enduring love song. The nation's relish in reminiscing about this world-renowned beachside town in its heyday is impressive, and annoying. It is not a criticism but a sense of ownership ("our Acapulco") made poignant by tragic loss.

However, while the evidence of Acapulco's decline is all over the center, this is not a topic to be discussed, especially by foreigners, without extreme sensitivity and tact. "Acapulco no *era, es*, la Perla del Pacífico," Hugo Maldonado corrects me in his office at the exclusive Hotel Princess, which opened in 1971 on Revolcadero Beach, at least half an hour's drive from the bay and old town.

Yet just a couple of minutes before, he had been explaining to me that Acapulco itself wasn't the holiday destination—the idea was guests would go to the belching and reeking center of town only once and then stay to relax in the familiar comforts of the hotel where you mostly heard English spoken.[4] Passionate, contradictory claims, flare higher in the golden oldie hotels such as the nostalgic, cliff-top Hotel Los Flamingos. "The days of splendor might have been the fifties, but Acapulco will always remain number one," says Adolfo Santiago by way of challenge in the quiet patio of the borscht-colored hotel. "Firstly, it has the best climate in the world; two, it has the best beaches in the country; and three, it is close to Mexico City, only three hours by road." Cancún merits the utmost scorn. "It's just an arm of the U.S.," he says, adding that I must not quote him. I take this with a pinch of salt when he then says he wishes Acapulco were an arm of the U.S. because "if we had a bit more of a U.S. flavor round here, we might get tourism all the year round!"

Despite his earlier assertions, Adolfo reflects glumly that Acapulco is primarily a magnet for national tourism, and that Europeans prefer cultural cities such as Mérida and Oaxaca. "There is very little here in Acapulco, just playas and *chupe* (booze)." We are interrupted by four coach-loads of pink-faced cruise passengers who have come to see the memorabilia. This hotel was formerly the 1940s home of La Pandilla de Hollywood ("the Hollywood gang"), Johnny Weismuller, John Wayne, and their lawyer and agent Boo Roos. "They gave him the hotel. He was just the *mozo* (servant boy)," said my companion Arturo Zuñiga, a local historian, as we peer in at the locked Casa Tarzan. "But he doesn't like anyone to know this."

YESTERDAY

"Tarzan lived, and died, here," announced Ignacio Sánchez one sultry November night in the Taquería La Quebrada. We are a stone's throw from where Acapulco's great icons, the cliff divers, plunge elegantly into the Pacific for tourists to see. Five times a day, every day of the year. Ignacio, known as Nacho, is a veteran cliff diver, a *clavadista*, who started his career in 1961 at age twelve. He was too young to be present at the 1947 shoot of Johnny Weismuller's *Tarzan and the Mermaids*, but he knows the lore: "Roberto Ramírez, one of the cliff divers in those days, dared Tarzan to dive, but Weismuller said, 'I'm no diver, I'm a swimmer.' Well, the rumor got out—Acapulco was a small town in those days—and this *tipo*, José Estrada he was called, challenged him to a swim, from the *Malecón* (seafront) to the Naval Base, and Tarzan won."

Nacho smiles approvingly, as though the triumph of the foreign star were also his. "He won by a long shot. He was a tall man, you know. He had arms like oars." The professional diver, by contrast, is bantam-sized and fine-boned, with thick white frizz on his head and a stern gaze. He has fractured his wrists four times from the awkward impact of entering a mere four

1. Technicolor photograph of Ignacio Sánchez, Acapulco's veteran championship cliff diver, ca. 1970. PHOTO COURTESY OF IGNACIO SÁNCHEZ.

meters of water from a height of approximately 35m, and perforated his ear drum once. Nacho is careful to sketch out the divers' association's version of a spectacle that is still, along with the stunning blue bay, the grand image of Acapulco for all-purpose tourism promotion.[5]

It is a history that has been repeatedly appropriated and tinkered with by entrepreneurs and hoteliers and by the tall tales of the tourism mythmakers. For example, José Salgado, manager of the 1930s Hotel Mirador, which overlooks the diver show, told me cheerfully the following morning that the first dive from La Quebrada was done at the behest of Richard Nixon— which does not tally with Nacho's tale, nor that of any other clavadista.

Once I have listened to the important facts, Nacho indulges me with a snippet or two of gossip. "Errol Flynn used to hang out with the clavadistas. And Frank Sinatra had a house close by. He came around with his body-guards, and Mexican TV criticized him because he was always giving money away. When people found out he was having supper here in the Mirador, they would line up outside as they knew he would leave handing out dollar bills." Nacho—who tells me in dignified tones that a cliff diver nowadays will earn between 3,000 and 8,000 pesos a fortnight[6]—manages to convey that he considers this situation unbecoming, if only to be expected.

It dawns on me Nacho was already diving at age fourteen, when Elvis

Presley's movie *Fun in Acapulco* was made.[7] "*What do you remember about Elvis?*" I ask him. "Presley never even set foot here," Nacho remarks scornfully. He shifts uncomfortably in his seat, a cheap metal chair, and glances around at the employees, who are idly chatting. He is not sure if he should say this to me. "If it's not an impropriety . . . they say he once made a comment that he would rather be with a dog from the street than with a Mexican woman."

I wipe the smile off my face and push the little that's left of the tasty twenty-peso ($2) serving of five pork, onion, and pineapple *tacos al pastor* around my plate. "So you see why he was not welcome here in Mexico. And the actress in that film, Elsa Cárdenas, was Mexican!"

The following night Antonio Velázquez is shooting the breeze with the taxi drivers in the plaza La Quebrada. "They know I'm a hell-raiser," he says proudly as he struts beside me in his red satin shirt. This former clavadista— who won't tell me his age—steps in and out of the rosy picture he conjures of his past, alternately enthusiastic and disenchanted. His career began when he was fourteen, encouraged by his mother so he could pay his way through school. He duly finished his education and tried to be a teacher. "But I was used to the fast life!"

He has been dry for twenty-eight years now, he tells me, and retired from diving three years ago. But he likes to reminisce about the bad old good old days and the stars—Frank Sinatra, Brigitte Bardot, James Caan. "We were hated in Acapulco!" he recalls with fervor, "We were *mal vistos*. It was *envidia porque andaba con pura güera!*" (envy, because we got all the white chicks). "Ask me more about La Quebrada and the stars," he urges me. "I've been beside presidents of various countries!" Suddenly the dapper sixty-something Velázquez plays it cool, as though he betrayed too much zeal. "It was all "friendly, but not a real relationship." Then he grins at me, "I did get emotionally excited, though when, as a Clavadista de La Quebrada, the celebrities asked *me* for an autograph!"

On my last afternoon, which was bleached of color by the blasting hot sun, I seek out Mónico Ramírez, a veteran diver of a more portly build. He talks with me in the clavadistas' air-conditioned offices but seems sapped of energy by the heat. Of his four children, two are males. The oldest—also called Mónico Ramírez—is a cliff diver too, while the other is studying computing. "It's changed a lot, Acapulco, after they sent the tourism to Cancún," Mónico Sr. grunts laconically. "We are part of the symbol of Acapulco's yesterday."

Acapulco today is world famous. The rich and beautiful people of this earth come to her shores. As I write this, Dr. Henry Kissinger is honeymooning with his talented and beautiful wife, . . . Prince Charles has just sailed away on a British frigate and Ronald Reagan and black civil rights leader Jesse Jackson present their views to the Young Presidents' Organization's convention at the Hotel Princess.

Yes, I would say Acapulco is a known place, an "in" place.

TEDDY STAUFFER, *FOREVER IS A HELL OF A LONG TIME*, 1976

For me—and many thousands of others—the stunning bay, the sassy people, and the yesterday make the perfect cocktail. "Acapulco has always been an international center for people," says Hugo, resident manager at the Princess Hotel. "It knew how to open its arms, unlike other places."

Foreigners played a role in the port's life for four hundred years before the modern tourism industry was born, Francisco Escudero, an academic, reminds me, as we move in from the sun on my balcony at the once-notorious hotel Villa Vera. "And in 1945 there were many postwar widows who wanted beach boys. We learned our English in bed," he says, eyes gleaming, following up with a slightly apologetic shrug.

But this is no place to be modest. The Villa Vera, which has just set up its own "museum" to the stars of the silver screen who were her guests and boasts the world's first swim-up topless bar, was inextricably linked to the Swiss playboy Teddy Stauffer. Stauffer is still known as "Mr. Acapulco" for his role in creating the city's dual image of perennial optimism and debauched hedonism. His autobiography is dedicated to 150 women—first names only—in alphabetical order and goes on in the same vein, with tales about the Kennedys and models, dead bodies found on the hills, priests in whorehouses, and the text of his will, which bequeaths fifty thousand dollars to "any young lady" with whom he might be making love when he dies.[8]

What is striking is that its superficial, dilettante appeal seems to encapsulate the air of the town, for both the foreigners and Mexicans who were part of the scene.[9] At the same time that Mexico's golden age was characterized by heightened patriotism, *mexicanidad,* and state-sponsored cultural nationalism, Acapulco, which was "very much a part of this new image," was learning its English in bed.[10] The Stauffer story appears to contradict the assertion that "the United States was invariably the 'silent partner' in the

2. Teddy Stauffer (with hat) along with (left to right) unidentified diver, the two-time champion Ignacio Sánchez, and the "hell raiser" Antonio Velázquez, ca. 1970. PHOTO COURTESY OF IGNACIO SÁNCHEZ.

most dynamic sectors of Mexico's postwar economy." There was little "silent" about the world of Mr. Acapulco.[11]

Ron Lavender, a U.S. real estate developer, has been involved in Acapulco's growth since 1953, when he came here to set up a Dairy Queen that built a roaring trade selling ice cream and hot dogs. He doesn't see neocolonialism or resentment to the outsider as part of the picture, he says, "because there is so much exposure to the foreign community here."[12]

Ron remembers that it was mostly Americans buying, from the mid-sixties onwards, but did not notice any "problem" in local reactions to foreigners buying up land and homes in their town. "They loved to see the gringo dollar coming in." Arturo, a local historian, notes that it wasn't just foreigners who fattened at Acapulco's feast: "Acapulco grew too much from the fifties to eighties. Everyone made money, Acapulqueños too—lots of us in hotels." Stauffer makes the same point.[13] At the same time, everyone in town is well aware that this is the period that saw the division into two Acapulcos, rich and miserably poor, which blights the resort now.[14]

"When I came to Acapulco at age fourteen, I was selling the truth," says don Pablito, as he takes a seat by his customer's feet. Tonio, who is seated here in the old square getting his beige boots shined, enlightens me: "*La Verdad* was a newspaper." Amid the raw screech and chatter of tropical birds in thick foliage above, the two elderly men squabble happily about everything, from which of the six different brushes Pablito, eighty-three, should select for the task at hand, to who has the healthiest diet, to the corruption of neighborhood leaders.

Pablo Sánchez Castañeda came to Acapulco in 1936, from the rural village of Teloloapan, seven hours away, he says, on the road to Tierra Caliente (the hot lands). He soon went from selling newspapers to shining shoes—a unionized job—with a few stints in construction. In 1962 he bought a *terrenito* (a small plot of land), paying in installments, back in the hills of the edge of the city. "*Arriba*, where they bring the mangoes down from." Later he gave part of the land to his son to build a home too, and sometime in the eighties the neighborhood got electricity. "We had to fix the road that went up to the antenna ourselves," says Pablito, his eyes glassy with cataracts, the dull stain of old tattoos on his skinny arms. Acapulqueños tolerate tourists because they know on which side their bread is buttered, he'll have me know. "Yo cuido el turismo porque por ellos comemos" (Thanks to them we have food on our plate), he says, adding pointedly, "Even if the money doesn't come directly into our hands."

Javier Rodríguez has worked as a steward in the Villa Vera for twenty-eight years. He remembers Al Pacino, Sylvester Stallone, Linda Ronstadt, Sting, and Michael Jackson, who didn't come down from his villa. "Mr. T. could be aggressive with white Americans, but embraced people of color, the stewards." He remembers when a wife of "one of the James Bonds" was *muy tomada* after drinking ten margaritas, refused help, got lost in the hotel's winding gardens, and fell over. Engelbert Humperdinck talked with everyone and gave Javier a cassette with his music. "Baby mi baby," Javier remembers. "That was why I stayed here. It was nice to be near these people. We made an effort so that our presence wouldn't bother them."

Javier had many offers to go and work in the United States, but he has been bringing up his children, all three of whom now have university bachelor's degrees. "The tourism seminars we take teach us not to get too close to the guests, but my experience teaches otherwise. People in offices don't see this, but we as receptors of needs know we have to watch carefully, and judge by each situation what the tourist *really* wants." I ask him whether guests seek contact with locals and he says that sometimes U.S. visitors want to see how the people here live. He has taken groups of foreign tourists to the hills where there is "lots of poverty, garbage—because it is not collected often—not much hygiene, and child malnutrition."

"*What do they learn?*" I ask him. "I'm not sure, but they want to see the quality of life. It's not really because they want to help. It's curiosity. Just that." "*Does this bother you?*" "No!" he laughs. "It pleases me that they know how we live, our lack of education, that our governors spend money on other things." He listens kindly as I relay some of the discrepancies and downright *ironías* (a word I had just learned, as a polite euphemism for lies) I am trying to sort through—the sense I am not to believe what I see, much less what I hear. "We are in election time, señora Bárbara, when people make promises, and other people don't believe them."

When another Acapulco historian I am consulting finally reads the project I had sent him before he gave me an interview ("I explore ways in which contemporary Acapulqueños have re-mythologized their city by appropriating stories of the rich and famous," I wrote) he erupts in spleen. "I do not agree!" he writes me. "Acapulqueños are respectable people, do not consider the Hollywood stars as celebrities; when they were or are on the streets or shops, we do not even go to them asking for autographs, but tourists did and do."

We had talked about my interest in the other classic Acapulco tourist experience, a seven-dollar roundtrip on a glass-bottomed boat to La Roqueta Island. Brimming with gossipy information and bawdy humor, the tour is a rare immersion in popular culture and local mythology, although the hour-long patter is hard for a nonnative to understand. The trip, designed for the national tourist market, reminded me of the old Butlin's holiday camp in England,[15] combining convincing information on the first hotel in town, Frank Sinatra's house, where Tarzan was buried, and so forth, with mother-in-law, drinking, and seasickness jokes.

The highlight is as famous among Mexicans as Acapulco's cliff divers are worldwide: crowding at the glass bottom of the boat to see a sunken statue of a Virgin, reputedly from a shipwreck. It is tacky but honed to perfection, with plenty of variety and high spirits. I was interested in the script, which the boatmen had told me was now an ad-libbed version of an original text by the town chronicler whose surname was Clavel, and whom I could find in the shady cafeteria La Astoria in the square. "Don't bother," said this historian contact at the time. "He's deaf and you'll have to write down all your questions. Besides, he has fallen into disrepute as his texts are full of errors and get the dates all wrong." But once my project started to alarm him, he wrote to say: "The people you heard on the glass bottom boat are not Acapulqueños. They came from different parts of the state, looking for a better way of living and with the illusion that in Acapulco, there are jobs and a higher minimum salary. The latter is true, but jobs are not abundant, so they invent anything to take food to their homes, like selling silver on the beach (that is not silver), prostitute their children or inventing stories about anybody looking for a tip." This is not all: "I am also worried about being mentioned when you will talk about the decadence of Acapulco as a tourist destination," he wrote me. "Yesterday, I had breakfast . . . with a friend that is running for governor of the state and if he wins, he may call me to help in the tourism area and being cited as a source will not help me."

Some tourism professionals adopt a faraway look when you ask about Acapulco's decadence, as though they are doing you the favor of pretending they didn't hear you. Others ingeniously shift the topic on to more positive ground, with the aid of those vast wells of myth and questionable information that derive from plentiful and mysterious sources. After his initial suspicion José, the Mirador manager, entered the spirit of my quest, encouraged by his elderly breakfast companions, who concurred that it was about time someone wrote about Acapulco's past, again.

Racking his brains, he came up with the gem that this glorious location, of individual chalets encrusted into the rocks of La Quebrada, was where a great song was born. "Begin to Begin" was composed by an American songwriter of the past, "who was very famous over there," José told me, never suspecting I might be an admirer of Cole Porter. This songwriter, so the story goes, was in a bad alcoholic way when he stayed at the Mirador, gazing blearily at sunsets, permanently in his cups. A *mesero* (waiter) took pity on him: "Begin to begin," came the kindly advice, night after night. Finally the mood lifted, the message penetrated, and the "compositor yanqui" scribbled out a beautiful tune—on a number of napkins—and then called for the piano and played it, drawing the chic guests of the day down the stairs from their rooms in wonderment.[16]

Needless to say, the tune was named after the wise words of the Mirador's mesero. I took a large bite of my *sope*, not to counter with *my* memory that the song is called "Begin the Beguine," and that the "beguine," I thought, was some sort of dance. This *could* have been a later transformation of the song's title, I supposed, lulled by the gamboling waves. And besides, brazen Acapulco has proven to be beyond contradiction.

Oaxaca: Tourism in the "Arts and Culture Laboratory"

Despite being hard to pronounce, Oaxaca ("wah-ha-kah") City is probably Mexico's most cherished inland tourism destination.[17] The picturesque colonial city has been a favorite with foreign and national visitors for generations. Contemporary tourist activity has its roots in the excavations of the archaeological zones of Mitla and Monte Albán in 1928 and 1932 and were accelerated by the development of the Pan-American Highway in the 1940s. The current surge in tourism dates, from a government point of view, to the creation in 1992 of the Ministry of Tourist Development under the state governorship of Diódoro Carrasco, who announced his determination to make Oaxaca fashionable in Mexico and in the world.[18]

The word that defines Oaxaca for tourism promoters and guests alike is "magical,"[19] and for foreigners in particular, the city seems tailor-made for tourism as a "sacred journey."[20] One of the sources for this enchanting otherness is its significant indigenous population, with over fifteen different ethnic groups living in the state. However, others are its geographical isolation, extreme poverty, and lack of modernization.[21]

Although there is no doubt that Oaxaca City's primary market is cultural tourism, slightly different opinions as to which, or what type of, cultural attractions provide the mainstay of the city's appeal have subtle political ramifications. Just as there are disagreements on how culture should be valued, as a commodity, as "forms for expressing humanity," as the traditions that add pleasure and meaning to daily life, there are also different opinions on how "culture" should be protected and maintained: for whom? And to what ends?

Between 2000 and 2005, Oaxaca established a reputation in Mexico for resisting the homogenizing trends of international tourist development. Its vociferous refusal of plans for a McDonald's to be opened in its sixteenth-century plaza made national and international headlines in 2002.[22] The debates about globalization raised in this battle and its aftermath illustrate the larger terms of the debate about tourism and imperialism in Oaxaca.

Through interviews with artists' foundations and cultural "defense" organizations, tourism officials, and Oaxacan women who serve different aspects of the tourism industry, I wanted to explore what Oaxaca's tourism "success" means to some of those at home. I found that rural abandonment and the burning issue of migration in this state enter investigations into Oaxacan tourism at every turn, further complicating the discussion about cultural preservation and the types of paternalistic or conservative discourse used to resist change.

"EL OTRO MEXICO"

While Acapulco is worldly, Oaxaca is otherworldly, stirring reactions primarily on the aesthetic and sentimental planes, and, many would say, the spiritual too. It is as though it was "lowered from heaven in a napkin," as the English novelist D. H. Lawrence wrote in the 1920s.[23] The city is especially admired by the European visitor—much coveted by Mexico's tourism industry—and hoteliers happily boast a high rate of repeat visitors.[24] There is even a modern tourist superstition, echoing that of tossing coins into Rome's Trevi Fountain: "If you eat *chapulines*, you'll come back to Oaxaca." Chapulines are savory little grasshoppers for sale in all of Oaxaca's colorful markets, and, while they are very palatable, foreign tourists tend to approach their ingestion as a slightly gruesome rite of passage into a magical world. This attitude represents a level of wanting to join in and overcome the "them-and-us" difference, at the same time that the tourist wants to boast of the feat, which accentuates the difference.[25]

Tourists who are drawn by Oaxaca also seek a fairly high host-guest interaction, one that furnishes a certain level of host satisfaction. "We don't have ugly Americans in Oaxaca, 'cause that's really a resort thing," says Donna Radtke, a Canadian who owns the small Hotel Azucenas near Oaxaca's Basilica to the Virgin of Solitude. Donna, an anthropologist-turned-hotelier, has three decades of experience of Mexican tourism destinations and makes a fair point in a characteristic manner. Years of dealing with what is felt as Mexican indirectness leads her to make pithy and shrewd generalizations—a recognizable trait of foreigners who have chosen to set up home and business in Mexico. Oaxacans will express a similar perception about their guests more gingerly, saying they are proud to receive a "turista de calidad" (quality tourist).

This colors host-guest relationships in that the Oaxacan host has a generally positive experience of the foreign guest, doesn't expect the worst, doesn't fear conflicting morals will affect her or his own communities, and is on the whole less cynical than the Acapulco host.[26] It also means Oaxaca is in a good position to develop various subvariants of tourism, ones thought to lend support to communities and encourage local autonomy, such as ethnic tourism (also known by other names, including "local color tourism") and eco-tourism.[27]

Known throughout Mexico as "the land of the seven moles" (mole being a sauce prepared with many different ingredients), Oaxaca is distinguished for its cuisine, for its famous sons, such as President Benito Juárez and the painter Rufino Tamayo, for its strong indigenous presence in dances, textiles, landscapes, endemic species of plants and animals, and for its ancient civilizations, notably the Zapotec and Mixtec peoples. Its large indigenous population,[28] spread throughout the large state in hundreds of small villages, maintains many centuries-old traditions. The best known internationally are those associated with Day of the Dead at the beginning of November and the dances performed annually in the Guelaguetza dance festival in July, but there are many more, primarily related to seasons, harvests, and social events such as marriages or coming of age, and manifested in the slaughter of animals and preparation of food, dances, and other rituals.

Armed thus with an exceptionally strong sense of regional identity and pride, many Oaxaqueños find it hard to imagine that tourism could erode traditions when they see that these are a great magnet for the tourists. This makes Oaxaca a fruitful destination to probe local perceptions of tourism as an imperialistic practice, or as one of the harbingers of globalization. Unlike Acapulqueños, many of whom are acrimonious about Cancún, Oaxaqueños, at least until the disturbances in 2006,[29] tended to be bright with hope and confidence in their city and state's future as a tourism destination.[30]

"We lack nothing here," says Paty Coronado, a local guide who has worked in Oaxaca for over twenty years, mostly assisting French tourists. "We know we have deep roots; we are one of the oldest cultures of Mesoamerica. Our city is a World Heritage site, we have an extensive oral tradition, and we have illustrious men who are recognized on the international stage." While Paty's job entails her being well rehearsed in the region's strengths,[31] such comments—especially on ancient cultures, gastronomy, and native sons—are heard from many throughout the city, including from market vendors. "I think Oaxaca is 'El Otro Mexico,'" said Jaime Katz, then the new subsecretary for Oaxaca state tourism. For the tourism promoter there is every confidence that "the south and southeast have a different, stronger, and weightier culture—with the Zapotecs, Mixtecs, and Maya."

However, with the perpetual problems of difference, there is a less savory side to being defined as what the main thing is *not*. Oaxaca has gathered a reputation in recent years as more Mexican than Mexico itself (or "the many

Mexicos" put together). A gringo joke asks, "What does *mañana* mean in Oaxaca?" with the response: "The same as in the rest of Mexico, only it's less urgent." As even this flippancy suggests, this does not work wholly in Oaxaca's favor. The state is seen as backward, and so it is, to put matters bluntly. Inhabitants point out that it's not as perfect as it seems to outsiders. "To someone who comes, like you, for a few days, Oaxaca seems ideal, a 'great place to live,' but live here and you'll find it problematic. Come back in March, when there's no water," grumbles Miguel Ángel Vargas, a graphic designer.

Oaxaca's trying geographical isolation was one of the major reasons for the state's ability to preserve its indigenous identities and traditions for so long. But, as Miguel says, "This was also used as an excuse not to do things. It preserved typical things, but also prevented advances." One of Oaxaca's dilemmas as a tourist destination is the degree to which touristically attractive culture—the "magic" its European guests relish—goes hand in hand with a backwardness that inhibits tourism infrastructure, planning, and development of lucrative attractions that might bring steady tourism dollars (and what is feared by some as "mass tourism").

HELP OR HINDRANCE—OAXACA'S VERSION
OF THE IMPERIALISM DEBATE

Of Mexico's many tourism destinations, Oaxaca City is probably the one in which the debate about, and concrete actions toward, the preservation of cultural heritage are the most developed. In this respect it provides a marked contrast to Acapulco, whose exotic history and varied cultures have been completely absent from the tourism lexicon and only recently have begun to be promoted as attractions. The discussion in Oaxaca is riddled with both conflict and irony, however, against a background in which tourism is only secondary.

The major issue affecting the state economically and socially is migration —to Oaxaca City, to Mexico City, and over the border to the United States— as a result of poverty and abandonment of the countryside. However, tourism and migration converge on the issue of patrimony, or cultural heritage. Many of the apparent contradictions that arise in the ensuing conversations depend upon how interviewees interpret the relationship of each of the above (tourism and migration) with patrimony. For example, tourism feeds on and arguably exploits, distorts, and erodes Oaxaca's patrimony, by decontextualizing and simplifying culture into tourism attractions. Migration

—especially when over the border—uproots and transforms patrimony, often watering it down and within a couple of generations eliminating it, but also, it can be argued, migration reinforces and revives aspects of Oaxaca's patrimony.

One interpretation would be that patrimony is what brings tourist dollars to Oaxaca, but it is not enough to keep Oaxaqueños home. What is magic for visitors could be ball and chain for those at home. (Further ironies appear to spring from a still more complex dynamic of lived culture and the relationship of Oaxaqueños with outsiders, which I will look at in the next section.) According to Rodrigo Esponda, an official with the Mexican Tourism Board, it is only recently that tourism has been regarded by Mexico's tourism authorities as a serious tool for the preservation of cultural traditions.[32] Discussing the topic with people in Oaxaca, be they market vendors or hoteliers, it is soon evident that those active and effective in preserving cultural heritage have not been tourism departments but rather the outspoken artists and intellectuals of the city, who tend to feel that they have had to work in spite of these departments. "There is an advantage here over other states, not as a result of entrepreneurial tourism, but because a strong group has put cultural heritage over economic gain," says Fernando Gálvez, director of Oaxaca's Institute of Graphic Arts (IAGO).[33]

The group of artists he is referring to is an NGO known as PRO-OAX.[34] PRO-OAX is closest to articulating that tourism in Oaxaca is in danger of functioning as a form of imperialism, although the word "imperialism" doesn't really have much resonance in Oaxaca, ever since *globalización* has begun to be used (around 2002) to denote contemporary ills of a similar ilk.[35] At the same time it is not in PRO-OAX's interests to declaim against tourism as an imperialist practice but rather to point out that tourism can bring along some of the bad sides of globalization, namely, cultural homogenization as "native" cultures are swallowed up by "Western values." Their stance —much of their rhetoric recognizably "old left" and parodied by Mexican press as "globalifóbico" (global-phobe)—tends to be that tourism should be put in its place as secondary to the preservation of culture, where it will do less harm and grow in a measured and beneficial way.

These stakes and stances—the simplistic approbation of tourism for its positive economic effects upon the arts and crafts industries, the role tourism could take in encouraging local autonomy, and the use of traditional cultures to empower communities and build resistance to outside profiteering through tourism—informed the conflict around tourism in Oaxaca at the end of 2004, when the new state tourism administration (although the incoming state government was from the same party, the PRI) was taking the reins. The influential voices here are tourism officials, spokespeople for artists' groups, and tourism service providers, foreign and Oaxacan.

"Cultural heritage" is considered by PRO-OAX to be the main attraction of the state and the key to its economic future, which is where the political ramifications of the question "What makes Oaxaca so attractive to tourists?" begin to become evident. The tourism office lists the city's top two attractions as pre-Hispanic culture, as in the archaeological sites of Monte Albán and nearby Mitla, followed by the architecture of the viceregal period, that is, colonial buildings and convents.[36]

Donna the hotelier disagrees: "Pre-Hispanic sites may be why the *Mexicans* come here, but North Americans come here for the variety of attractions." From what the Canadian tourism service provider has seen in the last three decades, this variety includes museums, art galleries, cuisine and markets, a wide range of handicrafts, textiles and clothing, language and cookery courses, churches and colonial architecture, dance and music, attractive streets, squares, and shops and—essentially—Oaxacan people, and the many ethnic groups, especially when they wear traditional clothing. "Tourists don't come for hotels, they come for history, indigenous tradition, gastronomy. The government needs to see that culture could be the motor for this state's development," states Jorge Contreras, a museum coordinator and PRO-OAX spokesperson.

I think the coincidence of the hotelier's opinion with that of PRO-OAX, and in contradiction of the official tourism authorities, is telling, although it can also be interpreted as a result of Donna's viewpoint as a foreigner (more aware of the appeal of Oaxaca's enchanting otherness) and the fact that her business is small (she is not under pressure to increase occupation of a large hotel off-season). PRO-OAX follows Mexico's National Institute of Anthropology and History (INAH) in defining cultural heritage, or patrimony, as that which is "tangible" (old buildings, plant species) and "intangible" (eating customs, musical traditions).

In recent years, Oaxaca has gained a national and international reputation for defending this so-called intangible patrimony from commercial interests, foreign megastores and food chains, and what has been presented by PRO-OAX as unhealthy and debased consumerist habits from the United States.[37] The highlight occurred in 2002 when, after colorful protests that involved handing out free tamales (a traditional food made of steamed maize), the city refused to allow a McDonald's in its *zócalo* (historic main square). Although this is not properly an issue of tourism—foreign visitors were eager and vocal supporters of successful efforts by the cultural community to reject the fast-food chain—resultant passionate feelings have contributed to a posture on the part of PRO-OAX that labels foreign tourism as part of the menace.

A position that may have fallen out of fashion in academia nevertheless has weight and conviction here—that tourism is one of the perpetrators of "our perverse age of modernization."[38] It was local entrepreneurs who sought the McDonald's franchise, and it was local government that was about to authorize it, but the discourse of resistance has characterized the issue as one of globalization *as an outside threat* (giving transnational corporations power beyond nation-states). Tourism participates in this threat by bringing in outsiders (however friendly and appreciative) with supposedly debased tastes, encouraging locals to associate these tastes with privilege and mobility, thus making them desirable and contributing to the erosion or distortion of traditions.

A suspicion on the part of PRO-OAX that tourism in Oaxaca can function as a form of imperialism (whereby foreign companies have more say than local people) is rarely articulated in these terms, probably because tourism and tourists have also proved a valuable ally of cultural projects. It would clearly be counterproductive to alienate well-meaning and wealthy outsiders when it tends to be Mexicans, rather than foreigners, who are behind the initiatives that PRO-OAX opposes. Rather than analyzing tourism practices as imperialist per se, the issue tends to be regarded in the Oaxacan context as the degree to which it ushers in globalization.

Oaxaca's first income is not tourism but *remesas* (money sent home by Oaxaqueños working elsewhere). Tourism comes next, but it gives outsiders an uncomfortable feeling if they become aware that, while they can afford to come to this beautiful state to enjoy its culture and traditions, its native inhabitants can't even scrape together the merest living for their families and have to leave. "Oaxaca is expensive for people who are from here, even though it is cheap for the tourist," says the tour guide Paty. "The minimum wage is just impossible, so everyone has two jobs. Even government secretaries sell shoes."

It is surprising therefore that one senses little detectable resentment against the tourist or the tourist entrepreneur among ordinary Oaxaqueños such as tourism service providers, vendors, or villagers. Jorge has seen tourists trampling over graves during Día de Muertos and locals disturbed but not overtly angry—although he, a PRO-OAX spokesperson, is taut with fury at the tourism marketing that has produced this situation. While the Acapulqueño may ironize his own welcome of tourists, saying he knows on which side his bread is buttered, this is not an outlook found readily in Oaxaca. IAGO's Fernando—also a spokesman for PRO-OAX—agrees that the preponderant attitude in the Día de Muertos fiesta, one of Oaxaca's four peak tourism seasons, is welcoming, with mourners feeling truly proud and honored that foreigners are really interested in their traditions.[39]

"The problem is not the tourists but bad regulation, weak legislation, and unscrupulous business entrepreneurs," he says. His comments suggest that groups of outsiders coming into a quiet graveyard flickering with candle flames to look at Zapotec people on the night they remember their dead is a little repugnant but nowadays inevitable. By focusing on the lack of regulation and sensitive planning, he avoids taking a position on whether those who want to preserve culture should support graveyard tours in this fiesta. Instead he suggests, quite reasonably, that someone who profits by bringing busloads of tourists to the gravesites (whose money does not go toward the local economy, as foreigners are advised not to eat on the street) could at least help fund some temporary latrines nearby to deal with the influx of outsiders. There are numerous examples of poor management and dismal coordination.[40] However, the very evident resentment, and even hostility, of some of the PRO-OAX spokespeople comes from a belief in principles that are misunderstood and a real sense of being under attack.

Seated in a tiny corner of shade in the first courtyard of Oaxaca's stylish and internationally prestigious Museum of Contemporary Art (MACO), of which he is the coordinator, Jorge mentions July's Guelaguetza dance festival as symptomatic of the widespread malady that makes culture subservient to tourism: "The attitude is 'We organize the Guelaguetza to bring tourists and make money.' Spectacles are valued as fun, instead of as forms for expressing humanity," he says, adding, "I am sure mass tourism poses a problem for Oaxaca." Jorge paints a picture whereby when culture is valued and promoted as a commodity, it loses its authenticity, that is, its social and human functions. While the subvariants of tourism mentioned above could help bridge this gap (spectacles valued as fun *and* forms for expressing humanity; or spectacles valued as fun *because* they are forms for expressing humanity), Jorge does not see evidence of a more community-focused tourism in Oaxaca, only the menacing spectacle of mass tourism.

I relay Jorge's plea to the new tourism secretary, Beatriz Ramírez: "Let cultural activity work its own way—as that's what brings prestige to Oaxaca." "I agree with them," Ramírez declared sweepingly, "Culture is above tourism." But her comments would not still the artists' doubts: "I know how to sell what I know," she said, pointing out that the new state government has set up a separate culture ministry, headed by Paty Zorote. So I must remember not to ask her, Beatriz, about culture, as this is Zorote's job.[41]

Oaxacan hotelier Lety Ricardez is happy about Beatriz's appointment because she is, as Lety says, "a business entrepreneur and not a politician." While the distinction may seem tenuous, given that most politicians are fueled by business, to Lety, a young businesswoman who has shown acumen and proven management abilities without excessive politicking is like a breath of fresh air. Besides, politicians in Oaxaca have an even worse reputation than usual after the former governor, José Murat, was alleged to have staged his own assassination attempt in March 2004.[42]

The one public figure to enjoy a noble reputation here, it seems, is the artist—as incarnated in Francisco Toledo, a renowned international talent and impressive benefactor of his home state. Mexico has a distinctive tradition of artists as public figures and spokespersons whose opinions and influence is not seen amiss in politics, one well-known example being the influence of Diego Rivera in the reception of Trotsky. Oaxaca, perhaps owing to its isolation and *caciquismo* (near-feudal power structures with strong local bosses), tends to intensify this situation.[43]

"I think Oaxaca is the only Mexican city where the voice of artists is so listened to," Jorge reflects. This is because "artists have known how to win the place, but also because they are a moral authority, seeking to benefit Oaxaca unconditionally." He is referring principally to Toledo's influence through PRO-OAX, whose achievements are legion. Nevertheless, the centrality of this painter, "the most generous and least loved man in Oaxaca,"[44] is a complicated phenomenon explained and probed (for example, Toledo's problematic role of the *cacique*), by the art historian Selma Holo.[45] Although Francisco Toledo, now seventy, lived for fifteen years in Paris and is married to a Dane, he is said not to like foreigners. The rumor is relevant to the myth around him and this suspected—primarily by the cultural community—discrepancy between the interests of Oaxaca's tourism industry and its cultural heritage. Although PRO-OAX's Fernando absolves the tourist of destructive imperialistic intent, he insists that a part of tourism profits should go toward maintenance of cultural goods. This point has been developed with considerable perception and clarity in Holo's discussion of the success-ful management by Nelly Robles of the Monte Albán archaeological site on the edge of Oaxaca City. The issue was not just preservation in the face of tourism as an "irreversible phenomenon in the globalized world" (thanks to Robles, 30 percent of ticket venues went toward the site) but also of negotia-tion of community demands and local politics.[46]

But even if one does absolve foreign tourists from destructive intent as their dollars encourage locals to make everything a show and thus wrench human value from ritual, tourism as an industry is intrinsically bound up with a crucially related tangle of heritage and sovereignty, local politics and law. "Why are we even listening to someone who is only going to create 120 jobs? What about Mexican people, us, who with our taxes have invested millions in the pyramids of Teotihuacán, which is the world's heritage?" Fernando asked, in response to the heated Wal-Mart debate of the moment. (In November 2004, Wal-Mart—the world's largest retailer and in control of 55 percent of Mexico's retail market—opened a superstore very close to the ancient pre-Aztec ruins of Teotihuacán, leading to arguments about profan-ing cultural heritage as well as the destructive influence of global companies on Mexico's local economies.)[47] "They are saying, 'We go where we want and governments are subordinate to us.' This is *angustiante* [disturbing]."[48] Fer-nando is undeterred by accusations of paternalism, and feelings are running high.[49] In his view these discussions about legal and moral authorities, and the current legal battles, are not yet over.

THE LOCAL PERSPECTIVE

The more one digs—into the fraught issue of migration, and the economic possibilities (especially for tourism) about to be opened up by new roads to the Isthmus and the Pacific coast—the more one realizes Oaxaca is still only at the beginning of a major change. By now, Oaxaqueños, at the same time that many who are enthused by the respect their city and state have gained in recent years and are seeing benefits from tourism revenues, sense that things can't go on at this level: "We know the tourist is happy. They write back after their visit about the magic here, but we in Oaxaca can feel that the spell is breaking," says the hotelier Lety, who expresses her concerns about the loss of the tradition of going to market with one's baskets.

Markets and cuisine are crucial aspects of cultural patrimony in this discussion because they affect both the daily and the sacred life of Oaxa-queñans, their childhood memories, their sense of home and identity—and they are also an essential part of the tourist/consumer culture arena.[50] Even in a country with so rich and varied a gastronomical inheritance as Mexico, Oaxaca—as the land of the seven moles, chapulines, iguana tamales, *tlayudas* (large white tostadas), chocolate, mezcal—stands out for its unique dishes and exotic ingredients. Food and recipes are genuinely treasured here and help bind communities.

With Paty, the local tour guide, a conversation about traditional clothing, within a breath, becomes a passionate description of food. A chat about the beautiful *Tehuana* (from the Isthmus of Tehuantepec, a remote and distinctive region of Oaxaca state) costume—brought to international attention by Frida Kahlo—leads naturally into the observation that, in Oaxaca, a traditional *tamal* (a meat or fruit-filled dumpling) is steamed and served in a banana leaf rather than a corn husk. She tells me that if I go on market day, a Saturday, to the "Central de Abastos" where tourists rarely go—not the 20 de noviembre market, which is a standard attraction for visitors—I will see a wealth of traditional costumes. But before she finishes this sentence, she interrupts herself to discuss the politics of markets and attempts by local authorities to control where they may be held, a discussion that leads to the new megastores, like Sam's Club (part of the Wal-Mart empire that caused such controversy at the time), which can be found increasingly on the outskirts of the colonial city.

Paty starts to argue with a foreign friend who believes these stores will be the eventual death knell of the markets. Locals still go for vegetables, cheese, and meat but venture into Sam's for novelties like Christmas trees, clothes, and detergent, Paty believes. But she agrees that, with time, there is reason to be pessimistic after all. "We probably can't keep going at this rhythm. Now young girls are leaving for the border too," she reflects, spurring the sad observation that her generation may be the last in which women are able to be proud guardians of this aspect of culture.

We are dining in the inexpensive, cozy, and romantic Zandunga restaurant, owned by a Tehuana woman, Aurora Toledo, who cooks typical *Istmeña* (Isthmus) cuisine behind a tiny screen; you can hear the sizzles and see the steam. Paty's appetite is whetted and she is thinking nostalgically of the markets she visited in her youth and identified proudly with the Zapotec Indians from there, even though she is *mestizo* from just outside the city: "We still sell iguanas, rabbits, armadillos, and quails in markets at the *Istmo*. At one a.m. the market is awake. The same as if it were one p.m." Aurora is half Zapotec Indian and half Zoque, she tells me, and understands the

Zapotec language perfectly well although she is not confident about speaking it anymore. She has a deep, caressing voice in Spanish and has the trademark Tehuana quality of making you feel seduced and mothered at the same time.[51] In addition to offering rare dishes, such as *estofado* (stew), she also sells embroidered *huipiles*, which she sews upstairs, and would like to write a book of anecdotes about food and markets. "Not recipes," she says in her luscious, deep growl. She wants to record when and how the cow is spliced up in preparation for the local feast, to write about rites of passage for girls who want to join the powerful community of female cooks, and to note down some of the ribald conversations that burn the ears of these young female initiates. "You *have* to go to the Istmo" (the Isthmus, about six hours by bus to the southeast of Oaxaca City), she urges me, with a wink. "El mercado es un mosaico [a mosaic] . . . the way people talk! They call you 'Mamá' and 'Papá.' If a young lad is walking by, they'll shout to him: 'Manito, compra camarón pa' que se pare tu pito" [little brother, buy my shrimp so you get a nice hard on].[52]

Indian identity and tradition are debated among a wide range of social groups in Oaxaca, not just influential intellectuals and artists. Although the demographic and political context encourages this, it is notable in comparison to states such as Puebla, Michoacán, Veracruz, and even Yucatán.[53] Oaxaca has among the largest variety of ethnic groups of any Mexican state, and it also has a dauntingly huge number of municipalities, so there are many competing and conflicting identities in small political and ethnic subgroups. It is only when one has assured a certain level of economic independence and social acceptance that the signifying political classes, for example, are happy to don the garb of indigenous identity without the fear of the denigrating aspects rubbing off on them. Although one should also be wary of idealizing the phenomenon—to be called "indio" in Oaxaca is an insult to anyone with middle-class pretensions, as in the rest of Mexico[54]—the very dynamism and relative sophistication of the debate could put Oaxaca in a strong position to define and develop its own variants of "ethnic," "indigenous," or "community" tourism.

In the pretty Sánchez Pascua market, slightly north of the Oaxaca City center, Marta Ramírez runs a food stall in the morning. In the afternoon she works in the Institute for Public Education. Marta remembers a restaurant she went to where the *entomatadas* (fried, folded tortillas in a fresh tomato sauce) were prepared with catsup. "Así no es," she said, shaking her head gravely. "A la mujer moderna, les da flojera" (modern women, they just can't be bothered anymore). She was moved to correct the owner, she said, because the cuisine advertised was Comida Típica Oaxaqueña, so "they are *desprestigiando* [lowering the reputation of] our food." Marta says her mother taught her how to cook using a *metate* (a long grinding instrument made of volcanic stone), "but everyone uses a liquidizer now. Everything is *corre* [rush rush] *y commercial*," she laments. "McDonald's, for example," Marta says, "creates a different youth" from their parents' generation. Hamburgers and that kind of food "just bloat you up." She makes sure her sons know how to eat properly, she says, and has just sent a recipe by email to her youngest son, who is studying for a year at a university in Madrid, she adds proudly. The oldest is now a lawyer.

Both Paty and Marta, mothers of adult children, share a concern for the preservation of their culture and participate in the transformation of it. While they worry, they do not wholly agree with the premise that local cultural values are being destroyed. Paty enjoys shopping at Sam's and also relishes going—on foot—to the market, and she very much resists the notion that the consequence of the former could result in harm to local economies. While Marta berates the women who let culinary traditions slide, Paty observes the link between poverty and tradition and the complex, and apparently contradictory, negotiations required of Oaxacan women to defy one and maintain the other. "Oaxaca is different from Veracruz and Jalisco also because it's poorer. Poverty, like in the *pueblos*, can help maintain traditions. Men want the old customs, but women have to do the legwork! There is definitely a pressure on the women—to maintain traditions of cooking, for example. At the same time, everyone wants a fridge, TV, car and liquidizer too!"

It is clear that globalization and migration are perceived as major threats to traditional culture. At the same time they provide hope for a better future—from liquidizer and car to higher education for their children—for thousands of Oaxaqueños. It is likely that tourism has only a tangential role in altering people's lives and impacting on their traditions in comparison with the major force of large-scale (poverty-related) migration and gradual globalization. Oaxaca fits the typical scenario whereby its success as a tourist destination attracts rural migration to the city, with increasing strain on already insufficient water resources and lack of adequate housing.

Migration even feeds a new kind of tourism or travel-related demands, such as in the village of Ciénega de Zimatlán, many of whose inhabitants have risked their lives by going to the United States in search of work and then sent money back to build houses. The former hosts return as outsider guests, seeking services that suit their new gringo-influenced tastes. It is an ugly hodgepodge of a place, Paty finds, with modern houses growing up in the middle of traditional architecture. Although the village has nothing to attract tourists, there is a travel agency and a new restaurant that advertises "international" fare. The former "exists for the sole purpose of selling tickets to Tijuana, from which Oaxaqueños cross the border," says Paty, while the latter sells hamburgers, catering to the new habits of those who have come back.

For many people of different social standing, the debate in Oaxaca has advanced far beyond the simplistic approbation of tourism for its positive economic effects upon the arts and crafts industries. That tourism can boost traditional industries by providing an expanded market for native products is a discussion Oaxaca and Mexico had years ago, and Oaxaca has provided examples to the world with its experiments in this arena.[55] Again, this has been a result of the devotion of artists and intellectuals who are understandably rolling their eyes in exasperation as they carry on their efforts without state support, such as the *fonotecas* (music libraries) of the IAGO: "There is not a single program to support villages that have musical tradition, just for people to sell handicrafts," says Fernando, resignedly, of official tourism promotion. The well-known weaving village Teotitlán del Valle, very close to Oaxaca City, is a success, he says, not because of tourism strategies but because of the villagers' own initiative and creativity in the face of the need to migrate. Because of migration they made contacts abroad, and they export their carpets and woven goods. "This is the *only* case of a successful pueblo," he asserts.

When a larger discussion of ethnic tourism takes off in Oaxaca, these villagers actually keep a distance from the tourist gaze when they can afford to. This presumably allows them to perform the simplistic role of "magical, folksy Oaxaca" promoted by the state tourist industry, which assumes what the tourists want to see (to the exclusion of Big Brother on television, jeans, email addresses and iPods). "You know, the successful weavers in Teotitlán have two houses?" says Donna. "One that they welcome tourists to, and further away from the road that they really live in." This looks like a clear demarcation of territory, underlining a desirable distance between tradition and village life, from selling and performing for tourism. Thus, despite the genuine welcome that foreigners and Mexicans alike feel from Oaxaqueños, there is—at least here—a local interest in differentiating culture as lived (and enjoyed privately, with personal meanings) and culture for sale (simplified, packaged, and performed).

Discussions and new examples of how to create sustainable tourism could help here, in the tense arena of patrimony and participation, and Oaxaca has an experienced, national prize-winning resource at its fingertips in the form of the eco-tourism website founder, researcher, and promoter Ron Mader.[56] But, as is the case with the artists, government officials are reluctant to open spaces for dialogue, which, essentially, would mean sharing power. Fernando said at the end of 2004 that he had never seen the new culture minister inside the IAGO even though it houses the best art library in the country. When I asked Ramírez if she was aware that the respected Mader lived just up the road, she drew a hesitant blank.

There is a potential irony latent in the use of a moral, conservative discourse to protect culture.[57] The interests of the tourism entrepreneurs who value traditions as capital and culture as commodity can appear to overlap with the outraged arguments of the Oaxacan artists. When questioned whether tourism was proving a destructive force in Día de Muertos celebrations, Jaime Katz replied that he had seen no such evidence and countered with his own idea of cultural impoverishment. His example was Oaxacans who had gone to the other side ("el otro lado") and back, selling Asian imports in the market and playing loud norteña music.

Not surprisingly, the artists are a few steps ahead, with a more subtle and fluid understanding of culture. Their work shows that culture recreates itself and has a dynamic and hybrid nature, while the entrepreneurs have a greater interest in culture as static. It's hard to market and sell something that keeps changing, especially when it mutates to incorporate elements of the forces you are trying to differentiate or "defend" it from. Nevertheless, neither—especially now with the stakes so high—seems equipped to value the jarring (grotesque for others) cultural spectacles that are taking shape before everyone's eyes.

Paty's cheery comment sums this up: "You can compare us to pre-Hispanic people. There's not much difference—just some money and some plastic." Rather than flippancy, this speaks to me of a resilient humor, combining tenderness and the absurd. It could be interpreted as indicative of a sense of impending defeat. But it could also be a gush of hope that things are more than black-and-white contradictions. The cartoon image evoked by this colorful thinking may be typical of poorer people for whom it is a luxury to warble on about patrimony because they have mouths to feed—but who do not believe that everything they want or need has to be at the expense of something else they also value. It points to a hope against hope that you can "have your cake and eat it too."

This romanticized view reflects the familiar foreign enchantment with Oaxaca's otherness and "magic." But it also hints at something more important: Oaxacans' views of themselves and the intellectual and emotional spaces they preserve for the coexistence of what might seem irreconcilable realities (having the cake and eating it; being pre-Hispanics armed with plastic; looking forward and backward at the same time). To a degree all Mexicans are grappling with this,[58] but Oaxaca offers clarity, persistence, and optimism that is hard to find elsewhere in the republic.

Ron Mader reminded me of the difficulty of getting a handle on tradition as we hiked past the morning glory, bougainvillea, *guaje* trees, and *pochote* on Oaxaca's Cerro del Fortín. Alebrijes, the fantastic creatures made of copal wood—one of Oaxaca's best known and most ubiquitous handicrafts—do not originate here and only began to be made in Oaxaca in the eighties, he told me. "You can tell a Oaxacan that you ate a *memela* (a kind of bean taco) in the market, and he'll ask you 'but was it a traditional memela?' And it turns out that if it has beans and isn't made with pork dripping, it is a nontraditional variant that started in the late eighties." Ron leaves me at the Sánchez Pascua market where I perch at Lourdes's stall and order a tasty memela (which she does smear with beans). I notice the vendor is squabbling with her daughters over her own breakfast, which is Kellogg's Choco Krispis.

As the anthropologist Davydd J. Greenwood writes, "To this end, the evaluation of tourism cannot be accomplished by measuring the impact of tourism against a static background. Some of what we see as destruction is construction; some is the result of a lack of any other viable options; and some the result of choices that could be made differently."[59]

While Oaxaca is not yet inundated by plastic trinkets and "airport art"— sights its ideal tourist does not want to see—Wal-Mart, catsup, norteña music, and Choco Krispis are part of the contemporary spectacle that tourism promoters, cultural defenders, and travel writers are reluctant to acknowledge. The tendency to disparage a hybrid contemporary culture that is mutating to include the past as well as modern commodities seems to me the first way to guarantee the loss of "authenticity" that tourists to Oaxaca are seeking.[60] A static and simplified crafts, costumes, and customs focus is patronizing and inadequate, while its highbrow equivalent—in favor of a rarified and exoticized culture—is also distorted, or re-created (at best) by "the codes of exoticist primitivism."⁶¹ Some Oaxacans seem as able to play the tourist gaze as they are able to resist, or join their own voices to, proscriptive mandates regarding what their culture "should be," as seen in the villagers of Teotitlán, who maintain two simultaneous worlds or spheres— keeping their sold culture separate from their lived culture.

Amecameca: Not for Outside Consumption

Tourism in Mexico can be highly political, drenched in denial and myth, flaring furiously with informed cultural debate. But there are also ambiguous destinations where it is met with relative indifference and farcical ineptitude. Amecameca in the state of Mexico is a faded attraction—an example of tourism suffering at the hands of a nature's forces—where efforts to get the industry on its feet again simply do not fly. Tourism entrepreneurs and professionals are cowed under a heavy weight of fatalism, while locals don't care that much. In fact it's hard to avoid the sense they wish you'd go away and let them get on with it.

Only one hour east from Mexico City, this town "under the volcanoes" is also "the other Mexico"—one that wouldn't dream of performing for the tourist gaze.⁶² Despite having its own particularities, it bears certain familiar traits from the other destinations. Handicrafts are for sale, but almost exclusively for passersby from nearby towns; it is steeped in "magic,"⁶³ although outsiders are not welcome to view these secret rites nor often told about them. Amecameca has a historically important religious icon, the Black Christ of Sacromonte (the Sacred Hill), but pilgrims tend to come only from nearby municipalities or the surrounding states of Puebla, Morelos, and the Federal District. Some customs live on, with locals who go to work every day in the city and eat their "traditional fast food," but the town is also modern, its market full of jeans, Asian imports, and plastic trinkets.

The area is breathtakingly beautiful and buried in garbage. It is both remote (it is a favorite spot for spiritual retreats) and accessible, with a long history of travelers passing through. Townsfolk seem suspicious and are frankly unfriendly but no one cares if you talk about the decline of tourism in Amecameca. If you go to the area known as Popo Park, that's all anyone talks about. Eco-tourism is loosely understood to be the key to the region's future, although there is no agreement as to what this means. You won't catch many locals using such a prissy term, anyway, when "day out in the country" will do quite as well.

Mexico City has an icon too, and I don't mean the rusty gray smog that foreigners still associate—to the bitter but familiar mortification of tourism promoters—with the capital. The colossal twin peaks of Popocatépetl and its neighbor Iztaccíhuatl have been a shorthand to represent the Valley of Mexico for centuries, from paintings of the early colonial period, through famous works of Mexico's muralists, and into contemporary art and advertising.[64] Before 1995, Amecameca was a popular stop-off for people hiking up to Popocatépetl's crater, an exhilarating experience and not too arduous. But in 1994 the volcano (known as Popo) started to smoke again, building up to a spectacular although minor eruption on December 18, 2000. Tourism in the area plummeted.

Local business people seethed at being abandoned by federal and state authorities, asking why the belching volcano wasn't promoted as a sightseeing attraction, as are active, erupting volcanoes in Costa Rica and Hawaii. Others considered themselves victims of sensationalist newspaper coverage. "The journalists came and enlarged the boulders that flew from the mouth of the crater to make everything seem more dramatic," said Miguel Ángel Reyes, manager of the formerly fine hotel Los Volcanes, one year later. "That sort of thing is typical of us here in Mexico."

In the seventies, the Parque Nacional Iztaccíhuatl-Popocatépetl was the place to go, receiving an average of 580,000 visitors per year from 1976 to 1982, from seventeen different countries.[65] By 2002 this had fallen by 90 percent and by October 31, 2004, the park had received only 42,000. I first visited in fall of 2001 to update—or delete—a guidebook entry on the mountaineering and eco-tourism attractions of the area. I was struck by how beautiful and empty it looked. Volcanoes shimmered sublimely above fleecy clouds that looked down indifferently upon the large empty restaurants and the decaying hotel below. The area would have great potential, I thought, once the volcano calmed down a bit. I looked for the tourism office. There was none.

After badgering taxi drivers and fruit vendors on the main square I was pointed in the direction of CONANP, the national park's office. Here, Alejandro López, an anthropologist and the town chronicler, as well as director of the park, told me that he was hoping for a decision to reduce the volcanic alert. This would help rejuvenate tourism in an area fertile with waterfalls, trees, lakes, chapels, haciendas, and other places of interest, he said, especially opening the doors to eco-touristic ventures that Mexico wanted, and needed, to promote. It seemed to have all the ingredients for a great feature article and I planned to return, but meanwhile I was hungry and asked where to eat. There wasn't anywhere (apart from the market, fine for me, but not my readers) and isn't—unless you go out of town to a site where a Swiss entrepreneur has a deer park and petting zoo, and even a little volcano museum in an old hacienda where you can munch on venison sausage. But I found this out later, by accident. No one in town saw fit to give it a mention. I asked where I should stay next time and was recommended to the same hotel I had just thankfully vacated, where I froze my guts in a large, foul-smelling room whose carpets seemed never to have been cleaned. "None of the other hotels are up to international standards," I was told.

THE TOURISM DEPARTMENT

When I returned at the end of 2002, nothing had changed, but I learned more. The town is a pre-Hispanic settlement with the church of the Black Christ of Sacromonte being the site of an earlier temple. Its major fiesta, held on Ash Wednesday, has clear roots in the precolonial "Primer Viento" (First Wind) held in spring and is the first of four ancient festivals that were transformed into pilgrimages after the conquest.[66] The other attraction, drawing day-trippers primarily from Mexico City, is a flourishing trade in Christmas trees, whereby visitors cut their own tree and pop into the market to buy some regional food such as *cecina* (cured, salted meat, usually pork), or simple clay pots and craftware.

Amecameca—often shortened to Ameca—was a passenger town. Hernán Cortés came through here in his triumphant march to conquer the Aztec capital of Tenochtitlán, and chroniclers show Popo was active then too. The first train line went through here, an important provider of ice, and there were *mesones* (inns) and *pulquerías* (the equivalent of an ale house). "People are not hostile to outsiders—they are used to strange faces," Alejandro told me, but they can be *gandalla* (greedy). "They'll charge prices according to how you look," he said, "and sell you rancid nuts, even when there are fresh ones."[67]

Ameca has an internal life, and an external one, said Alejandro, speculating that this is a result of exposure through trade with the capital. Overpopulation led to a loss of a sense of community and "a dramatic loss of heritage."[68] In 1940 local authorities knocked down the church atrium and ripped up the graveyard to build the municipal market. The atrial cross, a colonial legacy marking the central square, disappeared one night and hasn't been seen since. "Estas de Ameca son terribles!" laughed Alejandro. At the same time, the car park near the bus station is unusable in the morning because food vendors pack it with stalls selling fresh juice and *mixiotes*, traditional fast food (at just over three dollars) for commuters who catch the early bus every morning to work in the capital. Poorer folk who work locally have a cheaper fast-food option both in the same car park and on street corners, the traditional tamales and *atole* (hot drink made from corn paste), costing only a dollar. Alejandro was sure that tourism—when there was any—had no contact with the traditions that are left.

For my article, I tracked down the venison sausage, which was tasty—although the restaurant was open only for lunch. I slept in an ugly, but clean and warm motel. I saw saplings and soldiers and plentiful evidence of good park maintenance. I heard how all teenagers want to get out of there and go to the big city. I heard about the garbage problem and scattered incidents of violence with machetes. I saw an altar to Don Goyo, a local nickname for Popocatépetl, and chuckled at the colorful tale that last year "he" had asked for a mariachi suit as an offering to appease his wrath, which was duly presented. I even heard the volcano growl, but the latter highlights were in areas out of bounds to the public and, of course, tourists.

"There is stuff written on tourism in Ameca, but it's not available," Alejandro said. His own book, a carefully researched and intriguing anthropological study, was out of print even then (and it was still unavailable at the end of 2004). I couldn't squeeze a travel article out of this and wrote an ecology feature instead. However, Alejandro thought I would be interested to see the ancient and authentic Ash Wednesday traditions. In 2004 I decided to try my luck and phoned him; he recommended that I contact the tourism office.

The tourism office? Yes. There had been elections and the new municipal government had made some changes. There was a "Regidor" (alderman or director) for tourism now, although I should speak with "Teresita"—here was the phone number. The line was busy or out of order. Thanks to intervention by the CONANP offices, Teresita and her boss called *me*, at strange times of the day, on crackling lines. "We think we have a room for you in the town's best hotel," I was informed in one of these calls. It was the only one that was up to international standards.

The lady—perhaps in her late forties—who greeted me in a small cubicle in the hectic town hall was wearing a frumpy skirt and top, beige stockings and sensible shoes. Beaming, she showed me a new color promotional leaflet in Spanish for tourists to Amecameca. There were no phone numbers for the hotels and restaurants, nor any of the "important places" recommended (the address of the general hospital was merely *conocido*, that is, "known"). While waiting for the Regidor—we couldn't call him—Teresita let me know that there was only one phone line for the whole town hall. It had been out of service and now was out of bounds, because so many of the staff had used it for long distance calls, primarily to family in the United States. The bill had been too high to pay out of the last month's budget, which was why the tourism office had been *incomunicado*.

MI CASA ES SU CASA

The Regidor looked like he'd walked straight off his farm and wished he hadn't left his shotgun behind. "So where do you want to go?" he asked me, clearly thinking that spending the afternoon showing me around was beneath him and unmanly (hosting is a female task, it appears). I suggested one of the five waterfalls named in the leaflet. He said this was a printing error and this waterfall wasn't really of that name and was the same as—in fact—the second fall on the list. But, not to worry, he knew where he would take me, to La Castañeda, a Porfirian mansion used in the past as a loony bin. There was a waterfall there. I'd heard legends about the place, taken brick by brick from Mexico City, and agreed. Only we were not allowed in. No one there seemed to recognize the Regidor or care who he was. It turned out to be a cult retreat, related to the doings of the president's wife, Marta Sahagún—and not answerable to yokel local politicians.

Eventually an authorized affiliate came to show us the waterfall. The Regidor stood by helplessly as we were told how tons of garbage had to be removed from the falls when they changed from local authority management to private hands. I wasn't allowed to take a photo of the mansion, as we hadn't requested permission in advance.

I asked next to see the great cultural center in honor of the region's major historical figure, the seventeenth-century poet and nun Sor Juana Inés de la Cruz. Oddly, it seemed to me, the museum—built in 1995 by distinguished architects and named after Mexico's most famous woman[69]—was not mentioned in the new leaflet (because it happens to be in the adjacent municipality of Nepantla, I was told). Neither of my hosts had been there before. We arrived at a grand and harmonious building with library and flowing gardens, and while Teresita was curious, the Regidor spent the time giggling like a schoolboy, uncomfortable in the solemn atmosphere and poking fun at references to women's rights to education. On the way back, seeing further scores of fields afloat with garbage, I finally asked about the plastic detritus ubiquitous to Ameca and its surroundings and received a stare as though I had just uttered an incongruous observation about UFOs. It seemed I was the only one who saw it.[70]

That evening the Regidor cheered up, pointing out "mi humilde casa" (my humble house). I was briefly taken back by the old fashioned courtesy—as the Mexican saying goes "Mi casa es su casa" (My house is your house). It was fiesta day tomorrow, and he had been collecting, knocking on doors, for months, he grinned. "What for?" I asked. "La Quema de la Salva," he replied with a sly smile—I'd soon find out tomorrow. But he bickered a little with Teresita, over a disagreement he had with the parish priest. "I *know* God wants souls and not firecrackers, I told him. But these are our traditions, and we have to hold on to the ones we have left."

We were welcomed with a tequila against the cold at my familiar hotel and invited to join the gossip. That night the leader of Mexico's Green Party had been exposed in a tourism corruption scandal in Cancún, revealed to be inviting a bribe in return for some land meant to be under ecological protection. This was considered a great opportunity to enjoy hoots of derision at the—deservedly—much maligned party. No one was shocked at the crime itself, it was clear, merely delighted that the guy had been caught with his pants down on TV.[71]

THE SACRED FIESTA

The spectacle the next morning entails following shadowy forms up the Sacred Hill to the little church lit up with red bulbs and neon, where Mass is about to start. At 5:30 a.m. the Black Christ is already out of his cave, ornately dressed and surrounded by sweet-smelling jungles of exotic flowers. The faithful—many of them elderly *campesinas* with striped *rebozos*, flimsy skirts, thin brown legs, and graying plaits—pay Him their respects and then join in the service. There are also dancers dressed like Pocahontas, in American Indian conchero costumes, but with sweaters, and town families in casual garb, stamping their feet in the predawn chill, many wearing colorful crowns of red or white flowers on top of the hoods of their parkas. I am the only foreigner I can see, but the priest welcomes nonlocals, pilgrims who he says have come from Chimalhuacán, Puebla, and Cuautla—in the same state or two neighboring states—"people who have for centuries adored Nuestro Señor del Sacromonte."

The sky is turning white at the edges of Popocatépetl and Iztaccíhuatl and I can see the snow on both. There are many pale fluttering shapes on the flanks of the dusty hill, a thick carpet of plastic bags and garbage on a closer look. Under an hour later bells ring frenetically and then a band strikes up "Las Mañanitas" (Mexico's "Happy Birthday") to El Señor, while armies of men, some with black ash smudges on their heads, line up at the edge of the hill ready to light thousands of firecrackers with cigarettes. This is the Regidor's Quema de la Salva, which translates roughly as "the burning salute." Soon the air is thick with smoke and the sharp smell of sulfur. Wide celestial slats of light divide the sky around the volcanoes, and it looks as though Amecameca is on fire, as mist shrouds the houses in the valley. "Did you hear?" the Regidor says to me, appearing beady-eyed out of the crowd. "These ones whistle," as though he was talking about the chirping of a rare bird in the woods. I mention the garbage I'd spied. "I told you it will take a week to clean up after this fiesta," he replies irritably, even though the filth is evidently old.

That afternoon we go to another waterfall, the Viveros. There is no water at all, but the scenery is glorious, there are no metal fences or guard dogs to stop the public getting there, and it is immaculately clean. However, I would never be able to find it again nor describe to my readers how to get there. "Isn't there a signpost?" I ask the Regidor. "Oh no, we know what will happen to it, if your gang starts coming here," he says with a devious sideways glance. *What?* "Your neighbors from Mexico City—they will fill it up with garbage within a week," he says triumphantly, onto my game. I call Teresita the next week to thank them for their hospitality, but the phone is out of order ("there is no need to report this," the recorded message tells me).

"What did you think I would see?" I asked López months later, trying to make it clear I appreciated the pair's utmost kindness and patience but that it had been a little like spending two days with Laurel and Hardy. "But it's not for foreigners!" he laughed. By then, the Wal-Mart imperialism controversy had made it to Amecameca, the town recently putting a stop to construction of a branch of the foreign chain store on the main square—just as Oaxaca had stopped the McDonald's two years earlier and as protesters had failed in the area around the pyramids of Teotihuacán the previous month.[72] "How did you manage it?" I asked. "Aha! Because the town hall had granted permission secretly, so it wasn't fully legal" Alejandro explained, "And people found out on time." Also, he pointed out, it was the nature of the location. The plaza was not a historic colonial square, as in the case of Oaxaca, but nevertheless was a heritage site because, "everyone knows, once you start to excavate, you'll find the pre-Hispanic city beneath." So the formal reason was that the application procedure didn't follow established requirements. But the debate would continue for some time, as institutional excavations were going on and "they will find something, offerings from a burial," Alejandro was sure.

Meanwhile, progress was being made on rejuvenating tourism, he said, with a nationally funded study by the Tourism Department of the State of Mexico University. "We *have* tourism, but a tourism we don't want," Alejandro said, echoing the Regidor's comments about my neighbors. "They bring their piece of the city, noisy sound systems, their food and leave their garbage on the road." Garbage actually had been a political priority of the previous mayor, who had a campaign, "Amecameca sin basura." It was successful for a while, even winning the state cleanliness prize, but then, Alejandro said, "People robbed the bins."

Soon the park's office was going to take over the Sacred Hill, he said dully. "It's the last thing we need—that area is full of problems. We'll have to fork out for special vigilance. You can't use the police because all they do is extort money out of people." The Sacred Hill was not being conceived of as a tourism destination or as a local historical treasure that would bring tourism income but rather as a burden and as a messy (socially, as well as in terms of pollution) area in need of protection.

THE RIGHT AND THE WRONG SORT OF TOURIST

Ameca delivers authenticity, warts and all, which makes it unsuitable for outside consumption. Colloquial expressions of hospitality here cloak an absolute lack of curiosity about what the outsider might want to see. Garbage is a serious concern from the point of view of foreign tourism—with Acapulco being a great offender, and Oaxaca cleaning its act up a good deal at the time (2004–2005).[73] Ameca's nonchalance about the matter is largely a reflection of its indifference toward outside tourism. However, it ought to be surprising that the only interest the head of tourism shows in the town's major fiesta is the noisy firecrackers, and not at all in what it could mean as a tourism attraction!

But there is a level on which Ash Wednesday is already very successful.

Thousands come into town to trade and pray and witness the procession of the Christ in the evening, even though there's nowhere for them to stay (none came to my hotel, which *did* have international prices, if not standards). These "tourists," or visitors, are outsiders, but not from that far afield. Some are pilgrims from the same or nearby states who may return home the same night or doze at the bus station or bus stop until the first early morning service rolls up. Others snooze on the streets or on the floors of fiesta organizers the night before. The Cristo del Sacromonte is likely to be important to these visitors for vows they are making, or favors they are requesting or repaying that He has already granted. Still others are *conchero* dancers (members of a society who perform ritual dances, processions, and incantations during seasonal festivals around Mexico City) who arrive—many from "Neza" (Ciudad Nezahuacóyotl) on the outskirts of Mexico City—packed in little cars and rickety vans and sleep in these, in tents, or in someone's hallway or backyard (that of another dancer from a local "camada," as the troupes are called), all semi-informally arranged outside the ambit of local tourism. The Sacromonte is significant to these visitors because of its origins in precolonial religions and sacred sites, as well as the timing of the festival. Many more are tradespeople who arrive as many nights before the festival as they can to find prize locations for their stands, sleeping beneath these—much as folk at the circus are famed to do, and with something of the same welcome and status. Still others are buyers, who will set aside a day to combine some business and pleasure, squeezing in a night here to catch the fair in the morning, or a midday and dash of afternoon there, to relish, purchase, note, make contacts and, perhaps, continue on.

So who wants tourists anyway? Especially when your main experience is with "the wrong sort." The freedom of indifference to tourism in Ameca highlights some issues relevant to the other destinations—first, unwelcome tourists, the "wrong" type being national, especially those from Mexico City. Mexican nationals make up about 80 percent of the country's tourists, yet, en masse, they are considered the type of vulgar visitors who will tend to trash a place on leaving it (as well as behaving like "ugly Americans").[74]

This is largely Acapulco's problem—its "social tone"[75]—and hence the hysteria of my historian contact when I wanted to write about La Roqueta, a *clase popular* (loosely meaning working-class) attraction, and his strident claim that "these people" weren't even Acapulqueños.[76] It is also, conversely, part of Oaxaca's prestige, as this city nabs the European tourists, who are very much "the right kind."[77] On the rare occasions that foreigners might doubt their welcome in Mexico (at worst they are likely to be treated as minor irritants, as in Ameca), they could reflect that at least they are not *chilangos*, the nickname, rarely complimentary, for inhabitants of Mexico City. In the recent past, "Haz patria, mata a un chilango" (Support your country and kill someone from Mexico City) was a popular phrase, posted, for example, on car bumper stickers in places further north such as Guadalajara.

A more complicated development in the tensions between the foreign outsider and the national outsider, the right and the wrong tourist, is afforded by the following example. Mexicans in service—domestic or tourism—often find that they are treated much worse by other Mexicans than by foreigners. A driver told me about an occasion when he was working as a night watchman in a prestigious hotel in Acapulco and saw that a wealthy young guest from Mexico City had fallen down some steps and vomited from having taken too many illegal drugs. He went forward to help this man, who the next day accused him before his employers of assaulting him. Luckily another employee testified in his defense but he says he still feels nauseated when he smells the expensive aftershave the young man was using that night.

These common abuses can become even more poignant when gender relations are involved. I was told about an incident in a hotel in Oaxaca where a Mexican tourist from Mexico City demanded a meal service the hotel did not offer. The staff on duty at the time, all women, all local, explained this wasn't possible, only to be yelled at that they were "Hijas de Bush!" (Bush's daughters). The worst insult this Mexican tourist could hurl at these Oaxaqueña tourism service providers was that they were as repellant as *gringas*, or North American women. However, given the context, it was not that they were colonized flunkeys, identifying in a servile way with the white outsider, who caused the offense, but because they felt secure in *not* serving him beyond their established duties. He evidently felt superior to these brown-skinned provincial women, as a paying client but also as a male who was "whiter" and urban, from the capital. It was the nonsubmissive attitude of these Mexican females that incensed him.

Magic Tricks

Travel and tourism—I make the distinction as national travel is often not leisured, even the pilgrimage has trade components and is not always straightforward fun—in Mexico take place in heavily charged regional and class structures. The foreigner, while an outsider (and usually ignorant of these matters), doesn't fail to contribute to the significations being permanently contested here. He or she not only belongs to the privileged classes, as someone who is not working and has money to spend, but also sets examples for aspiring middle-class nationals and can unwittingly (and will inevitably) cause frictions in host communities. However, Amecameca reinforces the sense that the debate going on in Oaxaca is not because of tourism but is fed by it and can participate usefully in it. The decline of culture in Amecameca, and cultural pride in Oaxaca, also suggest—despite many differentiating factors—that tourism *can* help this debate, especially when conducted by "experts" in culture (who are sensitive to local politics) and where, as in Oaxaca, you have the "right type" of tourists.

In the last few years, Mexico's federal tourism office—with an eye on Oaxaca—has devised a strategy to get the right type of tourists. "Pueblos Mágicos" (Magical Towns) is a project started in 2001 to promote to inland destinations outstanding for their history, art, and cuisine and to encourage "pride in the Mexicanness of the town."[78] Customs and traditions are emphasized, the community has to be involved, and, if possible, a *"padrino"* (godfather) is sought.[79] Unfortunately, the program has a magical quality of its own, namely, a penchant for disappearing acts.

Perhaps I should have been alerted to this when Guillermo Tarrats, the ministry's Director of Regional Programs, asked me in spring 2004 how I had heard of the project. It was, apparently, a public program concerned with promotion, so it did not occur to me that there could be anything secretive or confidential about it. But then I received a congratulatory letter from a reader of an article I had written on Pueblos Mágicos, who said he had been trying to find out about the program for months.[80] As it happened, Pueblos Mágicos made another trip into the ether shortly afterward and I couldn't get any more news. Manuel Díaz Cebrian, director of the Mexican Tourism Board's London office, told me mid-December 2004 that it had not yet filtered into regional promotion strategies because the only pueblo in the program that was ready with its material was Izamal, in Yucatán.

One of the most surreal experiences I had in this endeavor was phoning the municipal tourism office in Valle de Bravo, a beautiful lakeside town west of the capital in the State of Mexico, at the end of 2003 to see if they were on the list as a Pueblo Mágico. "I need to know if Valle is a Magical Town," I said to the young man (in Spanish) in the tourist office at the town hall. There was a muffled pause and then hoots of mirth from the other side. If tourism departments in wealthy tourist destination towns hadn't even heard of the program, something wasn't going too well. But there was nothing new in this example of weak coordination at and between all levels of government.[81] In three months, from August 30 to December 2, the Pueblos Mágicos/Regional Programs office was not capable of getting back to me for an update, which I think speaks clearly enough for itself.[82]

However, the attempt to devise a program such as Pueblos Mágicos, which consciously tries to take a leaf or two from Oaxaca's book, shows a willingness on the part of Mexico's tourism authorities to go beyond the "beach, beer, and burn" (or sex, sun, and sea) model established in Acapulco at the rise of Mexico's tourism industry. It suggests a perception that greater emphasis on culture and community, going beyond a simplistic view of culture as commodity and even including elements of community participation and local decision making, could lead to a new direction toward authenticity and preservation.

But those same "many Mexicos" that the Tourism Board advertises to show the country's great diversity of appeal tend to thwart any attempt to produce authenticity as a consumable commodity. The many Mexicos are not just sun and beach here, dances and cuisine there, mountains and pilgrimages over there. They come loaded with real people with strong regional and local identities—and poignant comments—whose marginalization and discontent erupt through the veneer to reveal malnourished children in the hills of Acapulco, cultural disintegration on top of flaring land disputes and human rights abuses in Oaxaca, and self-satisfied macho indifference and environmental destruction in Amecameca.

The many Mexicos also include age-old traditions that are far from picturesque, of unaccountability and corrupt practices, racial prejudice and deeply ingrained sexual inequality. Any quest for the "authentic" (which tourists do not formulate in this way but rather as some variant of "how people live" or "what it's like for people here") can unearth these quickly enough, in, say, a conversation between a tourist and a taxi driver, or a female traveler having her hair braided on the beach. And last, the many Mexicos include the unmentionable modern character, an alarming protagonist in the industry's realm, the Mexican tourist—deplorable because s/he is not even exotic, unwanted because s/he spends little and trashes the place.

Oaxaca's success, insofar as it could be seen as a model, probably did not develop from official tourism strategy but from a unique series of geographical, historical, and social factors that cannot be transplanted onto other destinations, despite their scenic beauty and intriguing history and other similarities, like Amecameca, which shared a minor version of the patrimony versus Wal-Mart debate.

Irony if not downright cynicism is part of Acapulco's contemporary modus vivendi as a tourist destination. The tourist legend now spreads itself beyond the boundaries of credulity in a brazen effort to hide its social divisions and decline. Outsiders are welcome as always, as long as they do not comment on the town's decadence. Townsfolk's defensive strategies, however, are comical and creative, complementing brash denial with creative mythmaking.

Dreams, Doublethink, and Resistance

"Tourism is selling dreams," one tourism-sector entrepreneur who owned hotels in Mexico City, Cancún, and Puerto Vallarta told me enthusiastically in the late 1990s. His firm belief was that Cancún was the success story and path to Mexico's tourism future. In the case of Acapulco, dreams seem to be the province of the inhabitants and tourism service providers who negotiate memories of former grandeur with palpable evidence of deterioration. Their doublethink, contrariness, and often dark humor appear to me a defense mechanism against mostly outside forces that are beyond their control and have been that way for a long time.

In Oaxaca the dream is crumbling, or the spell is breaking as Lety, the hotelier, said although, until 2006, the city appeared to sustain a high host-guest interaction and satisfaction. Thanks to its politicized and high-profile cultural movement and the affluence of foreign tourists, Oaxaca seemed well situated to defend itself against some of the negative effects of mass tourism. However, as I have suggested here, forces more influential than tourism were transforming the state of Oaxaca, and the acute sense of conflict between culture and tourism had even deeper roots. Perhaps the combination of Oaxaca's "magic," cultural preservation, rural abandonment, poverty, and social injustice was just too contradictory to last. I thought at the time that Oaxaca was seeing a positive reconstruction of indigenous identity—not merely as exoticized but as strong in numbers, loyal, devoted to family and home and tradition, and creative. With its high and satisfactory host and guest interaction, it seemed to be doing things right, but when being backward is part of the attraction of a tourism destination, perhaps it should not be surprising that potentially explosive social and political problems lurk behind that backwardness.

At the same time, in contrast to the marked lower "social tone" of Acapulco, Oaxaca also highlights the role that the class, and nationality, of the tourist has in stamping a destination in Mexico. By attracting "quality tourism" Oaxaca is literally attracting "the quality"—that is, a higher social class of foreign traveler, affluent and cultured. Acapulco's lower social tone is widely lamented by tourism authorities, but the existence of cheap hotels and holiday activities for lower-middle-class folk from Mexico City has helped tide over the threat posed by Cancún.

In these destinations one can see how foreign tourism, and its influence on the behavior of Mexican tourists, reactivates and accentuates class and race and gender issues that one can convincingly argue have been part of Mexico's makeup at least since the conquest. Although these are uncomfortable, they also feed a positive debate and increase consciousness that contribute to Mexico's gradual unshackling from paternalism and authoritarianism. Insofar as tourism includes culture, culture includes people, and modern Mexican people are not easily commodified. This country's people are in the throes of major social and political change, and since the beginning of the twenty-first century they have vastly increased expectations of democracy and accountability, even in the provinces and remoter areas.

With the exception of Amecameca, whose defense strategy is indifference, behind which almost certainly lies cultural resistance, I see little evidence of tourism continuing in Mexico in a self-enclosed bubble. Mexicans are interested in more than the tourism dollar, and tourists are interested in more than having their stereotypes confirmed. Even the most unadventurous mass tourist has a hankering for a little contact with Mexicans beyond ordering a meal or going on a packaged boat trip or museum tour, and even the most indifferent Mexican entertains a vague curiosity about what the outsider thinks of his or her country and culture (and hopes they like it, especially the food!).

Some strategies for defense I have noted (by which I mean not only defense against negative impacts of mass tourism but also maintaining self-esteem while selling one's town, one's culture, and one's time and services to wealthy outsiders) are brazen contradiction and cynicism in the case of Acapulco, in contrast to a creative looking both backward and forward—not cynical, but perhaps idealized—in Oaxaca.

This double thinking (whether conceived of as a desperate measure and imposed, or creative and optimistic) relates to the hybrid cultures that pervade most of the many Mexicos. There are different and seemingly contradictory "realities" going on at the same time in Mexico, and Mexicans have to adapt as the moment dictates, back and forth between "traditions not quite past and modernity not yet wholly present."[83] Amecameca also shows evidences of a hybrid culture, but its attitude to tourism appears to be one of indifference. While the city can afford this because tourism is not the driving force of the local economy (as it is in Acapulco and Oaxaca), this same apparent indifference may also work as a form of defense, as a form of passive cultural resistance.

Notes

This chapter is dedicated with love and gratitude to Alejandro López (1945–2009), activist, town chronicler, ecologist and free spirit of the volcanoes: For your profound humanism and unflagging passion for Mexican popular history and living folklore; your respect for all voices; and your inspiring belief in people.

I conducted all interviews for this essay from 2004 to 2005.

1. Acapulco is the most popular tourist destination on Mexico's Pacific coast, although Nuevo Vallarta has the highest hotel occupation rate, according to statistics provided by the Informe de Sector del Turismo en México (SECTUR) for 2003. Statistics for the year 2000 named Acapulco as the second most visited resort after Cancún (SECTUR's 2003 Informe Annual, the most recent available, does not include destinations by amount of visitors). Tourism is Mexico's third industry, after oil and manufacturing, producing (in 2002) an estimated 8.2 percent of GDP.

2. The realtor Ron Lavender estimates that Acapulco's population has doubled from one million in 1988 to two million in 2004. While there are no official figures for the slum population on the outskirts of the city and on the side of the mountains not visible from the bay, it is considered to be slightly less than one third of the greater population.

3. Press revelation of high levels of fecal pollution (on fifteen other beach resorts, not just Acapulco) in spring 2003 was a great embarrassment to federal tourism officials and infuriated state governors, rousing antiforeigner rhetoric especially from Guerrero's governor René Cisneros. Within six months, Mexico's tourism minister, Leticia Navarro, had resigned and the country's environment minister, Victor Lichtinger, had been replaced.

4. Hugo Maldonado, resident manager, Hotel Acapulco Fairmont Princess, interview, November 16, 2004.

5. The divers of La Quebrada became known as a spectacle in 1934, with the association first organized in 1942, under the name Club de Clavadistas y Salvavidas de la Quebrada. In 1981 it became la Unión de Clavadistas de la Quebrada de Acapulco, S.C. and now is officially Clavadistas Profesionales de la

Quebrada Acapulco, S.C. For example, the divers' image forms the center of the logo of Acapulco's Conventions and Visitor's Bureau (OCVA), the main tourism office in charge of Acapulco's promotion abroad, and features first on the state promotional video run on the Estrella de Oro bus line.

6. Equivalent in November 2004 to between US$267 and $714.

7. *Fun in Acapulco*, Paramount 1963; musical comedy with Elvis Presley, Ursula Andress, and Elsa Cárdenas.

8. Teddy Stauffer, *Forever Is a Hell of a Long Time: An Autobiography by Teddy Stauffer "Mr. Acapulco"* (Chicago: Henry Regnery Company, 1976), 298.

9. Many influential Mexicans in the tourism industry and foreigners in Acapulco (including John McCarthy, CEO of FONATUR; Jean Berthelot of Hilton Hotels, Latin Division; Hugo Maldonado, Fairmont Princess; and the realtor Ron Lavender) concur with Stauffer's vision and are surprisingly unembarrassed by his story's egotism, naivete, and soft-porn tendencies.

10. Andrew Sackett, "The Two Faces of Acapulco during the Golden Age," *The Mexico Reader: History, Culture, Politics*, ed. Gilbert M. Joseph and Timothy J. Henderson (Durham, N.C.: Duke University Press, 2002), 500–10. While I agree, the role of foreigners in the private sector and especially pioneering individuals (many of whom were foreign) is being underemphasized. Foreigners were not silent in Acapulco, and it seems they were not required to be. Alemán [Miguel Alemán Valdés, president 1946–52], considered the grandfather of "Acapulco," was on very close and friendly terms with these foreigners, from Stauffer to Lavender.

11. Stauffer may have been European in origin, but he came to Mexico through the United States and went back to try his hand at Hollywood success; he was associated with the United States. As a foreigner, he gained the title "Mr. Acapulco"—uncontested by Mexicans—for his promotional skills and role in attracting desirable stars, most of them foreign, to the resort. The Villa Vera and Hotels Princess were built by Carl Renstrom and Daniel K. Ludwig of the United States, and the Flamingo was made famous by "The Hollywood Gang."

12. "When the tourist industry is managed by outsiders, to whom the profits flow, tourism becomes a form of imperialism . . . and may develop into neocolonialism." Valene Smith, ed., *Hosts and Guests: The Anthropology of Tourism*, 2nd ed. (Philadelphia: University of Pennsylvania Press, 1989), 8.

13. Stauffer, *Forever Is a Hell of a Long Time*, 282.

14. "With Alemán, Acapulco was divided in two. Locals had no drinking water, their roads were dirt, and electricity was always 'just coming.' While tourism flourished, the municipality fell behind. Federal government funded all the big works, and then the money went back to them. Nowadays, the state of Guerrero has 76 municipalities, all poor." Interview with Francisco Escudero, November 17, 2004; see also Sackett, "The Two Faces of Acapulco during the Golden Age," 502–3.

15. These camps became a legend of working-class tourism, further popularized by the BBC television series *Hi-de-Hi!* See John Urry, *The Tourist Gaze*, 2nd ed. (London: Sage, 2002), 34.

16. From Luz de Guadalupe Joseph, *En el viejo Acapulco* (Mexico City: Editora de Periódicos, S.C.L., La Prensa, n.d.).

17. INEGI statistics for 2000, provided by the Secretaría de Desarrollo Turístico, Oaxaca, state. Oaxaca center had a population of 472,624, with a total of 878,132 in the central valleys. In 2004, estimates put the population of greater Oaxaca City as between 700,000 and 800,000. SECTUR's 2000 edition of "Informe de sector del turismo en México" puts Oaxaca first as the "most visited and recognized" inland destination, and sixth of "all destinations," including beach (after Cancún, Acapulco, Ixtapa-Zihuatanejo, La Paz, Mazatlán, and Puerto Vallarta).

18. Oaxaca's first tourism office was founded in 1937. The city was granted UN World Heritage Status in 1987. The change in soil use in its historic center, permitting tourism activity, took place in 1994, during Carrasco's administration, with the declaration of Oaxaca and 141 hectares of the central valleys as a priority tourism development zone by Mexico's federal government. Information courtesy of Martin Ruíz Camino, minister of tourism for the state under Carrasco, December 19, 2004.

19. "Oaxaca means magic, color, indigenous arts and markets." Manuel Díaz, regional director for Mexico Tourism in Europe, interview, December 14, 2004. "What I hear all the time from foreign visitors—even the most literal and least poetic people you could imagine—is that Oaxaca is magical." Donna Radtke, hotelier, interview, December 4, 2004.

20. Some complain that the anthropologist Nelson Graburn's positing of tourism as belonging to the sacred (based on Durkheim and Leach) is passé. But his focus is on "the more extreme examples of tourism such as long distance tours to well-known places or visiting exotic peoples in most enchanting environments" (Graburn, "Tourism: The Sacred Journey," in Smith, *Hosts and Guests*, 24), which applies well to Oaxaca. And I find relevant his observation that "vacations involving travel . . . are the modern equivalent for secular societies to the annual and lifelong sequences of festivals for more God-fearing societies." Moreover, I would argue that a reading of tourism as sacred journey has greater resonance in a country, and state (such as Oaxaca), where the tradition of the pilgrimage/ returning to the hometown for the religious fiesta is still so alive.

21. Some say sixteen ethnic groups (Jaime Katz, subsecretary of tourism in Oaxaca 2004–5), others seventeen (i.e., Ron Mader, founder of Planeta.com). Oaxaca is Mexico's fifth largest state but one of the poorest and least industrialized. It also has a history of violent land disputes, intervillage massacres, human rights abuses, deforestation, political assassinations, and arrogant old-guard leaders with little sense of accountability. For example, Amnesty International reported

in 2004 that five Zapotec Indians in Oaxaca were killed as a result of human rights abuses (*La Jornada*, December 26, 2004).

22. Tragically, Oaxaca made international headlines again in 2006 with a violent social and political conflict that began as a teachers' pay dispute in May but soon grew into a much broader protest against poverty and social injustice in the state. A radical left-wing group (APPO) calling for the resignation of the state governor took over the city center, with the governor responding, according to human rights groups, by ordering a number of paramilitary-style shootings. APPO said in November that fourteen activists had been killed during the conflict, including a United States cameraman, whose death helped trigger federal police occupation in October.

23. Not a traveler easy to please, Lawrence produced some of his most contented and lyrical writings about Oaxaca in *Mornings in Mexico* eight decades ago (London: Penguin, 986; first published by Martin Secker and Warburg, 1927).

24. According to 2004 statistics from SEDETUR, of the 133,819 foreign visitors received in Oaxaca between October 2003 and October 2004, 56.27 percent were from Europe and 34 percent from the United States and Canada. "Key European markets such as German and French tend to deliver a higher income traveler (as well as the budget traveler, but weighted to the higher income, more discerning person)," according to a tourism consultant, Victoria Pratt, in December 2004. Ruíz Camino adds that to Mexico's tourism industry, European tourism means market diversification, to try to avoid dependence on the North American market.

25. The "brotherhood" implied indicates fellow travelers who share a solidarity with Oaxaca, and I think it is significant that this modern-day tourism lore (around thirty years old) resonates in the intimate cultural realm of gastronomy, one of Oaxaca's great treasures.

26. High host-guest interaction is also typical of destinations that receive a large proportion of European guests (Ruíz Camino). There is a high level of host satisfaction in part because serving tourists is not yet massified in Oaxaca, and so not overly monotonous for the host. Moreover, in Oaxaca's culture, service is not seen as degrading (it is part of the existing class structure and normal economy).

27. Smith lists five types of tourism in the introduction to *Hosts and Guests*, with considerable overlaps between what she defines as ethnic tourism, cultural tourism, and environmental tourism (4, 5). Later, she notes, "Cultural impact studies can serve tourism well and indicate which elements of a specific culture are 'public' and can be marketed as 'local color' without serious disruption" (15, 16). Within Mexico there is not yet any consistency between federal tourism board and state tourist boards as to what is meant by eco-tourism or ethnic tourism. For the purposes of this discussion, I will consider community and ethnic tourism as tourism in which local people and ethnic groups form a significant part of the attraction, e.g., their clothing, cuisine, traditions, customs, and craftworks.

While this overlaps with "local color tourism" (Smith, *Hosts and Guests*), it is distinguished by greater local participation in decision making.

28. Language has always been the yardstick for measuring the indigenous population; according to the 2000 census, approximately 1,120,000 persons spoke an indigenous language. That is 37 percent of the state's population, and a little over 19 percent of all indigenous-language speakers in the country. However, taking into consideration other criteria (descent, membership in a historically recognized indigenous community, etc.), most scholars add another million. On the other hand, a recent study by Consejo Nacional de Población (CONAPO) puts the figure at 56.3 percent for Oaxaca, making it the second in the country behind Yucatán at 65.5 percent (information courtesy of Ronald Waterbury, December 2005).

29. In 2006 a dissident teacher's strike developed into a social rebellion of the radical left whose members took control of Oaxaca City for six months until it was crushed by federal forces. Protesters claimed over twenty of their numbers were killed by armed groups associated with the state governor. The city center was sealed off and the tourism industry all but disappeared during that period. Following the violence, by the second half of 2006 Oaxaca's tourism's hopes looked very bleak: "Meanwhile, Oaxaca's tourist industry has effectively shut down. British and other foreign diplomatic missions have posted travel warnings about a city once considered a jewel among Mexico's tourist attractions—mixing architectural splendor with colorful indigenous traditions and culinary exoticism." Jo Tuckerman, "Fresh Flare Up in Mexico's Cultural Jewel," *Guardian*, November 27, 2006.

30. Hoteliers then were proud to announce that in 2004 Oaxaca gained *Travel and Leisure* magazine's prize for best city in Mexico, Central America, and South America, on a par with Rome for Europe; New York for the United States and Canada; Sydney (which won the world's best city prize) for Australia, New Zealand, and the South Pacific; Bangkok for Asia; and Cape Town for Africa and the Middle East.

31. Of the nine illustrious men Paty mentioned to me in an interview on December 1, 2004, only four are recognized internationally: Benito Juárez, Mexico's first Indian president; former president Porfirio Díaz; and the artists Rufino Tamayo and Francisco Toledo.

32. Rodrigo Esponda, New York office of the Mexican Tourism Board (MTB), interview, August 2005.

33. This statement spurs a surprising amount of agreement, among different—and competing—sectors within Oaxaca and the country at large, including the state's tourism secretary, Beatriz Ramírez (interview, December 3, 2004).

34. PRO-OAX is composed of all the major artists and many of the intellectuals of the city and aims to defend the culture and natural environment of Oaxaca. It began its work in 1992 and issued its first newsletter in 1995.

35. These would be aggravating the social inequalities established by European colonial domination, cultural homogenization, increased power to transnational corporations beyond nation-states, and the weakening of regional control over domestic affairs and self-determination.

36. Interview with Jaime Katz, state subsecretary for tourism, December 3, 2004.

37. This was a major feature of arguments used in Oaxaca's refusal to allow a McDonald's in its zócalo, which received more media attention (national and international) than any other event in the state until the violent disturbances of 2006.

38. Davydd J. Greenwood, in the epilogue to his essay "Culture by the Pound" (Smith, *Hosts and Guests*), questions the vision, born of "moral anguish," that tourism was "just one more example of our perverse age of modernization," noting that "the objectification of local culture via tourism does not always destroy it" (183).

39. Day of the Dead, or the Muertos holiday, is one of Oaxaca's four peak tourism seasons, taking place on November 1 and 2.

40. Hierve del Agua, a natural geological formation, was at the time the best-known example of poor planning, in terms of spoiling the natural area as well as exacerbating existing conflicts between local communities, resulting in violence (interview with Ron Mader, December 2004). "We never phone the tourism office for information. They don't even know when Easter is!" (Radtke interview, December 2004).

41. Interview with Beatriz Ramírez, December 3, 2004. She refers to Patricia (Paty) Zarate, Oaxaca's new state secretary for culture as of December 2004. Mader notes: "This is a good example of how tourism stakeholders conveniently divide the tasks. If we learn anything from the prior administration it is that the tourism office did a poor job of in-house communication in regard to ecotourism or 'alternative' tourism. The tasks of development and promotion have significant overlap and I would argue that the same can easily be said for 'tourism' and 'culture.' "

42. The incident illustrates the isolation of Oaxaca state in its own backwards, political world. Oaxaqueños from the city tend to laugh cynically about the incident (locally it is said that Murat was drunk at the time) but the former governor was also publicly mocked throughout national media and by a morning TV host, "Brozo," and made international news. The staged attempt was so serious in part because it occurred close to the date of, ten years previously, the assassination of Mexico's presidential candidate Luis Donaldo Colosio; in that context Murat's behavior was deplored as an act of exceptional frivolity and arrogance, disregarding the importance of outside perceptions of Mexico as politically stable. See "Questions Arise over Attack on Oaxacan Governor," *Chicago Tribune*, April 20, 2004.

43. Alan Riding sketches some of the reasons and procedures by which in Mexico

the arts are "so tied to politics" in his chapter "Culture for Some and for Many," *Distant Neighbors: A Portrait of the Mexicans* (New York: Vintage Books, 1986). In Mexico, "Academics, writers, painters and musicians of minimal renown inherit the right . . . to participate in politics, to give opinions on subjects far removed from their areas of talent, to sit in judgment of the regime, even to denounce the system" (295).

44. The achievements of Toledo with his colleagues, primarily through the civil association PRO-OAX, are legion. However, he is also said to be "the most generous and least loved man in Oaxaca" (interview with Ron Mader, 2004).

45. Selma Holo, *Oaxaca at the Crossroads: Managing Memory, Negotiating Change* (Washington, D.C.: Smithsonian Institution Press, 2004).

46. "For protesters with no education, the idea of protecting the patrimony is a luxury of the educated" (ibid., 215).

47. By November 2004, Wal-Mart was Mexico's largest private employer. The public debate that raged in national and international press included how to preserve local food, crafts, and buildings in the face of the trend toward homogenization. See Sara Silver, "Chain Reaction," www.travelandleisure.com, February 2005 (accessed June 5, 2009).

48. It was local entrepreneurs who wanted the McDonald's, and it was local government (Town Hall) that was about to authorize it. One of the reasons PRO-OAX won the day in this instance was a feud going on at the time between the local authority and the state government. The latter took advantage of the protest to back the artists and civil groups and score some media points. One implication local government's support for the international chain is that tourism as an industry makes local power wielders, politicians especially, willing to sell their heritage off cheaply (before someone else makes a killing with it).

49. "It's not a matter of some local people wanting these things and others not. It's a matter of the law. A mob lynched two policeman in Mexico City last week, because they wanted to—does that make it right?" Fernando Gálvez, Director of IAGO, December 2, 2004. Two weeks later, Toledo used the "national heritage" debate to protest in national press the allegedly illegal sale of tourism land in Cancún (*La Jornada*, December 16, 2004).

50. Although some are dying, the large weekly market (where people of remote communities conduct important social rituals in addition to trade) is still a tradition that survives in Oaxaca, such as the market in Ocotlán that bursts into color every Friday. The next step up is the *fiesta patronal* or Feast Day, where markets are set up usually for an extended period of time.

51. "Mesmerising and magnetic" (Isabella Tree, *Sliced Iguana* [London: Hamish Hamilton, 2001], 121), women from the Isthmus of Tehuantepec have a far more independent role in their society than found in the rest of Mexico.

52. Ribald humor and frank sexuality is part of Tehuana culture, with women taking a leading role as protagonists and spokespersons.

53. The exception would be the adjacent state of Chiapas, home of the Zapatista uprising in 1994.

54. However, while the barely ambivalent figure of the "peon"/peasant is seen as a stereotype of Oaxaca's hopeless Third World condition, the state's indigenous people have also gained a reputation for being ubiquitous, entrepreneurial, and valiant survivors.

55. One of the outstanding examples is the female ceramic artists of Polvo de Agua: "This was a social effort to create artists, to lift people out of a desperate situation; and to help them see the possibility of dignified, creative, large lives in the middle of the dissolution of their pueblos through emigration and through government neglect and betrayal" (Holo, *Oaxaca at the Crossroads*, 204).

56. Ron Mader, founder of Planeta.com, the Web's first site focusing on global ecotourism, pioneered a dialogue commissioned for the World Ecotourism Summit in 2002 and has received honors from the Mexican government and groups including Conservation International and the Council of Latin American Geographers for his work.

57. "Every generation produces moralists claiming that there is the epoch when culture has collapsed, when traditions have been destroyed and values lost. Though the anthropological critiques confidently announced this theme, it is troubingly difficult to separate this moral discourse . . . from other forms of intellectual and political conservatism, even though the rhetorical tone of the critique of tourism is politically left of center." Greenwood, "Culture by the Pound," 182.

58. Or even the whole of Latin America; see Nestor García Canclini's work on the "modern and authentic" in *Hybrid Cultures: Strategies for Entering and Leaving Modernity* (Minneapolis: University of Minnesota Press, 2005).

59. Greenwood, "Culture by the Pound," 182.

60. In Mexico the political advantages of being culturally authentic are still being developed. See Greenwood, "Culture by the Pound," 183–84.

61. In "Disentangling the Strangled Tehuana: The Nationalist Antinomy in Frida Kahlo's 'What the Water Has Given Me,'" *Genders* 33 (2001), Jeffrey Belnap examines the way in which the Tehuana is an example of a specific kind of "antinomial tension between the Mexican nation's claims of cultural continuity with pre-contact times, and the exoticizing fantasy of a 'tropical Mexico' linked to tourism and the art market," 5.

62. According to Alejandro López, the municipality of Amecameca had 46,000 inhabitants in 2000 and estimates for 2005 were 60,000 of whom 75 percent were expected to live in the town (Amecameca de Juárez), that is, 45,000 persons (interview in 2005).

63. One of the town's moderate claims to fame is its local shamans, called *granizeros* (hailmakers), who intercede with the volcano, interpreting "his" wishes, appeasing his wrath, and setting up offerings on altars.

64. The volcanoes appear on the Tiffany curtain in the white marble Palace of Fine Arts, which opens every weekend to reveal Mexico's world-renowned folkloric ballet. They are a constant figure in the large collection of viceregal art in Mexico City's Museo Nacional del Arte (MUNAL), and the murals by Diego Rivera in the National Palace, for example.

65. Information from the Comisión Nacional de Areas Naturales Protegidas (CONANP).

66. Black Christs are, from a historical point of view, highly significant in this region and to the south. Amecameca is known to historians and art historians almost exclusively for the Sacromonte. However, the tourism industry, such as there is one here, does not take its cues from historians and art historians, and tourism officials and entrepreneurs do not value or trade in the same priorities, which is why the Black Christs and Santos have not been used as focal points for tourism. As this vignette will show, local chroniclers have no expectation that this festival will attract foreigners and, moreover, there are a number of reasons why the town cannot sustain foreign visitors.

67. Recalling Oriol Pi-Sunyer's observation in "Changing Perceptions of Tourism and Tourists in a Catalan Resort Town," about the application of stereotypes, in this case the "outsider," seen as a mere resource whom "anything is good enough for" (in Smith, *Hosts and Guests*, 96).

68. In 1895, 90 percent of people spoke Náhuatl—the most common indigenous language in the valley of Mexico—while in 1995 the percentage had declined to about 0.01 (interview with Alejandro López). Also see Alejandro López, *Mongrafía Municipal: Amecameca de Juárez* (Toluca: Gobierno del Estado de México/Asociación Mexiquenese de Cronistas Municipales, 1999).

69. Known by her contemporaries as "the Phoenix of Mexico," Sor Juana is renowned as the finest Latin American poet of the baroque period and was an early pioneer of women's rights to study, teach, and write. See *Sor Juana Inés de La Cruz: Poems, Protest, and a Dream, Selected Writings* (New York: Penguin Classics, 1997). In recent years Frida Kahlo's fame has overtaken that of Sor Juana.

70. Indifference to garbage to the point of blindness is a common phenomenon in Mexico and very gradually changing with various government programs, such as "Mexico Limpio y Querido" (Mexico Clean and Loved). SECTUR started "Mexico Limpio y Querido" following the result of a ministry study, "Profile and Levels of Tourist Satisfaction." See SECTUR, *Tercer informe de labores*, September 1, 2002–August 31, 2003.

71. The behavior of the "Niño Verde" (Green Boy), as Senator Jorge Emilio González Martínez is widely known in the press and in public, caused this kind of delight when revealed as it confirmed public perception of his party as "a profitable

family business disguised as a political party" (editorial, *La Jornada*, February 25, 2004). González's father, Jorge González Torres, founded the Green Party in 1986 and in 2001 handed over the reins to his son in a disputed vote.

72. A Wal-Mart opened near the Teotihuacán pyramids in November, following high-profile protests at the end of October 2004.

73. Tourist professionals in Oaxaca noticed that foreign tourists were especially offended by the sight (and smell) of dead dogs on the roads leading out of the city. A program to address this took effect in 2003, and it is said that greater investment in cleaning streets made an impact in the same year. Graffiti was the major complaint at the end of 2004 (Radtke interview).

74. SECTUR's work report for 2003 (*Tercer informe de labores*).

75. John Urry explains that mass tourism represents a "democratization" of travel and the process by which, in the twentieth century, a "resort hierarchy" developed. "Major differences of 'social tone' were established between otherwise similar places." While Urry is discussing industrialized Britain, this is relevant to 1970s and 1980s Mexico too, for example, the accessibility of Acapulco to Mexico City, while Cancún is an expensive plane journey away: "On the face of it a reasonable explanation of these differences would be that those resorts which were more accessible to the great cities and industrial towns were likely to be more popular and this would drive out visitors with higher social status." Another reason Urry gives for the lower social tone is "highly fragmented land ownership," also an issue for Acapulco. See *The Tourist Gaze*, 16, 21–23, on the problem of social tone with regard to Acapulco.

76. The class associations, and attempts to overcome them, with seaside tourism described in Urry's chapter "Mass Tourism and the Rise and Fall of the Seaside Resort" are surprisingly applicable to Acapulco, although there are strong interests there against such work being published (Urry, *The Tourist Gaze*, 16–37).

77. European tourism, in addition to higher spending, has a cultural exchange and social aid component, providing a working example of tourism "as an instrument of understanding between peoples" (Ruíz Camino, December 2002).

78. Guillermo Tarrats, director of regional programs, SECTUR. Interview, February 12, 2004.

79. Tarrats admitted that a "committee" cannot be foolproof—there can be conflicts between the municipality and the state, for example—so one effort to help give the project continuity was to look, where appropriate, for a "padrino" (or madrina!) for the project, such as a local businessperson or public figure. This could work similarly to the support the artist Toledo has given to Oaxaca's tourism in recent years, one of the most successful models for quality tourism development in the country, Tarrats said.

80. Barbara Kastelein, "Travel Talk" column, the *Herald* (*El Universal*, Mexico), March 21, 2004.

81. Mader notes that Mexico *should be* the case example of things done right, but that collaboration agreements tend to yield few results, in part because the liaison personnel tend to be in flux, and that lack of continuity typically threatens successful coordination between institutions. "Exploring Ecotourism," www.planeta.com (accessed on June 5, 2009).

82. After five emails and eight phone calls, I gave up.

83. "Latin American countries are currently the result of the sedimentation, juxtaposition, and interweaving of indigenous traditions (above all in the Mesoamerican and Andean areas), of Catholic colonial hispanism, and of modern political, educational and communicational actions. Despite attempts to give elite culture a modern profile, isolating the indigenous and the colonial in the popular sectors, an interclass mixing has generated hybrid formations in all social strata." García Canclini, *Hybrid Cultures*, 46.

ANDREW GRANT WOOD AND DINA BERGER

CONCLUSION *SHOULD WE STAY OR SHOULD WE GO?*

Reflections on Tourism Past and Present

This indecision's bugging me	Esta indecisión me molesta
If you don't want me, set me free	Si no me quieres, líbrame
Exactly who'm I'm supposed to be	Dígame que debo ser
Don't you know which clothes even fit me?	¿Sabes qué ropas me queda?
Come on and let me know	Me tienes que decir
Should I cool it or should I blow?	¿Me debo ir o quedarme?
Should I stay or should I go now?	

THE CLASH, "COMBAT ROCK"

Tourist practices are embedded in a global political economy that
suggests that they should stay home, and in a competing moral
discourse that demands that they keep traveling.
JULIA HARRISON, *BEING A TOURIST*

The Caribbean writer Jamaica Kincaid pulls no punches in her portrayal of
the modern tourist as an agent of neocolonialism. In her masterful po-
lemic *A Small Place*, she calls the tourist "an ugly, empty thing, a stupid
thing, a piece of rubbish pausing here and there to gaze at this and taste
that . . . never [realizing] that the people who inhabit the place in which you
have just paused cannot stand you, that behind their closed doors they laugh
at your strangeness."[1] At the same time, Kincaid makes clear that those
traveled upon are also fundamentally envious of tourists. "That the native
does not like the tourist is not hard to explain," she writes, "for every native
of every place is a potential tourist, and every tourist is a native of some-

where." Yet not everyone can travel, she notes, because "most natives in the world—cannot go anywhere. They are too poor."[2]

While those of us with means to travel do so for increased self-awareness, knowledge of other places, relaxation and pleasure, a truly ethical approach to tourism must consider not only the traveler's perspective but also those who are "traveled upon." Given the fact that nearly four billion of the world's population live in extreme poverty, can fairness in the tourist exchange be realized today?[3] The situation is truly complicated but that need not indicate that meaningful tourism is not possible. Economic inequality, while important, does not wholly determine the politics of tourism. Rather, the subjectivities of guests and hosts must also be taken into account.

In 1967, W. A. Sutton Jr. wrote one of the earliest pieces on tourism and concluded that the industry has both its negative and positive dimensions.[4] Since then, many scholars have not taken such a fair view. Some, such as the historian Daniel Boorstin, snobbishly longed for the olden days when wealthy "travelers" journeyed abroad in contrast to more commonplace "tourists" of today.[5] More recently, academics have suggested that we eschew the negative characterization of the modern tourist and instead allow for the possibility of something positive coming from the broad range of tourist encounters. As one historian has written, at least "tourists are trying, with varying degrees of commitment to be sure, to find out about other people and places."[6] Moreover, tourists today are much more aware and critical of "staged authenticity," the attempts to satisfy a longing for "imperial nostalgia."[7]

Far from idealizing the "traveler" of old, we might consider for a moment how sojourners can be linked to imperial encounters in Mexico and elsewhere. When Hernán Cortés and his collaborators made their way from the Veracruz littoral to the Mesoamerican interior, for example, chroniclers such as Bernal Díaz de Castillo unofficially took time out from the violent machinations of their colonizing mission to indulge in the occasional "ethnographic" side glance and to observe the scenery and different cultures they encountered. As travelers, the Spanish certainly did not win lasting favor among all the various native peoples they met. Instead, they largely left a legacy of death and destruction in their colonizing wake.[8]

No doubt the chapters in this volume fit into a larger history of conquest, colonization, and capitalism in the Americas as European expansionism propelled countless individuals of various stripes around the globe. Those who "went beyond" acted as go-betweens in a process that largely subjugated African, Native American, and Asian peoples to European power.[9]

Over time, local cultures persisted as they incorporated into the ever-widening web of European colonialism, but not without undergoing various degrees of cultural, social, political, and economic restructuring to fit with the larger demands of capitalist logic. This centuries-long process of "globalization" has proven a history in which eventually nothing lay outside, a process giving rise to a near constant reconfiguration of virtually all local cultures and social relationships.[10]

Yet the sixteenth-century European colonizers were not tourists. Similarly, modern-day travelers should not automatically be considered nitwitted agents of imperialism despite the deep inequalities that may exist. As a development that runs somewhat parallel to the "reflexive turn" in the humanities and social sciences beginning in the late 1970s, tourists over the past few decades have become appreciably more self-aware, more sensitive to complex cultural, ecological, social, and political issues.[11] Some no longer want to bargain for rock-bottom prices, live out exotic sexual fantasies, or insist upon 300-thread-count creature comforts offered by the large corporate hotels. Just as a growing number of individuals have concerned themselves with finding solutions to world poverty and environmental degradation, more socially conscious travelers, in other words, have begun to explore alternative ways of interacting. Attuned to legacies of conquest and colonization, some even seem to take seriously the need to respect and honor those encountered through tourism. Many tourists today increasingly do not automatically assume that the world is *their* oyster but instead understand that "they are there by invitation only."[12]

From the first modern tourist encounters sometime in the mid-nineteenth century, guest-host exchanges in Mexico have given rise to a variety of responses as residents have, through fits and starts, become incorporated into larger social, economic, and political networks over time. Several of the chapters in this volume demonstrate the multidimensional impact of tourism as individuals, families, and communities shape different reactions to the industry's advance. Some avail themselves to tourism. Others resist. Many find themselves torn or somewhere in between.

Taken as a whole, the contributors in *Holiday in Mexico* attempt to trace these intricacies by offering specific examples of this larger process; they detail the different manifestations of social power in a way that does not necessarily view tourism in pejorative terms but sees it as a growing industry encompassing a wide range of social interactions over time and space. In the end, there seems to be no simple answer to the question of whether one "should stay or should go." Perhaps not surprisingly, it depends on the situation and the people involved.

As Andrea Boardman makes clear, the mid-nineteenth-century invading U.S. forces traveled, above all, for military objectives. Yet she argues that the *gringos* also acted as "proto-tourists" when they, like their sixteenth-century European predecessors, took time to contemplate the Mexican natural landscape along with selected archaeological and historical sites. What differentiates the U.S. military invasion at that time—and how it ushered in a new era in the history of travel—is the growing array of published travel accounts available. By the mid-nineteenth century, Henry G. Ward's *Mexico in 1827* had gained wide circulation. In 1843 Fanny Calderón de la Barca's *Life in Mexico* along with William Prescott's *The History of the Conquest of Mexico* further established Mexico in the minds of "Americans." Adding their own experiences to the record, reports by U.S. soldiers back home did not disappoint. In fact, they helped contribute to a new wave of literature that stimulated interest in foreign travel. As Boardman writes, "The collective impact of their writings helped to root Mexico in the American imagination." With the United States gaining hegemonic status in the hemisphere around the beginning of the twentieth century, an assortment of self-appointed travel authorities charted previously unfamiliar areas and presented their findings to the public. These accounts crystallized an outsider's "idea of Mexico," which, similar to European colonial pursuits at about the same time, proved an essential discursive element in mapping the course of American empire.[13]

Those incorporated into imperial orbit need not simply be thought of as victims. Indeed, Mexicans also worked diligently to develop an incipient tourism infrastructure around the turn of the century. As Christina Bueno writes, the one hundred year anniversary of Hidalgo's *grito* in 1910 proved a watershed event that brought many foreign visitors including a host of envoys from Europe, the United States, Russia, Norway, and Japan to Mexico City. They enjoyed a variety of the *Centenario*'s planned activities with itineraries that also included what would become one of Mexico's most important tourist attractions: the recently excavated ruins at Teotihuacán. Conscious of the inherent touristic appeal, designers saw to it that site construction included not only the uncovering of the actual ruins (however crudely done at the time) but also the building of a museum and Japanese garden. Similarly, workers painted and posted an array of signs to orient visitors. For the Centenario the renowned anthropologist Manuel Gamio also crafted what must have been one of the first Mexican tourist guides. In the end, President

Porfirio Díaz and his distinguished guests had helped to unleash a small but steadily growing stream of tourists drawn to Mexico by Mesoamerica's ancient past. Shortly after Porfirian elites celebrated the Centenario, however, revolution broke out. Further development of Mexico's tourist industry would have to wait until the relative calm of the 1920s.[14] At that time, a new generation of foreign travelers took interest in not only social-scientific descriptions of Mexico's natural landscape and traditional peoples but also contemporary events, politics, and burgeoning modern culture.

As Helen Delpar has described, a wave of political and artistic sojourners made their way to Mexico after the revolution. People such as Frank Tannenbaum, Anita Brenner, Edward Weston, Katherine Anne Porter, Hart Crane, John Dos Passos, and Aaron Copland, among others, found the country a fascinating place. The excitement of revolutionary politics, artistic dynamism, and social change did much to captivate their imagination. At the same time there occurred a reciprocal wave of Mexican travel on the part of artists such as Diego Rivera, Lupe Vélez, Dolores del Río, Agustín Lara, Miguel Covarrubias, David Alfaro Siquieros, and others.[15] Although they largely sought to advance their careers rather than simply see the sights, they nevertheless helped pave the way for future touristic exchange, however unequal, between the two nations.

By midcentury, economic growth and advances in diplomatic, business, social and cultural initiatives all helped encourage Mexico's tourism industry. Also hugely important by this time was the development of mass media. Radio, newspapers, and illustrated magazines featured advertisements for a wide range of products as well as tourist destinations and special events. Parallel growth in leisure travel by Mexican nationals during the early twentieth century can be seen, for example, in the popular celebration of Carnival in the Port of Veracruz, where a growing tourist trade stimulated commerce, cultural awareness, and civic pride.

The upsurge in tourism to Mexico during and after World War II significantly expanded the range of informal social contact among Mexicans and their hemispheric neighbors. From high-class political, academic, and business travelers to an increasing number of middle-class individuals taking their first trip, the diversity of tourist encounters sparked festive gatherings and cultural exchange. Going beyond strictly state-centered definitions of diplomacy, tourism, as Dina Berger argues, "acted as a nexus of cooperation between the United States and Mexico." Well before presidents Franklin Delano Roosevelt and Lázaro Cárdenas made official pronouncements promoting inter-American travel, social and cultural exchange brought about by businesses on both sides of the U.S.–Mexican border has proven to be of critical importance. Certainly much time and money is spent on various public diplomacy events. And going beyond these staged affairs one can hope that transnational, get-to-know-your-neighbor-type relations would play out in a positive manner.

A look at tourism in San Miguel de Allende is an interesting case in point. After the war, veterans went to this town to study. Some of them courted and married local women, much to the dismay of certain elders who were concerned with maintaining traditional practices. Speculating on the outcome of these couples, Lisa Pinley Covert imagines that many may have managed in a positive way to bridge differences between the two cultures. Yet when residents of San Miguel heard word of a touring cadre of rebel poets a few years later, they assumed a defensive attitude. In contrast to the servicemen in town, Allen Ginsberg, Neal Cassady, and Jack Kerouac's legendary long hours at La Cucaracha bar probably did little to advance transnational understanding. Subsequent word of their exploits in Mexico nevertheless helped inspire—for better or worse—a young generation of gringo travelers.[16]

In another important form of cultural diplomacy, traveling art exhibitions have been used by government, business, and a variety of cultural agents as a leading strategy to promote a national agenda that included tourism, international goodwill, and cross-cultural understanding. This type of cultural commerce, however, was not without its difficulties. Perceptions generated by these types of shows, as Mary Coffey points out, have tended to cast Mexico in exceedingly romantic terms. Mexico, for many, represented a predominantly rural, timeless, traditional land inhabited by colorful, largely unsophisticated people.

Blockbuster mid-twentieth-century shows at the Met and MOMA in New York City saw organizers wishing to promote Mexican folk art as not only an essential expression of national culture but also an increasingly cultivated taste among foreign consumers. Moreover, these exhibitions, Coffey observes, also served to "set the rhetorical and display strategies" for future relations in most other areas including "political negotiations between nations and the private interests of corporations." Here, art, in the early-twenty-first-century context of the Great Masters show, not only offers an "inducement to travel" but also provides an overarching framework for U.S.–Mexico relations—one that reinforces neoliberal economic policy and the power of transnational corporations. Do major expositions like these eventually merge with other, more commonplace promotional efforts such as advertisements seen in Sunday newspaper travel sections offering information on package tours, luxury enclaves, and "exotic getaway" vacations where consumers can purchase a carefully planned, secure experience free from unwanted contact with local residents?

Undeniably, tourism has a darker side, which scholars have had good reason to emphasize. Tourism studies rightly highlight the myriad ways in which tourists—often foreigners from the global north making their way in the global south—make insensitive, ignorant, and usually unfair use of their economic and social advantage to exploit and demean their hosts. It also shows how domestic leaders are willing to "offer up," or sacrifice, their own citizens and ideals for the sake of tourist development. The essays in this volume do not contradict these revelations. Nonetheless, they do much to illuminate specific processes by which tourism has dispossessed, despoiled, and degraded environments—both natural and social. They detail particular travel experiences, infrastructures, and international communication about tourism. They also show that responsibility for the negative impact and the ugly effects of tourism lies on both sides of the border.

In fact it was the *veracruzano* Miguel Alemán Valdés, serving both as minister of the interior and then president between 1946 and 1952, who did much to further Mexico's tourism industry. As the once humble port town of Acapulco became a pet project of Alemán, it changed into what promoters termed "the Mexican Riviera"—soon attracting celebrities from around the world. Yet behind Acapulco's so-called golden age is a telling tale of urban renewal and gentrification at the hands of the federal government. As Andrew Sackett reveals, behind a progressive façade featuring leisure, glamour, and oceanside relaxation for well-to-do travelers, backstage relationships involved in the making of tourism has often involved exploitation and abuse. Sackett disentangles the methods by which the state agency, Junta Federal, and President Miguel Alemán forcibly took prime land from *ejidatarios* in order to grow the tourist infrastructure. When landowners resisted, the police resorted to violence.

With World War II being fought, U.S. officials promoted the idea of travel "down Mexico way." Heading up the official promotion of the country as a tourist destination in 1939, Luis Montes de Oca and the Mexican Tourist Association (AMT) aptly conceived a strategy that blended "old" and "new" aspects of Mexico's culture. In the programming that ensued, AMT boosters framed the nation as a fashionable mix of modern hotels, night-clubs, and culture (largely in the capital) in combination with the traditional local appeal of archaeological sites, provincial towns, architecture, and markets as well as probably the most primary forms of touristic exchange: food and drink.[17]

Analyzing Anglos' consumption, Jeffrey Pilcher describes how this process has engendered a powerful transnational semiotic; one that often exoticizes *mexicanas* as objects of desire. Thus, the power to consume culture, going back to Jamaica Kincaid, illustrates the socioeconomic gap between hosts and guests. Indeed, the history of tourism in Mexico is one that cannot ignore the heavy demand for commercial sex and drugs, despite leaders' attempts to move the gaze to more refined offerings in Mexico. Taking a hard look at this darker side of transnational travel, Eric Schantz's account of how Mexican hosts cleverly catered to foreigners' desires shows how vice tourism became an exploitative, unsavory tradition founded upon greed and corruption. Many, including Presidents Lázaro Cárdenas and Manuel Ávila Camacho, have attempted to reform the "border leisure complex." When Baja California gained statehood in 1952, Governor Braulino Maldonado Sández renewed moralization efforts as well. His appeal to national tourism elites resonated with many of the plans initiated by the AMT years earlier that sought meaningful cultural exchange between the United States and Mexico as an antidote to vice. Yet little long-term improvement seems to have resulted, as north of the border demand for diversion has remained profound.

More recent developments in Mexican tourism further reveal the ugly underbelly of tourist development, namely, how the choices of domestic actors—tourist developers, politicians, and businesspeople—however well intentioned, can adversely affect the well-being of people and the environment. As scholars point out, tourism is about economic development and it fulfills goals of not only modernization schemes but also of neoliberalism. Mexico does not have to fabricate its beauty. According to the classical liberal model of comparative advantage, Mexico specializes in spectacular beaches, colonial architecture, and pre-Hispanic pyramids. It also specializes in hospitality. Not only are people just really nice and welcoming in Mexico, but many are struggling economically such that a large portion of them migrate to cities to work in the service industry. The combination of a comparative advantage in tourist sites and a population willing, however begrudgingly, to play the consummate host makes for a nation that (understandably so) opts for tourism as a form of economic development.[18] As the chapters here illustrate, promises of economic growth sometimes trump the greater good. Government agencies and corporate interests are often blinded by short-term economic benefits. Therefore, as scholarship by Alex Saragoza, Bianet Castellanos, and Barbara Kastelein suggest, there is a cost to the allure of tourist development.

Alex Saragoza's work on Cabo San Lucas, in particular, illustrates the political and economic reasoning that drives tourism as development. As Saragoza points out, designs for the resort complex of Cabo Real and the broader Escalera Náutica, drawn up by the beer mogul Eduardo Sánchez Navarro and given a stamp of approval by the Fox administration, suggested the extent to which Mexican visionaries imagined wealthy American tourists as the newest answer to a failed Cancún. But he also demonstrates how the fragility of relationships—between center and periphery and between visionaries and realities—can bring about unexpected consequences. One result, Saragoza argues, is that the development of luxurious Los Cabos produced a kind of placelessness in which one is hard pressed to find anything uniquely Mexican. This was certainly a far cry from initial goals of tourist development of the 1920s that sought to play on Mexico's unique attributes.

Other consequences of tourism are illustrated by M. Bianet Castellanos and Barbara Kastelein, namely, tourism's effect on local peoples and the environment. In Cancún members of rural indigenous Mayan communities who migrate to the city to labor in the service sector often return changed by their experience. Quick to note that their transformation is not always detrimental, Castellanos does show how expectations of seasonal migration and experiences of work in Cancún often collide as does the positionality of cultural identity. One of her most interesting conclusions is the way in which the identities of community members as indigenous shifted upon arrival to Cancún, where they positioned themselves as simply poor campesinos in contrast to well-off tourists. Upon returning, however, migrants distinguished themselves from hedonist tourists by reaffirming their beliefs in traditional indigenous values.

Kastelein, likewise, reminds us how the failure to adequately develop what locals believe to be the right kind of tourism can affect the environment. In her travels to Amecameca, the holy site of the Black Christ, she finds that local officials view national tourism as the wrong kind of tourism because Mexicans tend to make the quick day excursion from the capital, bring their own food, and leave tons of garbage in their wake. Meanwhile, Kastelein finds, Acapulco's heyday in the mid-twentieth century and exploitation ever since have amounted to a declining city where water pollution and violence marks it. From the days of Hollywood glamour, Acapulco now plays host to Mexican tourists who, locals say, further its reputation as a tourist destination in decline. Not surprisingly, these conclusions also yield important observations about how international tourism is perceived in comparison to a national one. As is often the case, international tourists are seen as far more profitable and preferable than domestic ones, whose spending power and cultural practices are deemed, often unfairly, as less advantageous and less refined.

As many of these chapters illustrate, tourism is Janus-faced: it is at once visible and invisible, detrimental and beneficial, transparent and corrupt. Considerations of the history of tourism in Mexico, then—from the countless explorers, administrators, evangelizers, settlers, and scientific adventurers to the solidarity seekers, artists, writers, and thrill seekers—engage a legacy of inequality and exploitation. Even those who see themselves practicing a more refined type of travel must face the fact that they, too, are ostensibly participating in unequal, unsustainable, and, yes, sometimes exploitative relationships. No matter how inconspicuous, sensitive, environmentally and socially conscious one might be, we foreigners inevitably enjoy an elite status as we make our way by car, ship, rail, jet, or perhaps an expensive touring bicycle![19] Relying on a tourism infrastructure that has often had a negative impact on local social, cultural, and natural environments, we satisfy our needs for shelter, meals, and security as privileged out-of-towners. The money we bring—or now have quick access to via electronic bank transfers and ATM machines—is earned abroad under radically different economic conditions. Perhaps Dina Berger's essay arguing for the diplomatic effect of tourism represents a way out of the present-day tourist conundrum. Arguing that the development of tourism proved "profitable, modernizing, and democratizing" during the war years, might contemporary industry players choose to valorize these same ideals again in any mutually beneficial manner? The historical record, however, more than hints that such a trajectory will prove extremely difficult. Nonetheless, we live in a world today that begs for cross-cultural understanding.

When reflecting on the dawning of the so-called post-9/11 age, the musician and lifelong civil rights activist Harry Belafonte has said, "America can no longer afford to be as arrogant as we've been [and] we can no longer exempt ourselves from the global family of concern."[20] How should this idea of global engagement be practiced? Will certain kinds of tourism serve as a goodwill vehicle for increased awareness of different places and peoples? The future is uncertain.

However clichéd it might sound, learning from mistakes of the past is not necessarily impossible. Today there are ventures on the part of artists, journalists, students, church groups, city officials, and nongovernmental agencies, among a host of other players, that offer promise.[21] Concerned people are taking action and are working to break down barriers across cultures. Future scholars of tourism will do well to document such things so as to complicate our appreciation of the industry and its history. It seems that the message we might wish to take from these and other works on the history of tourism is that despite the many, many unequal and exploitative characteristics of the travel experience, there remains the possibility of something positive in the tourist exchange and, at the very least, an acknowledgment that historical actors are their own agents.

We hope that this volume on the history of tourism in Mexico (however eclectic) will help readers understand the depth and breadth of colonial legacies and the seemingly immutable political, economic, and cultural determinations that favor wealth and privilege. Having said that, does this mean we are fated to repeat the mistakes of the past? Are all forms of tourism the same? Is the new age yuppie post-tourist just a dressed-up (or down) version of the allegedly cruder, all-consuming package tourist? Knowing something of the dark side of tourism, should we perhaps think about just staying home? In *The Art of Travel* Alain de Bottom argues that the occasional traveler may gain a certain understanding of a particular culture.[22] Describing the French writer Gustave Flaubert's nine-month stay in Egypt in 1849–50, he remarks, "We are taught to be suspicious of the exotic reveries of European men who spend nights with locals while traveling through Oriental lands." Yet "none of Flaubert's attraction to Egypt had been misconceived . . . he simply replaced an absurdly idealized image with a more realistic but nevertheless still profoundly admiring one, he exchanged a youthful crush for a knowledgeable love."[23] Let us hope that, perhaps like Flaubert, travelers today find a way to do something similar.

Notes

1. Jamaica Kincaid, *A Small Place* (New York: Farrar, Straus and Giroux, 1988), 17.
2. Ibid., 18.

3. According to the World Bank, poverty is measured by a consideration of one's purchasing power. In 2005, the World Bank estimated that 1.4 billion people lived at or below the poverty line, currently defined by those who live on $1.25 or less per day. "World Bank Updates Poverty Estimates for the Developing World" found at www.worldbank.org/research (accessed on June 3, 2009).

4. W. A. Sutton Jr., "Travel and Understanding: Notes on the Social Structure of Touring," *International Journal of Comparative Societies* 8.2 (1967): 218–23.

5. Daniel J. Boorstin, "From Traveler to Tourist: The Lost Art of Travel," *The Image: A Guide to Pseudo-Events in America*, ed. Daniel J. Boorstin (New York: Atheneum, 1973), 77–177, 79–80.

6. David M. Wrobel, "Introduction: Tourists, Tourism, and the Toured Upon," *Seeing and Being Seen: Tourism in the American West*, ed. David M. Wrobel and Patrick T. Long (Lawrence: University of Kansas Press, 2001), 12.

7. See Dean MacCannell, *The Tourist: A New Theory of the Leisure Class* (Berkeley: University of California Press, 1999), first published in 1976, as well as Renato Rosaldo, *Culture and Truth: The Remaking of Social Analysis* (Boston: Beacon Press, 1989), 68–87.

8. On the complicated history and many misperceptions of the conquest, see Matthew Restall, *Seven Myths of the Spanish Conquest* (Oxford: Oxford University Press, 2004).

9. The term "go-betweens" is borrowed from Alida C. Metcalf, *Go-Betweens and the Colonization of Brazil, 1500–1600* (Austin: University of Texas Press, 2006). For a concise treatment along these lines, see Dennison Nash, "Tourism as a Form of Imperialism," *Hosts and Guests: The Anthropology of Tourism*, ed. Valene Smith (Philadelphia: University of Pennsylvania Press, 1989), 37–52.

10. Néstor García Canclini, *Transforming Modernity: Popular Culture in Mexico*, trans. Lidia Lozano (Austin: University of Texas Press, 1993), 7–9.

11. The emergence of more self-conscious "reflexivity" in anthropology and other related disciplines has a long and important scholarly trajectory related to intellectual work achieved in Europe (i.e., Foucault, Derrida, Lacan) and in regard to ethnographic methods specifically (Turner, Geertz, Clifford, Marcus).

12. Julia Harrison, *Being a Tourist: Finding Meaning in Pleasure Travel* (Vancouver: University of British Columbia Press, 2003), 212.

13. As Mary Louise Pratt has observed in commenting on European travel and scientific writings of a century or so earlier, this type of writing tended to emphasize an inherently political progression from "poetics" to "discovery" and then "mastery." Mary Louise Pratt, *Travel Eyes: Travel Writing and Transculturation* (London: Routledge, 1992), 5, 18, 27–29, and passim; Harrison, *Being a Tourist*, 191–93. For a response to Pratt in characterizing exploration and travel in Africa, see Johannes Fabian, *Out of Our Minds: Reason and Madness in the*

Exploration of Central Africa (Berkeley: University of California Press, 2002). Also helpful is David Spurr, *The Rhetoric of Empire: Colonial Discourse in Journalism, Travel Writing and Imperial Administration* (Durham, N.C.: Duke University Press, 1993).

14. Of course, a few brave individuals such as the journalist John Reed did visit Mexico during the conflict.

15. Helen Delpar, *The Enormous Vogue of Things Mexican: Cultural Relations between the United States and Mexico, 1920–1935* (Tuscaloosa: University of Alabama Press, 1992).

16. Jack Kerouac, Allen Ginsberg, Gregory Corso, Peter and Lafcadio Orlovsky met in Mexico in the fall of 1956. Already in Mexico City living on money supplied from the G.I. Bill was William S. Burroughs. Glimpses of expatriate Americans in Mexico City after the war can be seen in his novel *Queer* (New York: Picador, 1987). The section "Passing Through" in Kerouac's *Desolation Angels* offers some reflections of the writer's time spent in Mexico (New York: Riverhead, 1995 [1965]). Subsequent Cold War suspicion of expatriate communist conspiracies brewing in San Miguel—not to mention the export of rock and roll music to Mexico—further complicated relations between the two nations. See Eric Zolov, *Refried Elvis: The Rise of Mexican Counterculture* (Berkeley: University of California Press, 1999).

17. See Dina Berger, *The Development of Mexico's Tourist Industry: Pyramids by Day, Martinis by Night* (New York: Palgrave Macmillan, 2006).

18. The same can be said for many South Asian countries like Thailand and Vietnam. Mexico, though, has a much more diverse economy so that tourism is not the only development option.

19. Those friends who embark on "eco-friendly" biking tours nevertheless rely on air or car travel to reach their destination. On the worsening impact of jet travel, see George Monbiot, "Flying into Trouble: Why Most Airplanes Must be Grounded," *Nation*, May 7, 2007, 33–34.

20. Sarah Ruth van Gelder, interview with Harry Belafonte, *Yes*, Spring 2002. http://www.yesmagazine.org (visited June 9, 2009).

21. Recent efforts, for example, by the photographers Miki Gingras, Patrick Dionne, and Jacques Pelchat, whose travels to Nicaragua (Gingras and Dionne) and Yucatán (Pelchat) incorporated on-site participation by residents. Their works were exhibited in Montreal during the winter of 2007 at the Maison de la culture Frontenac and Maison de la culture Mercier. In the journalistic realm, the U.S. photographers Susan Miesalas, Bill Gentile, and the late Randolph "Ry" Ryan have all made documentary films that explored the Nicaraguan revolution from a "before" and "after" perspective. Their work poignantly examines the tragedy of opportunistic relations between guests and hosts while also making a plea for

continuing, yet more humane, relations. Alfred Guzzetti, Richard P. Rogers, Susan Meiselas, dir., *Pictures from a Revolution*, 1992; Peter Raymont, dir., *The World Stopped Watching*, 2003.

22. Alain de Bottom, *The Art of Travel* (London: Hamish Hamilton, 2002), 93. Here, he considers Gustave Flaubert's extended stay in Egypt as an example.

23. Ibid., 97.

CONTRIBUTORS

DINA BERGER is an assistant professor of history at Loyola University Chicago. She is the author of *The Development of Mexico's Tourism Industry: Pyramids by Day, Martinis by Night, 1928–1946* (2006) and a variety of essays on tourism in Mexico. She is working on a study of U.S.–Mexican relations through the Pan American Round Table.

ANDREA BOARDMAN is the executive director of the William P. Clements Center for Southwest Studies at Southern Methodist University, Dallas. She was a writer-producer for the Emmy Award–winning PBS production *The U.S.–Mexican War, 1846–1848*. She is the catalog author and exhibition curator of *Destination México— "A Foreign Land a Step Away": U.S. Tourism to Mexico, 1880s to 1950s* (2001).

CHRISTINA BUENO is an assistant professor of Latin American history and Latino and Latin American Studies at Northeastern Illinois University in Chicago. She is currently writing a book that examines the Porfirian government's use of archaeology and Indian antiquity in nation building.

M. BIANET CASTELLANOS teaches in the department of American Studies at the University of Minnesota. She coedited a special issue on gender and migration in *Latin American Perspectives* and published an essay on adolescent Maya migration in *Frontiers: A Journal of Women Studies*. She is currently working on a book that examines the foundational role indigenous people play through their labor and culture in the development of tourism, transnational spaces, and the modern nation-state.

MARY K. COFFEY is an assistant professor of art history at Dartmouth College. She has published numerous essays on museum exhibition and the politics of culture in the U.S. and Mexico. Her publications include chapters in *Popular Eugenics: American Mass Culture in the 1930s*, edited by Sue Currell and Christina Cogdell (2006), and in *Foucault, Cultural Studies, and Governmentality*, edited by Jack Z. Bratich, Jeremy Packer, and Cameron McCarthy (2003). She is currently revising a manuscript titled

How A Revolutionary Art Became Official Culture: Murals, Museums, and the Mexican State, to be published by Duke University Press.

BARBARA KASTELEIN is a Mexico City–based writer and travel columnist. She has contributed to numerous guidebooks on Mexico and the surrounding region and has published articles in the *Boston Globe*, the *Houston Chronicle*, and the *Observer* as well as a variety of media in Mexico and Latin America. She has just finished a manuscript on the history, spectacle, and lives of the world-famous Acapulco cliff divers titled *Héroes del Pacífico*.

JEFFREY M. PILCHER is a professor of history at the University of Minnesota. He is the author of *!Que vivan los tamales! Food and the Making of Mexican Identity* (1998), *Cantinflas and the Chaos of Mexican Modernity* (2001), *Food in World History* (2006), and *The Sausage Rebellion: Public Health, Private Enterprise, and Meat in Mexico City, 1890–1917* (2006). His articles have appeared in the *American Historical Review*, *The Americas*, *Dimensión Antropológica*, and *Food, Culture and Society*. He is currently writing a book on the globalization of Mexican cuisine.

LISA PINLEY COVERT is a graduate student in history at Yale University. She is completing her dissertation on identity and culture in postrevolutionary San Miguel de Allende.

ANDREW SACKETT is a historian and lawyer working in Washington, D.C. He is the author of "The Two Faces of Acapulco during the Golden Age" in *The Mexico Reader: History, Culture, Politics*, edited by Gilbert M. Joseph and Timothy Henderson (2002). He is completing a study on the history of tourism in Acapulco at Yale University.

ALEX M. SARAGOZA is a professor of history and ethnic studies at the University of California, Berkeley, and author of *The Monterrey Elite and the Mexican State, 1880–1940* (1988). He is finishing a manuscript on the origins of the media conglomerate Televisa.

ERIC M. SCHANTZ teaches history at California State University, Los Angeles. He is the author of "All Night at the Owl: The Social and Political Relations of Mexicali's Red-Light District, 1913–1925," *Journal of the Southwest* (winter 2001).

ANDREW GRANT WOOD teaches at the University of Tulsa. He is the author of *Revolution in the Street: Women, Workers and Urban Protest in Veracruz, 1870–1927* (2001) and the editor of *On the Border: Culture and Society Between the United States and Mexico* (2004) and *The U.S.–Mexico Border: An Encyclopedia of Culture and Politics* (2008). Wood is currently completing a study on the Mexican popular musician Agustín Lara.

INDEX

Dina Berger is an assistant professor of history at Loyola University Chicago.
Andrew Grant Wood is an associate professor of history at the University of Tulsa.

Library of Congress Cataloging-in-Publication Data
Holiday in Mexico : critical reflections on tourism
and tourist encounters / edited by Dina Berger and Andrew Grant Wood.
p. cm. — (American encounters/global interactions)
Includes bibliographical references and index.
ISBN 978-0-8223-4554-1 (cloth : alk. paper)
ISBN 978-0-8223-4571-8 (pbk. : alk. paper)
1. Tourism—Mexico. 2. Americans—Travel—Mexico.
3. Mexico—Relations—United States.
4. United States—Relations—Mexico.
I. Berger, Dina. II. Wood, Andrew Grant.
Series: American encounters/global interactions.
G155.M6H64 2009
338.4'79172—dc22   2009032840